Praise for
The Bible

"What I loved best about this book—aside from the elegant prose and the abundance of startling facts—is the sense of a strong, wise mind behind it. Bruce Gordon has written a book that will engage anyone interested in the Bible, which is anyone interested in human history."

—Christian Wiman, author of *Zero at the Bone*

"This extraordinary book is both a stupendous intellectual achievement and a marvelously accessible guide that will delight everyone interested in how the Christian texts became the Bible, and why it has played such an enduring role in reading and worship in the millennia since."

—Andrew Pettegree, coauthor of *The Library*

"Even the best-informed readers will have much to learn from Bruce Gordon's erudite and accessible history of the Bible, which ranges knowledgeably across eras and Christian traditions, and indeed across continents. It deserves to find the widest possible audience."

—Philip Jenkins, author of *The Next Christendom*

"With stunning prose and relentless insight that could only come from this rightly celebrated historian, Bruce Gordon has given us the book that we need at this moment, a real history of the Bible. In Gordon's capable hands, the Bible becomes a sojourner through history who constantly makes history, and through whom history can be fruitfully understood in all its depths. This book is, quite simply, an intellectual feast."

—Willie James Jennings, author of *The Christian Imagination*

"If the word of God is alive, it has now met its best modern biographer. Filled with surprises, and sometimes aching with beauty, this is a book to take you wide-eyed round the world and then lead you back to that old leatherbound volume on your shelf."

—Alec Ryrie, author of *Protestants*

"This is the best survey yet written of the global transmission, and impact, of the world's most influential book. *The Bible* is readable enough to be enjoyed by anybody, while any expert is likely to learn something new from it."

—Ronald Hutton, author of *The Witch*

"From papyrus and purple-painted parchment, through six centuries of print and forward as far as an app, Gordon guides us on the boundless, unending odyssey of the 'Book of Books.' *The Bible* is a testament to the power not only of Scripture but of the written word itself to connect humanity, to educate, to liberate, and also to repress. Gordon bears witness to the individual lives leavened by the ever-changing form of the 'Book of Life,' from Frederick Douglass to today's football fans in Africa. This is a compelling account of two millennia of Western book culture, and the places and, above all, the people the Bible has touched."

—James G. Clark, author of *The Dissolution of the Monasteries*

"This is a stunning love song to the Bible. Bruce Gordon has managed the rare feat of telling a complicated story that spans two thousand years in an engaging and accessible way. His book brings new perspectives and a fresh energy to the rediscovery of the Bible and how it has been shaped and reshaped by countless communities in different decades and centuries around the world. It made me want to savor this precious book of books even more, and it reignited my enthusiasm for telling the unknown stories about its nature and origins. In years to come, this will be a classic text for anyone intrigued by the most popular book of all time."

—Chine McDonald, author of *God Is Not a White Man*

THE
BIBLE

ALSO BY BRUCE GORDON

Zwingli: God's Armed Prophet

John Calvin's "Institutes of the Christian Religion":
A Biography

Calvin

The Swiss Reformation

Clerical Discipline and the Rural Reformation:
The Synod in Zürich, 1532–1580

THE
BIBLE

A GLOBAL HISTORY

BRUCE GORDON

BASIC BOOKS

New York

Basic Books
Hachette Book Group
1290 Avenue of the Americas, New York, NY 10104
www.basicbooks.com

Printed in the United States of America

First Edition: September 2024

Published by Basic Books, an imprint of Hachette Book Group, Inc. The Basic Books name and logo is a registered trademark of the Hachette Book Group.

The Hachette Speakers Bureau provides a wide range of authors for speaking events. To find out more, go to hachettespeakersbureau.com or email HachetteSpeakers@hbgusa.com.

Basic books may be purchased in bulk for business, educational, or promotional use. For more information, please contact your local bookseller or the Hachette Book Group Special Markets Department at special.markets@hbgusa.com.

The publisher is not responsible for websites (or their content) that are not owned by the publisher.

Print book interior design by Bart Dawson.

Library of Congress Cataloging-in-Publication Data

Names: Gordon, Bruce, 1962– author.
Title: The Bible : a global history / Bruce Gordon.
Description: First edition. | New York : Basic Books, [2024] | Includes bibliographical references and index.
Identifiers: LCCN 2023056240 | ISBN 9781541619739 (hardcover) | ISBN 9781541619722 (ebook)
Subjects: LCSH: Bible—Influence—History. | Bible—Use—History.
Classification: LCC BS445 .G67 2024 | DDC 220.09—dc23/eng/20240415
LC record available at https://lccn.loc.gov/2023056240

ISBNs: 9781541619739 (hardcover), 9781541619722 (ebook)

LSC-C

Printing 1, 2024

For Rona

CONTENTS

Contents

What a book the Bible is, what a miracle, what strength is given with it to man! It is like a mold cast of the world and man and human nature, everything is there, and a law for everything for all the ages. And what mysteries are solved and revealed!

—Fyodor Dostoyevsky, *The Brothers Karamazov*
Translated by Constance Garnett

INTRODUCTION

Annie Vallotton has been declared the world's bestselling artist.[1] Her name may be little known, but her stick-figure illustrations have captured the global imagination. The Swiss artist fought with the French Resistance during the Second World War and sketched pictures on the walls of prison camps. Her artistic success was not immediate. Her French publisher had despairingly thrown three thousand copies of an early work in the Seine River. Her reputation today is a result of her engagement, after a ten-minute meeting at an airport, to illustrate the Good News Bible, a translation into everyday English that first appeared in the 1960s. To date, the Good News Bible has sold close to two hundred million copies worldwide.

Vallotton's characters deliberately reveal no ethnicity, having little in the way of faces—or any other detail—and yet they are full of life and personality. In simple, moving, and unsentimental images, her figures dance, pray, struggle (as in the image of an anguished Job striking the earth), and raise the dead. Her aim, she once remarked, was "to give maximum expression with a minimum of lines." She depicts the crucifixion in eight simple lines, the thorn-crowned head hanging forward, the single line of a shoulder below. Two right angles form the cross. The effect is devastating.

For millions of readers worldwide, Vallotton's line drawings capture the humanity of the Bible. They see themselves in the emotional universe She depicts. No one in our age has better captured the Bible's invitation to readers to encounter themselves in its pages.

The Bible remains the most influential book in the world. Today, it is the foundation for a global religion with two and a half billion adherents, almost a third of the world's population. But across Catholicism, Eastern Orthodoxy, Pentecostalism, liberal and conservative Protestantism, and nondenominational Christianity, it is not one book but a sacred text with multiple voices, open to widely divergent interpretations. In human hands it has been a book of both liberation and condemnation as the convictions it has inspired have been both praised and damned, depending on dominant orthodoxies of belief. A single book is the source of salvation and blasphemy, faith and heresy, in the eyes of those who judge. Where some find God's purpose for humanity and the certainties of an ancient faith, others see antisemitism, patriarchy, and imperialism. Still others believe the Bible needs to be radically reconceived for a modern world.

The Bible is God's word to humanity, but that is only part of the story. When God called to Adam "Where are you?" he began a direct conversation with his people. That conversation continued until Jesus's departing charge to "go and make disciples of all the nations." With Jesus's return to heaven, the conversation came to an end—at least, directly. Although there has never been a shortage of men and women who have claimed to have heard from God, they are exceptional, and their professions of faith are mostly disputed or ignored. Instead, the conversation between God and his people continued in the form of a book. But unlike the stone tablets given to Moses, which God wrote with his finger (Exo. 31:18), this was a book coauthored by people. God charged humans with writing down what they had heard and seen, and they did so with the promise that the Holy Spirit was their guide. Those writings became the Bible, divine words written by human hands—a complex partnership.

Once that book emerged, its impact was sublime and perplexing. No other book provides such a comprehensive vision of humanity from its moment of creation to the end of time, when all shall be gathered. Yet it perplexes and confounds. Where else can one find the anguished pain of Psalms or the erotic passion of Song of Songs mixed with the bloody slaughters of Numbers and Joshua? What other book would require us to believe that the God who struck down thousands in anger and demanded the sacrifice of innumerable animals was the same God who dined with prostitutes and preached that the meek shall inherit the earth? Nowhere in ancient literature is there a comparable scene to the one in which the son of a carpenter reads the words of the prophet Isaiah in a synagogue and then declares that he is the fulfillment of the Jewish scriptures. Ancient myths of the Near East sit alongside eyewitness accounts of miraculous healings. Even early Christians wondered whether the God of the Old and New Testaments was the same deity. And yet that is the declaration of the Bible, a book that transforms its readers with luminous wisdom, bewilders with contradictions, and teaches that men and women should defy long-standing assumptions about how to live.

The bewilderment is due in no small part to God's human coauthors. All of those writers believed they had recorded God's words and the deeds that had transpired, but like the testimonies of witnesses in a criminal trial, their stories always diverge. It is also the product of two thousand years of wandering, restlessness, and change. The Bible today—the one that we hold in our hand, see on Grandmother's shelf, or open on our smartphones—is an approximation, a version of what once was but is now lost. It is a transmission of centuries of transmissions. Unlike the genealogies it contains, the Bible has no known first parent. It is a sacred text that has been repeatedly translated, corrected, and copied around the world. It is the legacy left to us by distant, unknown ancestors who, like modern Christians, wanted to know what God actually said.

The history of the Bible, then, is a history of humanity's repeated and wondrous striving to hear God speak—not only hear, but see. It is the story of humanity's grasp for the impossible: the perfect Bible. The restless search for the divine always remains partial and always falls short. Each version of the Bible gathers the pieces and arranges them in different ways. Translations are replaced by translations in the search for greater faithfulness and proximity to the Hebrew and Greek in the common languages of the people. Illustrations express the imaginations of their ages. Only God can end this search. The image that comes to mind is the Tower of Babel, the effort to reach heaven foiled by the cacophony of languages. Striving to hear God results in division and fragmentation, and the yearning of men and women to hear God through the creation of Bibles has brought separation. In hearing and reading, transcribing and printing, illuminating and illustrating, studying and interpreting, people are constantly renewing and reimagining the Bible. Each Bible is a new creation, a fresh yet always partial attempt to capture the uncapturable, the pure word of God. Each Bible is a glorious achievement and a noble failure, an admission that it cannot be what it aspires to be. It may, like the Vulgate, the Luther Bible, or the King James Version, have a long life, but inevitably its time will come: it will be retranslated, corrected, reread, and perhaps even discarded.

The Bible is constantly becoming itself, eternal and perfect, but each version or edition reflects what it cannot be because it is the work of humans. In the seventeenth-century story of a utopia called *The New Atlantis,* Francis Bacon describes a perfect Bible that is found at sea. It was written just after Jesus's resurrection and perfectly conveys scripture in all languages at once. It's a fantasy. Though early, medieval, and modern Christians have all dreamed of such a book, it is never to be found. No one has seen the original Hebrew of the Old Testament or the original Greek of the New Testament. They have only seen the versions that have survived and been passed down to us.

This book is called a history precisely because that is what we have—the history of a Bible that has evolved over the centuries and taken innumerable forms in different communities and cultures. That is why the Bible can be thought of as a book in exile, a refugee that has washed up on many shores. Its oldest sections were created in ancient Palestine in languages that Christians have hardly ever been able to read or understand; its life has always been in translation. Not infrequently, it shaped the languages into which it was brought. That has been its strength. It constantly speaks to new communities in their tongue, allowing the people to claim and find their story. Those stories have patterns but also vary enormously. For many, the story of Exodus and the promised land speaks of liberation and freedom. Others see themselves as the Canaanites, conquered, their land taken.

This is a global history precisely because, from the beginning, the words that became the Bible have restlessly traversed all known frontiers. The book of Matthew relates that by the sea of Galilee Jesus took his leave from his disciples with the command "Therefore go and make disciples of all nations, baptizing them in the name of the Father and of the Son and of the Holy Spirit, and teaching them to obey everything I have commanded you. And surely I am with you always, to the very end of the age" (Matt. 28:19–20, NIV). And go they did. According to the earliest traditions, Peter, Andrew, Matthew, and Bartholomew preached in the region of the Black Sea while Thomas, Thaddeus, and Simeon the Canaanite reached modern-day Iran, possibly India. John and Philip lived and died in Asia Minor. The Egyptian Coptic Orthodox Church believes that the apostle Mark went to Alexandria less than twenty years after the crucifixion and was martyred there. Today the Bible is physically and virtually present in "all the nations," even where proscribed. It is the most global of books. With every communications advance it crosses new boundaries in ever-changing forms. As it always has, the Bible embraces new technologies and expressions of human imagination. Whether ancient codex or modern app, or whatever comes next, the Bible has never had a fixed abode.

The followers of the Bible embraced it as a book, from earliest times gathering their sacred texts in a codex. At first, this was so that a persecuted people could spread their faith by concealing the Word in a pocket or satchel. Later, the book became a sacred object, embodying the God for which it witnessed. The material form of the Bible tells the story of an uneasy relationship. It reflects the impossibility with which we began. The Bible today is a book, website, or app, where once it was parchment discarded in a rubbish dump or a precious vellum object dyed purple and inscribed with silver. Each physical manifestation reflected a moment in time that aspired to eternity.

Its form has constantly shapeshifted, reflecting the needs and aspirations of peoples across time. But the story of the Bible is not merely the story of a book. It is a story of the divine conversation that was never limited to bound pages. Throughout most of its history, the Bible has been read by only a few. Most people encountered it in oral and visual forms—they heard it, talked about it, prayed with it, or saw it in worship; its stories were told in paintings and drawings both crude and exquisite. Across the centuries, generations of Christians have been highly biblically literate without reading. This book argues that the story of the Bible is thus the story of a life force, experienced positively and negatively by all the human senses.

This book is also an attempt at the impossible: to tell the journey of the Christian Bible. It can only tell a partial story of the world's most influential book. It is not a history of editions or the long tradition of interpretation. Instead, it seeks to tell something of ongoing human effort to hear God. It is the story of a book that, in the presence and absence of faith, has left no one untouched. Gregory the Great, the seventh-century pope and doctor of the church, captures the paradox of this story: "[The Bible] is, as it were, a kind of river, if I may so liken it, which is both shallow and deep, wherein both the lamb may find a footing, and the elephant float at large."[2]

CHAPTER 1

BECOMING A BOOK

When Jesus went to the coast of Judea, a great multitude followed in his wake, including numerous men and women he had healed. According to Matthew 9:3–12, the Pharisees also joined the crowd, not as admirers but with a darker intent. They were not interested in the healing powers of a rabble-rouser. Rather, they sought to ensnare him. What better way to expose a hypocrite than to reveal that he had twisted the scriptures to dupe the people? Is it lawful, they baited him, for a man to put away his wife for every cause? Aware of the trap, Jesus reminded them of the holy texts, where at the Creation God brought forth men and women that they should marry and become one flesh. What God had joined together, he declared, "let man not put asunder." The Pharisees, however, also knew their scriptures. If such a union was not to be broken, then why did the Torah (the Law of Moses) permit divorce? Jesus replied that this was not God's intention but a concession to the hardness of their hearts.

The exchange by the sea reveals that Jesus, his disciples, and the Pharisees knew the Hebrew sacred texts by heart.[1] But in offering their rival interpretations, to what, exactly, were the parties of this dialogue referring? To some extent there was a fixed body of sacred books for Jews and the first Christians, or at least there existed a flexible consensus about which texts counted as sacred. But they never had a Bible in the way we might think of it—no fully agreed-upon sanctioned text, or, to use a later Greek word, no official "canon." To understand how the Bible became a book, we need to understand how Christians revolutionized the nature of a sacred text. In so doing, they separated themselves from Jewish traditions and the Roman world. Christianity became a religion of the book unlike any other.

How did the Bible acquire its contents? Was there always agreement on what was included?[2] Did Christians in the eastern lands of Syria, along the Nile in Egypt and Ethiopia, and across western Europe gather together and worship with the same texts? To these questions, there are no straightforward answers. Walk along library shelves where the bewildering number of books on the formation of the biblical canon stand shoulder to shoulder, and your first impression may be that there are as many views as scholars.[3] You would be correct. There are books written about books; as Ecclesiastes 12:12 has it, "Of making many books there is no end; and much study is a weariness of the flesh" (KJV). But there was also a time before books.[4] The biblical writings were not written to be collected in a book but rather emerged out of particular circumstances for particular purposes. They became binding for Christians as they came to define their identity in their religious, social, and private lives.[5]

In the fourth chapter of Luke's Gospel, Jesus enters the synagogue in his hometown of Nazareth. Upon being handed a scroll of Isaiah, he points to the words of the ancient prophet: "The Spirit of the Lord is upon me, because he hath anointed me to preach the gospel to the poor; he hath sent me to heal the brokenhearted, to preach deliverance to the captives, and recovering of sight to the blind, to set at liberty them that are bruised" (4:18). Having spoken, Jesus rolls up the scroll and sits down. In the silence all eyes are fixed on him, and he speaks: "This day is this scripture fulfilled in your ears" (Luke 4:21, KJV). The clerical elites are aghast. What did he just claim? This stunning moment of divine self-revelation occurred during the ancient practice of reading the sacred text from a scroll, following Jewish tradition and widespread custom in the Greco-Roman world. Jesus himself never held a book and he never wrote anything. His followers, however, would participate in a communications revolution. The Christian scriptures would eventually be written not on papyrus or parchment scrolls but on leaves gathered into a collected volume.[6] Theirs was to be a faith of the book.

Today, if you scroll through Amazon.com seeking to buy that book, you will be presented with an overwhelming range of choices. There are different translations, layouts, print sizes, and cover colors. You will find illustrated versions, electronic versions for different handheld devices, and Bibles with a seemingly endless variety of accompanying commentaries. Such options might seem like a modern expression of consumerism that emphasizes choice and convenience, and that is true, but the diversity of biblical options is as old as the Bible itself. For two thousand years Christians have been making choices about the forms of their Bible, and there has never been a single one for the whole of the faith.

For the faithful believer, understanding God and thereby living a godly life are all-consuming interests. The fifth-century North African church father Augustine named such living the highest act of love. The first step in appreciating how diverse materials became the sacred Bible is to grasp the compelling force of those interests. Rightly understanding God was and remains of everlasting importance, which is why the Bible stands in sharp contrast to all secular works, including this one. Those interests also help us see a common thread from the outset of Christianity through the centuries of history since. Sometime in the second century after Christ, what began as a tradition of stories, prophecies, tales, and wisdom retold and reenacted generation after generation without fixed form eventually became a codex, a collection of texts bound together in a meaningful order. Then and thereafter, the desire for greater proximity to the lessons, commands, and intentions of God marked diverse and sometimes competing claims for the Bible's sacred contents.

The word "bible," derived from the Greek *biblia*, means "books," plural. The individual books that make up the Old and New Testaments were already circulating among communities from Syria to North Africa in the second century and had been given the special status of scripture, a place of honor that set them apart from other ancient texts, however instructive. But the Bible has remained plural; it was and is a book of books. We can think of it as a library of the sacred. Even today, Catholic and Protestant Bibles contain different numbers of books, as do the Orthodox Bibles, with sixty-six to seventy-three books. At the far end of the spectrum is the Bible of the Ethiopian Orthodox Tewahedo Church, with eighty-one to eighty-four books, a good number of which other churches have rejected or lost.[7]

Despite these differences, agreement did cohere around the inclusion of the Hebrew books of the Rabbinic Bible, the four Gospels, Acts, and the Epistles. In the case of the New Testament, by the end of the second century, witnesses such as the church father Irenaeus of Lyon attested that four "gospels"—accounts of the words and deeds of Jesus attributed to Matthew, Mark, Luke, and John—had emerged as preeminent.[8] Irenaeus's approach was based on what he called the "rule of faith," which included belief in one God; Jesus Christ, who became incarnate for our salvation; and the Holy Spirit, who spoke through the prophets of the coming of the Son of God.[9] The brilliant and prolific writer Origen of Alexandria (ca. 185–253), who died in Palestine after being imprisoned and tortured by the Romans, was clear that while heretics had many gospels, the true church had four. Such seemingly conclusive statements contain, however, some nuance. A range of other writings recounting the life of Jesus, including the Gospel of Thomas, the Gospel of Judas, and the Didache, were read approvingly and circulated widely among early Christian communities.[10]

Likewise, by the end of the second century there was a consensus around the scriptural status of letters attributed to Paul the Apostle. There were fourteen or, more likely, thirteen—some believed the Epistle to the Hebrews was not written by Paul and should be dated later than his letters, a view that largely prevails today. Doubt also surrounded the book of Revelation, possibly written by John the Apostle, which appeared in some collections and not in others. Other writings, such as the Shepherd of Hermas and the First Epistle of Clement, stood on the threshold, occasionally permitted entry but ultimately left outside.

For the Hebrew Bible, Jesus is our witness when he clearly refers to the basic three-part division of Hebrew scriptures into the Torah

(Law), Nevi'im (Prophets), and Ketuvim (Writings): "These are the words," he tells his followers, "which I spake unto you, while I was yet with you, that all things must be fulfilled, which were written in the law of Moses, and in the prophets, and in the psalms, concerning me" (Luke 24:44, KJV). Jewish influence was decisive in the formation of the Christian Bible; its crucial distinctions were mostly adopted by early Christians. The first evidence of a clear list of the books of the Hebrew Bible comes from the controversial first-century Jewish Roman historian Josephus (ca. 37–100 CE), who recorded the existence of twenty-two books (five books of Moses, thirteen books of the prophets, and four hymns and precepts).[11] He did not, however, list the books to which he was referring, so how he arrived at this number is not entirely clear. Today, thirty-nine books are commonly recognized as composing the Hebrew Bible. Josephus also provided no hints as to the order of these books—a more recent invention, for the Hebrew scriptures existed as scrolls that could be placed in any arrangement.

Early Christians, like their modern descendants, were often unsure what to make of certain narrative works that were not written in Hebrew.[12] Compelling stories and works of wisdom—texts that include Tobit, Judith, 1 and 2 Maccabees, the Wisdom of Solomon, and Ecclesiasticus—the apocryphal and pseudepigraphal writings have always defied easy categorization. Neither Jesus nor any of the writers of the New Testament cite them, but they appear as part of the Septuagint, the third-century BCE Greek translation of the Hebrew Bible, which was originally prepared in Egypt for Jews who no longer spoke Hebrew.[13] The Septuagint was widely used by early Christians, who also did not know Hebrew, and remains the established form of the Old Testament in the Orthodox tradition. In the fourth and fifth centuries, Augustine, perhaps the most eminent Western theologian, considered the apocryphal books to be part of the Bible, while his contemporary Jerome, the great translator of the Bible into Latin, did not. Jerome acknowledged that these texts fostered piety and thus placed them between the Old and New Testaments, in a second tier, where they were recognized as helpful and instructive but not inspired by the divine.

In traditional stories of the formation of the Christian canon, perhaps no figure plays a more important role than the controversial and combative bishop of Alexandria, Athanasius (ca. 296/298–373).[14] Exiled no fewer than five times during his forty-five-year tenure, Athanasius managed to incur the wrath of four successive Roman emperors and has long been championed as the father of true or orthodox Christianity, the man who saved the church from error. He was an inveterate opponent of heresy, in particular Arianism, which held the Son to be distinct from, and therefore subordinate to, the Father.[15] He also had his sights set on the Gnostics in Egypt, who circulated a large body of texts that challenged essential teachings defended by Athanasius as orthodox. His appointment as patriarch, the spiritual father and head of the Orthodox churches, was rejected by the Melitians, or "church of the martyrs," a name that reflected their belief that the true church was founded on the blood of those who gave their lives for their faith, as well as their repudiation of Christians who they believed abjured their beliefs too readily. The Melitians accused Athanasius of beating their bishops and desecrating their sacred objects. For nearly his entire tenure, this militant bishop had more enemies than supporters.

Athanasius is remembered for a letter he sent out at Easter 367 CE that contained a bundle of instructions and pastoral advice. Crucially, in that year's episcopal epistle he listed the twenty-seven books of the New Testament he regarded as "canon," a word he introduced for the texts he held to be scriptural as well as the twenty-two books of the Hebrew Bible. (The difference in number from Josephus was because Athanasius often counted several books, such as the minor prophets, as one book.) Together, he wrote, they formed "the fountains of salvation, that he who thirsts may be satisfied with the living words they contain. In these alone the teaching of godliness is proclaimed. Let no one add to these; let nothing be taken away from them."[16] In providing a list of Old and New Testament books, Athanasius sought to confirm the legacy received by his people. These writings were canonical, he recorded, because they were "accredited as divine" and "handed down."[17] The bishop was particularly concerned that the faithful were reading the apocryphal books along with the true biblical books, which had originated in apostolic times and had been continuously used by Christians since then. The apocryphal books, he wrote, such as the Shepherd of Hermas, Tobit, the Didache, and the Wisdom of Solomon, were instructional and edifying but not canonical.

Athanasius's was the first such definitive list and is often regarded as a turning point in the determination of the Christian Bible, establishing what was in and what was out. However, by no means did this list define the contents of the New Testament for all Christians, nor could it.[18] A letter issued in Greek-speaking Egypt was not binding on the wider church, which stretched from Persia in the East and Ethiopia in the South across North Africa to the Mediterranean. Given the geographical breadth and cultural diversity of these regions, it is unsurprising both that there existed many lists of biblical books and that these lists varied in significant ways from Athanasius's.

For early Christians, the canon was not simply a list of acceptable books. It was a way of reading, praying, and thinking about what a book was. Each biblical book was not just a collection of words but a living body of the written and spoken, a shared set of beliefs about Jesus Christ expressed in communal living and prayer. The books were alive. "Canon" is a dry word, but it could take many forms. The first martyrs were living expressions of the Gospels. They were themselves holy books.[19] The canon embodied the written and oral. It was the whole of life.

Across communities the canon could look very different. In the eastern Syriac churches, for example, there was no tradition of reading the Gospels separately. Rather, the faithful used a harmony of the Gospels created by the second-century writer known as Tatian the Syrian (ca. 120–180). This book, named the Diatessaron, was an effort to combine the material of the four Gospels into one continuous narrative, which often required a little creative editing and writing.[20] Although there is little sense that Tatian intended his book to supplant the four Gospels, it was widely used among the Syriac churches in worship.

Rather than decreeing how the Bible should be, Athanasius, like Josephus, is better understood as recounting the norm in his part of the world. In other words, he was being descriptive rather than prescriptive. But creating a list of biblical books was also an act of aggression. Which texts were chosen reflected the expansive reading practices and devotional convictions of the fragmented world of Christians in the fourth century.[21] Rival hierarchies of power, as well as differing views of the Bible, posed a serious threat to Athanasius's hopes for a centralized church under the bishop of Alexandria. His attempts to define the Bible formed part of a bitter struggle for authority and control against inveterate opponents. The letter of 367 was not just a list of books but part of an effort to define Egyptian Christianity against those whom Athanasius regarded as heretics and therefore its greatest threat.

For all the necessary talk of bishops and theologians, the early story of the Bible is not primarily about which books were deemed scripture and which were excluded by the sole discretion of religious authorities. The revolution of the Bible lay in Christians' distinctive attitude toward their sacred writings. Words are powerful, particularly holy ones, and for Christians this meant both spoken and written. The Gospels and the writings of the New Testament authors circulated among communities orally and as leaves. In comparison to the Jewish tradition, early Christians did not have such a reverential attitude toward the written words of scripture. The writings of the New Testament were not the preserve of learned scholars but for the people. Written in common language, they were neither elegant nor refined, reflecting both their authors and their intended audience. The Christian revolution was that scripture was meant for all, whether literate or not. You did not have to be able to read or study them. They could be transmitted orally in daily conversation, prayer, and worship. They were not intended for the desk but for caring for thy neighbor.

The Bible grew organically into canon, fostered by the worship, reading, and devotional practices across Mesopotamia, the Mediterranean, and Africa.[22] Canon formation was a social act by which communities granted certain texts a status of authority for a wide range of reasons, although most prominently out of the belief that those works came from the earliest writers of the faith and carried the true teachings of Christ.[23] They were sanctioned to be read in worship. In other words, the Bible was not created by fiat. Instead, it took shape in diverse communities in which certain texts gradually emerged as its essence, even if there was not (and would never be) full agreement about that essence.

At the end of Matthew's Gospel, Jesus departs the world with a command and a promise: his followers were charged to teach what he had taught them with confidence, for, he pledged, "I am with you always, even unto the end of the world" (Matt. 28:20, KJV). Over the next centuries, Christians would turn to the Bible to understand what Jesus's words meant for their lives. Tertullian wrote of the constant benefit of scripture: "With the sacred words we nourish our faith, we animate our hope, we make our confidence more steadfast; and no less by inculcations of God's precepts we confirm good habits."[24] Christians heard the words of Jesus read, preached, and taught. They enacted Christ's presence in worship through hearing the scriptures, praying, and eating his body and drinking his blood. The book of Acts provided a model for how communities were to live in the Spirit and also for how individuals should die. Beginning with the martyrdom of Stephen and continuing through the fates of Peter and Paul, the scriptures taught the faithful not just to remember their Lord but to live his life, even if that meant perishing at the hands of their persecutors.

The New Testament itself explained how Christian communities were to engage with scriptures. Thus, writing to Timothy, Paul urged his younger colleague, "Till I come, give attendance to reading, to exhortation, to doctrine" (1 Tim. 4:13, KJV). The letter to the Colossians came with reading instructions: "And when this epistle is read among you, cause that it be read also in the church of the Laodiceans; and that ye likewise read the epistle from Laodicea" (Col. 4:16, KJV). In the book of Revelation, John of Patmos opens, "Blessed is he that readeth, and they that hear the words of this prophecy, and keep those things which are written therein: for the time is at hand" (Rev. 1:3, KJV).

Scripture was the launching point for communal worship by Christians in Rome, as second-century Christian apologist Justin Martyr recorded:

And on the day called Sunday, all who live in cities or in the country gather together to one place, and the memoirs of the apostles or the writings of the prophets are read, as long as time permits; then, when the reader has ceased, the president verbally instructs, and exhorts to the imitation of these good things. Then we all rise together and pray, and, as we before said, when our prayer is ended, bread and wine and water are brought, and the president in like manner offers prayers and thanksgivings, according to his ability, and the people assent, saying Amen.[25]

But the fathers of the early church also exhorted Christians to incorporate scripture into their home life. In the third century, in perhaps one of the least appealing pieces of marriage counseling, Clement of Alexandria advised a couple to avoid intercourse at any point of the day when they might otherwise be studying the Bible.[26] His successor in Alexandria was more specific: Christians at home should devote no less than two hours a day to reading and meditating on the Word. John Chrysostom in Constantinople wrote of reading scripture in the household as a "spiritual meadow and a garden of delight." This conversation with God created a paradise that surpassed the Garden of Eden. Indeed, he continued, "the reading of the Divine Scriptures rescues the soul from all evil thoughts, as out of the midst of a fire."[27]

The rich evidence from the Egyptian community at Oxyrhychus, where papyri were found in a rubbish dump, suggests that biblical texts were frequently copied and widely owned.[28] It is difficult to judge the quality of such early biblical manuscripts, some of which have survived precisely because they were discarded with the refuse. But it seems likely that literate Christians read extensively, combining scriptures with apocryphal texts and pagan literature.[29] Christians did not live in isolation from the communities around them. Reading in the early Christian world would have been a social event, with biblical texts shared aloud and discussed in groups of men and women. Pieces of papyrus with Christian writings were owned by rich and poor, men and women, free and enslaved. Indeed, women seem to have been prominent as owners of written texts.

Those who possessed such texts incurred grave risks. During periods of persecution, churches were ransacked and texts confiscated or burned. Those who guarded them faced martyrdom, and fear drove some Christians to collaborate with their enemies. During the Diocletian persecution of the early fourth century, for instance, church leaders who willingly handed over copies of scriptures to the Romans were denounced by other Christians as *traditors*, from which we get our word "tradition" (literally, that which is handed down from generation to generation) as well as "traitor." Although many of the cooperators were ultimately forgiven, the Donatists of North Africa—often maligned as the radical opponents of Augustine—regarded their mendacity in surrendering the holy texts as permanently invalidating their priestly functions.[30]

This profound reverence for religious texts was a trait that Christians inherited from the Hebrew tradition. Josephus wrote, regarding the books of the Jews, that "no one has ventured either to add or remove, or to alter a syllable; and it is an instinct with every Jew, from the day of his birth, to regard them as the decrees of God, to abide by them, and, if need be, cheerfully to die for them."[31] For most early Christians, the belief that the Bible was inspired came from the Bible itself. The text most often cited was Paul's second letter to Timothy, in which the apostle confirmed that "all Scripture is given by inspiration of God" (2 Tim. 3:16, KJV). The early fathers of the church extolled the Bible as unchanging, fixed, and reliable.

This exaltation of the Bible's constancy was at odds with practical realities as the scriptures spread geographically and were passed down through the generations. Even the best scribe transcribing the text onto papyrus or parchment could make errors, unwittingly creating yet another version. The result was predictable. Each copy of an Old or New Testament text was unique. And then there were the people, real or imagined, who willfully corrupted God's Word for their own purposes. Christians shared with non-Christian writers of antiquity a fear that their books would circulate in pirated or adulterated forms. Indeed, the Bible itself bears witness to this anxiety. In the book of Revelation John of Patmos expresses a wish of many authors, ancient and modern: "If any man shall add unto these things, God shall add unto him the plagues that are written in this book: And if any man shall take away from the words of the book of this prophecy, God shall take away his part out of the book of life, and out of the holy city, and from the things which are written in this book" (Rev. 22:18–20, KJV). Similarly, the third-century Egyptian church father Origen wrote of Rufinus, who threatened his copyists with eternal perdition, making them swear by their "faith in the coming kingdom" and "the mystery of the resurrection from the dead," with the prospect of "the everlasting fire," to "add nothing to what is written and take nothing from it."[32] Such was the suspicion of false texts that early Christians were deeply wary of anonymous writings.

In a letter to James, head of the church in Jerusalem and brother of Jesus, Peter noted both the problem and its solution: "I beg and beseech you not to communicate to any one of the Gentiles the books of my preachings which I sent to you nor to any one of our own tribe before trial; but if anyone has been proved and found worthy, then to commit them to him, after the manner in which Moses delivered his books to the Seventy who succeeded to his chair. Wherefore also the fruit of that caution appears even till now."[33] The letter never made it into the canon, as it was likely not written by Peter the Apostle, but it was nevertheless regarded by many as worthy of great respect. The fear of error was legitimate because so much was at stake, but Moses himself provided the model of faithful transmission when he brought the tablets bearing God's commandments to the people. He had conveyed God's exact words. Christians could believe that through the work of the Spirit, the truth was preserved. Thus, Augustine in North Africa, like many others, accepted that scriptural texts had been clearly handed down through the generations in an unbroken chain and accurately preserved.[34] Authorship, authority, and transmission worked together in relaying the authentic voice of the patriarchs, prophets, Christ, and his apostles.[35]

While private networks of early Christians likely transcribed and circulated texts, they later developed scriptoria, rooms in monasteries or households where scribes copied sacred works.[36] The earliest Christian scriptoria were found in Pachomian monasteries in Egypt, where copying biblical and other religious writings was part of the economic life of the religious houses, which engaged in brisk trade up and down the Nile.[37] In late antiquity scribes often were enslaved staff in elite households, a subordination also present in the first great Christian scriptoria, such as that of Eusebius of Caesarea.[38] However, with the rise of the monastic orders, scribal work became integral to holy living, and only those of the greatest skill and piety were appointed to inscribe the Word with ink on parchment. Scribes were not simply copyists. They participated in every aspect of preparing the Bible and frequently made editorial choices. Their skills, together with those of illuminators, ultimately determined the quality of the Bibles they produced, and it was widely believed that scribes would be richly rewarded for their fidelity on Judgment Day.

Putting ink to vellum was an act of prayer that bound together scribe and Word. This intimate relationship was known among the church fathers as the "inner library," with each faithful person becoming a repository of the divine Word.[39] The Irish saint Cummian spoke of copying scripture as "entering the Sanctuary of God."[40] Scribes were akin to the valiant saints of the deserts of Syrian and Egyptian Christianity. They were victors in a battle who had persevered, in solitude, in heroic acts of patience and of physical and spiritual endurance. It has been estimated that the Lindisfarne Gospels, produced in medieval England, took one scribe about five years to complete alongside his monastic duties. As Michelle Brown has written, "The act of copying and transmitting the Gospel was to glimpse the divine and to place oneself in its apostolic service. . . . As such these books are portals of prayer, during the acts both of making and studying."[41]

Scribes may have shared a sense of divine commission, but across early medieval Europe they adopted different approaches. In the Celtic realms, preparing manuscripts was closely associated with ascetic disciplines such as mortification of the body and isolation on remote islands; the Irish saints Canice and Columba were declared "hero scribes." The Bible shaped their harsh disciplines. Monks would recite the Psalter while standing in the freezing Atlantic. In other regions scribes worked in communities under the watchful eyes of the leaders of the religious house.

Not all scribes were men.[42] One of the first accounts of a female scribe comes from the sixth-century *Life of Saint Caesarius*, in which the bishop's sister is praised: "The mother Caesaria, whose work with her community so flourished that amidst psalmody and fasting, vigils and readings, the virgins of Christ lettered the divine books, having the mother herself as teacher."[43] In the eighth century St. Boniface wrote to the abbess of Minster-in-Thanet in England to request that she send to him a copy of the Epistles of Peter in gold script to impress converts. To that end he sent her the gold for the nuns to use. The evidence is clear that some of the wondrous, precious Bibles in England were prepared by women. In Gaul, too, women were involved in the creation of liturgical books for monasteries.

Communication of the faith was not only a divine command but also a performance of holiness. To copy a sacred text was an act of piety and self-sacrifice; it was grueling work that came at considerable personal cost. As one scribe recorded in a Visigoth manuscript from the eighth century, "O, you lucky reader, before you touch a book, wash your hands, turn the pages carefully and keep your fingers well away from the letters! For someone unable to write cannot imagine what an immense labor it is." He proceeded to detail the pain of the work: "Oh how hard is writing: it blurs the eyes, squeezes the kidneys, and tortures every limb. Only three fingers write, but the whole body suffers."[44] For the scribe Pionius, to whom tradition has often attributed the account of Polycarp's martyrdom, the painful act of writing connected him with the suffering of Christ. Self-sacrifice became a hallmark of Christian scribes, who saw their work as an arduous spiritual exercise that opened the gates to eternal life: "I gathered [the text] together when it was nearly worn out by age, that the Lord Jesus Christ might also gather me together with his elect into his heavenly kingdom," recorded Pionius.[45] This identification had a long history that reached from the Middle Ages to the age of printing. Scribes did not merely copy books; they created them.

From the second century, the Bible as a book, or rather codex, was a product of evolving technologies and new knowledge.[46] The codex was not invented by Christians but emerged from their interaction with Roman society, where bound volumes or notebooks were widely known.[47] What was innovative, however, was the zeal of Christians to make the book form their preferred way of gathering their sacred texts. It enabled a new way of reading, distinctive from scrolls, that allowed persons to move easily from one part of the Bible to another and back again. The codex became a means by which Christianity distinguished itself from Judaism and Roman culture.

By the fourth century the codex had replaced scrolls as the standard form of Christian scriptures. Today, we are so familiar with books that the revolutionary nature of the change is not immediately obvious. The codex, like language, embodied the distinctive attitude of Christians toward their sacred writings. Instead of consisting of separate scrolls, the codex brought together the books of scripture into one collection, emphasizing that the center of the story is Jesus Christ. That story was highly transportable. Christ had commanded his followers to go into the world, and they could now do so with a book that could be carried in a pocket or a bag. Early Christians placed their faith in a new technology that enabled them to perform the fundamental obligation. With roughly bound texts, they missionized the world.

A codex might be composed of papyrus, made from plants, or parchment, made from the flayed skins of animals. Vellum, a form of parchment, generally came from calves and lambs and was regarded as higher quality. Although papyrus continued to be used in North Africa, by the third century the breakdown of trade networks had limited the amounts available in the West, and papyrus was also not favored for prestige codices. Parchment and vellum were also much easier to form into pages than papyrus.[48] The enormous Codex Sinaiticus of the fourth century originally comprised 730 sheets of parchment, requiring animals in numbers available only to a few scriptoria.[49] The skins were scraped until sufficiently thin and all marks and evidence of veins were removed. Given the skill, material, and financial resources required, it is hardly surprising that such complete Bibles were a rarity in the early Christian world.

Codices were made from sheets of parchment folded to create leaves, with each side of a leaf forming a page; if it contained more than one fold, the folded sheet would be cut to create individual leaves. Stacking together folded sheets created a quire.[50] A codex might consist of one quire of folded sheets or of a number of quires, sewn together into a whole. If a new quire followed one for which not all the leaves were required, the blanks might be cut and removed, too precious to remain unused.[51] Expertise in making codices evolved over a long period, and it is unclear whether parchment quires were inscribed before or after they were bound together. Once completed, the codex was bound, its size and shape determined by the folding of the original sheets of parchment. For the early codices that have survived, the original bindings, which were probably also made from animal skins, have largely been lost.

A series of complex decisions left little room for error in constructing a codex. Most pressing was the question of which Old and New Testament texts to copy, with the plethora of existing manuscripts offering a variety of options. Even within each section, the scribe faced a dizzying array of choices. A scribe might prefer different readings from different texts, creating something of a biblical smorgasbord. The selection of texts for copying was accompanied by exacting preparation of the parchment. Just like a modern typesetter, the scribes had to determine the precise number of words and lines in a text in order to fit the text on the parchment perfectly. These calculations had to be done before the ink was applied to the parchment, as errors were not only aesthetic blemishes but also costly. Other practical concerns also required decisions. The whole codex existed as a mental plan before its execution.

Many hands ensured that a codex might be produced more quickly.[52] But unevenness was both a visual and a spiritual concern: variation in the appearance of letters could seriously diminish the aesthetic value of the Bible while also compromising the holy labor of copying the scriptures. To fix the inevitable slips and inconsistencies, the creators of the codex had to improvise, often seeking to avoid unsightly gaps. Each book of the Bible began on a new quire, and therefore the books existed separately until the quires were sewn together. Running heads were added later to provide greater coherence. This practice meant that the scriptural books did not have to be produced in canonical order.

From the second to fifth centuries, Christian collections of their scriptures transformed from rudimentary and practical stitched-together collections into precious volumes that sought to convey the piety and influence of both their creators and their creators' patrons. In these bespoke, luxury Bibles, which came likely from the eastern Mediterranean, the Old and New Testaments were for the first time placed together in a manner familiar to us. These creations, astounding both then and now, did not reflect how most Christians knew the Bible—in parts that circulated separately. They were akin to the nineteenth-century Russian imperial Fabergé eggs; they do not tell us how most Christians of the period made an omelet.[53]

But beautiful codices were designed not simply to look *at* but *through*. Both in the Orthodox tradition of the East and among Latin Christians in the West, the Bible became an icon, a window into heaven. The book was held aloft in worship, carried in the processional, and kissed. It was regarded as sacramental, like the baptismal water and the Eucharistic bread and wine. At the church councils of the fifth century, the physical presence of a Bible among the gathered fathers was an awe-inspiring symbol of the presence of Christ and the Holy Spirit. It had come a long way from a rubbish dump in Egypt.

The two great surviving codices of this period—the Codex Sinaiticus and the Codex Vaticanus—are integral witnesses to the varied traditions of Christian versions of scriptures. It is with these works, from the fourth and fifth centuries, that our story of the Bible as book really begins. And they remain part of our story right up to the twenty-first century. Surviving through centuries of appropriation and revision, they constantly carried the convictions and judgments of the cultures into whose hands they fell.

The unknown scribes who prepared these particular works made crucial decisions about which of the numerous versions of the Greek

Old and New Testaments to use.[54] By their choices they preserved versions of the biblical texts whose originals are now long lost.[55] They thus created not simply versions of the Bible but also museums or libraries of knowledge. Consequently, they have been invaluable for biblical scholars seeking the best version of the text. They are not, however, easily explored: reading the Codex Vaticanus is complicated by the absence of any standard orthography, with words spelled in different ways and their roots hard to trace, making it difficult for scholars to distinguish legitimate variants from scriveners' errors.[56]

The enormous Codex Sinaiticus, which was originally an almost complete version of the Old and New Testaments, reckoned at about 750 folios. As it has aged, it has grown thinner. Only 346 vellum folios—that is, 694 pages—survive, bearing about half the Old Testament, a complete New Testament, and a complete collection of those books known as deuterocanonical, such as 1 and 2 Esdras, Tobit, and Judith, which are not part of the Hebrew canon. The codex also contains two popular works that are not part of the Christian canon: the Epistle of Barnabas and the Shepherd of Hermas. Their inclusion does not mean they held equal status to the texts they sat alongside, for the codex was viewed not as a fixed Bible but rather as a library of books.[57] In addition to the missing parts, Sinaiticus is not entirely complete, and at some point it was abandoned unfinished, for reasons that continue to puzzle scholars. Although the Codex Vaticanus also bears scars—by the fifteenth century twenty pages of Genesis were missing, and its New Testament lacks several Epistles and the book of Revelation—it preserves a much more complete version of the Greek Old and New Testaments.[58] There is significant difference in size: Sinaiticus measures fifteen by thirteen inches, while the smaller Vaticanus is ten by ten.

For whom and by whom were these codices created? One long-favored theory links Sinaiticus and Vaticanus to Constantine the Great, the preeminent emperor of Christianity.[59] In his *Life of Constantine the Great*, Bishop Eusebius of Caesarea preserves the only textual evidence for the emperor's wish from the year 331 to have fifty Bibles for his churches in Constantinople: "You [Eusebius] should command to be written fifty volumes on prepared vellum, easy to read and conveniently portable by professional scribes with an exact understanding of their craft—volumes, that is to say, of the Holy Scriptures, the provision and use of which is, as you are aware, most necessary for the instruction of the Church."[60] The bishop was to carry out the task "as quickly as possible." The imperial demand was staggering, and the numerous delays tried the emperor's patience. Finally, the codices were dispatched to Constantinople in wooden boxes and by means of the *cursus publicus*, an ancient UPS.

Were Sinaiticus and Vaticanus among the Bibles sent to Constantine? The possibility has drawn supporters and skeptics. The balance of the evidence seems to be against it, however, and there are sufficient grounds for suspicion that we are dealing with an apocryphal story. As large single volumes, or pandects, the Codex Sinaiticus and Codex Vaticanus would have been extremely heavy, not really fulfilling Constantine's desire for versions that were "conveniently portable." The emperor may well have had just Gospels, rather than complete Bibles, in mind for his churches. Perhaps Eusebius in Caesarea had originally wanted to fulfill the emperor's request by providing beautiful Greek Bibles on the scale of the Codex Sinaiticus. The logistics of doing so, however, would have been eye-watering. As the skins of approximately 350 calves or sheep were required for just a single such text, Eusebius would not have had the resources in Palestine for fifty Bibles of this magnitude. Perhaps here lies the explanation for why the Codex Sinaiticus is unfinished: Was it abandoned and a more modest codex prepared, perhaps even the smaller Codex Vaticanus? An intriguing theory, but there are further problems: if the codices were part of this production, they would have been created and sent from Palestine to Constantinople in the 330s; that possibility does not sit easily with the more recent dating of the codices to the later fourth or early fifth century.[61]

While the chapter on the codices' infancy is missing, their biographies are gripping. Their journeys from somewhere in the eastern Mediterranean to their current homes in the West—London for Codex Sinaiticus and, as its name reveals, Rome for Codex Vaticanus—show how Bibles live in exile, distant from the place they were created. Originally envisaged for one purpose, the codices have been subjected to centuries of appropriation and revision. As clay in the hands of generations of scribes, collectors, and scholars, they have been molded according to the convictions, expectations, and assumptions of different cultures. Let's begin with the tale of the Codex Sinaiticus.

In 1844 a German professor, adventurer, and possible thief entered the great hall of St. Catherine's Monastery in the Sinai Desert, an ancient religious house located near where God had appeared to Moses.[62] Founded by Emperor Justinian, the sixth-century St. Catherine's sits at the foot of Mount Horeb and is one of the longest continually inhabited monasteries in the world; its first building was a chapel erected under the patronage of Helena, mother of Constantine, in the early fourth century. Over the centuries it has been patronized by Byzantine emperors, the prophet Muhammad, Catherine the Great, and Napoleon Bonaparte, all before our German adventurer crossed the threshold. For over a millennium and a half, its library has housed some of the greatest treasures of Christianity.

Accompanied by a Bedouin guide, Constantin von Tischendorf (1815–1874) had traversed the desert from Cairo to reach the monastery. His arrival was not entirely unexpected. Europeans searching for manuscripts were well familiar to monks in the East. Indeed, there was brisk trade in biblical texts between religious houses and Europe. But Tischendorf was a man with a purpose—he was in pursuit of the oldest versions of the Bible.

By his account, the German professor observed two baskets filled with parchment in the library at St. Catherine's.[63] He was horrified to learn from his host, he reported, that many other leaves had already been tossed into the fire for heat on cold desert nights. Picking up the parchment, Tischendorf immediately recognized that he was holding pages of the ancient Greek translation of the Old Testament sacred to the Eastern Orthodox Church. Sensing a rare treasure, he persuaded the monks—so he claimed—to allow him to take away some of this bundle, and he left the monastery with just over forty unbound leaves, a fraction of what he had seen. Tischendorf believed he had found, in the words of a Shakespearean sonnet, "bare ruined quires where late the sweet birds sang."

The monks' guarded response alerts us to an alternative telling of Tischendorf's story. The manuscripts were hardly awaiting rescue from the hands of benighted and clueless clerics. And the baskets in St. Catherine's Monastery were not necessarily for tinder, for they were the customary place for storing manuscripts. Furthermore, burnt parchment emanates a foul, acrid smell, making it an unlikely indoor fuel. There was also the issue of language. The German's heavily accented, stumbling Greek was no doubt difficult to follow, and it is not clear that he fully understood what he was being told. The monks may have been playing with this eager but impatient European.[64] In any case, there is no doubt that they were fully aware of the texts for which they cared, as well as their importance.

Tischendorf's "discovery" story fits a wider pattern of nineteenth-century colonialist tales that still heavily influence accounts of the Bible's past.[65] Numerous stories tell of lost treasures in the hands of backward "others" or "natives," be they Arabs or monks, who had no idea of what they were the accidental custodians. Although monasteries such as St. Catherine's had housed ancient manuscripts for a thousand years, we are told the monks treated them with contempt, a frequent Protestant trope. The burning of manuscripts or the smashing of objects to find gold are commonplace in European "discovery" narratives. The locals' interest in these treasures was purely venal, so the Westerners reported. Mercifully, despite their ignorance, the light of the past had been uncovered. The university-trained Europeans and Americans alone understood the value of what they found, sufficient reason to relieve the monks of their treasures.

Returning to Europe with his new trove, Tischendorf was intentionally cagey about his exploits in the Sinai.[66] He was obsessed with what remained to be "found" in St. Catherine's. A third visit, in 1859, following his second in 1853, was sponsored by the Russian czar Alexander II, a patron of the monastery. Tischendorf hunted in vain until a brother opened an unexpected door to show him a manuscript far more extensive than anything he had yet seen. "Full of joy, this time I had the self-command to conceal it from the steward and the rest of the community. I asked, as if in a careless way, for permission to take the manuscript into my sleeping chamber to look over it more at leisure," recalled Tischendorf. "There by myself I could give way to the transport of joy which I felt. I knew I held in my hand the most precious biblical treasure in existence. . . . I cannot now, I confess, recall all the emotions which I felt in that exciting moment with such a diamond in my possession."[67] The abbot of the monastery was less enthusiastic and denied Tischendorf permission to copy the text, leading the German to appeal to higher authorities in Cairo. Tischendorf called the St. Catherine's work Codex Sinaiticus to honor the site of its discovery, the Sinai Desert.[68] Eager to study this new codex in the proper scholarly European world, Tischendorf took the codex to St. Petersburg, where he had patrons in the czar and czarina and where the accusations of theft began.

The nineteenth-century European scholarly world viewed the Bible as a historical document to be mined for traces of the earliest scriptural texts, a disposition that they had inherited from Renaissance humanists and Enlightenment scholars. The optimistic view that there was much to be discovered was not unfounded. The holy grail was the oldest and therefore most authoritative manuscripts of the Old and New Testaments. In this respect, Tischendorf had stumbled on a treasure. Tischendorf understood that what he had encountered at St. Catherine's was similar to the Codex Vaticanus, which had been brought to the papal library in Rome by Greeks in the fifteenth century. Both codices were invaluable witnesses to ancient versions of the Old and New Testaments. They were libraries of lost biblical texts. They took scholars further back toward the vanished originals.

Some, however, believed the Codex Sinaiticus to be a fake. In the 1840s and 1850s, Constantine Simonides (1820–1867), a brilliant Greek paleographer and forger, was involved in selling faked ancient documents, including two he asserted were the original Gospels of Mark and Matthew, written shortly after Christ's ascension.[69] In the fevered nineteenth-century market for ancient Christian and classical texts, Simonides was able to profit significantly. Among his duped customers was the king of Greece. In time Simonides was unmasked, and he fled Greece for England. In 1862 he claimed in the *Guardian* that he was the author of the Codex Sinaiticus, which he had completed at the age of nineteen in a monastery on Mount Athos, before Tischendorf's arrival in the Sinai. Tischendorf robustly attacked Simonides in print, dividing scholars into the credulous and the skeptical. The uproar was calmed only by crucial support offered to Tischendorf by the distinguished Cambridge scholar Henry Bradshaw, who in a letter to the *Guardian* the following year conclusively exposed Simonides's hoax.

The Codex Sinaiticus had not yet reached its final home. With the 1917 revolution in Russia, there was considerable anxiety in the West about the fate of the Codex Sinaiticus in the hands of the godless Communists. In 1925 the archbishop of the Sinai traveled to Moscow to ask for its return but was met with hostile silence. The Communists set store by the treasure, if not for religious or cultural reasons: it was an invaluable asset to be used to raise much-needed capital for the first Five-Year Plan. They put the Codex Sinaiticus up for sale. After complex negotiations, the British Library, backed by Prime Minister Ramsay MacDonald, offered £100,000, twenty times the prime minister's own salary. MacDonald hoped that such a triumph would lift the despondent mood of the post–World War I British population.

The transfer of the Codex Sinaiticus to London required a confluence of political, economic, and personal interests, but it arrived in the end, in December 1933. Long queues to see it formed outside the British Library. The *Times* reported that "the crowd appeared to be drawn from all sorts and conditions of men and women, and of many nations and languages. As they approached within sight of the many parchment sheets, on which under the electric light, the dark color of the script—four columns to the page—showed up distinctly, not a few were moved out of reverence to take off their hats."[70] The desire of the monks of St. Catherine's to have Sinaiticus returned continued to be dismissed.

The journey of Codex Vaticanus was no less adventurous, though little is known about the path it traveled from its origins in Roman Palestine to a papal library newly founded in the fifteenth century. Even if it was not one of the fifty Bibles sent to Constantinople after 331, it likely remained in the imperial city for centuries. It was restored sometime in the ninth or tenth century, when a Byzantine scribe traced over the original letters, obscuring some of the original text. While it may have been taken to a religious house in Sicily before making its way to Rome, the evidence is scant. Greek churchmen and diplomats went to Italy in the mid-fifteenth century to attend the Council of Ferrara-Florence, which was convened in 1438 in a desperate attempt to heal the schism between the Western and Eastern churches as the Ottomans pressed ever closer to Constantinople. It is plausible that they carried the Codex Vaticanus with them. The council involved an elaborate ceremony in the presence of the Byzantine emperor and the pope, although there is no record of the codex being presented on this occasion.[71] We know for certain only that it found its way to Rome.

By the time the Codex Vaticanus entered the Vatican library, it was certainly not in good condition and was rapidly deteriorating. Scribes restored the missing pages of Genesis, although they would not have had access to the manuscripts from which the codex had been made. Restoration included the introduction of significant changes, such as divisions through markings in the margins. Further, the collapsed binding led to the loss of part of the book of Psalms. Yet despite its condition, the Codex Vaticanus was evidently prized in Rome. Contemporaries realized they were in possession of a dilapidated witness to ancient versions of scripture.

In 1809, following his conquest of Italy, Napoleon Bonaparte ordered the Codex Vaticanus removed from the papal library and brought to Paris, where it was among the plunder he gathered to create a Paris worthy of his glory. Once their codex was returned after Napoleon's defeat and exile in 1815, the papal librarians continued to shield it from scholarly eyes—particularly those of Protestants, with their scrutiny of biblical texts. The English biblical scholar Samuel Prideaux Tregelles railed, "They would not let me open it without searching my pockets, and depriving me of pen, ink, and paper; and at the same time two prelati kept me in constant conversation in Latin, and if I looked at a passage too long, they would snatch the book out of my hand."[72] The frustration of another scholar was laced with anti-Catholic venom: "The history of the Codex Vaticanus B, No. 1209, is the history in miniature of Romish jealousy and exclusiveness."[73] Another said he saw nothing of it except the red morocco binding, while the British scholar Henry Alford was allowed to look at the codex but not use it.

The wall erected around the Codex Vaticanus left the ancient codex in limbo, with scholars unable to draw on its value as a guide to early versions of the Old and New Testaments. Some were skeptical that it was of any great importance. That error was dispelled in the late 1880s, when a photographic facsimile of the Codex Vaticanus, prepared in Milan, appeared in three volumes; another facsimile followed sometime between 1904 and 1907. In the wake of these publications, the Codex Vaticanus stood as one of the most important witnesses to the Greek text of the New Testament. Ninety years later, Italian scholars produced a beautiful color facsimile that enabled study of all the qualities of the codex, including its format and construction. And in 2015 the Vatican Library made the Codex Vaticanus available online in digital form with open access.[74]

Christians did not invent the book, but they very much made it their own. In the words of the fourth-century Cypriot bishop Epiphanius of Salamis, "The acquisition of Christian books is necessary for those who can use them. For the mere sight of these books renders us less inclined to sin, and incites us to believe more firmly in righteousness."[75] Far from a world of scrolls without any official canon, the early Christians had turned to the codex. For three centuries, these codices were often rough collections of biblical texts and interpretation that were rather scrappy in nature and intended for regular use. These were the daily fare of the vast majority of the faithful. With the creation of Sinaiticus, Vaticanus, and other great codices such as Alexandrinus, a sea change occurred. The bespoke Bible took center stage as an object of great beauty, reverence, and holiness. It demonstrated the artistic gifts of scribe and illuminator and the piety and power of their patrons.

With time, the codex had become a sacred object. Nothing conveys this change more dramatically than the crucial church councils of the fifth century, at Ephesus in 431 and at Chalcedon in 451. The physical presence of a Gospel codex at the assemblies legitimated these gatherings of church leaders. The codex was itself a holy artifact, divine and proximate to God. These works were not the complete Bibles of Sinaiticus or Vaticanus, which were rare, one-off productions. But no one regarded the Gospels as merely a part of the Bible—they represented Christ and therefore the fullness of the Bible. The litigants at the councils swore on the Gospel book, whose presence was required to confirm the assemblies. By the fifth century, the Bible as book had become an incarnation of the divine, its physical presence in the world.

CHAPTER 2

TONGUES OF FIRE

Huddled in a house in Jerusalem, Jesus's disciples had yet another surprise in store for them. As if the Resurrection and Jesus's risen appearance were not astonishing enough, they were about to receive an unexpected visitor. According to the book of Acts, "Suddenly there came a sound from heaven as of a rushing mighty wind, and it filled all the house where they were sitting. And there appeared unto them cloven tongues like as of fire, and it sat upon each of them. And they were all filled with the Holy Ghost, and began to speak with other tongues, as the Spirit gave them utterance" (Acts 2:1–4, KJV). Each began to speak a different language, so that all present heard them talking fluently in the various languages of the known world. The terrified followers of Jesus would thus be able to speak to people in every nation under heaven: "Parthians, and Medes, and Elamites, and the dwellers in Mesopotamia, and in Judaea, and Cappadocia, in Pontus, and Asia, Phrygia, and Pamphylia, in Egypt, and in the parts of Libya about Cyrene, and strangers of Rome, Jews and proselytes"

(Acts 2:9–10, KJV). The skeptics present thought the disciples were drunk, clearly aware that it is always easier to speak a foreign language after a couple of glasses of wine.

The millennium following the onrush of the Spirit in Jerusalem saw the languages in which the Bible was written proliferate across Asia, Africa, and Europe. Eventually, of course, this would result in several famous (infamous, to some) translations: Jerome's translation of the Bible into Latin, the language of the West; Luther's translation of the Bible into German; the King James Bible in English; and Samuel Ajayi Crowther's translation into Yoruba, a widespread language of West Africa. But diversity of translation was a hallmark of Christianity from the start. From their origins in Hebrew and Greek, with breathless speed the scriptures embraced Syriac and Persian in the East, Coptic and Ge'ez in Africa, Armenian and Georgian in the Caucasus, and Latin and Gothic in the West. The Bible was the book of the people and was constantly translated. For Christians, there was no holy language; there were many languages.

As explored in the previous chapter, the faithful's desire to understand the lessons, commands, and intentions of God drove a process by which the Bible came together as a set of fragments to form the unity of a book, with a designated canon and meaningful order of texts. As the Bible began entering new languages in the following centuries, however, the act of translation inevitably resulted in renewed interest in greater understanding, as well as increased fragmentation. Each new rendition, created within a new cultural context, acquired a life of its own. And each new translation loudly sold its wares: greater fidelity to the original, more accessible language, more appropriate for particular readerships.

Indeed, most Bibles today continue the ancient practice of providing the translator's explanation of their approaches to the languages and the strategies they used. Recognizing the difficulties of reading the Bible, translators have sometimes also offered paraphrases or even rewritings, such as the bestselling paraphrase The Living Bible (1971) with its "in other words" approach to scripture. To make the famous opening of John's Gospel more accessible, Kenneth Taylor came up with "Before anything else existed, there was Christ, with God. He has always been alive and is himself God" (John 1:12, TLB). People loved it, and The Living Bible has sold forty million copies.

Perhaps it says something about the human desire for certainty that the pull of an "official" form of the Bible has long had a deep hold, that certain translations are enshrined as "authoritative." But our willingness to accept claims to expertise and objectivity can obscure the truth that translators are never impartial and are always present in their work. They make crucial decisions, their choices shaped by cultural contexts and religious inclinations. They domesticate the biblical text by accommodating it to their specific audience, aware of the words and phrases spoken in the home and in the marketplace. As the wave of translations proliferated during the Bible's first millennium of existence, these choices revealed different communities, each struggling to hear God in its own language.

Each community needed God's word in its tongue, removing the Bible far from its origins in Hebrew and Greek. This guaranteed a life of exile for the book and new lives far from its homeland in Palestine. Like any migrant, the Bible continued to speak with its original accent, but it was quick to gain fluency in the languages of the known world.

One of the less familiar stories of the spread of the Bible beyond Hebrew and Greek concerns the influence of Semitic languages, spoken across North and East Africa and the Arabian Peninsula. Indeed, Semitic heritage is deeply embedded in the New Testament. The authors of the Gospels wrote in a style heavily influenced by Hebrew, typical of the Greek they spoke. Jesus spoke Aramaic, a Semitic language, and his words were orally transmitted and written in that language and later translated into Greek. The Gospels contain many sayings of Jesus that reveal his Aramaic background, but there are some intriguing moments that confirm that he was a polyglot. In the temple he reads from Isaiah in Hebrew and likely spoke that language with Jewish leaders in Jerusalem. We are not told how he conversed with Pilate, the Roman governor, but as there is no mention in the Gospels of any problem with communication, they probably spoke Greek, the language of Roman imperial rule and the elites in Judea. The writers of the New Testament appear to take for granted that Jesus was comfortable in the vernaculars of his region.

With the spread of early Christians eastward into Asia, the scriptures entered another Semitic language, Syriac, which is closely related to Hebrew and Aramaic.[1] From the second to eighth centuries, there were at least eight significant attempts to translate the Bible into Syriac, of which three tackled the Hebrew Bible and five the New Testament. As a result, some of the earliest surviving manuscripts of the New Testament are in Syriac. The second-century Syriac translation of the Old Testament suggests that it was the work of Jewish scholars.[2] A complete Syriac New Testament manuscript appeared in the early fifth century and contains the twenty-two books recognized by the Syriac churches but lacks 2 Peter, 2 and 3 John, Jude, and Revelation, which they did not accept. These two translations, known as the Peshitta, remain the Bible of Syriac Christianity today.

Further translations into Syriac followed over the sixth century. They included the "Philoxenian version," sponsored by Bishop Philoxenus of Mabbug, which restored the biblical books omitted by the Peshitta. Another version was the work of Thomas of Harqel, who after being deposed as a bishop in Syria went to a monastery in Egypt to find refuge, seek the life of the Spirit, and translate the Bible. Thomas was more a scholar than a pastor, and his work was much admired for its linguistic accuracy and for his notes. Of his Bible, he wrote: "This book is of the four holy evangelists, which was translated from the Greek language into the Syriac with much accuracy and great labor. . . . It was revised afterwards with much care by me, the poor Thomas, on [the basis of] three Greek manuscripts, which [were] very approved and accurate . . . for the profit of my sinful soul and of the many who love and desire to know and to keep the profitable accuracy of divine books."[3]

Syriac monasteries, with their remarkable libraries of books, ensured the richness of the Eastern tradition in other lands. The Syriac language provided the basis for translations of the Bible into Aramaic, Armenian, and Geʻez, as well as Persian and, later, Arabic. These translations of the Bible were carried by monks and merchants east to India and west to Africa.

Eastern churches had especially extensive contact with churches in Egypt and the ancient kingdom of Aksum, which covered much of what is today northern Ethiopia, southern Sudan, and Eritrea. The first translations of the Bible into Geʻez (classical Ethiopic), the ancient Semitic language that remains the liturgical language of the

Ethiopian church, appeared, it seems, in the fourth century.[4] But Christianity in Ethiopia grew from strong Jewish and Semitic roots. The fourteenth-century Ethiopian history *Kebra Nagast* (*Glory of the Kings*) tells how the queen of Sheba had an intimate affair with King Solomon and converted to the religion of the Israelites. She bore him a son, Menelik, believed to be the founder of the royal house of Ethiopia.

According to the *Kebra Nagast*, as a young man Menelik visited Solomon in Jerusalem to be educated in the Jewish faith and to be instructed in how to be a king. As the descendants of Menelik, all the monarchs of Ethiopia down to Haile Selassie I, who died in 1975, have taken the title "Lion of Judah." This tradition is embodied in the Revised Constitution of 1955, in which article 2 reads: "The Imperial dignity shall remain perpetually attached to the line ... which descends without interruption from the dynasty of Menelik I, son of the Queen of Ethiopia, the Queen of Sheba and King Solomon of Jerusalem."[5]

The book of Samuel recounts that Solomon sent Menelik back to Ethiopia accompanied by a son of the high priest Zadok (2 Sam. 15:24–29). Legend relates that the son agreed to accompany Menelik only if the Ark of the Covenant was taken from the temple in Jerusalem and brought to Ethiopia. The sacred ark was replaced with a replica and carried to the city of Aksum, where it is said to remain in the main church as a symbol of the legal inheritance of Israel. To this day, below the altar of every Ethiopian Christian church there is an ark, known as the tabot, that holds wooden or marble tablets with the Law. On feast days of the Ethiopian church, the tabot is processed with joyous singing and dancing, as King David had danced before the Ark of the Covenant.

The origins of the Ethiopian Bible are closely tied to the tradition of the Nine Saints, who led the conversion of the land. Although the stories of these saints likely date from a thousand years later, they continue to occupy a central place in the historical imagination of the Ethiopian church. In the miraculous tales, one of the saints, Abba Garima, flew to Aksum in 480 CE aided by the archangel Gabriel.[6] Whatever their origins, these early translations had an effect on the Ge'ez language, shifting the direction of writing to left-to-right, replacing the right-to-left of most Semitic languages, and introducing vowels into the language, making it easier to read.[7]

The Bible of the Ethiopian Orthodox Tewahedo Christian church today consists of from eighty-one to eighty-four books. Its scale reflects the early translations of the Ethiopian Bible from Greek into Ge'ez, which included not only all the books of the Hebrew Bible but also the books known collectively as the Apocrypha, as well as some others, including Enoch, Jubilees, the Ascension of Isaiah, Baruch, the Epistle of Jeremiah, Shepherd of Hermas, the Epistles of Clement, Didascalia Apostolorum, and the Apostolic Constitutions. The early tradition of the Ethiopian church made no distinction between these books and the Hebrew books of the Old Testament. They were all held to be inspired and canonical. Although Enoch and the book of Jubilees were known to early Christians, they survive only in their Ge'ez translations, a precious inheritance from the Jews who came into the land.

Across North Africa the Bible spread in Arabic, another Semitic language.[8] One Muslim writer of the ninth century recounted that one of the best-known Christian scholars from Baghdad, Hunayn ibn Ishaq (808–873), translated part of the Old Testament into Arabic. Another remarked, "This text has been translated a number of times into Arabic by earlier and more recent scholars, among them Hunayn ibn Ishaq."[9] The reference to the Bible being translated many times suggests a lively culture of Jewish and Christian scriptures that have not survived, though there are traces of these translations in references to the New Testament in Muslim literature. Influence also flowed the other way. Many of the early Arabic translations of the Bible reveal distinctively Muslim qualities of style and word choice. It is possible that as Arabic Christians became more enculturated in Islamic culture and linguistically and stylistically fluent, they lost contact with their traditional languages, such as Syriac and Greek.

The Sinai monastery of St. Catherine's, home of the Codex Sinaiticus encountered by Constantin von Tischendorf in the nineteenth century, possesses the earliest-dated Arabic biblical manuscript, a copy of the Gospels. The Epistles and Acts that followed contain a colophon—a description of a text's production usually placed at the end of the text—that provides an invaluable account of their origin and purpose:

The poor sinner Bishr ibn al-Sirrı translated these fourteen epistles from Syriac into Arabic, and provided an explanation of their interpretation, as much as his inadequate abridgement would allow, for his spiritual brother Sulayman. He finished it in the city of Damascus in the month of Ramadan in the year two hundred and fifty three. Praise be to God the Father, and the Son, and the Holy Spirit, forever and ever, Amen. May God have mercy on anyone who prays for mercy and forgiveness for the author, translator, and possessor [of this book].[10]

Notably, the writer dates the work according to the Islamic calendar, and the translation was from Syriac, not Greek, reflecting the strong Eastern influence on Arabic Christianity. Notes made in the margins over the following centuries reveal that the Epistles and Acts were used for worship and to instruct the faithful. Although we cannot know the full extent of production of Arabic translations of the Bible during the early period of Islamic rule, all evidence suggests a flourishing culture—one estimate is that there were 150 Christian translations of the Torah alone.[11]

In addition to the various Semitic translations that appeared during these early centuries, the Bible appeared in Coptic, the language of the Egyptian church. Coptic, which evolved from the ancient language of pharaonic Egypt and was spoken in Egypt from the second century CE, was written in Greek letters (with some additions) and adopted many of its Christian terms from Greek.[12]

Coptic emerged as a biblical language in the third century. There was, however, no one form of the language into which the Bible was translated but instead a range of dialects. One surviving witness from the fourth century is a translation of the Gospel of Matthew, one of the earliest to be found in any language. The spread of Coptic Bibles is known from the early fifth-century Akhmim Codex of the four Gospels, written in the Sahidic dialect of Coptic. Found at the end of the nineteenth century in the Egyptian town of Akhmim, on the Nile, it was subsequently transported to Berlin.

In 1945, some sixty miles further up the Nile, an Egyptian farmer at Nag Hammadi discovered a set of jars that proved to contain fifty-two treatises in thirteen leather-bound codices.[13] Written in Coptic, these writings reveal a world in which sacred works excluded from the Bible gave voice to a broad diversity of beliefs. These Gnostic texts had been explicitly condemned in 367 CE by Athanasius, whom we met in the last chapter, who made it his mission to suppress such heresy. The Theodosian decrees of the 390s further tightened the screw of doctrinal orthodoxy, excluding the Gnostics from churches.

Although many of the Gnostic texts are esoterica and difficult to fathom even for the trained eye, others are relatively easy to follow.[14] They contain the voices of Christians who struggled with the orthodox churches. These Christians held to beliefs—about the Creation, the powerful separation of matter and spirit, a feminine God, and Jesus Christ—that set them at odds with church leaders. Salvation was achieved, they believed, in gnosis, a divine self-knowledge.

Much as the Semitic translations of the Bible spread throughout North Africa and the Middle East, the Bible in Greek served as the foundation for translations north in Armenia, Georgia, and Slavic lands. Yet there is one important difference: the Greek Bibles of the Byzantine Empire formed the basis for new churches that did not possess a written vernacular culture, and thus they became symbols of a shared religion. They embodied the Byzantine Orthodox faith and the authority of the patriarch in Constantinople, demonstrating the perennial link between language and power.

Consider, for instance, the ancient kingdom of Armenia, which stood between, on one hand, the classical worlds of the Greek and Roman Empires and, on the other, the East, notably Syria, Persia, and, later, Islamic nations. Here the Bible actually created a language. The Christianity of the Caucasus was a product of religious syncretism but also bore a distinctive character shaped by holy men, doctrinal divisions, and war. The creation of the Armenian Bible (known as the "Breath of God" in Armenian) was complicated by the absence of a written form of the language.[15] Scripture was therefore initially only available in monasteries and in Syriac and Greek. Divided between the

Persians and Byzantines in the late fourth century, Armenia faced the loss of its heritage: the Persians required Christians to worship in Syriac and forbade Greek, while the Byzantines did precisely the opposite. For the majority of people, neither language was comprehensible.

The great Armenian historian Movses Khorenatsi (ca. 410–490) records how Mesrop Mashtots (362–440), a soldier turned monk and missionary, responded to the plight of the Christians.[16] Encouraged by the saintly Isaac of Armenia (also known as Sahak the Parthian, 354–439), who had become patriarch of the Armenian Apostolic Church, Mesrop created a thirty-six-letter Armenian alphabet, mostly drawn from Greek with some Syriac. Together with Isaac, he translated the Bible into Armenian from the Syriac Peshitta, although they also had access to both the Greek Septuagint and the Hebrew. Later, several Armenian monks who had been sent to Constantinople and Edessa to cultivate their skills in preparing Bibles returned bearing invaluable Greek manuscripts. These prized possessions enabled the creation of a much-improved version of the Armenian Bible.

The Armenian Bible was part of Isaac's wider religious labors on behalf of his land. As patriarch, he sent monks far afield to study in Mesopotamia, Eastern Anatolia, and Constantinople, learning from both the Greek and Eastern churches. The Greek and Syrian liturgies were translated into Armenian, as were the works of the eminent church fathers Athanasius, Cyril of Jerusalem, Gregory of Nazianzus, Gregory of Nyssa, and John Chrysostom. Isaac's vision was an Armenian Christianity that assimilated the best of Persian and Byzantine cultures while remaining distinctively native.[17]

In the fifth century, the earliest author in Armenian, Koriun (also known as Koriwn), prepared *The Life of Mashtots*, which offers an account of Mesrop's labors from these early years. (Koriun, who later became bishop of Armenia, also attempted his own translation of the Bible.)[18] He recalls Mesrop's first efforts with his students: "[They] began the translation of the Bible, first the Proverbs of Solomon, which begins with the exhortation, 'to know wisdom and instruction, to perceive the words of understanding.'" With this beautiful translation, Koriun continued, "our blessed and desirable land of Armenia became truly worthy of admiration, where, by the hands of two colleagues, suddenly, in an instant, Moses, the law-giver, along with the order of the prophets, energetic Paul, with the entire phalanx of the apostles, along with Christ's world-sustaining gospel, became Armenian speaking."[19]

The classical translation of Isaac and Mesrop remained the Armenian Bible until the Middle Ages. The written text primarily existed, however, in the rarified world of the educated few. Most women and men encountered scripture through worship and by learning to recite biblical stories. This oral tradition is evident in the historian Ghazar P'arpetsi's (ca. 442–ca. 510) history of Armenia: "Our blessed teachers taught us the whole of the covenant of the church three or four times from the beginning to the end of the book, demanding the same from us, and forced us to repeat it like the Psalms of David."[20]

Though never popular items in their own time, more ancient Armenian Bibles survive today than any other ancient translation.[21] This translation also demonstrates the significant diversity of the Bible in these early centuries, as it includes numerous books elsewhere labeled apocryphal, including the Testaments of the Twelve Patriarchs and Joseph and Asenath. Its New Testament also contains the Epistle of the Corinthians to Paul and a third letter from the apostle to the Corinthians, though it lacks the last twelve verses of the Gospel of Mark, known as the "long ending."

In Georgia, biblical texts appeared by the end of the fourth century, and as in Armenia, the Bible played a crucial role in the formation of a written script.[22] The earliest literary texts bear witness to the great diversity of Georgian Christianity, with books about the lives of saints featuring characters who are Armenian, Iranian, and Arabian. Faith was by adherence to the sacred message of the Bible, not ethnicity.[23] The ninth to thirteenth centuries saw a flourishing of Christianity in Georgia, with churches constructed and decorated with magnificent frescoes, as well as a flowering of Georgian literary and biblical culture. One of the biblical treasures of the period is the Adysh Gospels—the oldest surviving biblical Georgian manuscript—with its first five folios illuminated.[24] Created in 897 at Shatberdi Monastery in a Georgian principality now in northeastern Turkey, they were moved to the village of Adishi in northeastern Georgia.[25] The Adysh Gospels lack Christ's agony in the garden, the woman taken in adultery, and the longer ending of the Gospel of Mark, as well as a number of passages found in almost all Greek New Testaments. Subsequently, during a period of increased Byzantine influence, efforts were made to bring the Georgian Bible in line with the Greek, primarily by Euthymius (ca. 955–1024), a learned monk from Mount Athos, and his followers.[26]

Byzantine influence was also instrumental in the gradual appearance of Slavic Bibles, including by providing access to Byzantine cultural resources, such as libraries and manuscripts.[27] The creation of the first Slavic translations is, however, obscured by myth.[28] As *The Life of St. Methodius* recounts:

> Rejecting all the tumults, placing his cares upon God, he [Methodius, 815–885] first took two priests from among his disciples, who were excellent scribes, and translated quickly

from the Greek into Slavonic—in six months, beginning with the month of March to the twenty-sixth day of the month of October—all the scriptures in full, save Maccabees. And upon finishing, he rendered due thanks and praise unto God, who grants such peace and success, and performed the elevation of the blessed Mystery, celebrating the memory of Saint Demetrius. For previously he had translated with the Philosopher [Methodius's brother Cyril, 826–869] only the Psalter, the Gospel together with the Apostolos, and selected church liturgies.[29]

This frequently quoted passage should not be taken at face value. The legend of Cyril and Methodius's complete Bible is troubled by the lack of any known complete Slavic Bible before the end of the fifteenth century.[30] Rather, the passage may well offer the saints' sanction for rendering scripture into the language of the people. For Cyril's contemporaries, no achievement outdid his creation of an alphabet (appropriately named Cyrillic), for which he invented letters that he, reputedly following God's command, employed to compose homilies.[31] That step was primarily driven by a desire to bring the Bible to the Slavs through missions, as part of a goal to unite the Western and Eastern churches.[32]

The influence of Byzantine on the spread of the Bulgarian Bible was less beneficent. Following the conversion of the Bulgarians to Christianity in 864 CE, the city of Preslav emerged as a key military, political, and religious center. By the end of the century, it had become the seat of Bulgarian rulers and flourished as the heart of Slavic culture, focused in particular on the Preslav Literary School, a base for scholars, including translators, as well as writers, poets, and painters. However, following the Byzantine invasion of Bulgaria, the

Bulgarian biblical culture that had flourished in Preslav was forced into exile, first to Mount Athos in northern Greece and then to newly Christian Rus. Many Bulgarian books were transported into foreign lands to be preserved. The Grand Prince of Kyiv also conquered parts of Bulgaria and took home with him books, manuscripts, and clergy, beginning a new story in the East. Here begins the story of the Bible in Ukraine and Rus.

In Africa and Asia, every new Bible lay at the crossroads of cultures, and no translation existed without inheriting linguistic, theological, ritual, and political legacies. Language both united and divided cultures, engaging peoples of different convictions. Move westward in the Mediterranean world, however, and the story of biblical translation unfolds rather differently. Across the sprawling Roman Empire, Latin dominated as lingua franca.

Yet even within a shared language, translation was not without controversy. In 403 CE Augustine, bishop of Hippo in North Africa (modern-day Algeria), wrote to the author of a new Latin translation of the Bible. The bishop was clear that new was not necessarily better. During a reading from the book of the prophet Jonah, he reported, a congregation had heard a "very different rendering from that which had been of old familiar to the senses and memory of all the worshippers, and had been chanted for so many generations in the church."[33] Members of the congregation had been deeply offended and had protested.

Augustine reported that the bishop had consulted with Jews in the town of Oea (present-day Tripoli in Libya), who told him that the traditional Latin translation was accurate. The new translation was wrong.

"What further need I say?" asked Augustine. "The man was compelled to correct your version in that passage as if it had been falsely translated, as he desired not to be left without a congregation—a calamity which he narrowly escaped." The response of outrage demonstrated the voice of the people in the choice of the sacred text. The author of the offending translation was none other than Jerome, now regarded as one of the greatest translators of the Bible but not much appreciated in his time. The almost church brawl in North Africa is but one story in a long history of the preference of a known Bible translation over the presumption of a better translation.

So what version of the scriptures was held in such deep affection by the people of Augustine's diocese? From the second century, Latin versions of the scriptures had spread across the North African and Mediterranean world.[34] These did not, however, originate among the early Christians in Rome—who up to the third century continued to speak Greek—but rather from North Africa. These scriptures from Africa are referred to as the "Old Latin."[35] The arresting diversity of these Latin versions owes to their multiple sources, Greek and Syriac, and to scribes exercising considerable freedom in copying the texts. The predictable result was all manner of variations with the Gospels of the New Testament. And the Latin Old Testament had been largely translated from the Greek Septuagint, which added its own variation of forms.

Contemporaries were fully aware the Latin manuscripts of the Bible diverged from locality to locality to such an extent that no one knew what was original or authentic. Such uncertainty was a source of considerable anxiety. Augustine in North Africa, who knew little Greek and ministered to a Latin-speaking diocese accustomed to the Old Latin, expressed his disquiet: "Those who translated the

Scriptures from Hebrew into Greek can be counted," he wrote, "but the Latin translators are out of all number. For in the early days of the faith everyone who happened to gain possession of a Greek manuscript and thought he had any facility in both languages, however slight that might have been, attempted to make a translation."[36]

Augustine's concern about the number of Latin versions was shared by a pope. Damasus I (305–384), eager to reform the church, was persuaded that an authoritative version of the Bible was essential for unity in the West under the auspices of Rome. The man to whom he turned was a brilliant, ambitious, and controversial figure untroubled by self-doubt. Jerome of Stridon (ca. 342–420) believed himself uniquely chosen and qualified to provide the church with a Latin Bible prepared from the original languages of Hebrew and Greek.[37] Such was the towering confidence of the man later made a saint and a doctor of the church that he saw in himself not only the synthesis of Eastern and Western Christianity but also the synthesis of Greece and Rome with the true faith.[38]

Jerome wanted his translation to be both faithful to the original languages and written in the very best Latin. But Hebrew and Latin are entirely different languages (Semitic and Indo-European) and extremely difficult to reconcile. The former reads from right to left and has no vowels, and its poetic beauty evades easy capture in Latin. How to make the prophets of Israel speak excellent Latin?[39]

Jerome's approach proved enduringly influential. He wrote of "Hebrew verity," by which he meant that the translator must be immersed not only in the language but also in the culture that produced it.[40] In other words, one must understand the world of the Hebrew Bible in order to translate its sacred text. Further, as there could be no direct equivalence between two radically different languages, and as Jerome thought one must avoid ugly and misleading literal translations, he believed that each language should be treated according to its own characteristics and beauty. The wonder of the Hebrew should be expressed in the finest Latin. In the sixteenth century Erasmus would name Jerome the "Christian Cicero."

Working in Jerusalem and greatly aided by Jewish teachers and assistants, Jerome prepared a Latin translation of the Hebrew Bible. It does not diminish his work at all to acknowledge that Jerome also made use of other translations, such as the Septuagint and the Hexapla of Origen. His New Testament, which followed later, was not entirely Jerome's work, as he made extensive use of Old Latin versions. The resulting Latin Bible had a somewhat compositive character, but it was nevertheless a landmark.

Jerome carefully cultivated his persona as an ascetic, monk, and scholar.[41] Translation, like the scribal work discussed in the previous chapter, is a form of spiritual torture. Struggling to render the words of God into the language of the people was not only intellectually and spiritually challenging but also physically painful. "Composing has become so difficult," Jerome recorded, "that with the clouded eyes of extreme old age, suffering to some extent what the blessed Isaac did, we can no longer read the Hebrew scrolls by the light of night. Indeed, even in the blaze of the daytime sun, we are blinded by the smallness of the letters."[42] Later Renaissance scholars would often speak of how translation brought them to the brink of death.

Bodily pain, however, was alleviated by the translator's love of the Bible. In a famous letter often included in medieval editions of his translation, Jerome spoke of his labors as "a foretaste of heaven here on earth." Each translation, he believed, was but a faint vision of God's Word, and one should not be put off by the flawed efforts of those who attempt the task. Nevertheless, translation was risky "as the educated person can take one meaning and the uneducated another from one and the same sentence."[43]

Jerome admitted his shortcomings in a letter to Paulinus of Nola in 394 CE: "I am not so dull or so forward," he wrote, "as to profess that I myself know it, or that I can pluck upon the earth the fruit which has its root in heaven, but I confess that I should like to do so." For the translator who modestly and constantly strives like a student, there is a promise: "'Every one that asks receives; and he that seeks finds; and to him that knocks it shall be opened.' [Matt. 7:8] Let us learn upon earth that knowledge which will continue with us in heaven."[44]

Despite Jerome's achievement, the dramatic transition from old to new that so concerned Augustine did not immediately take place. Over the next five hundred years, Jerome's translation continued to coexist alongside the Old Latin versions, often with both interwoven. One of the reasons for the diversity of texts is precisely that Jerome never produced a single codex of the Bible. He sent his texts to friends as individual books or collections of books to be distributed. When the books began to be compiled, they were often put together with versions of the Old Latin in varying combinations.[45] Another reason is simply that Jerome's translation possessed no particular authority, empowering scribes to feel at liberty to correct what they saw as errors and rely on the more familiar Old Latin translations. The medieval West in the first millennium still had no singular Latin translation but a vast multitude of local traditions of the Bible, regional in character.

Picking and choosing your version of the Bible was the norm. Pope Gregory (ca. 540–604), for instance, whose many achievements included reform of the Roman liturgy and missions from Rome to Anglo-Saxon England, noted in his commentary on Job (known as

Moralia in Job) that he used both the new translation (Jerome's) and the old (Old Latin).[46] Spanish scholar and cleric Isidore of Seville (d. 636), often referred to as the last great scholar of early Christianity, had a strong preference for Jerome, although he too made use of other translations. On the canon of the Bible, both Gregory and Isidore followed Jerome in regarding the Hebrew books of the Old Testament as of greater value and holding that while the Greek Apocrypha could edify, it could not form the basis for doctrine.

In time, however, concern arose in more elite circles that Jerome's authentic voice should be recovered, that it represented the supreme expression of scripture in Latin. Gradually, Jerome's translation became a powerful religious and culture symbol of becoming "Roman" and "civilized." The sixth-century patrician Roman senator Cassiodorus (ca. 485–ca. 580) led efforts to restore Jerome's Latin Bible to its original form. Following his retirement, Cassiodorus founded a monastery called Vivarium, from whose scriptorium he sought to make available the best possible text of Jerome's translation.[47] Jerome's Bible was a lifeline to the glories of Roman learning, a tradition eagerly sought by ambitious rulers of early medieval Europe.

When in the ninth century Charlemagne sought to restore the vanished glory of Rome and unite a deeply fragmented Christian world, he looked to Jerome's Latin Bible as the link to the essence of Roman Christianity.[48] It would serve as the foundation of a church united by worship, prayer, and education under his auspices. But the best text of Jerome's translation was required, for all blemishes detracted from the glory of God and emperor. At Christmas 801 the great Northumbrian scholar Alcuin (d. 804), who had been invited to the Carolingian court, presented Charlemagne with a single volume of the Bible that he had corrected and believed to be the most faithful to Jerome.[49] Writing to Charlemagne, Alcuin indicated he was presenting the emperor with the most precious of gifts: "Nothing appeared more worthy of Your Peaceful Honor than the gift of the Sacred Scriptures; which, by the dictation of the Holy Spirit and the mediation of Christ God, were written with the pen of celestial grace for the salvation of mankind."[50]

Alcuin's task was not a new translation, for there was no need to replace the work of the blessed Jerome. Instead, he sought to recover Jerome, an endeavor he undertook by referring to Bibles brought over from his native England, primarily Northumbria.[51] His remarkable pandect of the whole Bible was made in the scriptorium in Tours, which would produce complete Bibles of rare quality. Bibles were produced in Tours at the rate of two per year for over fifty years and soon spread across Europe. The Tours Bibles were very large, and their layout and script were brilliantly clear. Two to twenty-four scribes worked on each creation, and work continued long after the deaths of both Alcuin, in 804, and Charlemagne, in 814.

Forty-six complete Bibles and eighteen Gospel books from the period before 853 remain extant.[52] A fine example is the Moutier-Grandval Bible, made under Abbot Adalhard between 834 and 843, now housed in the British Library and available digitally online.[53] For the first time, the Bible was now referred to as a *bibliotheca*, or library, a name that gestures toward a set of books gathered according to a particular logic.[54]

At the same time as the great scholar Alcuin was producing his revisions of Jerome's translation, other corrected texts appeared from the hands of contemporary scholars. They were not competition but part of a shared effort to find the best text of the Latin Bible. Across France to the Rhineland and south to central Italy, a vast number of Bibles were produced in pursuit of providing the Carolingians with an accurate and reliable text.[55] Carolingian culture therefore possessed a rich variety of Bibles. Perhaps the most spectacular are the Lindau Gospels, now in the Morgan Library and Museum in New York. Created at the Abbey of St. Gall in Switzerland in the late ninth century for Charlemagne's grandson, Charles the Bald (823–877), the Gospels are bound with a jeweled cover of beauty almost unmatched in the Middle Ages. The front has a gold repoussé Christ on the cross with precious jewels. The richness of distant influences is reflected by the ornamental linings inside the front and back of the codex. The front cover has exquisite Byzantine silk lining while the back is Islamic design.[56]

Innovations during the Carolingian period included single-volume Bibles intended to be consulted by scholars and read from in lectures in major churches. Scholars restlessly annotated, edited, and transmitted the biblical text in the quest to improve the text. The volumes were a powerful statement of the Bible as a single story, unified in its account of God's creative and sustaining power. The physical form of the Bible as a single book was integral to what its sacred text was held to be.[57] Additionally, glossed Bibles were produced, with passages from writings of the church fathers copied into the margins or between the lines of the sacred text. One tenth-century Bible from Werden, Germany, contains commentaries by Jerome, the Venerable Bede (author, scholar, and teacher at Monkwearmouth-Jarrow Abbey), and Alcuin, which made it very much part of the educational purposes of the age.

The story of the Bible in England casts in relief a story of language we have encountered numerous times throughout this chapter. The scriptures were received in England by an oral culture that had little tradition of writing in the various Anglo-Saxon dialects. Latin was the language of the church and newly founded monasteries, but preaching was in the vernacular. The Bible also entered into popular culture through poetry and songs. Not surprisingly, the verse form of the Psalms made them a particular favorite. Long before the first translation of the Gospels into Anglo-Saxon in the tenth century, the Bible therefore circulated among the people as an oral text that they likely knew by heart and could sing and recite. Bede records the story of the monk Caedmon, who, unable to sing, withdrew from a gathering to be among animals. Having fallen asleep, he dreamed of a voice telling him to sing of creation. When he awoke, he was miraculously able to translate "passages of sacred history or doctrine" into "the sweetest of songs."[58]

King Alfred (848/49–899) laid the foundation for the first full translations of scripture into Anglo-Saxon by making the language an acceptable medium for governance and religion. But the first full translation of the Gospels into Anglo-Saxon—more precisely, into the Old English West Anglo-Saxon dialect of Northumbria—did not appear until the Wessex Gospels, begun around a hundred years after Alfred's death. Like the Armenians and Ethiopians long before them, the English sought to hear God speak to them in their own language.

The Bible, of course, provides the origin story for such linguistic fragmentation and the accompanying limits of our understanding: the story of the Tower of Babel (Gen. 11:1–9). It starts, "The whole world had one language and a common speech" (NIV). Then the people built a city with a tower that reached to the heavens, a tower that would bring them renown. God saw their hubris and pondered, "If as one people speaking the same language they have begun to do this, then nothing they plan to do will be impossible for them. Come, let us go down and confuse their language so they will not understand each other" (Gen. 11:6–7, NIV). With comprehension comes opportunity, for good and for ill. But every translation is contingent, a product of a moment that, unlike the Bible, is not eternal. At that moment the Bible holds something back. This was, at least, the experience of a vast cast of first-millennium missionaries, hermits, teachers, emperors, kings, queens, monks, priests, scholars—and translators.

CHAPTER 3

MANIFESTATION OF THE SAVIOR

Enter the Chora Church in the Edirnekapi neighborhood of Istanbul and you will find yourself in the presence of Christ Pantocrator ("Ruler of All"), one of the first depictions of Christ developed by the early Christian church.[1] In the image, which signifies the return of the Son of God and the Last Judgment, his face is melancholy and stern, his right hand is raised in blessing, and a bejeweled Gospels sits in his left. The inscription reads "Jesus Christ, the dwelling-place of the living."

This particular mosaic dates from the fourteenth century, a wonder of late medieval Byzantine art, but it depicts a remarkable transformation that occurred during the first millennium: the transformation of the Bible into a holy object.[2] Not only does the image portray the Son of God holding a book, but in doing so, his glorified body and the book, ornate and decorated with precious stones, are presented as one—both are gospel, the Word of God.

Jews and early Christians did not think of their scriptures primarily in terms of their physicality. The disciples had heard Christ's actual words, touched the wounds in his hands. The rolls and leaves stitched together spoke the ancient wisdom of Israel and the words of Jesus and the apostles, but they were just rolls and leaves. The book became Christ visible in the world.

From the fifth century, however, the Bible itself became an object of veneration. Together with the physical expressions of Christian imaginative piety—relics, wall paintings, and architecture—the Bible was seen as the ultimate symbol of the sacred. The architectural forms in the Bibles, with canon tables and illuminations, remind us that each book was a re-creation of the tabernacle, the entrance into the holy.[3] Like the bread and wine of the Eucharist, the Bible was Christ's physical presence in the world, reenacted daily in the liturgies of the churches across the Christian world. Indeed, by the eighth century, the scholar Alcuin at the court of Charlemagne could speak of the rare complete Bibles as "the font of life."[4] These Bibles contained, he claimed, "in one holy body all these things at the same time, the great gifts of God." As the Bible was God's gift to humanity, not unlike Christ himself, it became a holy object to be presented to others, such as princes, as priceless symbols of their divine authority.

But what caused this transformation? How did what were once mere pieces of papyri found in Egyptian rubbish piles become an object that was itself seen as the body of Christ? The Bible became a translation of human yearning for a text not just of words but of transcendent beauty. That beauty expresses holiness and encounter, a relationship between the beholder and the object that enhances the written word.

It demands a response. The Bible acquired a new voice, the speaking of physical beauty to move the faithful toward a transformation of life. The beauty of the Bible expressed and fed a visceral desire to receive and experience God through all senses. In word and image, the Bible became seductive and sensuous. It was the mutual attraction of lover and beloved of the Song of Songs, an image widely embraced by Christian writers.

Responses to the beauty of the Bible took place through individual and communal worship. Words and images of the book were harmonized with bodily movement and stimulated senses. As the message of the Bible could no longer be separated from its physical presence, the book itself came to play a central role in Christian liturgy. Beginning sometime around the fifth century, the Bible became a book to be seen, heard, and touched. Although it was held mostly in the hands of priests, scholars, and their patrons, the Bible had diverse ways of extending beyond the elites to invite all into its presence through worship. Standing in front of wall paintings and mosaics that visualized the biblical stories, hearing the voice of preachers and lay readers, or listening to the chant of priests and monks, the people were enveloped in the Word. In cultures dominated by spoken words, visual images, and tactile objects, common and elite Christians dwelt among representations of the divine in relics, paintings, architecture, and sacraments. The Bible as a book entered into this sacred landscape, taking its place in the sensuousness of the holy.[5]

In Coptic Egypt the intimate bond between the Bible and sacred space was realized in the great monasteries.[6] Among the most esteemed figures of this tradition is the Coptic monk Shenoute of Atripe (ca. 347–465), who was for over eighty years the spiritual father of a federation of three monasteries in Upper Egypt near the modern town of Akhmim, as well as a decisive figure in the establishment of Coptic as the literary language of Egyptian Christianity.[7] His voluminous writings were stored in the White Monastery for over a thousand years, and for centuries after his death, the White Monastery drew pilgrims to celebrate the feast of the desert of Apa Shenoute, which involved the association of Shenoute with Elijah and Christ.

Every part of the celebration was guided by scripture. The sharing of a simple midday meal was accompanied by passages from the Bible about food, drink, and cooking. At various stations, or stopping points, during their progression around his spiritual home, the pilgrims heard passages of scripture read or chanted, drawing them into the biblical narrative and the life of the "Father of these Congregations." From the twelfth chapter of the Gospel of John, they heard, "Walk while ye have the light, lest darkness come upon you. . . . While ye have light, believe in the light, that ye may be the children of light" (12:35–36, KJV).[8] And they walked into the light. Toward the end of the procession, likely in the evening, the pilgrims entered into the brilliantly illuminated church of the monastery, the Church of the Virgin and of St. George, where they sang hymns of praise to Mary, mother of God, and looked devoutly on icons of St. George, always accompanied by the reading of the Bible.[9] What began outside led to the monastery, the movement symbolic of internalizing the Word.

The ascetic St. Anthony in the Egyptian desert recited scripture in his imitation of Christ. In his battle against demons, he invoked Psalm 118—"The LORD is with me; he is my helper. I look in triumph on my enemies" (NIV)—as Jesus had rebuked the devil with scripture. So, too, the monastic houses consecrated time to the service of God and the rejection of evil. Their walls offered a world of isolation in which religious men and women led lives shaped in every way by scripture.[10] Scenes from the Old and New Testaments, from the Creation to the Last Judgment, were painted on walls, with biblical figures mingling with saints. Scripture molded the ritual worlds of these houses, transforming them into Jerusalems through sacred biblical time, making monks the earthly representatives of the heavenly host. As previously discussed, most Bibles were prepared in monastic scriptoria and were for monastic use.[11] And in the liturgies of the church offices the monks performed through the day and year, the Bible was read and chanted.

The sixth-century rules of St. Benedict, which laid out instructions for life in monasteries in the West, required monks to set aside two hours a day for the reading of the Bible, known as lectio divina, in the belief that contemplation of the words would lead to the transformation of the self into the life of God's Word.[12] One rule summoned monks to "cultivate silence" in order for scripture to take hold and bear fruit. Memorizing scripture made the mind, the soul, and the heart a sanctuary for the divine. Monks learned the Bible, above all the Psalms, by heart and lived out the biblical stories ritually, as in processions with the book. In liturgy and in the hours of monastic life, biblical scenes were daily reenacted according to an order that mirrored God's creative purpose.

But it was not merely monks, separated from the world, who celebrated and performed the scripture. For the majority of Christian men and women, this occurred through the liturgies of worship, the place where heaven and earth touched. The liturgy, for them, was not merely outward action but a manifestation and ritual reenactment of creation and redemption. In worship, the temporal became divine. It was structured time and movement in which they were in the presence of what created and sustained them. They were not passive spectators but actors in a divine drama.

From the beginnings of Christian worship, liturgy gave shape to worshippers' recollection and reenactment of the passion, burial, and resurrection of the Son of God. In mind and body, they participated in the biblical story. Over the ensuing centuries many writers recounted this experience, but a beautiful evocation of worship from the Hagia Sophia in the eleventh century in Constantinople survives from the hand of Nicholas of Andida. The holy rites, he observed, "signify all the manifestations that accompanied his entire saving life among us in the flesh: his conception, his birth and his life in the first thirty years, the activity of the forerunner, and his public appearances at his baptism."[13] In the liturgy the faithful were healed, their sins forgiven, and their inheritance of the kingdom of heaven assured.

The Bible is liturgy, the performance of God's words. The Byzantine liturgy was infused with biblical text and symbolism not only in what was heard but also in all that surrounded the worshippers visually: crosses, icons, the vestments of the clergy, the architecture of the church buildings, and the frescoes on the walls.[14] The anticipation of the end of time, when Christ will return to judge the whole of humanity, was conveyed in the sacred space in which the people stood. Churches were visions of heaven, the fulfillment of time and divine promises.

And in this cosmic drama, the Bible provided the holy narrative. For the medieval writer Nicholas Kabasilas (ca. 1322–1392), the Bible represented "the manifestation of the Savior, by which he became known soon after his showing." He described its role in the drama of the liturgy:

> The first showing of the Gospels, with the book closed, represents the first appearance of the Savior, by which he became known soon after his showing. The first showing of the Gospels, with the book closed, represents the first appearance of the savior, when, while he himself remained silent, the Father made him manifest . . . but that which is represented here (in the proclamation of the scriptures) is his more perfect manifestation, during which he mingled with the crowd and made himself known not only by his own words, but also by that which he taught to his Apostles. . . . That is why the Gospel and Epistle are read.[15]

Similarly, the Bible also played a central role in Egyptian Coptic worship, above all in the liturgy named for Basil of Caesarea (331–379), bishop and theologian.[16] In the Mass the Bible was read at several points, notably the Epistles of Paul, the Catholic Epistles (the letters of James, Peter, John, and Jude), the Acts of the Apostles, and the Gospels. At the conclusion of each reading, the congregation offered praise to Mary: "Hail to you, Mary, the fair dove, who has borne unto us God the Logos."[17] The priest incensed the Gospel, the icons of the saints, the congregation, and then the altar. Together, the images, words, and bodies form the sacred witness. Following the reading of the Acts of the Apostles, the altar was incensed, as the priest alternated between east and west, and then once more the icons and Gospel. The chronicle of the saints was read before the congregation sang a hymn to Christ: "Holy God, Holy: Mighty, Holy Immortal, who was crucified for us, have mercy upon us." For Christians, then as today, ritual presented the unity of heaven and earth that was the church as the body of Christ.

The acts of speaking and hearing in the ancient Armenian liturgy likewise have their roots deep in the Hebrew Bible, where God addresses Moses before the people at the foot of the mountain. According to the medieval Armenian theologian St. Gregory of Datev (1346–1410), the lectern that held the Gospels on the bema, the elevated platform from which the Bible is read, was Mount Sinai.[18] The deacon summoning the people to hear God's word was the thunder and lightning. The Gospel was the voice of God. The incense surrounding the procession and reading of the Gospel was the trumpets, while the coal providing the incense was the fiery presence of God on Mount Sinai. The rising incense symbolized the clouds around the mount, and in this unfolding biblical drama, the gathered faithful became the Israelites.

Although men and women heard the Bible read, performed, and interpreted in the liturgies of the church, they did so in particular ways determined by the churches. The Bible was not read from start to finish but in selected readings (or lections) arranged according to the seasons of the Christian year. The source of these readings was known as a lectionary and, with its collection of biblical passages, likewise became an object of veneration.

Bibles and lectionaries in the Orthodox churches existed in a relationship of mutual dependence. The lectionaries were a different form of Bible created by the church to guide the faithful along the sacred path of life. In many respects, the lectionaries were practical applications of the Bible, bringing scripture into human time through the year with the promises of eternity. Lectionaries, therefore, were not simply books for consultation or reference but sacred objects in the performance of the liturgy.[19] Sometimes illustrated and bejeweled, they were used in every church and monastery, and during the service they were carried into the sanctuary and placed on the altar by a deacon.[20] The priest would process with the lectionary through the royal doors, or "beautiful gate," before returning the book to the altar. The volume would then be removed from the altar once more during the readings from scripture and used to make the sign of the cross. Not uncommonly, the four evangelists are portrayed on the frontispiece of lectionaries, conveying the intimate bond between the authors and their words.

By the fifth and early sixth centuries the Bible had emerged as an icon.[21] The word "iconic" has become rather threadbare in our society, applied mostly as a cliché to sports stars and celebrities. But as applied to the Bible, it has a deeper meaning. For Christians, icons are sacred images that, far from being mere artistic representations, are portals to heaven. From early centuries, icons were a central pillar of the Orthodox tradition. They were thought to mediate persons and events of salvation directly and immediately, alongside the verbal images of scripture, hymns, and the stories of martyrs.[22] Icon "writers" (the name for artists) are described by Orthodox fathers as freeing matter, such as wood and paint, to offer it back to God. These writers followed prayerful steps, meditating during each moment of creating an image. The resulting icons, which bring together various sources to place the viewer in the world of the Bible, were often referred to by Eastern writers as "windows into heaven." They drew the viewer into an intimate relationship of prayer and contemplation, just as participation in the liturgy did, and served as a means by which Christ's luminosity was transmitted.

The use of biblical images was also deployed by emperors, conveying their divine presence and intimate relationship with the Logos, the Word of God. Biblical images suffused the Byzantine sense of the imperial and the unbreakable bond between the sacred and the political. The historian Eusebius recounts Emperor Constantine as unequivocal: "You are bishops whose jurisdiction is within the Church: I also am a bishop, ordained by God to overlook whatever is external to the Church."[23] Already by the time of Justinian, the Genesis figure of Melchizedek was invoked in speaking of the emperor as priest and king. On account of his special status, even Abraham, the father of all peoples, offered sacrifice to Melchizedek, which became a central theme in Byzantine art.[24]

Most icons were of Christ, Mary, and the apostles, signifying the central role of the Gospels in Byzantine Christianity. Matthew, Mark, Luke, and John were the most copied texts of the Bible, and together with the Psalms they formed the lifeblood of worship, continuously read through the year. So venerated was the Gospel book that it was itself regarded as an icon of Christ himself.[25]

The connection was immediate. From the fourth century the Gospels were often accompanied by portraits of the evangelists, uniting their iconic gaze with their written text. Traditionally decorated with an icon of the Crucifixion on the front and Jesus's descent into hell on the back, Gospel books in their beauty evoked the mysteries of the faith. Their symbolism as books reflected the conviction that the Bible was not the end in itself but a sacred guide to the spiritual world, at the heart of which is the mystery of Christ and new life in him.[26] The Bible brought the faithful to a personal encounter and communion with God through prayerful reading and worshipful hearing of the Word.[27] Recently, Archimandrite Sergei, head of the Joseph-Volokolamsk Monastery near Moscow, home of the newly opened Russian Museum of the Bible, spoke of their rich collection of Bibles: "Icons are national traditional treasures of Russia," he said, adding, "These books are also icons, only written in letters."[28]

Despite the importance of sacred images during these early centuries, their use was not without unease, even conflict. There was little consensus on whether and how the divine might be represented through human hands. Aspirations to convey God through artistry clashed with contrary convictions. Could the words delivered by God, the patriarchs, prophets, Christ, and apostles be rendered in visual form?

The Bible itself seemed to offer an uncompromising response. The second commandment God thundered to Moses on Mount Sinai emphatically declared, "Thou shalt not make unto thee any graven image, or any likeness of any thing that is in heaven above, or that is in the earth beneath, or that is in the water under the earth: Thou shalt not bow down thyself to them, nor serve them" (Exo. 20:4–5, KJV). While Moses was on the mount, the Israelites grew impatient, and Aaron's weak leadership led to the idolatry of the golden calf. In punishment three thousand men were put to death.

The Jewish tradition avoided representations of God, but Christians were less certain. Their God had entered into human flesh in order to be seen and heard and known. And yet the matter was not so easily resolved. The Orthodox churches of the East in the eighth and ninth centuries were torn apart by debate over the role of images in Christianity.[29] A council in Constantinople declared in their favor, but questions remained. Even if images of the divine were acceptable and edifying, what was their relationship to the written text? Were they of equal value? Views diverged. Gregory the Great (540–604) declared images on church walls and elsewhere to be scriptures for the illiterate.[30] Others, including Augustine in North Africa, were less persuaded. The bishop of Hippo inveighed against any form of equivalence. Images were a poor substitute for the words of scripture and could easily deceive or be misunderstood. For the common faithful they were a false friend. Over time, however, devotional artwork became a staple of the Christian religion and the Bible itself an important icon.

The sacred nature of the Bible developed not only through word and image but also through song. Singing lay at the heart of the Bible in the East and West. From the early period of Byzantine Christianity, with the works of Ephrem the Syrian (ca. 306–ca. 379) and Romanos the Melodist (d. ca. 555), hymns to the Virgin fostered considerable interest in women of the New Testament as worthy of song. Ephrem is even credited with founding a women's choir. The biblical figures of the Samaritan woman, Mary and Martha, and the Magdalene are all praised in Ephrem's hymns. In his *Hymns on the Nativity*, Mary is placed alongside Tamar, Rahab, Ruth, and Bathsheba as women whose childbearing was a scandal that ultimately led to piety. In one hymn of Mary and the Samaritan woman, Ephrem sings:

> *Mary, the thirsty land in Nazareth conceived our Lord by her ear.*
> *You, too, O Woman thirsting for water,*

Blessed are your ears that drank the source that gave drink to
the world.
Mary planted him in a manger,
But you planted him in the ears of his hearers.[31]

For Ephrem, the Samaritan woman was the first evangelist, leaving the well to tell others of Jesus's deeds.

Song was often poetry, and the poetic arts filled Byzantine Bibles. Archbishop Gregory of Nazianzus (329–390), for instance, wrote simple poetry to help teach the Bible to the faithful, in hopes that common people might internalize the words of scripture. Mostly composed toward the end of his life, Gregory's poems are agonizingly intimate, reflecting on his own brokenness and pain together with the promises of scripture.

I give them this single piece of advice, the best of all:
Throwing away every word, they should
Cling only to the divinely inspired ones,
As those who flee the storm seek the harbor's calm.
For if the scriptures accord so many opportunities,
This, O Spirit, is the one that seems most sensible to you,
Namely that this should be a defence against all
Empty talk on the part of those with evil motives.[32]

The greatest of the ancient Byzantine poets and hymnists was Romanos the Melodist, born in the Syrian city of Emesa to Jewish parents before moving to Constantinople, where he served in the Hagia Sophia.[33] He was reputed to have spent his nights in a field in prayer. Without talent as a singer or speaker, he was mocked for his feeble efforts, and while in deep despair he had a vision in which Mary appeared to him with a scroll that she commanded him to eat. Immediately, he was given the gift of understanding, composition, and hymnography, as well as a melodious voice.

Romanos was known as a master of the kontakion, poetry written on scrolls; he composed these poems in honor of his encounter with the Virgin. He brought epic style and dramatic paraphrastic retelling of biblical narratives in Christian poetry, which is still sung today in Orthodox churches. Working with contrasts and paradoxes, Romanos conveyed the wonder and mystery in the story of salvation. As one writer has commented, "Just as the inner structure of the Bible itself, his poetic structures aim at telling the story of salvation afresh."[34] Writing in simple Greek, Romanos sought to bring the Bible to the people, befitting his lifelong care for the poor as a deacon. His language is deeply emotive, with an intense focus on Christ:

Make my language clear, my Savior, open my mouth
And, after filling it, penetrate my heart so that my acts
May correspond to my words.[35]

For Romanos, singing was the enactment of Christ, opening his mouth to speak. Music and poetry penetrate the heart.

As the Bible was transformed into a holy object in worship and the arts, it also became a vessel for the flourishing of word and image. In the Jewish tradition, figurative representations are limited to certain books of the Bible and are never used in the Torah. All illustration is strictly limited by the traditional interpretation of the second commandment. In Islam, the Qur'an contains sacred calligraphy and decorative patterns but rarely images of humans or animals.

In contrast, Christians in both the East and West took up decorating their Bibles with literal and allegorical depictions.[36] The acceptance of images in the Christian world created a wide range of possibilities for Bibles in terms of types of decoration. The texts themselves became objects of beauty through the use of elegant calligraphy, with the embellishment of initial letters at the beginning of Psalms and Gospels. Animals, plants, and geometric patterns joined illustrations of biblical scenes and portraits of the Gospel writers. The complex relationship between text and image found a dramatic resolution in the canon tables devised by Bishop Eusebius of Caesarea in Palestine (ca. 260–339).[37]

The tables visually present the parallels between the Gospels, identifying similar passages. But they are more than biblical GPS. Widely used through the early and medieval periods of Christianity, the canon tables united text and image as Eusebius guided the reader through the four Gospels. Their purpose was not merely organizational but spiritual. The enhanced accessibility of the Gospels was intended to feed the soul of the reader, creating patterns that fostered a sense of divinity: the unity of the Word in the different accounts of the apostles.

Framed by elaborate architectural images, these tables themselves became icons—contemplation of their architectural forms and sumptuous colors inspired prayer and reverence. The Golden Canon Tables from sixth-century Constantinople offer a vivid representation of Eusebius's purpose. Each table is surrounded by inscribed arches and subdivided into smaller spaces framed by their own arches of gold. The evangelists are portrayed in medallions following the Roman form of portraiture. Strict geometric lines, energetic brushwork, and three-dimensional flowers and birds create the Gospels as an iconic form of the Word.

The canon tables were widely and variously employed across the Christian world and became a major inspiration for biblical illustration. The earliest examples of illumination come from Africa and the undisputed treasure of Ethiopian Christianity, the codices known as the Garima Gospels.[38] Particularly distinguished by painted birds native to Ethiopia, the canon tables of the ancient Gospels frame the whole codex. Comprising three copies—known as Garima I, II, and III—of the four Gospels in two volumes, they were long thought to be medieval creations that drew on Coptic and Byzantine influence, as scholars deemed their illustrations too sophisticated to be Ethiopian. Misidentified and misdated, these treasures were held for centuries in the Ethiopian monastery of Abba Garima.

Western condescension was not, however, shared by the Abba Garima monks, who always believed their Gospels to be much older. Among Europeans, the books' antiquity was first recognized by visionary scholar Beatrice Payne on her visit to the monastery in 1948, when she noted their similarities to the Syriac Rabbula Gospels, created in the sixth century. French priest Jules Leroy, whom Payne informed of what she had seen, was responsible for the first photographs, which appeared in 1960, and noted striking similarities with Armenian Gospel books, suggesting a common Syriac heritage. But a greater surprise lay in wait.

The decisive turn came in stages. First, the two volumes of the Gospels were restored in 2006. This involved a great deal of sorting.

Many of the pages were out of order within each volume, and some had migrated to the other volumes. The ornate illuminated pages, for example, were mixed between Garima I and III. The painstaking restoration took place in the courtyard of the Abba Garima Monastery's treasure house, where the Gospels were kept, and one conservationist spoke of the constant company of monkeys. Second, in 2013 the Ethiopian Heritage Fund announced at a conference in Oxford, to worldwide media interest, that radiocarbon dating had confirmed that the Garima Gospels were from the fourth to sixth centuries, making them among the oldest surviving illustrated and intact Gospel books in the Christian world.

The gold and jewels that decorated the Gospel covers indicate that books were objects of reverence, embodying the presence of Christ. The first volume, with a gilded copper cover, contains Garima I. The embossed copper cover is slightly damaged from heavy use and has a cross surrounded by leaves, into which would have been placed jewels, now long lost. The second volume, with a silver cover, contains Garima II and III, Garima III being the eldest of the three Gospels, perhaps created as early as 330. It is not certain whether the silver and copper covers are contemporary with the Gospels' creation. The two volumes are bound in what is known as the "Coptic twin method," in which each quire is stitched to the next. The ends of the stitching are joined to the boards and remain uncovered. This method was widely used in Egypt for the first codices and continues to be used in Ethiopia today.

It is now thought that both the scribes and the artists who made the Gospels were Ethiopian, and various aspects of the illuminations reflect a mixture of Aksumite, Nubian, Egyptian, and Greek influences. The Garima Gospels are remarkable examples of the distinctive culture of early Ethiopian Christianity, reflecting its diversity of sources and influences from Egypt, Syria, Armenia, and the Byzantine worlds, which in turn indicate Ethiopia's place at the crossroads of trade and religion between the Mediterranean and the East. By the fourth century, the technology for producing sophisticated codices with intricate metalwork and illustrations was evidently in place in the kingdom. The story of the Garima Gospels has not ended. During the current (as of this writing) conflict in Ethiopia, the Abba Garima Monastery has been desecrated, and their whereabouts are currently not known.

The practice of using canon tables like those in the Ethiopian Gospels was widespread across the Christian world but not universal. They are rarely found in the Coptic Bibles of Egypt, possibly because Egyptian leaders were suspicious of Eusebius.[39] Yet even within the early Bibles themselves there is diversity, as represented by the relationship between the canon tables and the portraits of the evangelists that accompanied them. Whereas the canon tables, with their cross-referencing of the Gospels, pointed to their harmony, the portraits, dispersed to the beginning of their Gospels, brought out their individuality and uniqueness. The portraits were embodiments of their divine message, to be viewed in relation to the text that followed so that image and word intimately interpreted one another.

The desire to illustrate and illuminate books of the Bible spread across the Christian world. An early treasure is the sixth-century Rossano Gospels.[40] A fragmentary volume of great opulence, it is one of the oldest surviving illustrated Gospel books. Written in silver on purple vellum, the text is decorated at intervals with gold letters. The fine, thin parchment is dyed purple to symbolize both Christ's royalty and the dignity of imperial patronage. The gold and silver of the written text are not merely precious commodities but are imbued with deep spiritual meaning as visual reflections of the heavenly kingdom.[41]

Requiring vast financial resources and the very best scribes and artists, these Gospels are among the greatest treasures of Byzantine Christianity and have been designated by UNESCO as among the prized objects of world artistic heritage. Many have looked to Constantinople as the provenance of the Rossano Gospels. Their distinctive features, however, point elsewhere, perhaps to Syria, in particular Antioch.[42] Another possibility is further west. Although the Gospels are clearly the work of Greek artists, some have suggested that the artists fled from the iconoclasm in their land to Rossano, on the Gulf of Taranto in southern Italy, in order to complete their labors in safety. It was in a monastery there that the Gospels were discovered in 1879. Like so many of the treasures of the first millennium, the Gospels carefully guard their story.

Not all is hidden, however. The Rossano Gospels were clearly intended primarily for worship. More specifically, they were made for the season of Lent, one of the most holy periods in the church year. The importance of Lent helps to explain why these Gospels were so elaborately prepared.[43] The miniatures are situated according to their liturgically related themes and visually bear enormous theological and spiritual power.

Despite the wondrous beauty of works such as the Garima and Rossano Gospels, many disapproved of illustrations in the Bible. Precious books as liturgical objects or as gifts to prestigious patrons were seen as contrary to the humble message of the gospel. Jerome, for instance, was hostile to lavishly decorated Bibles, seeing them as a sinful luxury that offended ascetic piety.[44] But a growing attachment to illustrated biblical manuscripts reflected a Christian love of images, perhaps stimulated by public Christian paintings.[45]

But illumination was never mere decoration. Today, these volumes are mostly removed from their religious contexts, housed in secular museums, where their aesthetic appeal is most prominent. To do them justice, however, requires imagining them in the contexts of worship and devotion for which they were created. The spellbinding images were married to the text they illuminated. Each illuminated Bible, whether whole or in part, proposed how scripture was to be read, envisaged, and experienced.[46]

The relationship between text and image that blossomed from the fifth to ninth centuries in the north and west owed much to the Byzantine tradition. In Ireland, Anglo-Saxon Northumbria, and Carolingian Aachen and Tours, and on the Iberian Peninsula, vernacular cultures drew on artistic and intellectual traditions from the Eastern and African churches to create new, intimate conversations between text and image. Some of the most remarkable illustrated Bibles of the early medieval world were products of Irish monastic culture, which, fired by the zeal of monks to convert, spawned a rich Celtic Christian culture that spread east across Scotland and Anglo-Saxon England to the Continent.[47] In Irish monasteries, liturgical books were kept in leather pouches in monks' cells, reflecting the bond between books and sacred space. Scribes prepared many less ornate copies of Psalms and the Gospels for Irish monks who journeyed across the northern waters, preaching and practicing their ascetic Christianity.

A long-standing tradition proposed that the Book of Durrow was written in twelve days by St. Columba (521–597), the evangelist of Scotland, but scholars date the Gospel book to a century later, to around 680–690, in Durrow Abbey, which had been founded by Columba around 553. Such was the beauty of the book that it soon acquired the status of a relic and was preserved in an ornate box.

In the seventh century, Bibles and liturgical books were increasingly found with lavish, often-bejeweled covers that indicated the preciousness of the book. They were the embossed masterworks of goldsmiths, whose labors both protected the text and conveyed its spiritual power. There was another powerful association. Biblical texts in ornate boxes were reminiscent of the relics of saints, confirming the sanctity of their physicality.[48] The connection with Israel was also arresting: the boxes evoked the Ark of the Covenant, into which Moses placed the tablets of the Law.

From the seventh to ninth centuries, Irish illumination and script were the very best in the Latin West, prompting the observation that "only there and at that period was a degree of perfection achieved that is comparable to that of Islamic or Chinese calligraphy."[49] The so-called carpet pages, entire pages of geometric patterns of great complexity and beauty placed at the beginning of each Gospel, were unique to insular manuscripts—manuscripts associated with the post-Roman monasteries of Ireland and Britain—but had striking parallels to both Jewish and Islamic books.[50] They acquired the name from their affinity to carpet patterns from the East. In the Book of Durrow, the carpet page at the beginning of the Gospel of John is a gold-rimmed disk with a Greek cross representing the victory of Christ. Surrounding the cross are Celtic spirals and images of animals—a fantastic mixture of bulls, wolves, butterflies, and dolphins—that in Celtic culture were imbued with mystical union of the divine and the natural world.

Celtic influence arrived across the sea with missionaries to the Continent. The Benedictine abbey at Echternach, now in Luxembourg, was founded by the Northumbrian monk Willibrord (ca. 658–739) in 698 and is home to another magnificent Bible of uncertain origin. The cover of the book is decorated with precious stones and pearls, emulating the garments of the Old Testament priests, and with illuminated initials of the opening words of the Gospels in gold. No other contemporary book possessed such a rich ivory cover that bound decorative pages and initials.[51] It opens with an image of Christ in majesty surrounded by the four great prophets (Isaiah, Jeremiah, Ezekiel, and Daniel), the evangelists, and the animals associated with the evangelists. Quite possibly it was brought from Ireland by the missionary Willibrord, under whose influence the scriptorium at Echternach became one of the most influential centers of what is known as the Hiberno-Saxon tradition.[52]

Another exquisitely illuminated volume, this one filled with elaborate architectural arches, decorated initials, and diagrams, comes from the England of Bede in the eighth century. It is the oldest surviving complete Latin Bible and was produced at the Benedictine monastery at Monkwearmouth-Jarrow.[53] Thought to be the purest version of Jerome's Bible from the fourth and fifth centuries, the Codex Amiatinus became the foundation for numerous editions across Europe.[54] It was also used as the basis for editions of the Vulgate in the nineteenth and twentieth centuries. The work of approximately nine scribes, the Codex Amiatinus weighs over seventy pounds; the skins of two thousand calves provided the vellum. Its illuminations are often theologically complex, such as a two-page representation of the temple in

Jerusalem with its integration of worship and architecture, as well as the fusion of Old and New Testament prophecies in light of Christ.[55] The Codex Amiatinus also offers one of the earliest visual representations of God the Father, long considered by Christians in the East and West as forbidden as a graven image.[56]

This work of tremendous beauty was intended for no less than Pope Gregory II. St. Ceolfrith, an Anglo-Saxon abbot, commissioned the codex and took it to Italy but died before he reached Rome. The Codex Amiatinus passed first to the monastery at Mount Amiata in southern Tuscany and then to the Laurentian Library in Florence. One of the greatest creations of Anglo-Saxon culture, it did not leave Italy until 2013, when it returned to England for an exhibition in the British Library.

Such codices were glorious creations but hardly typical. Given the availability of the Psalms and Gospels for liturgical worship and reading, there was little need for expensive complete Bibles, which tended, as in this instance, to serve as prestigious gifts that demonstrated the talents of the creators and the glories of the recipient.[57] Their symbolic roles were powerful, and as sacred objects they became central to ceremonial rituals, but they have survived largely because they were hardly used. They moved in the circles of the elite, never seen by the vast majority of the people—most of whom never saw any Bible.

Around the time the Codex Amiatinus was making its way to Italy, the crown jewel of Anglo-Saxon culture was created at the monastery at Lindisfarne, the "holy island" off the coast of Northumbria that had been founded as a daughter house of the monastery at Iona, a Scottish island.[58] Two cultures met on the pages of the Lindisfarne Gospels: the Latin of Jerome's Vulgate and the Anglo-Saxon language of the people. Likely produced to celebrate the physical transportation of the relics of St. Cuthbert to his shrine, the Lindisfarne Gospels were closely connected to the ascetic holy man, who had lived on the island until his death. They were the work of the monk Eadfrith, who died in 721, before his labors were completed, leaving his work unfinished. His achievement was, however, celebrated in verse:

> *Eadfrith bishop of the Church of Lindisfarne*
> *He, in the beginning, wrote this book for God and*
> *St Cuthbert and generally for all the holy folk*
> *who are on the island.*
> *And Æthilwald bishop of the Lindisfarne-islanders,*
> *bound and covered it without, as he well knew how to do.*
> *And Billfrith the anchorite, he forged the*
> *ornaments which are on the outside and*
> *bedecked it with gold and with gems and*
> *also with gilded silver-pure wealth.*[59]

Although the Lindisfarne Gospels, along with the relics of St. Cuthbert, went with the monks when they left the island monastery to escape Viking raids, the precious stones that decorated it had already fallen into the hands of Vikings and disappeared from history.

The Lindisfarne Gospels contain five full carpet pages, one before the prefatory material and one before the beginning of each of the Gospels. The vibrant illustrations reflect a wide range of influences, including Byzantine and Italian, and were made from forty-two colors, including a precious blue, a splendid range that speaks for the wealth of the monastic foundation.[60]

Among the book's glories is a full-page illumination of the four evangelists and the Chi-Rho symbol, which combines the first three Greek letters of the word "Christ" ☧.

The Gospels are a masterpiece of insular illumination of the Irish and British scriptoria of the age, resplendent with Celtic spiral patterns and birds. Such insular Bible illuminations were the jewels of European artistic culture from the late seventh to ninth centuries. They had no equal in the West.

Another of the great treasures of the insular tradition is the famous Book of Kells, now held at Trinity College Dublin. Its origins are debated, with some suggesting Ireland, Iona, or a monastery in Pictish Scotland.[61] Whatever its provenance, it was held at the Irish monastery of Kells, which was sacked by the Vikings in the ninth century. Indeed, work on the Book of Kells may have been interrupted by Viking raids on Scotland and Ireland, as some have suggested that the illustrations' emphasis on the Christ-centered themes of imprisonment and demonic temptation may connect the Gospels to the afflictions of monks in the Viking raids.[62]

The text is written in black, yellow, red, and purple ink, and the 340 vellum leaves include the canon tables of Eusebius, with their guide to the Gospels. Each page of the Gospels, which are mostly the Vulgate text with some Old Latin, contains spectacular illuminations. The intricate interweaving of ornamentation and extensive depictions of animals is characteristic of Celtic design. It is thought that the Gospels are the work of three miniaturists who prepared the metalwork and painted the portraits of the evangelists.

The artists made use of lapis lazuli, a precious stone brought by merchants from the mines of Afghanistan and prized as highly as gold.

The calligraphy, the ornamentation, the nests of birds, the portraits and symbols of the evangelists would never be surpassed in the medieval world. Influences from the Greek East and the Italian West were married to a rich Celtic tradition, resulting in remarkable originality. The Book of Kells marked the zenith of the insular style and was celebrated by the twelfth-century historian Gerald of Wales: "Look more keenly at it and you will penetrate to the very shrine of art. You will make out intricacies, so delicate and so subtle, so full of knots and links, with colors so fresh and vivid, that you might say that all this were the work of an angel, and not of a man."[63]

Back on the Continent, the Celtic influence is apparent in the Harley Golden Gospels, so named because they are written entirely in gold; the book is decorated on every page with patterns and animals. This Bible issued from Charlemagne's court and is an expression of the architectural vision it inhabited: the great palace erected during the 790s in Aachen, the center of Charlemagne's new Christian empire. The Bible as a creator of sacred space was intimately connected to the Christian architectural imagination. Books were tabernacles. At the heart of the palace was the Palatine Chapel, in which East and West came together in a vision of Christian unity. Of Charlemagne's palace, his medieval biographer wrote, "Hence it was that he [Charlemagne] built the beautiful basilica at Aachen, which he adorned with gold and silver and lamps, and with rails and doors of solid brass. He had the columns and marbles for this structure brought from Rome and Ravenna, for he could not find such as were suitable elsewhere."[64] In the Harley Golden Gospels, the Roman porphyry columns that Charlemagne brought back to Aachen to decorate his palace chapel are reimagined as the marbled columns framing the evangelists and the canon tables.[65] The portrayal of the evangelists as classical authors or even noblemen, through the modeling of their faces and the pens with which they wrote, expressed the desire for a full embrace of Christianized antiquity.

Britain and the Carolingian Empire were not alone in having a flourishing culture of Bibles in the early Middle Ages. On the Iberian Peninsula there was a tradition of Latin and vernacular Bibles shaped by the distinctive influences of contact with Jews and Muslims. Iberian Bibles, with their enormous size and pages rich with illuminations, have been identified as "countermodels" of the Qur'an, the dominant religious text of the southern parts of the peninsula.[66] They were also influenced by the Carolingian centers of Bibles, such as Tours, as monks and merchants took codices into Spanish lands. But Spain also had a long and distinct tradition of its own. Licinius Baeticus, who, like Cassiodorus, was a wealthy man who turned his estate into a monastery, sent men to Jerome in Bethlehem to obtain his Latin Bible. They returned in 398 with a copy of his Old Testament in papyrus codices.[67]

Over subsequent centuries, specific centers in Spain were connected with the production of books of scripture, gathered, for example, around the eminent scholar Isidore of Seville (ca. 560–636) and in the city of Zaragoza, where the seventh-century bishop John II commissioned a complete volume. While the historical record shows that Bibles were produced in the northern kingdoms of Asturias, Léon, and Old Castile, fragmentary evidence suggests that Bibles were also being produced in Catalonia, where they were heavily influenced by the importation of Bibles from the Carolingian Empire across their shared frontier.

While Iberian monasteries were certainly producing Bibles, in comparison to Ireland and the Carolingian Empire, biblical illustration was less widespread.[68] A Visigoth Bible known as the La Cava Bible, or Codex Cavensis, which dates from the late eighth or early ninth century, is entirely without illustrations. Its decoration is limited to the cross in four places.

In striking contrast is the Léon Bible of 960, a most remarkable example of Bible illustration from the Christian-Muslim frontier.[69] The codex is richly decorated, with a distinctive Spanish cross on the frontispiece together with human and animal figures in a series of medallions, and portraits of the evangelists. It is a luxury Bible whose eclectic illumination is difficult to trace but which is among the oldest in Spain.

A sense of achievement in an apparently cooperative effort is evident at the end of an illustrated Bible from around 960, where two scribes toast each other in celebration of the completion of the Bible: "Florentius Confessor. To the most cherished pupil, chosen by me, Sanctius the Priest. We bless the heavenly kingdom which allowed us to bring to an end this book"; and the response, "And I too say, Master, let us praise our Lord Jesus Christ World without End, who may lead us to the heavenly kingdom, Amen."[70]

Throughout early Christendom, word and image did not exist apart from the physicality of the books in which they dwelled. With lavish ornamentation and exquisite illuminations, the Bible became a living relic, an object that both transmitted the holy and embodied it. In liturgies of worship, as gifts for kings and emperors, and in monastic prayer, the Bible was not an inanimate object but a source and creator of sacred space in churches, chapels, monasteries, and palaces. As in Coptic Egypt, the lands of the Syriac monasteries, and the churches of Ethiopia, in western Europe, too, Bibles were regarded sacramentally, like the body of Christ in the bread and wine. They were precious books to be transcribed, illustrated, and displayed as befit their holiness.

CHAPTER 4

BOOK OF LIFE: MEDIEVAL WORLDS

Through Christianity's first millennium, what began as a set of stories, prophecies, letters, and wisdom retold without fixed form emerged as a sacred book. That book entered a multiplicity of languages as it spread through Europe, the Middle East, and Africa and, over time, came to be regarded by the faithful as not merely a container for the message of God but an icon itself. Along every stop, the Bible was always being appropriated and adapted, its readers continuously seeking the presence and intentions of their creator through the written word.

Moving into medieval times, the Bible continued to reflect and shape the worlds it occupied. But these were worlds undergoing rapid political, cultural, and technological change. From the People's Crusade of the eleventh century, when thousands of poor men and women followed the French priest Peter the Hermit to their horrid deaths, to the fifteenth-century wonder of Johannes Gutenberg's printed Vulgate, different segments of society developed new relationships to the Bible. As the Christian world grew ever more distant from the millennium, the act of biblical interpretation became increasingly important among teachers and scholars, giving rise to intricate commentaries and glosses, as well as a desire to turn back the clock and engage with earlier renditions of the Bible. As Christianity became the dominant organizing force of life in Europe, the Bible became omnipresent in everyday life—present in every aspect of culture, encountered daily by men and women in the hurly-burly of their lives. It is meaningless to say it was a religious book, for the medieval world knew no distinction between religion and any other aspect of life. And finally, with the advent of new technological developments such as printing, the Bible, though still sacred, also became an object of commercial life.

Across the medieval world, however, there was an emphasis on the simplicity of the Bible, a view that indicated the long shadow of Jerome. In his prologues produced with almost all Vulgate Bibles, he urged scholars and readers alike to adopt an attitude of humility. The Bible, he reminded Christians, was written in the humble language of fishermen. That had been the spirit of his translation and Augustine's preaching as a bishop in North Africa. This belief in the Bible's simplicity was repeatedly endorsed by generations of commentators to the end of the Middle Ages. But that did not mean the book was simple. The Bible was understood to consist of many parts of different origins and diverse voices. Rising above the distinctions, however, was an abiding devotion to the coherence of the sacred text and its story of creation and salvation. As the Franciscan friar Nicholas of Lyra (1270–1349) wrote, "The book containing Holy Scripture, although divided into many partial books . . . is properly called the Book of Life."[1]

For the medieval teachers, the Bible was the absolute authority, and they alone could interpret it. Scripture was not mere proof texts for their arguments. Their task was to elucidate it for the church. As the medieval philosopher and theologian Thomas Aquinas (1225–1274) wrote, "It must be said that Sacred Scripture is divinely ordered to this: that through it, the truth necessary for salvation may be made known to us."[2] Though the creation of the Bible involved many human authors and many different types of books, God directed the pen.

Medieval scholars often spoke of the fourfold way of reading scripture: the literal (or historical), allegorical, tropological, and anagogical.[3] Each cast light on the spiritual and ethical dimensions of the holy book. The literal/historical sense was deployed to understand what had actually happened. The allegorical sense was used to see how Old and New Testaments converged through foreshadowing and fulfillment. The tropological, or moral, sense offered instruction about how to live. And the anagogical, or eschatological, revealed promises to be fulfilled in the heavenly Jerusalem.[4] Deploying these four methods, scholars found that every story was pregnant with wisdom and anticipation of fulfillment. The liberation of the ancient Israelites from Egypt, for instance, represented the way out of sin through the Red Sea (baptism and freedom), the struggle of the Christian life (their wandering in the desert), crossing the Jordan (transition through death), and entering the promised land (the reward of paradise).

This method was no mere academic exercise—it was the discerning of God's words to humanity. What the theologians taught made its way to distant parishes through the preaching of priests and friars. The Bible was full of figurative language that could be grasped by those who contemplated with faith under the guidance of the church. The fulfillment of the Bible was in the intimate relationship between the writers of scripture and their readers. The church enforced that where a person or groups departed from the spiritual and mystical teachings of the Bible, prospects for error or heresy abounded. The path was dangerous with many snares, requiring the constant vigilance of priests and preachers.

By the eleventh century, the Bible in the West was Jerome's translation, but it did not exist in one form. A Bible in Spain might look quite different from one in England or German lands. Medieval scholars were fully aware of the problems they faced.[5] In his commentaries on the Old Testament, Andrew of St. Victor (d. 1175), an Augustinian canon in Paris, expressed his conviction that he had to do something to recover a Bible full of errors and variations that had accrued over the centuries. Andrew was one of the few men of his age with competence in Hebrew, which he had learned from Jewish scholars in Paris.[6] This gave him an enormous advantage because most scholars who shared his sense of urgency were only able to correct the Latin from the Latin—a losing proposition. Without access to Hebrew and Greek, Andrew understood, progress was impossible, and he urged his fellow scholars to learn these languages.

Andrew's zeal for a return to the biblical languages was enthusiastically embraced by one of the most brilliant and fiery figures of the age, a Franciscan theologian in Oxford, Roger Bacon (1219/20–1294).[7] Bacon was an excoriating critic of what he saw as the inherited corruption of the Latin Bible through poor or lazy copying by the commercial enterprises that had begun to compete with monastic scriptoria in producing manuscripts and books. He was also part of a broader religious movement, as the thirteenth century saw the founding of the orders of the great confessors and preachers of the medieval West, the Franciscans and Dominicans, known collectively as the mendicants on account of their vow of poverty. Their zeal for restoring the faith and combating heresy fired them to pursue the best version of the Bible. In Paris the mendicant houses devoted themselves to work on the Bible, an enthusiasm for scripture that, as one scholar has observed, "belies the assumption that the medieval period only corrupted the Bible text without attempting to improve it."[8]

Desire for the pure Word of God was not confined to Europe but stretched across the Christian world. The centuries following the creation of the Garima Gospels is often thought of as a "dark age" in Ethiopian Christian history—a period stretching from the late seventh to early thirteenth centuries. The Aksum kingdom was weakened and vulnerable, its ports captured by Islamic Arabs and its lands torn apart by internal rivalries, preventing trade and resulting in political and economic chaos. This so-called dark age ended, however, with a literary renaissance that accompanied significant political and religious reform.[9] During this period, the Ge'ez Old Testament underwent a major revision based on an Arabic translation of the Hebrew.[10] In other words, the existing Ge'ez translation, based on the Greek Septuagint, was revised with Hebrew-based Arabic. The result was that, by the fifteenth century, the Ge'ez Bible was a distinctive mix of Greek, Hebrew, and Arabic. Indeed, the Arabic of the Muslim world was particularly influential.

With this renewed focus on recovering the unadulterated Word of God, the medieval world developed a distinctive approach to reproduction, which involved placing the Bible in a frame of interpretation visible on the page. Following the Jewish tradition, the sacred text coexisted alongside the wisdom of past and present, offering a powerful image of how the Bible lived inside the architecture of understanding and authority. In the medieval West, this practice was most prominent in the twelfth century, when Bibles often included interlinear or marginal glosses, commentaries that provided learned readers the simultaneous encounter of scripture and interpretation. It was the medieval equivalent of the modern hypertext.[11] Through carefully designed marginalia drawn from the writings of the church fathers, scholars, students, and monks experienced the Bible in a manner similar to the way we might read the No Fear Shakespeare edition of *The Merchant of Venice*, with text and modern translation side by side—a favorite of students and actors. Like images and text, text and interpretation existed in creative tension, generating a dialogue.

As these works grew in complexity, with increasingly intricate dialogues between text and gloss, scribes developed elaborate systems of markings to guide the reader. The supreme achievement of this form of Bible study was the twelfth-century *Glossa Ordinaria*, begun by Anselm of Laon (d. 1117), which became a standard reference work for the rest of the Middle Ages and the early modern period.[12] Following the founding of the University of Paris in 1150 and its widespread use of the Bible commentary, the *Glossa* became a biblical reference book for the whole of the Latin West.[13]

In their quest to refine their interpretation of the Bible, medieval scholars and artists were also influenced by Jews and Muslims.[14] Cultural exchange, notably in Spain, was rich and exciting. Christians learned from their Jewish teachers and adopted Islamic artistic styles. In the twelfth and thirteenth centuries, a culture of Hebrew studies flourished in Spain, France, and England thanks to scholarly and artistic interactions with Jews. Herbert of Bosham (d. 1194) drew deeply from the work of the great French rabbinic scholar Salomon Isaacides (known as Rashi, 1040–1105), author of a comprehensive commentary on the Talmud and the Hebrew Bible.[15] Jewish scholars were thought indispensable both for language instruction and for an understanding of the historical sense of the Bible—less so for the allegorical on account of their failure to recognize Christ.[16]

Others, such as Roger Bacon and the Franciscan Nicholas of Lyra, engaged in extensive study of Hebrew and the rabbinic tradition. Bacon prepared a Hebrew grammar, while Lyra cited Rashi repeatedly in his *Postilla litteralis*, literal commentary on the Old Testament.

Christian fervor for the poetic Song of Songs, which the sermons of Bernard of Clairvaux (1090–1153) often engaged, provides further evidence of close attention to Jewish readings.[17] But there was a catch. What Christians saw as the Jewish tendency toward the literal sense revealed the blindness of Jews who failed to find the mystical presence of Christ in their scriptures. For Christians, Jews remained the killers of Christ, and on Good Friday they prayed for their conversion and acceptance of the New Testament.[18] Medieval Christians seem to have forgotten that Christ was a Jew. Vilification and persecution of Jews were repeatedly and vigorously undertaken, even as Christian dependence on them ran deep regarding essential linguistic, textual, interpretive, and ceremonial needs.

The most influential of all medieval writers on the question of Jewish interpretations of the Bible was Nicholas of Lyra, who came of age in the late thirteenth century, when Jews were being expelled from numerous European lands.[19] At the Lateran Council of 1215, the renewed papacy had sought to separate Jews from their Christian neighbors, and Christian rulers were pressured to enact strict measures, such as the wearing of the Star of David. Anti-Jewish sentiment was rife. Their books were censored and destroyed. The Talmud, the rabbinic tradition of commentary on the Law, was repeatedly put on trial and declared heretical, and in 1309 three wagonloads of

Hebrew books were burned in the Place de Grève in Paris (today the Hôtel de Ville). The same year, Jews were expelled from France. The ferocious attacks across Europe were largely directed toward forced conversion.

Lyra, speaking at the University of Paris, posed a question that would resonate through the late Middle Ages: Was it possible to learn of Christ from the Jewish rabbinic writers? If so, why did Jews remain ignorant of the Son of God? Nicholas was determined to make use of Jewish writers in an age of intense hostility. To do this, he adopted the established Christian conceit that rabbinic scholars could throw light on the Christian Bible while remaining in darkness about its ultimate truths. His perspective, though the most comprehensive response to the question of how to use the Jewish scholars he so highly valued, is somewhat chilling to modern eyes: "The Church is composed of different people, that is, Jews and Gentiles, the just and the unjust, those who rule and those who are ruled."[20]

Nicholas had critics, notably Paul of Burgos (1351–1435), a Spanish Jewish convert to Christianity.[21] A wealthy man, Paul had been a rabbi and erudite scholar of the Talmud. It is thought that he converted and was baptized following the massacre of Jews in Spain in 1391, but Paul sought to conceal that story. Not wanting to suggest that external pressure brought about his adoption of Christianity, he maintained that he had converted earlier. Numerous siblings of his and his children were also baptized, but his wife Joanna remained a Jew (although she was buried by her husband in a church). Paul studied in Paris and became a learned doctor of the faith. He then viciously turned on his people and became a fierce persecutor of Jews, removing their rights and reducing many to penury. For his efforts he obtained high office in the church and became a tutor to the Spanish king.

Paul was a man driven by hate, above all for the Jewish Talmud. His writings against the Jews had enduring influence and were cited by successive Christian churchmen, including Martin Luther. Such was his vitriol that he rejected Nicholas's desire to draw on rabbinic teaching as misjudged and dangerous. He wrote a series of additions to Nicholas's *Postilla litteralis* in which he sought to put the Franciscan scholar right. Such debates about the Jews and the Bible were not merely arcane questions of theology or hermeneutics. They had real consequences beyond universities, feeding into the pogroms and expulsions that took place in villages and cities across Europe.

Hostility toward Jews in the name of the Bible raises the broader question of the Bible's stance toward violence and coercion as perceived in the medieval world. The issue was not straightforward, and the Bible seemed to provide conflicting guidance. The wars of ancient Israel sanctioned by God stood in contrast to Jesus's admonition to turn the other cheek. The ambiguity ran through medieval society, which possessed a culture of ritualized violence, from feuds, vendettas, and executions to chivalrous combat. No greater challenge arose, however, than holy war—the Crusades.[22]

During the eleventh and twelfth centuries the Western church created a theology of holy war based on selected biblical texts.[23] The enemy was not only the Muslims occupying Jerusalem and the holy land but Jews at home, who in the name of a biblically based holy war were massacred in northern France and the Rhineland. The Bible played a central role in this conflict. Preachers, scholars, and bishops drew from scripture to exhort the faithful to depart Europe in the name of the Lord.[24] The prophet Ezekiel provided a well-known exhortation to those who hesitated: "Ye have not gone up into the gaps, neither made up the hedge for the house of Israel to stand in the battle in the day of the LORD" (Ezek. 13:5, KJV). On Palm Sunday, 1146, Bernard of Clairvaux, promising papal absolution of sins, preached to the assembled Crusaders at Vézelay, France:

> Christian warriors, He who gave His life for you, today demands yours in return. These are combats worthy of you, combats in which it is glorious to conquer and advantageous to die. Illustrious knights, generous defenders of the Cross, remember the example of your fathers, who conquered Jerusalem, and whose names are inscribed in Heaven. Abandon then the things that perish, to gather unfading palms and conquer a Kingdom that has no end.[25]

Those living in the largely rural world of the Middle Ages knew the Bible not as an object of interpretation and contestation but as an object central to worship.[26] Liturgy, with its rich symbolism and ritual movement, was an expression of the allegorical understanding of the Bible—its deepest spiritual mysteries. The biblical texts in reading, chanting, and prayer presented the faithful with an interpretation of the divine mystery of creation and redemption. The central drama of church life, the Mass, celebrated the sacrifice of Christ in the Last Supper, presenting the faithful with the ever-present Christ. In the rites of the Mass, the Bible was read two or sometimes three times, from the Old Testament, Gospels, and Epistles according to a prescribed cycle.[27]

The worship of Eastern and Western churches seamlessly integrated the visual and sensual—the rising incense that filled churches, for example, representing the prayers of the faithful. In missals, books that contained the liturgy, images of Christ's Passion and of Christ in glory opened the text. During worship, the priest often kissed these images to celebrate the presence of Christ in the Gospel readings. The sacred act of kissing the Gospel, which was common throughout the Christian world, was closely connected to the kiss of peace shared by the faithful present in the church—another way in which the Bible did not simply contain the words of God but was itself a sacred image of the presence of Christ in the worship.[28]

The central importance of the Gospels to the liturgical life of the Georgian church is confirmed by two thirteenth-century illuminated books from the region of Abkhazia on the Black Sea. The Mokvi Gospels (1300 CE), with almost 350 pages written in Nuskhuri and illuminated with a cycle of 157 gold miniatures, are one of the great cultural treasures of Abkhazia. Less elaborate but also a witness to a rich tradition of biblical works are the Vani Gospels, prepared in Constantinople for Queen Tamar of Georgia. Tamar (ca. 1160–1213) was the first woman to rule Georgia in her own right, though she is referred to in the historical chronicles as "king."[29] The illustrations of the Vani Gospels interweave worldly and heavenly authority with elaborate fountains, hunting animals, and exotic beasts such as elephants and monkeys, symbols of the leisured elite.[30] Similarly, from the twelfth century the Miroslav Gospel—a glory of medieval Serbian culture with its parchment, gilding, and exquisite miniatures of the holy authors—documents the liturgy of the Balkan Orthodox Church.

As the Gospel and Eucharist brought the bread of heaven down to earth, the liturgical processions of the priests enacted heaven. At the end of *Purgatory* in the *Divine Comedy*, the pilgrim Dante in the Garden of Eden watches a grand procession of the Bible: "Neither Scipio Africanus nor, indeed, Augustus ever gladdened Rome with so magnificent a chariot."[31] Twenty-four elders process in pairs, representing the twenty-four books of the Old Testament. The Gospels and evangelists take the form of four cherubim followed by figures from the other books of the New Testament. A chariot, greater than any of ancient mythology, is drawn by a griffin, who, like Christ, has two natures, and is attended by women representing the cardinal and theological virtues. Women dance and the animals from the book of Ezekiel follow. The procession moves out of the eternal heavenly realm and into the sublunary world of human time and affairs. Dante's poetry conveys the unity of body and word in medieval Christianity. The liturgical procession and reading of the Bible elevated the church out of the mundane.

The later Protestant attack on the medieval church in the sixteenth century circled around how the laity were kept from the Gospel, particularly because it was read in Latin, a language that few understood. Yet, for Christians of this era, understanding was not limited to a rational act. As the fourteenth-century *English Treatise of the Manner and Mede of the Masse* instructed, each person was to stand during the reading of the Gospel because even "when not understood, the power of God's word still avails."[32]

Understanding the language was only part of the encounter with the medieval Bible. Perhaps more important was the sense of divine presence. Even if they could not understand the Latin, men and women knew that the ritual of reading the Gospel marked a crucial moment in the service. As one Frenchman commented, the Gospel was "the banner which shows that God is certainly near"—signaling the approach of the most holy part of the Mass, the consecration of the host. The French theologian Jean Gerson (1363–1429) instructed the laity that "when the Gospel is said, you must listen quietly to his sweet word, which comes truly from mouth and heart. And men should rise and remove their hats when they hear it."[33] The

Gospel reading announced God's arrival, and the people knew what that meant. Protestant reformers placed an emphasis on understanding the Bible through text and reading that would have been foreign to the medieval world.

The Bible of medieval popular imagination was never limited to books of the two testaments but came to the people through the circulation of stories and encounters with visual representations. One of the richest and most widespread sources for the biblical imagination in the Middle Ages was from the hand of the learned twelfth-century Frenchman Peter Comestor (d. 1178), whose *Historia scholastica* was translated into every known language. Comestor prepared a biblical paraphrase that drew together scripture, classical sources, and the teachings of the church fathers to create a universal history. Not only was it required reading in the elite universities, but over the course of the Middle Ages it transmitted knowledge of the Bible into vernacular cultures through literature, drama, and sermons, for which it provided a compendium of stories. As one scholar has observed, "As a work of literature the *Historia* made the Bible, which can be very strange and intractable, into a coherent, orthodox, and entertaining narrative."[34] One of the most remarkable aspects of Peter's work was his extensive use of Jewish sources. Comestor's *Historia* illustrated that the worlds of learned Latin culture and of the wider populace were much less separate than one might assume based on later Protestant objections.[35]

Beyond books, the Bible found expression in the medieval world with the great cathedrals of the twelfth and thirteenth centuries, notably in northern France. The Cathédrale Notre-Dame in Chartres, rebuilt in Gothic style after a fire in 1194, offers a stunning experience for worshippers entering the nave. The stained-glass windows, with scenes from the Hebrew Bible and New Testament, cover over twenty-eight thousand square feet and are remarkably well preserved. The stained glass of the western wall tells the story of Christ, from his royal ancestors to his crucifixion, resurrection, and ascension.[36] The west rose window tells of the end of the world with its depiction of the Last Judgment and Christ as the judge of all humanity. It has been noted that this image of the end-time is illuminated by soft light at the end of the day, a daily reminder of Christ's return.[37]

Without a doubt, one of the greatest mistruths perpetuated by the Protestant Reformation is that the Bible disappeared during the Middle Ages. True, few in the medieval world ever touched a Bible, and even fewer read it. Yet the Bible was everywhere: heard and seen in worship, performed on temporary stages erected in village squares, recounted in song, shown in pictures on church walls. It was in medicine, colloquial speech, and roadside chapels and crosses. The medieval Bible was not limited to a seldom-seen book; it was the book of life. It was internalized in word and image through repeated experiences. When Dante sees the procession of the Bible, Beatrice commands him to "take care to write what you see, when you return."[38] And through so many media the Bible was embedded in popular memory, as Virgil exhorted. From the village square to courts and universities, scripture was quoted and sung from memory, requiring no written texts. For most men and women, the Bible was spoken and performed.

We know, for instance, that Geoffrey Chaucer likely did not have a Bible open in front of him for easy consultation for the plethora of scriptural references that pour from the mouths of his bawdy characters in *Canterbury Tales*.[39] His men and women quote scripture from memory, not from books they took with them on pilgrimage. The Pardoner echoes Isaiah with his admonition, "Now lat us sitte and drynke, / And make us merie, / And afterward we wol his body berie."[40] Most likely, this reflected Chaucer's own deep familiarity with the Bible, which he could assume would be shared by his readers and hearers.[41] In a mostly illiterate world, the Bible was simply known.

Such assumed familiarity was equally common among the great mystical and devotional writers who saw the Bible as a rich treasure of spiritual instruction and discipline and whose works contained rapturous expressions of God's love. Richard Rolle, the fourteenth-century English hermit and writer, received the Bible through a long tradition of mystical interpretations that he fashioned into his own idiosyncratic spirituality.[42]

The flourishing of spiritual and mystical literature in the medieval world spoke to the intimate relationship between God and the individual soul, often presented as a passionate love affair. This brought both familiarity and tension. The German mystic Mechthild of Magdeburg (ca. 1207–ca. 1282/94) wrote a work entitled *The Flowing Light of the Godhead*, a collection of prayers, visions, and experiences that spoke to the direct encounter with God. While the wealth of biblical images resonated with her readers and the circle gathered around her, opponents claimed that she was using her authority as a mystic to offer an alternative to scripture. This was never her intention, but mystics were often marginalized and considered dangerous. Frequently, such allegations against women mystics were tainted with traditional misogyny.[43]

In the East, the physicality of the mystical bond of word and soul was expressed in the Orthodox tradition of Hesychasm, which involved adopting bodily positions and breathing patterns to achieve a state of contemplation. The practice followed Christ's admonition in the Gospel of Matthew: "When thou prayest, enter into thy closet, and when thou hast shut thy door, pray to thy Father which is in secret; and thy Father which seeth in secret shall reward thee openly" (Matt. 6:6, KJV). Hesychasm was not distinct from the Bible but instead drew on scripture and the teachings of the holy fathers to find stillness and peace of heart. Indeed, it was based on Christ's words and the teachings of Paul in the New Testament. A crucial text is 1 Thessalonians: "But we urge you, brethren, that you increase more and more; that you also aspire to lead a quiet life, to mind your own business, and to work with your own hands, as we commanded you" (4:10–11, NKJV). The word *hesychazein*, meaning "quiet life," is the root of the term "Hesychasm."

This sense of the intimacy of word, image, and movement is poignantly experienced when entering the grounds of the late-medieval painted monasteries of Bucovina in Romania. Resting in the forested hills of the Cimirna Rivulet, which were occupied for generations by holy hermits, the Moldovita Monastery was built in 1532 by the illegitimate son of Stephen the Great, prince of Moldavia. Artists were commissioned to cover the exterior and interior with images of saints and scenes from the Bible and contemporary events.[44] Summoned to prayer by the knocking of the wooden semantron (used after the occupying Ottomans forbade bells), monastics and laypeople entered a chapel that was visually an open book of the Bible. They entered the church past an enormous Tree of Jesse, depicting the genealogy of Jesus and the holy family, and a mural of Christ summoning the whole of humanity at the Last Judgment. The liturgy was performed as the people were surrounded by the prophets and saints processing toward an enthroned Mary holding her child. Past and present merged as the ancient biblical scenes accompanied a mural of the 1453 siege of Constantinople and images of Stephen and other living patrons. The biblical characters bore the faces of the local population. With chanting and incense, the people stood to worship in a biblical cosmos.

A major source of this medieval devotion in the East and West continued to be the Psalms. Examples are legion. The Ingeborg Psalter at Chantilly, created around 1195, is complete with fifty-one full-page miniatures of the Old and New Testaments. Although the Danish queen of France for whom it was commissioned did not know French, she would have been able to follow devotionally through the images of biblical stories. The Ingeborg Psalter is representative of French art at the beginning of the thirteenth century, reflecting the shift in painting toward the Gothic style, simultaneous with a similar shift in architecture and sculpture.[45] It was the age of the great cathedrals of Reims, Chartres, and Notre Dame, a confident flourishing of culture in a France that had reclaimed most of its lands from the English and was experiencing a spiritual renewal. A vivid example in the Ingeborg Psalter is a miniature of the Tree of Jesse with scenes from the Old Testament, the life of Christ, and the coronation of the Virgin. The luminous blues and crimsons, shared by the stained-glass windows of cathedrals, point toward artistic perspectives of the future, leading to the Renaissance.

Orthodox Christians also found deep spiritual solace in the psalms. Gregory of Sinai (d. 1346) describes the regiment of the religious: "The solitary should first of all have as the basis of his activity these five virtues: silence, temperance, vigilance, humility, patient endurance; and his God-pleasing activities should be three: psalmody, prayer, reading, plus (if he is weak) handiwork."[46] Many of the Byzantine Psalters contain these words from a preface by Athanasius of Alexandria (296/298–373):

But the marvel with reference to the Psalms is this: beyond the prophecies concerning the savior and the nations, the one saying the other things is speaking as in his own words, and each person sings them as if written concerning himself and relates them not as if another were speaking and not as if they signified another. . . . I think that these words become like a mirror to the singer for him to be able to understand in them the emotions of his own soul and thus perceiving them to explain them.[47]

The fourteenth-century patriarch of Constantinople, Philotheos Kokkinos, relates that even as a child, the future saint Germanos (ca. 634–ca. 733/40) would secretly imitate the piety of his father, a tax collector: "In solitude he talked solely to God, holding in his hands the sacred book of Psalms."[48]

The spiritual power of the psalms was felt in daily life. Psalters came with instructions on how to pray with gestures and offered particular psalms as curatives: Psalms 53 and 54 were to deal with despondency; 34 and 37 to guard against lewd and rancorous thoughts; Psalms 12 and 16, against forsakenness; 70 and 72, against despair; and 139 to prevent blasphemy. Indeed, the Bible was widely regarded as a talismanic source of prognostication, healing, and defense against demonic forces. It could also control natural forces. The power of the Bible to address the depredations of life was recognized by all, including kings and peasants, clerics and laity.

From the twelfth century it was common to try to prevent lightning storms and bad weather by reading the opening of John's Gospel. There was, in fact, great faith in the ability of the fourth Gospel to ward off all manner of fearful threats, including hail, demons, and sudden death.[49] According to *The Hammer of the Witches*, the late-medieval handbook for witch hunters, the Gospel calms stormy weather, as Christ did for his disciples, but in this case stirred up by black magic.

Those who persecuted witches were convinced of the restorative powers of Bible verses to break demonic possession. Church exorcists would read passages of scripture, particularly from the Gospels, to drive out demons, and it was common for them to write out "In the Beginning," from John's Gospel, and hang it around the neck of the possessed until they were cured. While the priests might claim that God was doing the healing, many believed the curative powers were in the words themselves.[50] In societies primarily oral in nature, words were power.

The church repeatedly denounced the use of the Bible for divination as superstition, but to little effect. The practice was widespread both inside and outside the church. For instance, according to the friar and poet Thomas of Celano (ca. 1195–ca. 1260), St. Francis, seeking refuge from the crowds in a hermitage, turned to the Bible for a sign. He placed the Gospels on the altar and, prostrating himself in prayer, beseeched his heavenly Father to reveal his will for his servant that he might live in simplicity and prayer. With "reverence and awe" he removed the Gospels from the altar and randomly opened them, landing on the Passion of Christ. He had received his answer. Francis, like Christ, was called to suffer greatly. But, Thomas continues, "to avoid any suspicion that this might have happened by chance, he opened the book a second and a third time and found the same or a similar passage written." God was speaking to him through the book: "Then the man, full of the Spirit of God, understood that it behooved him through much anguish and much warfare to enter into the Kingdom of God."[51]

In the end, the church adopted a more flexible attitude toward divination, and clergy as often as laypeople looked to the Bible as a physical manifestation of God's will. It was common for the book to play a role at trials both religious and secular. At a twelfth-century Benedictine monastery in Austria, a copy of Psalms was placed on a table during procedures concerning theft and violence. Elaborate rituals were performed in which God was invoked to indicate guilt or innocence by moving the book toward the east or west. Such common practice was not far from the widespread medieval practice of trial by ordeal, in which men and women were subjected to enormous pain in order to determine whether or not they had committed offenses.

Although most men and women during the medieval period encountered the Bible not as a written text but through speech and ritual, the Bibles that were produced during this period, as in earlier centuries, were often remarkable objects that went on remarkable adventures. In the thirteenth century, for instance, the Shah 'Abbas Bible (also known as the Crusader Bible) made its way from France across Asia before returning home. Likely created as a picture Bible (it has no text) for King Louis IX, a zealous Crusader later canonized, the exquisite, rolled gold illuminations provide scenes from the Hebrew Bible, from Creation to King David. Blending past and present, the Israelite soldiers are shown dressed as thirteenth-century French soldiers. Further, the biblical scenes were set in thirteenth-century France, with vivid depictions of the daily lives of commoners and nobility. Scholars believe these beautiful images may have been produced by an artist who worked on the wall paintings and stained-glass windows of Sainte-Chapelle in Paris. Indeed, the images are so stunningly graphic in their portrayal of the violence of Crusader battles that the weapons depicted could be accurately reproduced from the art.

Like the codices Sinaiticus and Vaticanus, the Crusader Bible passed through many hands before vanishing from history for centuries. Having been taken to southern Italy by Louis's brother Charles of Anjou, it appeared three hundred years later in Kraków, Poland, in the bishop's court. In 1604 the Bible was presented by the pope to the shah of Persia in the hope of fostering an alliance against the Turks. The shah was so delighted that he had commentaries in beautiful Persian script added. The story of Absalom, however, who rebelled against his father, greatly displeased the shah, and he ordered it removed from the Bible lest his sons get wrong ideas.[52] The Crusader Bible is now housed in the Morgan Library and Museum in New York.

The largest medieval Bible (in fact, the largest codex) in existence today was also well traveled, journeying from a Bohemian monastery to a Swedish castle.[53] The aptly named Codex Gigas ("Giant Book"), crafted in the thirteenth century, is also known, infamously, as the Devil's Bible. Its name derives from a highly unusual portrait, not of Christ or an evangelist, but of Satan. Created in Bohemia, it is the largest and heaviest known medieval manuscript (weighing almost 170 pounds)—a complete version of the Vulgate bundled together with a collection of other writings. The devil is said to have had a hand in its creation: according to legend, he aided a scribe named Herman the Recluse in copying the Bible in one night in return for his soul. As a reward, the devil was given a portrait almost twenty inches high in the book. He is portrayed with a large green head, small red eyes, curly hair, white teeth, and two tongues protruding from the corners of his mouth. In the sixteenth century the Bible was taken from its Benedictine house to the library of Emperor Rudolf II, and then in the Thirty Years War, Swedish troops carried it off to Stockholm. In 1697 a fire destroyed much of the Swedish Royal Library. The Bible was saved by being tossed out of a window, but the devil continued to have his way: it landed on a bystander, causing serious injury.

The thirteenth century also saw the appearance of another form of Bible, the so-called Bibles moralisées, extraordinarily lavish works with exquisite paintings by some of the finest artists of the age. Indeed, one distinguished art historian has described one of these Bibles, held in Vienna, as "one of the supreme achievements of medieval art."[54] Their origins lie in the artistically creative Paris of King Louis VIII, his wife Blanche of Castile, and his son Louis IX, patron of the Crusader Bible.[55] The young queen, following the death of her husband, became the sole ruler of France in an age of civil strife. Surrounded by enemies and accused of being a whore, she fought to ensure her son's accession. Blanche's deep piety led her to commission and finance the St. Louis Bible, which is currently held at the Morgan Library and Museum in New York. On the dedication page, the enthroned Blanche and her beardless young son appear together in poses intended to evoke Mary and Christ. As patron Blanche provided teams of artists and scribes with studios to carry out their work.[56]

Though called Bibles, these sumptuous Bibles moralisées, such as the St. Louis Bible, do not contain the full text of the Old and New Testaments but, rather, selected scenes for interpretation. The scenes link biblical texts with images to draw together past and present to convey a range of moral admonitions, giving rise to the name of these Bibles.[57] These injunctions are not primarily theological but rather illustrate Christian life, reflecting the worlds of students in Paris, Christian-Jewish relations, the Crusades, and courtly politics.[58] The interpretations often spoke to the contemporary world, drawing parallels between the evildoers of the Bible and those vilified in medieval society, including corrupt priests, thieves, adulterers, and Jews. In fact, the anti-Jewish sentiments of thirteenth-century France were prominent in the moral messages and accompanying images.[59] No doubt Blanche had in mind the treacherous nobles seeking to overthrow her. Hostility to Jews was not limited to persecution. It was ingrained in the devotional world of medieval Christians.

Closely associated with the Bibles moralisées were the misleadingly named Bibles of the Poor (*Biblia pauperum*) that spread across Europe in the later Middle Ages. Hardly for the poor, they were beautifully illustrated with images depicting stories from the Pentateuch and the books of Kings together with scenes from the life of Christ, from the Annunciation to the Last Judgment.[60] The text was a heady combination of prayers and cryptic interpretations, although references are continuously provided to the biblical text. These Bibles assumed readers would know scripture well enough to grasp the images and verse.[61]

The porous boundary between the Bible and devotional books is most richly found in another creation of the thirteenth century. In the High Middle Ages, devotion to Mary, Mother of God, was reflected in elegant works known as books of hours.[62] Closely associated with the cult of Mary that flourished in the fourteenth and fifteenth centuries, these books contained sumptuously illustrated prayers, readings, and psalms known as the Hours of the Virgin to be prayed throughout the day.[63] To a certain extent, these books reflected the medieval expansion of monastic piety into the temporal world, feeding a growing appetite among urban elites and merchants eager for greater involvement in religion while also cultivating their desire for collecting valuable objects. The growing demand for religious literature among men and women reflected the prosperity of mercantile, urban communities.

In the books of hours, devout men and women were offered a form of the canonical hours of the religious orders, structured in eight "hours" a day of veneration of the Mother of God. Her story was told from the Annunciation to the Passion, when she remained at the cross of the crucified Christ. Illustrations, or painted prayers, were integral to the prayer book. The faithful, in the words of the historian Virginia Reinburg, "addressed the Virgin Mary and the saints, asking for their intervention before God, and in exchange offered them praise, tribute, or donations." Books of hours were "archives of prayer" as well as precious objects.[64]

By the late Middle Ages, the religious life of men and women involved a mixture of Latin and vernacular languages. In rural and urban areas, the Bible was available to the laity in both. Although men and women encountered the Bible in liturgy, unless they understood Latin, there remained a barrier, so it was primarily sermons in parish churches that made the Bible accessible in their tongue.[65] From the thirteenth century, preaching flourished in the medieval world in the form of scholastic sermons in which the biblical text was broken down systematically and interpreted in parts.[66] A phrase or even a longer text from the Bible might form the basis for a series of themes through precise divisions. Over the next century, preaching acquired a new character as a result of the work of the medieval schools and, later, the Dominicans and Franciscans.

Medieval writers on the art of the sermon continued to admonish clergy to preach on the Old and New Testaments without distorting the texts. The Bible was to be mined for authoritative passages. The themes of the sermon were to be based on these quotations, by which the preacher would prove his case. Through these sermons and their forms, audiences would be exposed to a great deal of the Old and New Testaments. As one medieval English writer on the art of preaching advised, "It is clear that scripture is of itself sufficiently rich so that one can easily and quickly understand what is necessary if one chooses a good beginning of one's discourse."[67]

In more popular preaching, biblical narratives were explained and expanded through the extensive use of stories, or exempla. These exempla were drawn from a mixture of the Bible, saints' lives, and local folklore. Many of the fairy tales later gathered by the Brothers Grimm had their origins in such sermons. These stories were collected in volumes and circulated throughout Europe, offering learned and humble preachers a vast repertoire of imaginative tales through which the Bible could be communicated into daily life.

The ubiquity of the Latin Vulgate in the Middle Ages as *the* medieval Bible tends to overshadow the spectacular growth of vernacular translations in the fifteenth centuries. Here again, this fact travels against the Protestant current, which recalls Martin Luther and William Tyndale as heroically bringing the Word of God into popular tongues. Less known are the approximately seventy German vernacular Bibles before Luther's September Testament of 1522. Seventeen of these Bibles were complete, appearing in one volume.[68] Full Bibles generally belonged to wealthy laity, including burghers and nobility, as well as to religious houses.[69]

In England, the appearance of the Wycliffite Bible in the 1370s caused great unease for church and king. Intended for a broader audience, it became associated with heretical ideas such as attachment to scripture alone. Wycliffe set out a radical agenda for the Bible and the people:

Christ and His Apostles taught the people in the language best known to them. It is certain that the truth of the Christian faith becomes more evident the more faith itself is known. Therefore, the doctrine should not only be in Latin but in the vulgar tongue and, as the faith of the church is contained in the Scriptures, the more these are known in a true sense the better. The laity ought to understand the faith and, as doctrines of our faith are in the Scriptures, believers should have the Scriptures in a language which they fully understand.[70]

Wycliffe's conviction that the Bible should be in the language of the people—the reason Protestant reformers referred to him as the Morning Star of the Reformation—was viewed as not only heretical and a challenge to the church's authority but seditious, encouraging popular discontent. The response to the Bible was fierce. Thomas Arundel (1353–1414), as archbishop of Canterbury, denounced Wycliffe:

That pestilent and most wretched John Wycliffe, of damnable memory, a child of the old devil, and himself a child or pupil of Antichrist, who, while he lived, walking in the vanity of his mind—with a few other adjectives, adverbs, and verbs, which I shall not give—crowned his wickedness by translating the scriptures into the mother tongue.[71]

In 1407–1409 Arundel's Oxford Constitutions damned Wycliffe and prohibited vernacular translations not approved by the bishop or church council. Despite these strictures, a large body (over 250 manuscripts) of Wycliffite Bibles has survived, putting in question the effectiveness of the prohibition. Nevertheless, on account of the ban, late-medieval England—unlike the rest of Europe—saw no vernacular translations until William Tyndale's in the 1520s, and he would be strangled for his efforts.[72]

On the Continent, the situation was different. German, French, Italian, and Spanish Bibles of the late Middle Ages emerged from vigorous relationships between printers, patrons, and the public. In the early years of print, vernacular Bibles accounted for a relatively small amount of production compared to the vast market for Latin Bibles. For instance, in Germany, France, the Low Countries, and England, they formed only about 10 percent of total production.[73]

The tradition of the German Bible remains fixated on Martin Luther, but he was something of a Johnny-come-lately. From the late eighth century, vernacular translations of parts of the Bible, notably the Psalms, were found across German-speaking lands.[74] These translations existed alongside other books with biblical material. *The Heilend* (The Savior), for instance, tells in verse form how Jesus was akin to a Germanic tribal leader who dispensed rings to his disciples. There are over a thousand known biblical manuscripts from German lands in the late Middle Ages, and Martin Luther made use of many in preparing his own translations.

Similarly, French versions of biblical literature exist from the eighth century and ninth century, around the time of the appearance of the kingdom. A stunning edition of the Old French Bible is the Acre Bible, produced in the thirteenth century for Louis IX (son of Queen Blanche) in the Crusader kingdom of Jerusalem. The partial Old Testament, an exquisite example of the so-called Crusader art that flourished in the Levant throughout the Middle Ages, contains scenes that display a mixture of Eastern and Western influences: the translations made from Latin reflect earlier traditions of French from Norman England and the different regions of the kingdom, while, strikingly, there are also a number of words and phrases taken from Arabic, reflecting the Bible's creation in the Near East.

The first full French Bible, known as the Old French Bible, appeared between 1220 and 1260. It was followed by Guyart des Moulins's *Bible historiale* (1291–1295). Together, they formed the basis for what became the most important French Bible of the late Middle Ages, *Bible historiale complétée*, whose manuscripts survive in great number. These less expensive Bibles reached a much wider readership, including lower social groups. Like all Bibles, these French editions did not exist alone but alongside a flourishing body of devotional literature recounting the life of Christ and his Passion, intended for clerical and lay readers.[75]

The Iberian Peninsula also witnessed a dynamic biblical world, and with a distinctive character provided by its rich Jewish and Islamic cultures.[76] Spain had a long but troubled history of vernacular translations.[77] During the Middle Ages, anti-Jewish violence and sentiments raged across the Iberian Peninsula. In an effort to mitigate this hostility in the fifteenth century, Don Luis de Guzmán invited the rabbi Moses Arragel to work with him on a Castilian translation of the Bible. The result, known as the Alba Bible, was an artistic and linguistic treasure. The translation of the Old Testament was largely the work of Rabbi Arragel, but the accompanying illustrations were produced in Toledo by Franciscans. Most amazingly, the Bible was accompanied by the commentaries of Jewish and Christian scholars, drawing from church fathers, medieval commentators, midrash, and the Talmud. Further, in the surviving Bible the correspondence between Don Luis and Rabbi Arragel, as well as between the rabbi and the Franciscan illustrators, had been inserted between the pages. Such Bibles were available only to elites, but manuscripts of books such as the Psalms and Gospels reached a wider readership.

By the end of the Middle Ages, vernacular Bibles had never before been so widely owned and read. Commercial prosperity sparked the growth of education, there was a distinct shift toward a reading culture, and the advent of printing placed a new emphasis on the Bible as a book to be read. In cheaper, more accessible manuscript form, Bibles reached a much broader audience, such as merchants and women, creating ever-expanding reading audiences.

The shift toward reading the Bible was also embraced by the church. In his *Miroir de l'âme* (1400–1401), the eminent pastor and theologian of the French church Jean Gerson explained how all people could access those parts of the Bible essential for salvation—the Ten Commandments, the Lord's Prayer, the Apostles' Creed, and the Hail Mary—together with short explanations.[78] In his *La montagne de contemplation* (1397), Gerson recommended that laity should read the Bible, particularly the Gospels, in their homes to cultivate the religious life.

Evidence for this wider reading audience is found in wills, which show how Bibles were passed from generation to generation, usually in parts.[79] For those who could read but possibly not afford biblical books, access was possible through libraries, hospitals, and other charitable institutions. Books were often exchanged. But Bible reading was not necessarily a solitary, silent activity. It was read generally aloud and shared in community, not only in homes but in workplaces.

This shift in the fourteenth century toward greater availability of Bibles and devotional literature for laymen and laywomen also involved a move away from monastic houses for the production of manuscripts to lay shops.[80] Such was the demand for religious literature that workshops developed under the patronage of the affluent, and manuscripts moved away from possessions of churches to commodities for the people. Religious literature was becoming a business in which the needs of the market were determinative.

Naturally, this culture of supply and demand for manuscripts and, later, books required financial investment, which inevitably increased economic risk. Not infrequently, vernacular Bibles were printed in parts and then collected and assembled by laymen and laywomen at home to create their own book.[81] Market considerations also required a close relationship between printers and their public. Printers chose the text to produce but did so with a mind to current tastes. In the Netherlands, for example, there was a highly urbanized, literate public with considerable demand for biblical and devotional literature. The Devotio Moderna, a spiritual reform group that was often suspected of heresy but remained within the church, produced manuscripts of vernacular readings from the Bible as an aid for laypeople to follow the Mass.[82] Accessible to both nuns and laypeople, these manuscripts were enormously popular, creating a market for printers, who were highly sensitive to demand.

How did this growing audience read their Bibles? Marginal reading marks indicate guides to learning scriptures by memory.[83] In other Bibles, prayers were added, reflecting individual devotional readings. The boundaries between the sacred text and daily life, or the sacred and profane, were certainly porous. Bibles were often used to store family and commercial documents, such as contracts, wills, travel accounts, and even records of building materials.[84] One reason why Bibles were so useful as repositories of information was because their margins and blank pages offered a source of much-needed paper.

The medieval world thus anticipated our modern sense of the Bible as a commodity. By the late Middle Ages, in particular with the advent of print, the Bible was well established as a commercial good produced by professional scribes who were independent of churches and universities. Their primary interest was in creating Bibles for sale, and they were thus little concerned with scholarly correctness.[85] But the commercial upside of these ventures paled in comparison to that of the first printed book in the West: Johannes Gutenberg's Bible.

Through the use of movable type, Gutenberg began the rapid transition to mass production of Bibles that could, in medieval terms, quickly reach to the frontiers of Europe. But the modern valorization of the advent of print tends to obscure aspects of the story that seem less exciting. First, though the advantages of print were quickly recognized, the resulting product was not immediately regarded as more valuable than manuscripts—in fact, quite the opposite. It is no coincidence that the Gutenberg Bible with its Gothic type was created to look like a manuscript. Printers did not enjoy the spiritual status of the scribe, whose painful labors were relieved by the knowledge that their efforts were holy. Printing never achieved that level of sanctity. As a consequence, printed books were not as valuable as manuscripts. An illustrated book could not match an illuminated manuscript. Further, by no means did print immediately kill off manuscripts; the two forms would coexist for centuries.

Jerome's Latin Bible was the first book to be printed in the West with movable type, produced by Gutenberg in the German city of Mainz from 1453 to 1455. Approximately 50 copies survive of the original run of 180. Perhaps surprisingly, the Bible contains no clues to its printer's identity.[86] Indeed, for all his fame, there are only a few historical traces of Gutenberg, such as his tax records, and he remains a somewhat elusive figure. Born in Mainz, he lived for over a decade in the Rhine city of Strasbourg. An early endeavor to produce mirrors for pilgrims in large numbers was a business failure, a harbinger of future financial flops. The idea, however, was a good one. Mirrors were widely used by pilgrims who found themselves tightly packed in crowds. They were both practical and sacred. By using mirrors like a periscope, pilgrims could get a glimpse of the sacred relics they had journeyed to venerate. But there was more. The mirrors, it was believed, captured the reflected rays emanating from sacred sites such as altars and shrines. Those rays could be preserved and taken home.

The genesis of the Gutenberg Bible, as well as Gutenberg's motives, are both familiar and debated. He took two loans in the early 1450s from Johann Fust to finance the production of a lectern Bible for use in churches and religious houses. Among clerics and monastic groups, there was a renewed taste for these large volumes in the spirit of religious renewal. Gutenberg, sensitive to the desires of the market, looked to rich possibilities in the Rhineland and Low Countries. He was aware that wealthy donors were willing to commission large, enormously ornate manuscript Bibles, and he alighted on a way in which they might be produced more economically.[87] Prudence prevailed, and Gutenberg sold his Bibles by subscription before he began production, raising the capital in advance.

The Bible itself was produced in two folio volumes with parallel columns of forty-two lines, the first volume with 324 leaves of text and the second with 319. The type was the Gothic of many contemporary religious books, such as the missal, produced in a size easy on the eye. The text was the Paris Latin Bible of the thirteenth century with some modifications. As such, the Gutenberg quickly became the exemplum for future printed Bibles, ensuring its fame.

Enea Silvio Piccolomini, later Pope Pius II (1405–1464), was among the first to see the Gutenberg Bible, at the book fair in Frankfurt, and described Gutenberg as "that miraculous man," adding, "Of the number I am not entirely certain; of the perfection of the books (if any faith can be placed in men) I have no doubt."[88] Soon the Holy Roman emperor was able to examine quires from Gutenberg's press. The effect was immediate, and the print run was sold out by subscription before the Bibles were produced in 1455. When Fust demanded that Gutenberg repay the initial loans, a court ruled that Gutenberg was required to make satisfaction against the collateral of his press and future profits. Their partnership ended, possibly amicably. Whatever the case, Gutenberg surrendered his printing press to Fust. By 1456 the Bibles were sent unbound to patrons across Europe, who then dug into their pockets to have the pages illustrated and red ink used for key words.

News of Gutenberg's work spread quickly to the French court, and the king sent engraver Nicolas Jenson to Strasbourg to learn the secrets of this new wonder. He went away empty-handed, but movable type was soon found in other German cities, leading to the appearance of almost a hundred Latin Bibles by the end of the century. The craft developed exponentially, allowing Bibles to appear in a variety of forms as printers became more adept with creating and employing type, moving away from the heavy folios printed by Gutenberg to more practical forms.

By the end of the century, print shops had sprung up across Italy and north of the Alps. The success of print did not, however, guarantee financial rewards. Just as Gutenberg did not profit from his innovation, many printers lost their shirts when a book failed to sell and they were saddled with unsold stock. The costs of paper, labor, and distribution were significant, and many books did not survive. Nevertheless, the availability of the Bible across Europe post-Gutenberg created a new world of readership. The speed of development was eye-watering. In a mere fifty years, the world of publishing went from Gutenberg's Gothic-print Bible of the 1450s, which was meant to resemble a manuscript, to the multilanguage polyglots, which contained multiple versions of scripture in different languages.

Printing also made possible the production of standardized Bibles. If a book was printed in Basel and sent to Scotland, Spain, and Hungary, it was the same book in all three lands. But there was a catch. While errors or omissions were an inevitable feature of hand-copying, printers also made mistakes, and the stakes for the latter could not be greater. If a printer made a mistake with a word, omitted a paragraph, or reproduced an error by the author, it was circulated in thousands of copies across Europe. Sometimes the error could become authoritative. It became commonplace in late-medieval and early-modern cultures for authors to curse their printers, perhaps not always fairly, for corrupting their text and printing embarrassing mistakes. What scholar wanted it to look like his Latin was not very good?

There is no doubt that the advent of print culture transformed human culture, but it is important to recognize that these effects were not immediate. Few in the medieval world ever encountered a book, and changes in society left most men and women untouched. When

Nicholas of Lyra spoke of the Bible as the book of life, he could not have envisaged Gutenberg, but in many ways his idea was more expansive. Far from a mere commodity or object, the Bible suffused everyday life in the Middle Ages, a universal bond among the faithful. Soon, however, with the coming fracture of the Reformation, the Bible would lose its universal status as the book of the whole Western church.

CHAPTER 5

RENAISSANCE AND REFORMATION

The stories contained in the Bible have a small geographical home in Egypt and ancient Palestine. Once they formed a book, however, they quickly traveled to distant lands and spoke in many tongues. Tradition holds that the apostle Thomas took the gospel to India. Early Christians made their way to China along the Asian trade routes. By the end of the Middle Ages, with the voyages of Henry the Navigator and Christopher Columbus, the Bible became global on a new scale. From the 1540s, Jesuit missionaries were found in the Congo, the Philippines, and China. Accompanying merchants and colonizers, the Bible entered cultures that knew nothing of it, such as India and Japan, which had their own traditions of sacred writings. At the same time, the Bible was tearing apart the Europe that these conquistadors and missionaries had left behind.

As the unity of Western Christianity was shattered by the Reformation, the Bible lost a straightforward narrative. Its future was fragmentation and contestation in debates over authority and identity. Fragmentation does not, however, necessarily denote decline but simply radical change. No longer a book of a universal faith, the Bible had power in its ability to transform communities and individuals.

The Bible transformed the life of Martin Luther, a professor at a remote university who lectured through the books of the Old and New Testaments. His own spiritual anguish and his careful reading of scripture started a revolution. In 1522 the former monk was a notorious fugitive with a price on his head for challenging the authority of the pope and the emperor. Hiding in Wartburg Castle deep in the Thuringian Forest near Eisenach, he took up his pen and over eleven weeks translated the Greek New Testament into German.[1] Scripture, Luther believed, should speak in the language of hearth, market square, and tavern. It should speak, he famously said, as a mother to her child. His was not the first translation into his people's tongue, but from his desk emerged a classic that changed the world.[2]

Isolation had not been entirely salutary. Luther recounted battling severe depression. But his demons were not only internal. The devil, according to an apocryphal story of uncertain origin, fumed to see Luther provide a version of the sacred text that all Germans could understand. He appeared in Luther's room in the tower, determined to tempt the former monk from his work, but Luther grabbed his inkpot and threw it at the evil one's head. He apparently missed and stained the wall. The Brothers Grimm, expanding on this story after Luther's death, claimed that the excommunicated professor had pointed the devil to the passage in Genesis where the serpent in the garden is crushed, and, outraged, the malevolent intruder had departed—after farting so powerfully that the room stank for days.

The flatulent devil had good reason to be angered. The forces of the Renaissance and the Reformation, epitomized by Luther's lonely project, changed the Bible forever. Within ten years of Johannes Gutenberg's first printing of the Vulgate in the 1450s, copies of scripture had spread across Europe in Latin and vernacular translations—often as a complete work, with Old and New Testaments firmly bound together. The late-medieval world, as recounted in the previous chapter, was awash with Bibles in German, Czech, Spanish, Dutch, French, and Italian. Widely read, heard, and preached in the languages of the people for the first time, the Bible fostered devotion, literature, art, and music. The Reformation fed this raging torrent and, in doing so, contributed to a flood of interpretive disagreement that could no longer be contained by existing religious authorities.

Even prior to the Reformation, the diffusion of the Bible during the Renaissance gave rise to important changes that fueled disagreement and division.[3] Renaissance scholars began to treat the Bible as a historical object—as a book with a history. They embraced the dangerous idea that the study of language, literature, and history, rather than church doctrine, provided the best path for unlocking the Bible's mysteries. At the same time, in the hands of conquistadors and Catholic missionaries, the Bible became truly global for the first time, a transformation that raised troubling questions about its veracity, as the Bible itself did not acknowledge the existence of this New World, let alone the peoples who lived there. The universal status of the Bible was thus already beginning to fray by the early sixteenth century, but with the Reformation this status would be forever torn asunder.

During the sixteenth and seventeenth centuries, the printing presses of Europe poured forth the writings of Protestants, Catholics, and more radical thinkers, each asserting the correct and exclusive interpretation of the Bible, creating a world of vitriolic religious polemic that went far beyond universities and princely courts to the lives of men and women in churches, cities, and villages.[4] The head-spinning diffusion of the Bible made scripture more accessible, but the hands that held the Bible were raised not only in prayer but also in anger against opponents. As in the medieval world, the Bible was brandished to repudiate those who thought differently, but the Reformation created a new order of conflict between Christians. The Bible became a symbol of what both united and divided. Just as a family might sit at home with the Gospels, armies marching into battle in a new age of religious wars sang psalms. The gaseous devil may have been banished by Luther's flying inkpot, but in the longer run he had reason for glee as the unity of Western Christianity came crashing down.

Disagreement reigned over not only what the Bible said but what it was. Against the consensus of the medieval Catholic Church, Luther and his followers took their stand that scripture was the sole authority for the church, the only standard by which all Christian teaching and living should be measured.[5] To the horror of the Catholic hierarchy, they loudly declared that the Bible should be directly accessible to all, because for faithful men and women its message of salvation was utterly clear. Catholics did not willingly accede to this claim. They countered with the long-standing argument that scripture could only be interpreted within the church and its traditions. Nevertheless, Catholic scholars both embraced the changes of the Renaissance and reaffirmed the church's relationship to the Bible.

One of the earliest statements of the reforming Council of Trent unequivocally declared the centrality of the Bible for the church. They were not prepared to lose the book.

Not since its early times had Christianity witnessed such fragmentation. The Bible was the child in a particularly ugly divorce. That child was also changing its identity. The medieval world knew the Bible as the foundation for the teachings, worship, and devotion of Christians. The form of the Bible may have varied, but its purpose did not. Now, new questions were raised. From the end of the fifteenth century to the eighteenth century, the period covered by the next two chapters, the sacred text faced investigations that challenged its very essence. What did the rapid growth of knowledge of ancient languages, the study of history, and the discovery of manuscripts mean for the Bible? Was the Bible still a coherent account of humanity's salvation, or was it an inchoate bundle of historical documents? Such questions shook the Western church but left untouched the Orthodox Eastern and African churches. The Reformation created two radically different views of the Bible: Was it the book of the people or the book of the church? There was no straightforward answer.

The roots of this seismic change lay in the Renaissance, a period that emerged during the late Middle Ages and was associated with the paintings of Botticelli, Michelangelo, and da Vinci, the glories of Medici Florence, and scandalous popes. The great nineteenth-century writer Jacob Burckhardt hailed the Renaissance as launching the modern world with its discovery of the individual human person. This, he argued, was a welcome return to paganism after the benighted monkishness of the Middle Ages.[6]

Indeed, there is a long tradition of looking to the Renaissance for the first stirrings of secularism. In truth, religion suffused the age. Beginning in Italy and spreading north across the Alps, scholars, artists, poets, politicians, and churchmen fell under the spell of the classical world and sought to make the glories of ancient Greece and Rome their own. For many, the paganism of antiquity birthed a renewed Christianity. In their view, antiquity had bequeathed to the West a wisdom that poured light on the Bible, from Plato to Virgil.[7] Like Jerome in the fifth century, Renaissance Christians believed that scripture could speak with the hortatory eloquence of classical orators. Its words could flow like Cicero's and Livy's, and its original, pure form could be recovered. Erasmus spoke of the ancient world being baptized in Christian waters.

In casting their gaze backward, Renaissance scholars began to see the Bible as a book with a history and became increasingly curious about how it was written and transmitted over time.[8] This idea, though not unknown in the Middle Ages, acquired new force as scholars embraced the tools of humanism, an educational ideal that revived the classical arts such as rhetoric and dialectic, and recovered the fields of poetics and ancient philosophy. The impact on the Bible was transformative. Medieval theologians had largely assumed a fixed text of scripture, although they were well aware of its deficiencies. Repeated efforts were made to correct the Latin from other Latin versions and, only occasionally, Hebrew and Greek.

The Renaissance offered a new way forward through the recovery of the original languages, against which the Latin could be tested, and through the study of manuscripts—including many brought from the crumbling Byzantine world or found by rummaging through monastic libraries.[9] To peel back the layers of the past and recover the Bible in its purest form, scholars turned not only to Hebrew and Greek but also to Aramaic (which Jesus likely spoke), Syriac, Coptic, and, later, Arabic. Even Ge'ez (Ethiopic) made its way to Europe. It became clear that languages were not static but continued to evolve and had a history. Knowledge of how languages worked and mutated, Renaissance scholars believed, explained the many variations in the Bible. It was in many ways a return to Jerome's fifth-century vision that the best possible Bible must be constructed from Hebrew and Greek.[10] Not surprisingly, Jerome became the patron saint of those who pursued this goal during the Renaissance, and once again, to many scholars, the Bible in its purest and most authoritative form appeared within grasp.

In retrospect, this idea—that the study of language and literature, not established church doctrine, offered the superior way to mining the Bible's mysteries—may appear to be overtly subversive, even mutinous. Yet almost all scholars working on the Bible in the Renaissance assumed that their work would bolster the church, not pull the lever of a trapdoor. By the seventeenth century, philology would be considered separate from church teachings, but in the Renaissance that possibility occurred to no one. Languages were the way forward to restore Christianity. Indeed, both Lorenzo Valla (ca. 1407–1457) and Desiderius Erasmus (1466–1536), the most influential advocates of humanist learning in the service of the Bible, maintained to their deaths their shared conviction that sound knowledge of Hebrew and Greek did not undermine the authority of the church but provided better access to the truth through a purified Bible.[11] For both, the church was the ultimate source of wisdom to which all should defer. Many would later invoke the name Erasmus to tear down the old order, but destruction was never the Dutchman's intention.

Nonetheless, the results of this approach were striking and often alarming. Eventually, some came to believe that historicizing the Bible exposed weaknesses in the traditional stories. By the seventeenth century, the question of whether Moses wrote the first five books of the Bible was openly debated, as was the reliability of the Hebrew text, such as with the antiquity of the pointing. Until the sixteenth century, most scholars assumed the vowel pointing, whereby vowels are indicated by signs not in the Hebrew alphabet, was ancient, perhaps dating to Moses or Ezra the Scribe. The brilliant Jewish scholar Elijah Levita (1469–1549) challenged this assumption by arguing that the vowel points, which influence how the Hebrew text is understood, dated only to around 500 CE and had less authority.[12] The ensuing debate involved questions about the antiquity and reliability of Hebrew. The issue was highly divisive for Christians and Jews. Responses to these debates about the Bible and its languages varied. Some churchmen and scholars held fast to the literal biblical text, while others were skeptical. A conspiracy theory espoused by the Swiss reformer Huldrych Zwingli and others held that the vowel pointing had been deviously created by Jews to confuse Christians. One solution to the problems of the historical Bible and its obvious uncertainties was to read it more as a spiritual or ethical book than as historically accurate.

Far from the scholar's study, the Bible in the Renaissance underwent an equally important transformation: in the hands of conquistadors and priests, it became the first truly global book. The late fifteenth century saw the rapid expansion of Spanish and Portuguese imperialism, and the Bible was at the heart of the age of discovery as Spanish scholars and churchmen sought to place their brutal conquests in biblical terms. How to justify entering another land? Medieval interpreters of the Bible had not broached the topic, leaving the Spanish to grapple with the question in new ways.

Indeed, the very discovery of the Americas posed challenges of interpretation. The Bible had nothing to say about their existence, or the existence of Indigenous cultures of great sophistication with ancient gods. How could these races with their religions and many languages be reconciled with biblical chronology? If humans were all descended from Adam and Eve, then how did they appear in faraway and isolated America? Some interpreters thought they might even predate Adam.

With respect to the question of conquest, the Bible itself provided ample interpretive resources. The 1493 papal bull from Alexander VI that divided the world between the Spanish and the Portuguese brimmed with references to the book of Genesis and the command to subdue the earth. The desire for conquest was thus biblical from the start, and the Spanish naturally turned to Israel and the promised land. When Columbus went ashore in Hispaniola, his commands were framed from Deuteronomy 20:10–13: "When you draw near to a town to fight against it, offer it terms of peace. If it accepts your terms of peace and surrenders to you, then all the people in it shall serve you at forced labor. If it does not submit to you peacefully, but makes war against you, then you shall besiege it; and when the Lord your God gives it into your hand, you shall put all its males to the sword" (NRSV).

More dramatic was the Requerimiento of 1513, a declaration by the Spanish monarchy that announced the pope as the chief religious figure of the world and ordained their right to take possession of the territories in the New World. The Requerimiento was read by officials to the subdued peoples, often in Latin and therefore incomprehensible. Although generally performed as a formality, or even not at all, it was an uncompromising declaration of intent. Once more, the language is directly from Deuteronomy 20: "With the help of God, we shall powerfully enter into your country, and shall make war against you in all ways and manners that we can, and shall subject you to the yoke and obedience of the Church and of their Highnesses; we shall take you and your wives and your children, and shall make slaves of them, and as such shall sell and dispose of them as their Highnesses may command."[13]

The Christian faith was to be carried to colonized lands and the Indigenous peoples converted. In 1519 the jurist Martín Fernández de Enciso, who significantly influenced the writing of the Requerimiento, wrote the first Spanish history of the conquest of the early 1510s. "The king," he claimed, "might very justly send men to require those idolatrous Indians to hand over their land to him, for it was given him by the pope. If the Indians would not do this, he might justly wage war against them, kill them and enslave those captured in war, precisely as Joshua treated the inhabitants of the land of Canaan."[14]

By the middle of the sixteenth century, vigorous debate had arisen around the biblical foundation for conquest and enslavement.[15] For instance, did the Bible's authority extend to lands where it was unknown? The Dominicans Bartolomé de Las Casas (1484–1566) and Francisco de Vitoria (ca. 1483–1546) argued against Spanish imperial expansion and defended the idea that the Bible's authority was geographically and morally limited. Opposing numerous other churchmen and colonial authorities, these Dominicans rejected any scriptural injunction for the forced conversion and enslavement of Indigenous peoples. At the famous Valladolid debate of 1550–1551, Las Casas explicitly refuted biblical warrant for the forcible conversion of "heathens." The account in the Bible of Israel's war against the Canaanites, he argued, was a specific historical event and not to be invoked for contemporary religious oppression.[16]

The Bible was largely kept out of the hands of the conquered peoples and not widely distributed. Spanish clergy used the Latin Vulgate, and translations in Indigenous languages did not appear until much later. Hostility toward local cultures combined with the fear of what was taking place in Reformation Europe, where vernacular translations were seen as a source of heresy. Efforts to convert Indigenous peoples were seen as a war on idolatry, and the Latin Bible was regarded as an essential defense of the true faith.

Conquest overseas inspired conquest at home. The interpretation of the relationship between ancient Israelite history and the present-day Jews also caused problems in Europe, where Christians justified their hostility by distinguishing between the Israelites of the Old Testament, the elect people of God, and the condemned, benighted people of their age. Nowhere was this more evident than in the work of the brilliant Johannes Reuchlin (1455–1522), the leading Hebraist of his age and student of Jewish Kabballah. Reuchlin wrote the first Hebrew grammar and Hebrew-Latin dictionary and was among the first Christian teachers of Hebrew to pave the way for the revival of the language across northern Europe. He was also the founder of a small but influential movement in the sixteenth century of Christian scholars of Hebrew and Jewish writings, who sought to restore knowledge of the language in the service of revealing Christ in the Old Testament.[17] Yet the revival of Hebrew in the fifteenth and sixteenth centuries did nothing to stifle traditional and often violent hostility toward Jews, and one of the most damaging accusations of the age among Christians was of "Judaizing."

Reuchlin was not himself a translator of the Bible, but in the years before Erasmus's 1516 New Testament and Luther's protest, he was nonetheless at the center of the bitterest conflict of the day. The Jewish convert Johannes Pfefferkorn (1469–1522/23) mercilessly attacked him for his defense of Jewish books. Pfefferkorn, seeking the support of Emperor Maximilian, sought to have these books banned and their possession made illegal. Reuchlin defended the rights of Jews not only to keep their books but also to live under protection of the law. The controversy did not end well for Reuchlin. He was condemned under imperial law and fined by the papacy, although his influence remained significant. Over the next century the study of Hebrew became essential for the work of translators. Jews paid the price for the Christian recovery of Hebrew to study the Old Testament.

As the Reuchlin controversy swirled throughout German lands, a sensation emerged from the Swiss city of Basel. Erasmus's 1516 *Novum Instrumentum Omne*, as it was named, was a New Testament in which the Greek text was placed opposite his own Latin translation, followed by extensive explanatory annotations.[18] Erasmus's New Testament was three major achievements in one volume: it made the Greek available, offered a new translation into Latin from the Greek, not the Vulgate, and provided annotations that presented the reader with interpretive guidance.[19]

Each part was controversial. Erasmus had insisted on the primacy of the Greek, but, more boldly, he dared to offer a different translation than the Vulgate, and his notes challenged the biblical grounds for important teachings of the church. He claimed his intention was to improve the Vulgate and serve the unity of Christianity. His opponents saw otherwise. Both advocates and opponents recognized the breadth and audacity of the project: according to some accounts, Erasmus's translation altered about 40 percent of the traditional Latin Bible through a mixture of corrections from the Greek, the use of different manuscripts, and his own assessment of what seemed better.[20] By placing the Greek and his Latin on facing pages, Erasmus invited learned readers to draw their own conclusions. His opponents were incensed.

The whole Testament was framed by Erasmus's ideal of the "philosophy of Christ," a profoundly biblical vision with deep medieval roots that focused the life of faith on the imitation of Christ as portrayed in the Gospels. It was a practical Christianity that advocated peace. Erasmus viewed the Vulgate Bible, with all its errors and crude Latin, to be wholly inadequate to the teaching of a Christ-centered faith. His controversial decision to include a new Latin translation of the Greek was intended to provide readers with greater clarity and a text they could trust.

History lionizes Erasmus as the father of reform, but his efforts were very flawed. Indeed, his approach to his work, so influential for biblical interpretation, was surprisingly haphazard, and the manuscripts he examined were deficient. It is fair to say that as a creation of humanist Latin, Erasmus's New Testament was a jewel. In contrast, as a piece of textual scholarship it was a flop.[21] Further, the approach adopted by Erasmus, of reading the Bible figuratively and presenting God as speaking to humanity, is better seen as a continuation of medieval tradition rather than a significant departure.

The response of the establishment, clerical hierarchies and universities, was swift and harsh. How dare Erasmus, who did not even hold a university position, challenge the Latin Bible of Jerome and the medieval church? Worse, it was simply execrable that he should use his private learning to raise questions about the teachings of the church. Erasmus knew he was in deep trouble. Through the successive editions of his New Testament, which came to be known as the *Novum Testamentum Omne*, he repeatedly argued that he would always follow the teaching of the church, even when the Greek suggested otherwise.

In the eyes of his critics, in advocating the study of languages and manuscripts as essential and primary, Erasmus's supposed call to rejuvenation was in fact undermining doctrines of the church and the authority of those charged with preserving orthodoxy. The Dutchman was fiercely criticized for virtually every alteration. At one point, in translating Ephesians 5:25 ("Husbands, love your wives, even as Christ also loved the church and gave himself for it," KJV), he made alterations to the traditional wording that led his opponents to claim that he was subverting the church's teaching on marriage.

"Pray, what sort of people are these men?" the exasperated Erasmus lashed out. "I write a modest few words [of] what is correct, never uttering a single word that anyone who finds 'dimitte' more agreeable . . . and these people rail against me in sermons before unlearned folk, provoking them to attack; they rave at drinking parties, they rant in servant's quarters, on ships, wagons, who knows where else. Christian religion is done and over with, they themselves studied theology in vain, for someone has appeared who does not shy away from corrupting the Lord's Prayer."[22]

Opponents lined up to denounce Erasmus's public mendacity.[23] The most effective approach was to publicly question his competence, to beat him at his own game. The Englishman Edward Lee wrote a trenchant attack in 1520 that systematically laid out Erasmus's errors, of which there were many.[24] The Dutchman's clever response was to discreetly adopt many of the corrections without attribution to Lee. The Englishman took Erasmus to task over the so-called Johannine Comma, a passage from the first Epistle of John that seemed to offer biblical proof of the doctrine of the Trinity. It has been long disputed whether the passage was original or a later addition, and it is found in none of the Eastern Bibles. Erasmus agreed and left it out, in contrast to the Vulgate, and was immediately denounced. Cowed, he returned it in later editions, although he seriously doubted its authenticity.

The brilliant and prominent Noël Beda in Paris likewise drew attention to Erasmus's errors, but his concern was more focused on the nearness of the Dutchman's views to those of the heretic Martin Luther, who had used the 1519 edition of the New Testament to create his 1522 German translation. Although Erasmus initially suggested that he and Luther shared certain views, he quickly backpedaled. By the early 1520s, having been censured by the theology faculty in Paris, he knew he risked losing everything if he, like Luther, was excommunicated. Erasmus's dance steps allowed him to elude formal condemnation while alive, but several decades after his death, his writings were placed on the Index of Forbidden Books. Many Catholics never forgave Erasmus for the Reformation.

In addition to his many enemies, Erasmus had many friends, rivals, and acolytes. None was more distinguished and venerated than his French contemporary Jacques Lefèvre d'Étaples (ca. 1455–1536), leading light of the Renaissance in France.[25] Although they shared an uneasy friendship, both were committed to the study of the Bible as the only road to reform of Christianity. More mystical and philosophical in disposition, Lefèvre was favorably inclined toward the teachings of the Reformation. Late in life, the Frenchman dedicated himself to the study of the Old and New Testaments and produced an edition of the Psalms in which he placed five versions side by side.[26] His labors were reminiscent of the lost Hexapla of Origen from the second century. Lefèvre's Psalms was effusively praised and became a standard reference for future generations of Bible scholars. His translation of the Bible into French laid the foundation for all vernacular Protestant versions to our time. Such was his towering reputation that the elderly Lefèvre was visited by the young and still-unknown John Calvin.

Erasmus's unwavering contention that his efforts were in support of correcting the Vulgate, which was the Bible of the Western church, was no fig leaf to cover his true intentions. Among Catholics and Protestants there was a shared belief that the Vulgate was the Bible, however corrupted. It possessed a weight of tradition unmatched by any other Bible. It was the work of Jerome, whom all admired, and as a Latin translation it was the model for all vernacular versions of scripture. On that, Catholics and Protestants could agree.

Indeed, while the Latin Vulgate, repeatedly criticized, might seem to be the beleaguered Bible of the Renaissance and Reformation, it was more akin to the phoenix of the age.[27] Just like repeated efforts to correct the corrupted text, the proliferation of vernacular translations did not unseat the Vulgate, which both Catholics and Protestants honored. It remained unchallenged as *the* Bible of the Western church, however lamentable its condition. Protestants, from Luther to Calvin, acknowledged the Vulgate as the Bible of the West.

The great reforming body of the Catholic Church known as the Council of Trent explicitly confirmed the Vulgate as the Bible of the church, although it was recognized that it was impossible to recover fully the translation of Jerome. In 1547 the fathers of the council declared that the Latin Bible, by its "lengthened usage of so many years[,] has been approved of in the Church, [and shall] be, in public lectures, disputations, sermons, and expositions, held as authentic."[28] This did not mean that church leaders were unaware that the Vulgate was in desperate need of correction, but it alone would be the Bible of the restored and reformed Catholic Church.

During the sixteenth century there were repeated efforts to produce the best possible version of the Vulgate. Most significant was the work of the French royal printer Robert Estienne (1503–1559), known as Stephanus, whose 1528 edition was based on the work of Erasmus and corrected according to the Hebrew and Greek.[29] His most celebrated edition came twelve years later, in 1540, with his Paris edition of the Latin Bible, a foundation for both Catholics and Protestants. Likewise, his Greek New Testaments of the 1540s were essential for every translator. The Frenchman's flight from Paris and embrace of the Reformation in Calvin's Geneva made him both the preeminent Protestant printer of his age and a traitor to France and the Catholic Church.

Catholic hands were not idle. The Council of Trent had declared the necessity of a restored edition of the Vulgate, launching numerous efforts toward this noble goal. Leading the charge was Johannes Hentenius (1499–1566), whose 1547 version was not from Hebrew and Greek but the best possible Latin versions. Between 1559 and 1579, his Bible was printed nine times and achieved the status of semiofficial in the Catholic Church in Europe. Unlike Erasmus's, it was approved by the theological faculty of Louvain in Belgium.

The first attempt to embody the reforming spirit of a church with global reach, from the Americas to Japan, was the edition of 1590. It was a textual attempt to enforce a common, global Bible that would unite the rapidly increasing worldwide population of Christians. It proved an embarrassing misfire. The careful work carried out by a team of distinguished scholars was upended by Pope Sixtus V, who fancied himself a Bible scholar. Papal delusion caused mayhem. He rejected the recommendations of the commission for his own version. The result was a rushed and botched edition riddled with errors, and the Vulgata Sixtina was widely derided and had to be withdrawn. Indeed, the situation was so disastrous that nine days after the pope's death in 1590, the cardinals ordered all copies destroyed.

Damage repair immediately commenced. In 1591 Pope Gregory XIV, who reigned for only a year, created another commission to revise the 1590 disaster. After a series of false starts, which included an original intention to use Hebrew, Greek, and Latin sources, the decision was made to correct Hentenius's 1547 Latin Bible.[30] The new edition of the Vulgate was promulgated by a papal bull of Clement VIII in 1592 and contained almost five thousand revisions of Sixtus's misguided effort.[31] In a wonderful attempt to spare blushes, the new version, known as the Sixto-Clementine Vulgate, was printed to look like the 1590 edition, in order to give the impression that nothing had happened.

The decision by the Catholic Church to work from the Latin should not be read as a rejection of Hebrew and Greek or as a denial that the Latin translation was flawed. Rather, the decision was taken in light of the calamity of the Reformation and the uncertainty generated by biblical scholarship. What the church needed, Popes Gregory and Clement decided, was not the cacophony of Protestants but stability and certainty. And that could only come from the Bible that had been the foundation of the church for a thousand years—the Vulgate.

Far from an elitist, remote Bible in Latin, the Vulgate fed the Catholic imagination following the Council of Trent. It was recited during the mystery of the liturgy and set to music by the great composers of the age, Giovanni Pierluigi da Palestrina (d. 1594) and Claudio Monteverdi (1567–1643). Among the people it was sung in devotion, and its wording inflected popular speech. The Vulgate provided the language and imagery for a vibrant Catholicism that embraced the senses and the body. Perhaps most dramatically, it was carried around the world by the Jesuits, from China to Africa and the Americas.

The power of art to evoke this new spiritual agenda was nowhere more evident than in the paintings of Michelangelo Merisi da Caravaggio (1571–1610).[32] Some of Caravaggio's realistic renderings of biblical figures were viewed as scandalous, even sexually provocative, by church authorities. Nevertheless, the intimacy of his biblical scenes drew inspiration from the great Catholic reformers Ignatius of Loyola (1491–1556) and Philip Neri (1515–1595).[33] In his *Spiritual Exercises*, Ignatius taught that a person should visualize episodes from the Gospels as if occurring before their very eyes and with their own participation in order to achieve a fully immersive process of contemplation. This spiritual bond between viewer and biblical character was most successfully achieved in Caravaggio's *The Supper at Emmaus* (1601) and *The Denial of Saint Peter* (ca. 1609/10).

While Rome opted for one Bible as the foundation of the church, there also emerged in the Renaissance and Reformation a form of the Bible that expressed unity in diversity: the polyglot Bibles of the sixteenth and seventeenth centuries.[34] First appearing less than fifty years after the Gutenberg Bible, they were marvels of printing that placed the sacred tongues of Christianity side by side. In producing these texts, Renaissance scholars had models. Origen had produced his Hexapla in the second century with its parallel texts of the Psalms in Hebrew and Greek, and more recently, there was a tradition of multilingual volumes in the Arabic world.

The polyglots were libraries of the Bible intended to demonstrate the breadth of God's revelation and the frontiers of human learning. Mapping the explosion in knowledge of languages in Renaissance Europe, they were not merely impressive but powerful embodiments of sacred history, a symbol of unity in fragmentation, of the ultimate oneness of Christianity.[35] These multilingual monuments, which reached their peak between 1500 and 1650, were also seen as physical incarnations of creation and revelation, and no expenses were spared in their production. The cost of one polyglot edition has been reckoned in the range of fifty thousand ducats, which in our time could be compared to NASA's budget in the 1960s of around $30 billion.[36]

No polyglot Bible was more breathtakingly audacious, if ill fated, than the Complutensian Polyglot from Alcalá de Henares in Spain. The vision of the powerful and farsighted cardinal Francisco Jiménez de Cisneros (1436–1517), it was begun in 1502 and took fifteen years to complete—a three-way marriage of learning, piety, and technology.[37] Like his contemporary Erasmus, Cisneros believed he was doing the work of Jerome in the service of the church and the Bible. He personally founded a university at Alcalá de Henares dedicated to the study of Hebrew, Greek, and Latin, and he brought leading Christian scholars together with learned Jews to prepare a Bible with all the known sacred languages. Cisneros's polyglot was produced in five languages in six volumes, the work of the extraordinary printer Arnao Guillén de Brocar (ca. 1460–1523). To produce the volumes, de Brocar set up a massive workshop in a monastery in Alcalá de Henares.

In the Christian West, the Complutensian Polyglot was unrivaled, a veritable titanic compared to what came before. Its six volumes of the Old and New Testaments were filled with the known biblical languages carefully arranged side by side, the unity of the sacred tongues aligned as a symbol of the one true church. For the Pentateuch, the Latin Vulgate is flanked by Hebrew and the Greek of the Septuagint. At the bottom of the page is Aramaic, and the text is accompanied by rabbinic commentary.

According to its preface, the Latin of the church represents Christ on the cross, while the Hebrew and Greek are the two thieves crucified with him. The message spoke of the triumph of the Roman Church over the obstinate Jews and the schismatic Greeks of the Orthodox East. The polyglot was prepared in Spain less than a decade after the expulsion of Jews from Iberia, leaving no doubt as to which thief was saved and which condemned.

The Complutensian Bible was a model for all future polyglots, but from the start it was bedeviled by problems. The project was a financial disaster, and had it not been for the support of Cisneros, the six volumes would never have been completed. When the cardinal died in 1517, work ceased, and the printed pages were left unbound. It was not until 1520, following the intervention of Pope Leo X, that the polyglot was assembled.

Sales were miserable, and it is reckoned that only 7 percent of the production costs were recovered.[38] Many of the copies of the finished work that were sent to the pope in Rome were lost in a shipwreck (again, like the *Titanic*), finding a home instead at the bottom of the Mediterranean. Almost worse, north of the Alps Erasmus was preparing his own version of the Greek New Testament with a Latin translation and extensive notes. Cunningly, Erasmus had received a papal privilege in 1516 for four years, meaning that the Complutensian Bible, which was completed in 1517, was shut out of the market until sanctioned by Pope Leo X in 1520. The results of this blackout period were financially crippling. As a Bible, however, the prodigious scholarship and printing expertise of those who prepared the Complutensian Polyglot made it a jewel of the Renaissance.

The growing expertise among Catholics and Protestants only heightened the desire for comparative study of the ancient languages in the pursuit of the best possible version of the Bible. In 1565, after the last session of the Council of Trent, a French printer living in Antwerp, Christophe Plantin (1520–1589), produced one of the great achievements of the northern Renaissance to rival the Complutensian of fifty years earlier.[39] Born in the year the Complutensian was finally completed, Plantin initially planned to reprint the Spanish polyglot with corrections and greater use of rabbinic commentaries. Eventually, he undertook something more ambitious.

Having consulted some of the most learned scholars of the day, Plantin sought the patronage of the king of Spain for his project. The most significant figure in the origins of the new polyglot was the Spanish scholar Benito Arias Montano (1527–1598), who was engaged to oversee the whole project. Nevertheless, the Complutensian Polyglot played a crucial role, providing the Hebrew, the Greek of the Septuagint, the Targum Onkelos (the Aramaic translation of the Pentateuch), the Greek of the New Testament, and the Latin Vulgate.[40] The new work was bolstered by more Jewish sources and the addition of Syriac, which was offered together with a literal Latin translation.

The result was spectacular: the Antwerp or Plantin Polyglot appeared in eight volumes from 1568 to 1573.[41] It included the Old and New Testaments together with an amalgam of glossaries and grammars. Arias Montano added a vast body of his own prodigious learning, offering interpretations of scripture and discussions of Jewish antiquities concerning the temple and the ritual garbs of the priests. Apprehensive that the discovery of the Americas might impugn the learning of the polyglot, he argued that the writers of the Old Testament had already known of the peoples of the New World. To prove his case, he provided a map with their biblical names.[42] The Antwerp Polyglot also acknowledged the position of the preeminent status of the Vulgate in the church, as it once more took its place between the Hebrew and the Greek of the Septuagint.

Twelve hundred copies of the Antwerp Polyglot were printed from 1569 to 1573. Although its patron was King Philip II, the leader of the Catholic reform, the polyglot combined scholarship with theological moderation. Unlike Spain, where heretics had been hunted down or expelled, Plantin lived in the hotly contested world of the Low Countries, where more than eighty years of strife between the Dutch and the Spanish continued. His perspective was a model of humanist, non-polemical scholarship. Such tempered views did raise the ire of some Catholics who believed Plantin had drawn too heavily on Jewish scholarship and gone too lightly in criticizing Protestants. In the end, however, papal approval was received.

The culmination of the Renaissance polyglots was the achievement of the English bishop Brian Walton (1600–1661), which appeared from 1653 to 1657 and is known as the London Polyglot. Nine languages were contained in its two volumes, and for the first time all on the same page. The polyglot was made possible by the flow of knowledge from the Ottoman Empire in the East and the continued uncovering of manuscripts available to scholars in the West. Financial backing was secured by selling subscriptions, signaling an enthusiastic readership. Walton sought nothing less than the compilation of all scholarly biblical knowledge. His extensive prologue offered a full account of the

Bible, its editions, and the history of its languages.[43] Like Plantin, Walton saw the vast accumulation of knowledge as serving wider Christendom. In an age of religious wars and revolution, his polyglot was intended as a symbol of religious unity.

More broadly, in an age of fragmentation, the polyglot Bibles were a poignant reminder of the search for unity, the truth that held everything together. They were temples of holiness and learning. Expensive, complex, and competing, they defeated the intention of unity by their very completion. By their nature, however, the great Renaissance polyglots were rare gems: precious and seen only by few. The Bibles that the vast majority of women and men came to know were printed in their own language.

In the castle high above the town of Eisenach, Germany, during the winter of 1521–1522, Martin Luther worked in the room where, legend had it, the devil visited him, translating Erasmus's Greek New Testament into German. Following St. John in the book of Revelation, the German referred to his drafty chamber as his Patmos. The image is evocative: the prophetic figure receiving inspiration directly from heaven. In the spring he returned to Wittenberg and worked through his translation with Philip Melanchthon, his close friend and a prodigious young scholar.[44] The Wittenberg printer Melchior Lotter employed more printers and established additional presses to produce the New Testament during the summer, and it appeared in the autumn of 1521, acquiring the name the September Testament.[45]

Luther's Bible had not come out of nowhere. From 1512 he had taught scripture at the University of Wittenberg, lecturing on the books of the Bible, notably the Psalms and Paul's Epistles. Combined with his spiritual crisis of fearing the judgment of God, his study and teaching of the Bible had birthed radical convictions. Humanity, he came to believe, is saved by the grace of God alone. Men and women can do nothing to deserve God's mercy apart from having faith in Christ. At the heart of this theological revolution was Luther's declaration that scripture alone is the foundation of Christianity. "Sola scriptura" became the creed of the Protestant Reformation, although what it meant was often disputed. When Luther stood before the young emperor Charles V in 1519 in the German city of Worms, he declared he would recant only that which could be proved erroneous on the basis of scripture.

Luther believed his translation of the Bible to be an achievement that would endure long beyond the grave. He was right. A brilliant stylist, the former monk was able to convey the words of scripture in the language of the people like no other. In order to translate the Bible for the common people, Luther remarked, "We must inquire about this of the mother in the home, the children on the street, the common man in the marketplace. We must be guided by their language, the way they speak, and do our translating accordingly. That way they will understand it and recognize that we are speaking German to them."[46] Indeed, practicing what he preached, Luther was known to slip into local villages to eavesdrop on conversations.

Never had the Bible been produced for such a broad swathe of society. Roughly three thousand copies of the September Testament were printed, and its success was immediate.[47] Despite (or perhaps because of) the pope's ban on the works of Luther, his Bible was eagerly sought, and by December it was necessary to produce a second edition. The intervening time allowed Luther to make a number of corrections. Like the September, the December Testament contained woodcuts for the book of Revelation from the workshop of the artist Lucas Cranach the Elder (ca. 1472–1553).[48] The images were highly polemical, with Babylon depicted as Rome and the Whore of Babylon shown with the papal tiara. The friendship between Luther and Cranach yielded a stunning combination of word and image. Over the next ten years and despite the tumults of the Reformation, Luther revised his New Testament repeatedly, producing more than fifty editions and reprints.

Luther's audacity extended well beyond his theological protests to the Bible itself. Though the Western church had no official canon of the Old or New Testament in the early and medieval periods, there was a general consensus, which Luther entirely disregarded. In his New Testament, he removed Hebrews, James, Jude, and Revelation from their usual place in the Bible and relegated them to the end of the Testament with the explanation that they were "disputed."[49] Luther created a hierarchy of biblical books, at the top of which he placed Paul's letter to the Romans, which he believed was the fullest expression of salvation.

Luther was writing his own legacy. By saying that some books of the Bible were more important than others in conveying God's word of salvation, he was essentially setting himself up as the arbiter of scripture. And having denied the Catholic Church its role in interpreting scripture, he made clear that the mantle had fallen squarely on his shoulders. Luther was able to present his complete German Bible in the fall of 1534 with his name on the title page—a first.[50] Among its notable features was the placement of the Apocryphal books between the two Testaments, where they would remain in most Protestant Bibles. In the Middle Ages, these books had been interspersed among others in the Old Testament.[51] The Luther Bible, as it would come to be known, would continue to be revised during his lifetime as the reformer and his colleagues continuously sought to improve the text. Although Luther never received any royalties from the sales of his Bibles, he was extremely concerned that pirated editions would appear—which they did. To guarantee the authenticity of his work, he included a woodcut cross in a heart in a rose on the title page.

Luther's Bible was an astonishing success. During his lifetime over 253 editions of the whole work or parts of it were printed, mostly officially but many not. The text had assumed a stable form by the end of the century, by which time over forty editions of the complete Bible had been printed. By 1800, there were approximately three million copies of the Luther Bible in circulation.[52]

Luther was fully aware of the problems presented by interpreting the Bible. His abiding conviction was that the Bible interprets itself, a major part of his legacy for Protestantism. Against Erasmus he had argued that on the message of salvation, the Bible was absolutely clear. The Dutch humanist was not persuaded. The Bible, he replied, is often ambiguous or obscure. To a degree, Luther conceded the argument. He understood that the clarity of the Bible depended on an authoritative voice. Luther, convinced of his role as a prophet, as a new Elijah, was sure that that voice was his. This conviction was both the strength of a movement and the source of discord. Luther had no time for those who dissented. Perhaps the most bitter debate of the early Reformation involved Christ's words "This is my body."[53] The hotly contested question concerned whether, at the Last Supper, when Jesus told the disciples to remember him when they ate the bread and drank the wine, he meant he would be physically present with his followers or only in Spirit. On this Luther and the Swiss reformer Huldrych Zwingli (1484–1531) could not agree, and the reform movement was irrevocably and acrimoniously split. Two men looked at the same text and came to radically different conclusions. It was the story of the Protestant Reformation.

Luther and Zwingli may have disagreed on significant points of theology, but they converged on the question of who can interpret the Bible.[54] The promise of scripture alone was intoxicating and attracted many from all stations of life. Yet, just as Catholics had predicted, the danger was chaos, a sixteenth-century tower of Babel. The Protestant reformers had promised the Bible to all and had then taken it back. All could have access to scripture, but not all could interpret it, they claimed. The need of every Christian to understand the text was paramount for the reformers, but they believed its truths had to be interpreted and communicated by them and the clergy.

The clericalism of the Catholic faith was quickly replicated by the Protestants, who held that ordination to the ministry and the study of Hebrew and Greek were essential to proper understanding. Protestant culture was dominated by the educated clergy who preached and taught, exhorted and cajoled. They were the new priests of a religion that insisted that the Bible had to be understood. Above all, they were to preach the Bible, for from the pulpit God spoke to the people. Ordinary men and women, once promised so much, were cast in the role of the obedient and unquestioning faithful. Luther had told the peasants who revolted in 1525 in the name of the Gospel that they had perverted Christ's words and misunderstood him. The Bible became a symbol of the top-down imposition of reform.

No group of Christians suffered more from suppression unleashed by the leaders of the Reformation than the radicals often known as the Anabaptists.[55] From the first years of the reform movement in the 1520s, many of those early converts embraced the Reformation's call for scripture and salvation by faith alone only to be left deeply disappointed. These men and women felt that reformers like Luther and Zwingli had wrongly retained the Catholic emphasis on the power of the church to interpret the Bible. In clerical Protestantism, ordinary believers were being denied access to the Word of God. The Anabaptists were nearly as appalled by how the reformers retained doctrines that were not biblical. The most contentious issue, as their names suggests, was the sacrament of baptism. The Anabaptists rejected infant baptism because, they argued, it was nowhere to be found in the New Testament. Their argument was compelling. Neither John the Baptist nor Jesus and his disciples baptized babies, only adults. Baptism, therefore, should only be for those who could make an affirmation of faith and demonstrate godly living according to biblical principles. In Anabaptist eyes, the reformers had betrayed the Bible they proclaimed. The reformers, in response, thought the Anabaptists were sectarians who threatened the state and immediately supported their execution. Anabaptists in Zurich were frequently drowned in a ritual of death that mocked their rejection of infant baptism.

The radicals had absolute faith in the Holy Spirit to guide them in understanding the Bible. John Claesz (d. 1544), writing from prison, urged, "Search the Word of God, and ask Him for His Holy Spirit, and the same shall instruct you in everything which is needful for you."[56] Understanding the Bible came about through life in the Spirit, careful study, and pious living. To this end, scripture needed to be in the languages of the people, and the radicals were active in producing their own translations and editions of the Bible. Everyone, not just scholars, had access to the teaching of the Spirit, but patience was required. Hans Denck (ca. 1495–1527) was a university-educated man who fervently believed that the Christian life lay in rigorously following the teachings of Jesus. Those who believed would be saved, and it was to them that the Holy Spirit opened scripture. He set out the model reader of the Bible: "If there is a part of Scripture that he cannot understand from the context of the whole, then he certainly does not despise the testimony of Scripture. Rather, he seeks its meaning with all diligence and compares [all parts of Scripture] with one another. But he surely will not accept them until they have been interpreted for him by the anointing of the Spirit. What he does not understand, he reserves judgment about, and expects revelation from God."[57]

Anabaptist communities were spread across Europe and were extremely diverse in their beliefs and practices. Uniquely among the reform movements, women often preached and interpreted the Bible. Often persecuted, the Anabaptists sought to create communities modeled on the Bible, in their case on the earliest Christians recounted in the book of Acts. Against the state churches of the Reformation governed by princes and city magistrates, their churches consisted only of those who demonstrated true faith. Dirk Philips (1504–1568), once a Franciscan friar, became one of the leaders of the Dutch Mennonites. A peaceful spirit by temperament, he was clear about who belonged to the band of faithful: "He who does not have the Spirit of the Lord does not understand the Word of the Lord and does not experience what is spiritual. How should he then be able to teach God's Word correctly or correctly distribute the gifts of the Spirit? . . . The other kind of fruit which a true teacher brings forth is a blameless life, walking in accordance with the gospel."[58]

The leading reformers—Luther, Zwingli, Calvin, and others—did not own the Bible. Indeed, they feared how easily the book might slip from their grasp. Protestant churches flourished in northern and eastern Europe, and a deep biblical culture took root. Yet the reformers and their followers were surrounded by opponents who relentlessly exposed their weaknesses. The Catholics denounced the chaos that ensued from untethering the Bible from the ancient authority of the church. The broad company of radicals, many erstwhile supporters of the Reformation, decried their betrayal of their own principles. Why, they argued, did the reformers retain doctrines found nowhere in the Bible, such as infant baptism and even the Trinity? Protestant leaders counterattacked fiercely, not fearing to dehumanize the Anabaptists as animals and voicing support for their execution. Their claims were fraught with peril. The Bible they claimed also put them on the defensive.

In a way, the story of the English Bible also began in Wittenberg.[59] Although too much has been made of William Tyndale's debt to Luther, the Oxford humanist scholar frequently invoked his name and claimed Luther as his inspiration.[60] Tyndale sought to translate the two Testaments from the Hebrew and Greek. Rejected in England, where vernacular versions of scripture were strictly forbidden, he fled to the Continent, where he encountered a sophisticated world of biblical scholarship and printing. Unlike John Wycliffe (ca. 1328–1384), whose Bible was translated from the Latin of the Vulgate into somewhat incomprehensible English, Tyndale sought, in his words, to bring the Word of God to the ploughboys in their own language. Tyndale took a sanguine view of how the common man and woman might understand God's Word through exposure to the text and the work of the Spirit. He made this point in his 1526 preface to his translation of the New Testament:

Give diligence, reader (I exhort thee) that thou come with a pure mind, and, as the Scripture saith, with a single eye, unto the words of health and of eternal life, by which (if we repent and believe them) we are born anew, created afresh, and enjoy the fruits of the blood of Christ. Which blood crieth not for vengeance, as the blood of Abel, but hath purchased life, love, favor, grace, blessing, and whatsoever is promised in the Scriptures, to them that believe and obey God, and standeth between us and wrath, vengeance, curse, and whatsoever the Scripture threateneth against the unbelievers and disobedient, which resist, and consent not in their hearts to the law of God, that it is right, holy, just, and ought so to be.[61]

Tyndale knew the task was herculean and beyond the efforts of one person, but he had a bold vision of what such a Bible might be. He sought English that aptly reflected the biblical languages while being idiomatic.[62] Tyndale "Englished" the Bible, not merely translating the language but creating a book in which everything from clothes and animals to plowshares and rural pastures reflected English culture.[63] He steered away from Latinate words, believing that simple English better captured the cadence and spirit of the originals: "The properties of the Hebrew tongue agreeth a thousand times more with the English than with the Latin."[64]

Tyndale possessed a remarkable ability to navigate the complexities of Greek and Hebrew to find colloquial English. He gifted the English language with such new words as "Jehovah," "Passover," "atonement," "scapegoat," and "mercy seat." For his New Testament he worked from

Erasmus, although the influence of Luther's translation is notable. Tyndale provided extensive explanatory notes for his New Testament to aid the reader in understanding the texts, which were divided into chapters and printed in pocket-sized books.

The first complete English Bible, which was built on Tyndale's work and appeared in 1534, was produced by Miles Coverdale. It was known as the Bug Bible or Treacle Bible on account of two notable passages: "Thou shall not need to be afraid for any bugs at night" (Ps. 91:5) and "There was no more treacle at Galaad" (Jer. 8:22). The effort, however, was something of a misfire. Unlike Tyndale, Coverdale had little facility in the biblical languages, and his translations were drawn from a series of Bibles in German, including Luther's, as well as from the Vulgate. Even worse, despite his linguistic shortcomings, Coverdale made numerous revisions to Tyndale's words.

Under Henry VIII, the 1408 prohibition on the Bible in English was enforced. Tyndale, who had promised to return to his native land and not cause trouble if the king permitted the people to have the Word in their language, was arrested in 1535 and executed for heresy the following year. At his execution, with his last breath he uttered, "Lord, open the king of England's eyes."[65] Two years later, Archbishop Thomas Cranmer made a request to Henry for a Bible in English, and Thomas Cromwell ordered the clergy to "provide . . . one book of the whole Bible of the largest volume, in English."[66] The first to appear was the Matthew Bible, to which the king assented. The work was produced by John Rogers, who assumed the name Thomas Matthew. It was largely Tyndale's and Coverdale's work, although the identities of the heretics were concealed. The 1,500 printed copies failed to meet the desired goal of an English Bible in every parish pulpit.

From 1539 to 1541, a seven-volume folio Bible appeared, known as the Great Bible, which was claimed to be the work of scholars who had labored with the Hebrew and Greek. The later addition of a preface by Archbishop Cranmer led to its being known as Cranmer's Bible. A remarkable frontispiece depicts Henry VIII delivering the Word of God to the people in their own language, a significant reversal of his attitude toward Tyndale. The work, however, was primarily Coverdale's, who revised Tyndale by removing words and phrases that displeased the bishops and by consulting a range of sources, most in Latin. Cranmer's preface was by no means a full-throated endorsement of the Protestant cause. His advocacy of the Bible for all was tempered by concern for the chaos of individual interpretations.

The most influential Bible of the next century was the work of a group of exiles in Calvin's city of Geneva.[67] Based on the work of Tyndale and the Great Bible, a New Testament appeared in 1557 from the hand of William Whittingham (ca. 1524–1579). The volume was replete with aids for the reader, notes that explained both diversities of reading and doctrinal points, and was the first Bible in English to be versified. The full Bible appeared in 1560, led by Whittingham but with the labors of the exiled Coverdale. It purported to be the work of eleven men, but we have no evidence of how they divided their labors. Best known as the Geneva Bible, it also, like the Bug Bible, became known for a particular verse: in this case, it was called the Breeches Bible on account of its translation of Genesis 3:7, "They made themselves breeches."

During the next century the Geneva Bible won the hearts of the people, going through 140 complete or partial editions. It was affordable, rich with notes, maps, and illustrations, and beautiful in language. It also introduced versification into English Bibles. With the divisions into verses, the Bible acquired a new form that would distinguish it from then on. The Geneva in many formats was available to the people in numbers previously unknown in England. It became the book of the household, market, and stage, as Luther's had in German lands.

The popularity of the Geneva Bible lay in its accessible English and extensive notes that were intended not for scholars but for ordinary laymen and laywomen. Its title boldly declared its intent:

THE BIBLE: THAT IS, THE HOLY SCRIPTVRES CONTEINED IN THE OLDE AND NEW TESTAMENT: TRANSLATED ACCORDING to the Ebrew and Greeke, and conferred with the best translations in diuers languages. With most profitable ANNOTATIONS vpon all the hard places, and other things of great importance.

The explanatory notes made the Bible accessible to the widest English-speaking audience, but they were controversial because the Calvinism of the Bible's origins in Geneva sometimes bubbled to the surface.[68] For instance, the explanation for Revelation 9:3 ("And there came out of the smoke locusts upon the earth: and unto them was given power, as the scorpions of the earth have power," KJV) would send a shiver down the spine of any Elizabethan bishop: "Locusts are false teachers, heretikes, and worldly subtile Prelates, with Monks, Friars, Cardinals, Patriarkes, Archbishops, Bishops, Doctors, Bachelors and Masters which forsake Christ to maintain false doctrine."

Beyond being responsible for the transparent Calvinism of the annotations, the production of the Bible in Geneva also explains its remarkable quality, as Geneva was a center of Bible translation and printing, a place where English exiles were able to draw on a wide range of resources. They had the Greek of Robert Estienne's New Testament (which became known as the *textus receptus*, "received text"), and they were also able to draw on decades of Hebrew scholarship by Protestants and Catholics alike. The Geneva Bible was a milestone both of scholarship and of the English Bible. Its Old Testament remained largely untouched after the first edition, but the New was revised by English politician Laurence Tomson (1539–1608) for a new edition in 1587. The Bible found a special home in Scotland, where English, not Scots, was to become the people's language of scripture.[69]

The greatest writer of the age, William Shakespeare, was a master of the Geneva text, and virtually all of his characters speak in the language of the Bible.[70] While it is often difficult to say exactly which version of scripture he references, clearly the Geneva sat open on his desk. He knew in detail its prose, poetry, and annotations, which echo throughout the plays and sonnets, and the references would have been unmissable for those standing in the Globe Theatre. In *Cymbeline*, for example, Pisanio says there is no need to draw his sword because the paper hath cut her throat already: "No, 'tis slander, whose sting is sharper than the sword, whose tongue out-venoms all the wormes of Nyle" (act 3, scene 4, lines 33–34). The Geneva provided the references: Psalm 57:4, "Whose teeth are speares and arrowes, and their tongue a sharpe sword," and Job 5:15, "But he saveth the poor from the sword from their mouth."[71]

Similarly, in his Sonnet 61, Shakespeare alludes to both the Geneva scriptural text and the notes. He writes:

It is my love that keeps mine eye awake;
Mine own true love that doth my rest defeat
To play the watchman ever for thy sake.

The phrase "keeps mine eye awake" is not only very close to the Geneva Bible text of Psalm 77:4—"Thou keepest mine eyes awake"— but also to the accompanying marginal note in the Bible: "Meaning, that his sorowes were as watchmen that kept his eyes from sleeping."

Despite its great popularity, the Geneva Bible with its Calvinist notes was not deemed suitable to meet Queen Elizabeth's injunction for a book of scripture in every parish. Bishop Matthew Parker commissioned a new translation, known as the Bishops' Bible because it was largely prepared by prelates. Although it appeared with a grand engraving of Elizabeth I, the work was of generally poor quality. It would, as David Norton has remarked, replace "the Great Bible in churches, but not the Geneva Bible in the people's hearts."[72] Nevertheless, despite its rather wooden quality, the Bishops' Bible would serve as the foundation of the King James of 1611, to which we shall come in a later chapter.

Although the English translations that prospered in England were Protestant, Catholics in exile also prepared vernacular renditions of the Bible, beginning with the Rheims New Testament (1582) and the Douay Old Testament (1609/10), the work of the linguistically gifted priest Gregory Martin (ca. 1542–1582).[73] This Bible, too, was grounded in Tyndale's translation, and it was similar to both the Great Bible and the Geneva. In large part, however, it was taken from the Latin Vulgate. Indeed, the Douay-Rheims Bible has been treated with some condescension on account of its literal and highly Latinate character. Nevertheless, it was expertly printed and offered a robust defense of Catholic faith. Following the Council of Trent, the preface argued that the Latin Vulgate, not Hebrew and Greek, should form the foundation for the translation, as the Latin was the Bible of the church.

For all the vitality of the Dutch biblical world, it was not until the Synod of Dort in 1618–1619 that the decision was made for a new translation of the Bible into Dutch from Hebrew and Greek. As with the King James in England, committees were formed to undertake the task, and the result was the Statenvertaling of 1637. Intended as the Bible of the Dutch Reformed Church, it was a collaboration of church and state, and until the separation of the two in 1796, the political rulers were obliged to ensure the church was adequately supplied with the Bibles. The translation process had striking similarities to the creation of the King James Bible in 1611: the scholars used a variety of vernacular versions (including the King James Version) while staying close to the Hebrew and Greek. In terms of the Dutch language itself, loanwords were to be avoided as far as possible.[74]

The world of the seventeenth-century Dutch Republic was extensively portrayed in the drawings and paintings of Rembrandt (1606–1669), a devout Protestant whose faith was deeply influenced by the religious tumults in his land.[75] Living in a diverse religious society, Rembrandt received the patronage of Calvinists, Mennonites, Catholics, and Jews, and he often portrayed Jews in his paintings, although not always with charity. In his *Peter and Paul Disputing* (ca. 1628), the two elderly men face one another in intense conversation. Peter, holding a Bible with three fingers marking pages, is looking attentively at Paul, who is speaking and points to the open text. Interpretations vary among scholars, but it's generally thought that Paul is explaining the fulfillment of the Hebrew Bible in the Gospels and the primacy of faith over law. Rembrandt followed the Calvinist scholars of his age in emphasizing the Christ-centered reading of the Hebrew Bible, in which the covenant with the Israelites is completed in the covenant of faith.[76]

In neighboring France, Jacques Lefèvre d'Étaples, discussed earlier in this chapter, was one of the great biblical scholars of the early sixteenth century.[77] His translations and commentaries on the letters of Paul brought the opprobrium of the Theological Faculty in Paris, which rained down condemnation. Sympathetic with the views of the reformers—although he never left the Catholic Church—he moved to the city of Meaux to join a group of scholars and churchmen dedicated to the study of the Bible. Lefèvre, more than any other figure, was responsible for bringing the philological study of scripture into France. While in Meaux, he produced in 1523 a French New Testament based on the Latin Vulgate, although he corrected it against the Greek. Five years later, he followed with a translation of the complete Bible that further fueled the controversy around his efforts and sympathies. His last work was a 1534 revision of his New Testament that proved highly influential on all subsequent French translations.

A more radical change was brought about by Pierre-Robert Olivétan (1506–1538), who produced a French translation from the Greek. A cousin of John Calvin, Olivétan was directly connected to the Evangelicals in France, that is, those dedicated to the cause of the Bible as sole authority. His most famous and influential translation of the whole Bible comes from 1535 and is known as the Serrières Bible after the village in which it was printed. Olivétan intended his Bible for laymen and laywomen and carefully prepared the text to offer a clear Evangelical interpretation of scripture. In an age when most writing in French involved long, complex sentences, Olivetán's Bible was a model of economical style and clarity.

Calvin himself was likewise committed to the creation of a French translation of the Bible. In 1540 he produced the Sword Bible, so called because its frontispiece has the image of a hand holding a sword, promising the defeat of demonic forces. The 1540 version is now rare, but the Bible was frequently revised and reprinted. Although Calvin oversaw the changes, the work was likely carried out by assistants. The hand of Olivétan is evident throughout: Calvin drew heavily from his cousin's Bible. Though there is disagreement about whether the reformer of Geneva was competent in Hebrew, he was certainly not able to translate directly.

The great strength of Calvin's Bible was its accessibility. It was produced in vast numbers and in pocket-sized format for easy transportation (including being smuggled into France). Low production costs and mass distribution made his Bible ubiquitous. But there was more. Calvin's great gift as a speaker and writer was his ability to explain complex ideas and difficult passages in plain language. He did this in his sermons, his commentaries on the Bible, and his translations. This small, affordable book was easy to read, greatly increasing its popularity. In addition, Calvin included prefaces directed at lay readers that offered clear instruction in the message of the Bible, and which provide the best introduction to Calvin's understanding of the Bible.

For Calvin, the Bible was written by human hands but dictated by God.[78] Far more than Luther and others, the Frenchman was fascinated by the historical contexts of the scriptural books. A child of the Renaissance, he fully realized that they were composed over a long period by various authors, and he was well aware of discrepancies between the biblical books, which he never hesitated to point out. Ultimately, however, he did not view them as significant. The authors of the Gospels might differ on certain points, or Paul might seem to contradict Moses, but for Calvin the core message remained undiminished. The heart of the Bible was the "divine oracles" or "wisdom," which was the word of salvation. He believed that one should deal with the questions of time, place, and authorship in studying the Bible but ultimately focus on what is said about God's glory and human obligation. Even where contradictions remained unresolved, one must trust in the Spirit.

Calvin spoke of the Bible writers as "scribes" of the Holy Spirit, and just as the biblical prophets shifted back and forth between speaking in the first person and speaking as God, so too did Calvin believe that both God and the human writers spoke.[79] Later in life, as a very ill man, Calvin often dictated his works and letters from bed, so he had firsthand experience of the mistakes that could be made through the act of recording. Even if God's words were without flaw, the writings of humans were not. In the end, however, Calvin was persuaded that the Bible contained God's self-revelation and could be received in faith. The Bible was always right, but humans rarely so. His calling, he believed, was first and foremost to interpret and preach the Word of God. Calvin preached most days of the week; over the course of months, his sermons covered every line of the Bible. Standing in the pulpit of St. Pierre, the main church of Geneva, he preached extemporaneously for several hours with only the Greek or Hebrew text in front of him.

For Calvin, the Bible was not for reading or preaching alone; it was to be sung. In 1545 he wrote in his "Epistle to the Reader" in the *Form of Prayers*, "And as music or singing is natural unto us, and therefore every man delighteth therein; so our merciful God setteth before our eyes, how we may rejoice and singe to the glory of his name, recreation of our spirits, and profit of ourselves."[80] We have seen how central the psalms were to the devotional world of the Middle Ages. For Reformed Protestants of the sixteenth century, they were daily manna.[81] Calvin oversaw the creation of the Geneva Psalter in 1539 while tending to a French congregation. Inspired by the versification of the psalms by Martin Luther, Calvin began to set the biblical poems to song for worshippers. Uncharacteristically critical of his own efforts, he turned to the French court poet Clément Marot (1496–1544). The full Psalter appeared in 1561 with all 150 psalms. By this point, the singing of psalms was widespread across the French, Dutch, English, and Scottish Reformed Churches.[82] Among the exiled and persecuted Reformed churches of Europe, the lamentations and praise of the psalms held particular worth for communities suffering under the cross.

The meter of the printed psalms was intentionally uncomplicated and the tunes, often four-part, were kept short. Psalm 24 from Robert Crowley's 1549 *The Psalter of Dauid Newely Translated into Englysh Metre* reads:

> *The earth and al that it holdeth, do to the lorde belonge*
> *The world and al that dwel therein as wel the olde as yonge.*
> *For it is he that aboue al the seas hath it founded:*
> *And that aboue the freshe waters hathe the same prepared.*

The simple form served the intentions of the reformers that common people would sing psalms in worship, in the home, and in the field. The key was memorization. Setting the psalms to popular tunes made the biblical message catchy. In an oral society, music was crucial to internalizing the Bible and bringing the sacred text into daily life. Through psalms and hymns the Bible lived in the popular world of ballads, poetry, and storytelling. In Lutheran churches, hymns were sung in worship and in the home. Without doubt, the most famous hymn of the Protestant Reformation was Martin Luther's adaptation of Psalm 46 ("God is our refuge and strength, a very present help in trouble," KJV):

> *A mighty fortress is our God*
> *A bulwark never failing*
> *Our helper he, amid the flood*
> *Of moral ills prevailing.*

Spain alone had no printed vernacular Bible in the sixteenth century, but not for want of trying. Mostly the works of Protestants on the run, Spanish translations were produced in exile, beyond the reach of the Inquisition. The first significant effort was a tragic tale.

The inspiration of Erasmus was powerful on Francisco de Enzinas (1518–1552), a young Spaniard, also known as Francis Dryander, who came to the Low Countries to study. There he came across the ideas of the German Reformation and was so attracted that he went to Wittenberg to study. While in Germany, he was fired with enthusiasm to translate the Greek New Testament into Spanish, which he achieved before returning to the Netherlands to have it printed.

Enzinas may have been naive or foolish, but in the flush of enthusiasm he offered his translation to Emperor Charles V, who promptly had him arrested as a heretic. The dedication of the New Testament to Charles was, however, a highly astute defense of having the Bible in Spanish. Among Enzinas's arguments was an appeal to the greatness of Spain, which was preeminent in the world in all things. Why should it not have a Bible in its renowned, global language? Further, he pointed out to the emperor that Charles had never explicitly forbidden the Bible in Spanish. Bible translations, Enzinas pleaded, were not the cause of heresy. Instead, false teaching came from those who departed from the will of the church. If he hoped that such ambiguous language might save him, it didn't work. Fortunately, he was a man with cunning and was able to escape from the Vrunte prison in Brussels.

Enzinas married an Englishwoman and taught in Cambridge under the patronage of Archbishop Thomas Cranmer before returning to Strasbourg, where he set up a business for Spanish printing. His dream was to produce a complete Bible in Spanish, but before he had the opportunity to do so, the dread hand of plague ended his life. His manuscripts passed into the hands of others, and his work deeply influenced future Spanish translations. The first complete Spanish Bible was the undertaking of a man who similarly risked everything for his work. Casiodoro de Reina (1520–1594) was a former monk in Seville whose study of the Bible led him to Protestant sympathies. Once his views became known he fled Spain to Geneva and John Calvin. In 1569 the first full Spanish translation of the Bible appeared in Basel, but anonymously, for fear of retribution. From behind the veil of anonymity, Reina claimed that no Spaniard had accomplished anything better.[83]

By the sixteenth century, Germany, England, the Netherlands, and France had well-established networks of printers and large urban commercial areas, which created markets for the flow of Bibles and religious literature from the presses. In the East, the lands of Bohemia, Hungary, Poland, and Lithuania possessed an equally creative culture of the Bible, but with a different dynamic. The influence of Wittenberg and Geneva was strong, and Bibles made their way east. Cultural contacts were further cultivated by the young men who made their way into German and Swiss lands to study at Protestant universities. Erasmus in Basel had an extensive network of correspondents in eastern Europe that included kings and noblemen who acted as patrons for translations of the Bible in the spirit of the great Dutchman.

The distinctive biblical culture in eastern Europe owed much to diverse political conditions and traditions of language. Unlike in the West, where clear lines of demarcation separated Catholics and Protestants, in the East there was a much more fluid culture in which a wide range of groups, from Jesuits to Unitarians, found space in lands such as Transylvania and Poland, where rulers were prepared to allow levels of religious toleration found almost nowhere else.

Humanist learning was similarly not confined to the West but flourished from Prague to Kraków.[84] The older tradition of Czech Bibles remained vibrant, notably through the work of Jiří Melantrich of Aventino (ca. 1511–1580), a printer whose work became closely associated with a golden age of Czech writing. The range of his labors is breathtaking: he published works of Renaissance humanists such as Erasmus, poetry and history, legal texts, dictionaries, and children's literature. Religiously broad-minded, he produced both Catholic and Protestant writings, although he was a Lutheran by conviction. In collaboration with the Catholic Bartoloměj Netolický, Melantrich translated numerous works of literature and religion, most famously a complete New Testament, which was reprinted five times between 1549 and 1577. Unlike earlier translations into Czech, Melantrich's New Testament, in the spirit of his embrace of humanism, was from Greek.

Further east, printing reached Russia in the sixteenth century in the age of Ivan the Terrible. Parts of the Bible appeared, but the glory of the age was the Ostrog Bible of 1580–1581. Its creator was the printer Ivan Fyodorov, father of Eastern Slavonic printing, who, when he was not creating Bibles, was an expert in making cannons. A monumental book of over 1,200 pages, it was a translation of the Greek Septuagint and the Codex Alexandrinus, and the first in Old Church Slavonic and Cyrillic. One of the Ostrog Bible's remarkable aspects is that it contains seventy-six books, far more than found in the West or other Orthodox churches, including numerous books not found elsewhere. It was lavishly decorated, and copies were sent to Czar Ivan and the pope in Rome. Only three hundred copies exist today. Its influence on the Orthodox world was enormous.

Looking back over the expanse of the Renaissance and Reformation, it is striking how many of the momentous developments of the Bible were the work of individuals or small groups in peril. Like Luther in the tower with the devil, so often the image of Jerome in the desert became the model of the Bible translator working in solitude, suffering for God's Word. But compared to the early scribes, whose suffering was largely confined to the scriptoria, men during the Renaissance and Reformation, like William Tyndale or the English exiles in Geneva, were producing Bibles on the run. They suffered persecution and exile, and even lost their lives. With its stories of God's providence and unending care for the persecuted, the Bible was a book for an anguished people. There would one day be a return to the promised land. And the Bible as a book permanently in exile came to be the symbol of a world torn apart by religion. The Bible's impact fulfilled Jesus's warning: "Think not that I am come to send peace on earth: I came not to send peace, but a sword" (Matt. 10:34, KJV).

CHAPTER 6

SCIENCE AND REASON

There is no better symbol of the centrifugal forces pushing apart faith in the possibility of a unifying, inarguably true Bible than Francis Bacon's utopian *New Atlantis* (1626). In the story, a cedar ark appears in the sea off the fictitious island of Bensalem.[1] Signifying the wondrous nature of this jetsam is a pillar of light and a cross in the sky. Naturally curious, the Bensalemites retrieve the ark and rescue a Bible accompanied by a letter from the apostle Bartholomew. Their find is truly miraculous. The letter tells them that this complete book of scripture appeared only twenty years after Christ's ascension. They have in their hands a pure and complete Bible, one that existed before the scriptures were even written! A Bensalemite official describes their discovery to his astonished European visitors:

> The Book contained all the canonical books of the Old and New Testament, according as you have them . . . ; and the Apocalypse itself, and some other books of the New

Testament which were not at that time written, were nevertheless in the Book. . . . There was also in both these writings, as well the Book, as the Letter, [that] wrought a great miracle, [to] conform to that of the Apostles, in the original Gift of Tongues. For there being at that time in this land Hebrews, Persians, and Indians, besides the natives, every one read upon the Book and Letter, as if they had been written in his own language.[2]

How could this be? A Bible before the Bible that all could read. Surely it was Pentecost in a book. And just as when the Holy Spirit came upon the disciples huddled in Jerusalem, everyone could understand the Word in their own language. The visiting Europeans were rightly astounded. The Bensalemites possessed what Christians through the centuries had desperately sought but could never have, a perfect Bible. Unlike theirs at home, which the Reformation had rendered an object of discord, it was not the creation of human hands across time and place in diverse and often incomprehensible languages.

The Bensalemite Bible, though obviously a fantasy, was a symbol of permanence and stability.[3] It was a sacred book from the time of Christ, unweathered by change, the ravages of time, or the perils of human transcription and translation. The previous chapter recounted how the Renaissance, by turning to the perplexing human history of the Bible, raised significant questions about the book's character and coherence, while the Reformation, with its belief that the Bible could stand alone, added fuel to an already-raging fire of fragmentation. This was the bewildering world into which Bacon's *New Atlantis* arrived in the early seventeenth century. But with the coming Age of Enlightenment, the Bible would be confronted yet again by a remarkably transforming world, one being changed by the rise of new scientific thinking, fresh perspectives on what it meant to be human and our place in the universe, and the spread of commercial empires.

It is tempting to think that, with the arrival of the age of science and reason, the story of the Bible had reached its zenith—that what remains is a tale of decline. Not so. The rise of natural philosophy and the Enlightenment brought to the fore the relationship between the Bible and reason. Though older and sometimes still-prevalent accounts of the eighteenth century cast it as a time of reason prevailing over religion, the vast majority of writers and their readers during this period believed that the two sat together in the same boat. The seventeenth century underscored what had long been known, that the text of the Bible was problematic, but few saw that as grounds for abandoning what they saw as the source of reason itself. There were, of course, skeptics like David Hume and Voltaire. But other leading lights of the age, such as Galileo, Bacon, and Newton, transformed our understanding of heaven and earth and did so with the Bible in hand. Indeed, as a panoramic view of the most important scientific, political, and philosophical thinkers of the age will show, efforts to marry religion and the Bible with science were far more prevalent than we today often take to be the case. The question with which these thinkers grappled was not really *whether* the Bible was still relevant in a world in upheaval but *how* it was so.

The rise of natural philosophy in the seventeenth century is closely identified with the notorious case of Galileo, the defense of Copernicus, and the decline of the belief in a geocentric universe.[4] This was the moment, so the story goes, when science took its leave from the benighted world of religion, marking the beginning of the modern world and the end of superstition. This account of the divorce of science and religion, which emerged in the nineteenth century, doggedly persists in our day. It is the stuff of textbooks and popular media. What better image of reactionary forces than when an elderly Galileo was forced to kneel in a humiliating recantation of his life's work on the grounds that it conflicted with the teachings of the church and scripture?[5] "I must altogether abandon the false opinion," he acknowledged before the inquisitors in 1633, "that the sun is the center of the world and immovable, and that the earth is not the center of the world, and moves, and . . . I must not hold, defend, or teach in any way whatsoever, verbally or in writing, the said false doctrine . . . after it had been notified to me that the said doctrine was contrary to Holy Scripture."[6]

The problem with this familiar narrative, often omitted by those who see religion as hostile to science, is that Galileo and his critics shared in common both loyalty to the church and resolute faith in the truth of the Bible. Despite his final forced recantation, the story of Galileo is about different attempts to claim and defend the Bible. His was a revolution from within rather than an external attack on scripture itself.

Galileo himself was no outsider to religion or politics.[7] He had moved through the rarified worlds of the ducal court at Florence and the Jesuit college in Rome and counted among his friends a future pope. The Jesuits, the great mathematicians and educators of their day, understood perfectly well Galileo's calculations and honored him as a colleague.[8] They, like him, did not see his great advances as threatening the Bible. Decades later, the great poet John Milton shared this optimism in *Paradise Lost* (1667). When the archangel

Raphael imparts information about the heavens, he does so with the words of Galileo.[9]

Galileo was adamant that nature and scripture could not be set against each other as separate truths.[10] If that appeared to be the case, it was the result of mere human weakness. Galileo put it clearly: "If some passages of Scripture were to sound contrary, we would have to say that this is due to the weakness of our mind, which is unable to grasp the true meaning of Scripture in this particular case."[11] To the Duchess of Tuscany he wrote, "The holy Bible can never speak untruth whenever its true meaning is understood."[12] In taking this position, he was no different from St. Augustine, who held that whatever could really be "demonstrated to be true of physical nature; we must show to be capable of reconciliation with our scriptures,"[13] or Thomas Aquinas, who regarded theology as the supreme science and encouraged his students to study Aristotle's *Physics*.

In his defense, Galileo also brought to the fore an old belief: that the principal purpose of the Bible was to teach not natural philosophy but salvation. In so doing, he considered himself to be appealing to Catholic doctrine. The Bible, he even suggested, had much to tell about the natural world. One just needed to be careful in how one interpreted it. Its words, such as the story of how God made the sun stand still in the book of Joshua, could not be understood literally. Indeed, Galileo deployed passages from the Bible to defend the Copernican system, writing, "And to prohibit the whole science would be to censure a hundred passages of holy Scripture which teach us that the glory and greatness of Almighty God are marvelously discerned in all his works and divinely read in the open book of heaven."[14] More generally, appealing to a long-standing principle shared with Protestants, Galileo argued that the Bible was God's accommodated language, spoken in words that the people can understand for their salvation. Images and words are used that cannot be taken at face value, such as the suggestion that the sun revolves around the earth. There was plenty of room to make mistakes, and interpreters often had.

So, too, had those investigating nature. All the more reason, he argued, for a healthy dialogue between science and the Bible. Religion speaks imprecisely about the natural world, and science has nothing to say about salvation, which comes from God's revelation, which is above all human reason. The church, Galileo adamantly maintained, was the guardian of that salvation and true interpretation. The Bible, however, does not teach science. He famously declared, quoting his Catholic opponent Cardinal Bellarmine, "The intention of the Holy Ghost is to teach us how one goes to heaven, not how the heavens go."[15] In the end, however, the commission of theologians employed by the Inquisition condemned him for holding Copernican opinions that contravened the true meaning of the Bible.

Though Galileo's understanding of the relationship between science and the Bible was rejected by the Inquisition, it was quite similar to that held by the celebrated author with which this chapter began, Francis Bacon (1561–1626).[16] Bacon was, like Copernicus and Galileo, a man of deep faith.[17] And though he has been long heralded for elevating science over religion, Bacon was actually more concerned that the two were being badly confused. He believed that those who looked only to nature were equally in the dark as those who only read the Bible. God should be understood as the author of two books, distinct but complementary. And Bacon thought they should be read quite differently.

The Bible must be read in terms of its literal and figurative senses.[18] Nature must be studied in all its particulars and not squeezed into prior categories. Truth was to be found through careful methods of experimentation, not through abstract philosophy or first principles. Bacon based his belief in the two books on Matthew 22:29, writing:

> For our saviour saith, You err, not knowing the scriptures nor the power of God; laying before us two books or volumes to study, if we will be secured from error; first the scriptures, revealing the will of God, and then the creatures expressing his power; whereof the latter is a key unto the former; not only opening our understanding to conceive the true sense of the scriptures, but the general notions of reason and rules of speech, but chiefly opening our belief, in drawing us into due meditation of the omnipotency of God, which is chiefly signed and engraven upon his works.[19]

For Bacon, the Reformation and science were God's gifts to humanity. The renewal of the Bible harmonized with the new knowledge provided by science. Together, they would restore humanity to the Garden of Eden—a wondrous new age that recovered a lost paradise.

Galileo and Bacon were not the only scientists with strong views about the Bible. Though Isaac Newton (1642–1726) is more commonly associated with an apple than with the Bible, from his early thirties he devoted more of his energies to writing about the Bible than he did to the science for which he is remembered.[20] This legacy is due in part to nineteenth-century Victorians, who embraced Newton as a hero of modern thought and paid little attention to his religious writings, which they regarded as an eccentricity, and in part to the fact that Newton knew his views about Christianity were unorthodox and might cost him his position at Oxford University.[21] As a result, his writings on the Bible remained unpublished during his lifetime.

But not for lack of conviction. Like Galileo and Bacon, Newton regarded his religious and scientific works as flowing from the same source. And like them, he argued that these works were distinct but mutually supportive. To his friend Richard Bentley he confided, "When I wrote my treatise on our system, I had an eye on such principles as might work with considering men for the belief of a deity and nothing can rejoice me more than to find it useful for such a purpose."[22] He regarded the work of the devout Catholic René Descartes as deeply dangerous, risking atheism. The attraction of bodies, so central to Newton's work, he explained in terms of an act of divine will, not the result of impersonal forces, as in today's science textbooks.

Newton also adopted the long-standing tradition of the two books. He saw himself as divinely chosen to read the difficult book of nature correctly. Likewise, he believed himself called to interpret the book of scripture, which also defied easy interpretation, for it is "contrary to God's purpose . . . that the truth of his religion should be as obvious and perspicacious to all men as a mathematical demonstration."[23] Newton regarded the stories of the Bible as true but requiring some sophistication on the part of the reader, as the Bible was neither scientifically precise nor exact in language. He agreed with Galileo: because scripture is God speaking to our human capacity, one needs to be aware of how language works in scripture.

Newton was also interested in the history of the Bible.[24] The Old Testament, he believed, was preserved by God's providence because the original sources from which it was compiled were lost. He had a particular attraction to the prophetic voices of the Bible. Prophecy, he believed, was not idle speculation of future events but understanding the fulfillment of what has already taken place—that is, Christ's fulfillment of the promises of the Old Testament. Prophecy and history were thus inseparable, and Newton sought to demonstrate the verity of biblical chronologies, drawing on histories of other civilizations and science, such as his work in astronomy, to establish correct dating. Newton shared the views of the scientists and biblical scholars of his age that the study of the natural world and of history and languages only enriched the understanding of the Bible.

Some scientists, such as the Dutch physicist and mathematician Bernard Nieuwentijt (1654–1718), took an even more extreme position that the Bible was the primary source of knowledge uncovered by science. In 1718, in a work titled *The Religious Philosopher; or, The Right Use of Contemplating the Works of the Creator*, Nieuwentijt set out the extraordinary claim that careful reading of the Bible could confirm scientific discoveries. It was hard work that required an acute eye. The Bible teaches that the Earth is a globe (Isa. 40:22 speaks of "the circle of the earth") and that its poles are flattened (Jer. 6:22: "Behold, a people cometh from the north country, and a great nation shall be raised from the sides of the earth"). In a similar manner, Nieuwentijt translated Isaiah 25 to say "he that created the air and its stretching into all directions" to prove divine knowledge of the "spring of air," whereas Job 38:31 ("Can you bind the sweet influence of the Pleiades, or loose the bands of Orion?") indicated Newton's theory of planetary attraction. In other words, where science had arrived, the Bible was already there. These were but a few of the arguments that proliferated in the seventeenth century as theologians and scholars wrestled with the impact of new learning on the Bible. The question was not, except for a very few, whether to side with the Bible or science but rather how to uncover their true relationship.

If Galileo, Bacon, and Newton all thought that the work of individual reason could make compatible nature and scripture, and that the Bible, though requiring some figurative interpretation, presented the Word of God, other contemporary thinkers were less sanguine. Thomas Hobbes (1588–1679), philosopher and political thinker, took a radically different view about both the Bible's origin and its interpretation than these scientific thinkers.[25] Best known today for his views on the brutishness of human existence, Hobbes immersed himself in the study of the Bible and, controversially, rejected its divine origins.[26] Stuart England, in his view, was living the effects of the Reformation, the instability caused by religion and politics, and he sought a resolution that denied religion any independent claims to authority. In Protestant England, that meant the Bible. To prevent the political conflict that arose from wildly divergent interpretations of scripture, he argued that the right to discern the sacred book lay with the sovereign. Religion could not be allowed to pose a threat to political and social order, and the king was to appoint qualified scholars to secure the Bible.

That was perhaps the least controversial of Hobbes's views about the Bible. He also denied that Moses was the author of the Pentateuch, as well as the traditional authorships of other books of the Hebrew Bible. Provocatively, Hobbes claimed the New Testament only became canon in the fourth century as a political act, roundly rejecting any providential role in the formation of the Bible. In so doing, he downplayed the role of the Holy Spirit and elevated

Emperor Constantine. Unity of scripture was only possible through the actions of an outside force, namely the ruler. Another provocation: scripture was no different from any other human text except for the type of supernatural responses it had elicited from the faithful. Naturally, no Catholic or Protestant would have concurred, but Hobbes was unrepentant. The Western tradition had held that the contradictions of the Bible were not so, and Galileo agreed. They were evidence of human weakness. Hobbes turned this argument on its head.

Left to their own devices, the churches in Hobbes's view were a source of unrest and possible subversion. He had no time for the Holy Spirit leading the faithful to truth and unity—the evidence pointed to quite the contrary. The Reformation might have been a good thing, and Hobbes was fervently anti-Catholic, but the upshot had been political chaos. For the sake of the state and the people, the Bible should be in the hands of the sovereign. Hobbes was no atheist, despite the accusations of contemporaries, but he was under no illusion about religion's place.

For Hobbes, a significant part of the problem lay with the nature of the Bible itself. The authors of the biblical books existed in particular contexts and wrote with the power of their own characters. Indeed, many of their prophecies were manifestly false. He rejected the idea, so prevalent among the Orthodox, that human time is caught up in divine time. This argument was not in itself new in an age when scholars were looking at the historical circumstances of the Bible. What Hobbes overturned, however, was the belief that these writers had any ability to convey the divine message. They reflected particular revelation to one person alone. Faith could not be communicated or shared. As Hobbes wrote, "The New Testament was not yet published in one

Body. Every one of the Evangelists was Interpreter of his own Gospel; and every Apostle of his own Epistle."[27]

The writers of the Bible had no particular authority because the demesne of religion belonged entirely to the individual who received the words. Those writing the biblical books might have been inspired by God, but that was entirely unknowable. The unity of the Bible was brought about by external, human forces, not by divine Providence, and was ultimately both itself political and grounded in political authority. "Those Books only are Canonicall, that is, Law, in every nation," stated Hobbes, "which are established for such by the Soveraign Authority."[28] No place here for the self-authenticating scripture knowable to those of faith. Calvin was certainly rolling in his unmarked grave.

Another way of approaching this issue of the historical and linguistic issues was offered by the Dutchman Hugo Grotius (1583–1645), an extraordinary polymath who made seminal contributions to the fields of political theory, philosophy, law, classics, and religion. Grotius was a student of the most brilliant scholar of biblical chronology and philology, Joseph Scaliger (1540–1609), who imparted the belief that rigorous examination of the biblical texts could foster faith.[29] Grotius's approach to the Bible was shaped by scholarly precision and a deep attachment to establishing peace between the warring Catholic and Protestant parties. Closely involved in the adoption of an edict of toleration in the Dutch Republic, he believed that divisive theological differences should be left to the individual conscience.

Grotius echoed Hobbes in acknowledging that a major problem for Protestants lay in their fundamental belief in the clarity of the Bible, a conviction that had led to controversy and violence.[30] Perhaps his most radical idea was that peace could be established between warring Christian factions through agreement on a few essential points of the Christian religion, such as an almighty God and Christ as savior. Internecine warfare over the finer points of doctrine should be set aside for private discussion, reserved for theologians and kept away from harming the faithful. Grotius believed that a more harmonious Christianity of antiquity offered a model for his day: "Tradition thus teaches us to reconcile what is said in Holy Scripture about grace and free will."[31]

Like Hobbes, Grotius believed that the differences in scripture had to be reconciled by an external authority. Unlike the Englishman, however, he believed that authority could not be the political authorities, who were hopelessly divided and in conflict. Grotius had what might seem a rather naive belief in the power of history and tradition to resolve tensions in the Bible. He was a formidable scholar, but his purpose was not merely study. In his view, interpretation of the Bible should foster peace among warring Christians in church and society. There would always be differing interpretations of scripture, he knew, but early Christianity and the church fathers had shown it was possible to live with diversity of views.

By the middle of the seventeenth century, debates over the reliability of the Bible were by no means limited to the world of scholars. In the Dutch Republic, a particularly animated controversy was fueled by several perplexing issues, including the age of the world. The controversy made its way into the public through sermons and tracts in Dutch. Was the Bible an accurate account of history? What might it mean to say it was not? Among learned writers, there was a well-recognized difficulty with the varying genealogies and chronologies of the Hebrew and Septuagint Bibles, and opinions varied on which was more reliable.[32]

Anxiety about the effects of such questions on the faithful left many scholars in a conundrum about what to do with their research. Some circulated their work in private and avoided publication in order to not cause offense. Others proceeded in the belief that there was no contradiction between serious historical questions about the Bible and acceptance of its divine nature. The Dutch scholar Étienne de Courcelles (1586–1659), who prepared an edition of the New Testament, wrote that hiding the differences would be far more damaging to Christians. Rather, and radically, he proposed that different interpretations should be placed before the people in order for individuals to choose for themselves: "But if everything has been diligently annotated, we can be sure that the true reading will be found among the variant ones, and that only an accurate examination is needed to distinguish it from the false ones."[33] De Courcelles sought to breathe life into the Protestant creed that the Bible interprets itself.

But there were strong countercurrents, most radically and influentially in the Jewish Dutch philosopher Baruch Spinoza (1632–1677). In crucial respects, Spinoza took up the ideas of Hobbes and others, but his conclusions were far more radical and far-reaching.[34] Spinoza was a careful reader of the Christian Bible and frequently quoted approvingly from it, and he was in frequent conversation with contemporary theologians.[35] Like others of his generation, he rejected the idea that the books of the Bible were written at once by divine command. They emerged over a long time. But that was only the beginning. Spinoza ventured further to claim that to understand the Bible and the prophets of Israel was by no means to understand the mind of God. At the same time, he said, "a man is more perfect in proportion to the nature and perfection of the thing which he loves before all others."[36] Spinoza put an axe through the Bible, a book he loved and that he argued had been selectively put together by priests and scholars. Only in terms of religion was the Bible the Word of God. Otherwise, it was a purely historical document to be explained only in human terms. There was no room for the supernatural.

Spinoza tossed overboard previous assumptions about the Bible. He rejected divine authorship and made the study of the Bible about its human authors, who were not divinely inspired. The Bible expressed humanity's image of God as the biblical writers and their contemporaries conceived of them. That was what could be known. It was a work of imagination that emerged out of particular historical contexts. Scripture could only be known on its own, historical terms. That was how it spoke.

Spinoza did not reject or discard the Bible. Quite the opposite. He held it in high regard, but as a humanly authored book with conceptions of God shaped by the particular circumstances, abilities, and limitations of its authors. Once one learned how to read those authors on their terms and understood how they lived in a very different world, one could discern the divine message and the appropriate response. Spinoza opened the door to the possibility that the Bible was no more inspired than any other book.

Spinoza had gone where no other had dared. His successor took up these radical views, but with a different purpose. Richard Simon (1638–1712), French Catholic priest of the French Oratory, a society of priests in Paris founded in 1611, perhaps most boldly demonstrates the effort of many in the seventeenth and eighteenth centuries to hold together the critical treatment of the Bible with a commitment to the faith.[37] A brilliant scholar who courted controversy his whole career, Simon brought to the fore the most contested questions of his time concerning the Bible. In many respects he followed in the tradition of Grotius, who looked to biblical learning as a way of resolving the inveterate hostility between Catholics and Protestants. A brilliant linguist, Simon believed that the Bible had to be studied through ancient languages, manuscripts, history, and knowledge of cultures. One could not, for example, understand the Hebrew Bible without a profound grasp of Judaism. Following the work of others, he placed the biblical authors in their historical and individual contexts, speaking of them as scribes who wrote down what they had received.

The question of authorship loomed large and brought down on Simon the opprobrium of his all-too-numerous enemies. His commitment to historical study, they repeatedly charged, threatened the sacredness of the Bible. Front and center were the first five books of the Hebrew Bible, which Simon claimed were not written by Moses but, rather, put together much later. One seventeenth-century Catholic writer made clear what was at stake: "Of all the paradoxes that have been advanced in our century there is no one, in my opinion with more temerity, nor more dangerous, than the opinion of those who have dared to deny that Moses was the author of the Pentateuch."[38] The question of whether Moses had written the whole of the Pentateuch was not itself new, but in the seventeenth century the debate became more urgent because the status of the whole Bible was at stake.

Simon was a master of detailed manuscript work, and his labors convinced him that the Bible was made up of books of widely different backgrounds and that some were more divinely inspired than others. Further, the long periods of transmission meant that the received text was deeply flawed. His goal was to restore the text of the Bible to the best of his ability, even as he recognized that the results would only be partially successful. He fully believed that the biblical text was inspired but that it had mutated through the centuries because of the work of human hands. His critics were not persuaded. One wrote, "All of his remarks tend towards an indifference to the dogmas [of the church], and a weakening of all its traditions and doctrinal decisions, and that is his true system, which carries with it, as you see, the complete subversion of religion."[39]

Simon responded that authority lay not in the text alone, a conviction that he believed had led Protestants into error. Rather, the historical circumstances of the Bible needed to be considered alongside the theological, which was authority of the church. As a Catholic, he accepted the authority of the church to rule in matters of faith even if the historical truth suggested otherwise. The authorship of Moses was a good example. Simon fully acknowledged that the Pentateuch was part of the biblical canon as the church taught, even if he did not think that Moses was the author. A related case was the Trinity, which he fully acknowledged while aware that the biblical evidence was ambiguous at best.

Simon shared the tradition of Renaissance and Reformation scholars that the study of the Bible through language and history would ultimately serve the church, not destroy it. In the conflict-ridden world he inhabited, he believed that the Bible pointed back to a time before theological conflicts to provide a basis for religious agreement.

In the eighteenth century the debate about the Bible and nature often turned to botany, archaeology, paleontology, and the conundrum of the account of the flood provided in Genesis. Discoveries of fossilized seashells, bones, and other oddities raised uncertainties about the dating of the Earth.[40] Further study of the erosion of coastlines as the cause of the shape of lands raised troubling questions about whether the flood had shaped the land. Eventually, natural scientists began to claim that scientific techniques offered alternative dates for Creation than the vague information in the Bible, though most who carried out this work remained committed to the biblical narratives.

Two significant discoveries near the beginning of the eighteenth century in British North America posed a particular challenge to the Bible.[41] The first was a collection of giant fossils, consisting of several teeth and bone fragments, unearthed in a field in Claverack, New York. Sensationally, these large bones suggested the existence of giant-like figures. The second, in Massachusetts, was a large boulder with written characters in an unknown language. The news of these discoveries quickly spread across the Atlantic to Britain and Europe.

Another find, near Albany, New York, was recorded by Cotton Mather, who argued in a letter to the Royal Society in London that they were the bones of the Nephilim, the wicked children of men who according to Genesis occupied the world before the flood. For Mather, the discovery confirmed that the Bible was correct and that key stories in the Old Testament had actually taken place in the Americas, an argument later made by Mormons.[42]

Such discoveries had been made before in Europe, but the American giants, Mather was convinced, were much larger—a very American assumption. His conclusion thrilled him: "The Giants themselves have come over to America!"[43] The importance of this thesis extended to contemporary times: the giants had plagued the earth before their destruction, which was a prefigurement of the extinction of Native Americans in his own time.[44] Mather had hoped that his discovery might lead to an invitation to join the Royal Society, but he was sorely disappointed.

Fossils and giants were aspects of a wider swathe of questions that natural science brought to the fore: Did the flood in Genesis cover the whole earth? Where was the Tower of Babel? And why did the patriarchs live so long? Of particular interest were the complexities that were raised by the destruction and repopulation of the earth. Richard Cumberland (1631–1718), philosopher, bishop, and opponent of Thomas Hobbes, addressed the question of how, after the deluge, such a small number of people had been able to repopulate the earth. His answer was disarmingly straightforward: In the time of Genesis, men were much more virile. They lived longer, were stronger, and were able to father children at a much older age. Cumberland's response, though amusing to modern ears, followed from a shared belief that there was a common humanity that led back to Noah. This belief would greatly complicate the issue of race and indigeneity in the premodern world and would also raise troubling questions about the historical accuracy of the Bible's chronology.[45]

Ancient cultures, such as Egypt, dated their culture to far beyond the biblical account, and there was also a growing awareness of the antiquity of the Chinese language. But no issue was more pressing than the so-called New World, which was nowhere mentioned in the Bible. How did people come to these lands, and why did they have no knowledge of the flood Moses spoke of in Genesis? These questions dominated the writings of seventeenth-century theologians.

One of the most creative and scandalous solutions came from the French theologian and lawyer Isaac La Peyrère (1596–1676), who posed a direct challenge to the Abrahamic origins of the peoples from Genesis.[46] A Calvinist of possible Jewish background, La Peyère put forward the thesis of polygenism, the multiple origins of peoples. According to this alternative history, the flood of Genesis did not extend to the whole earth, and certain ancient peoples had survived untouched. Although he claimed to have taken the story from the Bible and sought only to defend the holy book, for most his argument was seen as a repudiation of the Christian story; ultimately, his argument that there were sinful men before Adam landed him with charges of heresy.

The point of his Christian critics is not difficult to see. The Bible taught monogenesis, that all peoples were descended from Adam and Eve, and the suggestion that nonwhite lineages existed apart from the flood story undermined this claim. Though some believed that reason and religion could be reconciled and that scientific knowledge would confirm the common humanity of monogenism, this defense of Christian monogenism was no enlightened ideal. It was accompanied by clear ideas of the inferiority of Black people and justifications for slavery: for monogenists, widespread interest in skin color generally held that dark skin was a variation or degeneration of white, the result of long exposure to the sun. Indeed, the rise of Enlightenment reason only convinced many Europeans of their utter superiority and in some respects marked a turning point in racist thinking, as there was a distinct decline in earlier ideas of a common humanity based on scriptural principles.

Such a turn can be found, for instance, by looking at the work of Johann Friedrich Blumenbach (1752–1840), who coined the term "Caucasian race." Although he believed that Adam and Eve had been Caucasian and that the other groups he studied had derived from this race, he did not proffer a clear hierarchy. He was more interested in understanding the relationships between the "world's races," a term he came to use late in life. Although often seen as the source of what came after him in terms of race theory, Blumenbach was committed to the unity of humanity within a scriptural context. Nevertheless, he stood in a critical relationship to the Bible. How, he asked, could the sloth, which moves at six feet an hour, have made its way to South America after the flood?[47]

There were also more direct expressions of condescension. The Scottish philosopher David Hume (1711–1776) adopted a polygenist view of creation, and many have seen in his writings a distinct racist thread. In a remark that he subsequently removed from his writings, Hume spoke of ethnic inferiorities and mocked the Black people of Jamaica. In this respect, his critics saw his views on race as closely related to his anti-Christian sentiments. Members of the Scottish Common Sense school, including James Beattie (1735–1803), attacked Hume and fully rejected any idea that there were inferior races, which they saw as an offense to scripture. As they argued, "The only credible extant account of mankind is that which we have in scripture. And if we acquiesce in it, we must believe, that all the nations upon the earth are 'of one blood,' being descended of the same first parents."[48] Although Beattie clearly regarded Black people as inferior, he argued that they possessed a soul just as white people did.

Race was not the only matter of public debate that occurred through the prism of the Bible. Throughout the eighteenth century, Catholic and Protestant writers applied themselves with zeal to preparing detailed notes on scriptures and offering ways for profitably reading the Bible in light of the times. Some focused on the literal meaning of the text, while others looked to how the whole of the Hebrew Bible was shot through with figures of Christ. Among the most eminent and anticlerical of the philosophes, Voltaire (1694–1778), the Bible was mined not for revelation or miracles but as a crucial source for knowledge of ancient cultures. It was a passion shared by his mistress, Émilie du Châtelet, until her premature death. Romance and scriptural interpretation were apparently not wholly incompatible.

A gifted mathematician, Mme du Châtelet found a litany of numerical problems in the Old and New Testaments, including Matthew's account of Jesus's words: "All things are delivered unto me of my Father: and no man knoweth the Son, but the Father; neither knoweth any man the Father, save the Son, and he to whomsoever the Son will reveal him" (Matt. 11:27, KJV). The passage, she believed, was mathematical nonsense for which God should be awarded a zero.[49]

This approach to the Bible was, unsurprisingly, unusual. From Descartes to Gottfried Leibniz, pious philosophers and mathematicians generally avoided trying to read the Bible scientifically.[50] They did not believe in two separate truths but in different books to be read differently. The Bible was not irrational; indeed, repeated efforts were made through the eighteenth century to demonstrate the rationality of its teachings. Those who rejected wholesale the reasonableness of scripture were certainly to be found, but they were very much in the minority. For instance, Denis Diderot, who came from pious beginnings, eventually came to regard that which lay outside human experience as impossible—a point on which he agreed with Hume. Consequently, gone were miracles and the Resurrection, despite their presence in the Bible.

Much of the debate about the Bible's veracity surrounded those passages deemed unreasonable and beyond explanation. Figures such as John Locke excised them, as did Thomas Jefferson in his much-cut-down New Testament. Others, such as the great Hebraist Richard Simon, did not omit such passages, but Simon used his formidable skills as a philologist to reduce their importance. Clerics, scientists, philosophers, and educated persons (women and men) carried out a very public debate about such issues, and pamphlets and books were widely circulated across Europe, indicating an extensive lay readership. The rise of the coffeehouse and other public forums created ever more accessible ways in which supporters and critics of the Bible could air their views.

What makes the variety of positions and arguments, from both the apologists and critics, so fascinating is how scripture and reason were so protean. Different authors applied varying standards of what they thought "reasonable." Did it refer to inner coherence, an underlying divine plan, or accordance with human experience? The elasticity of the debate resulted in just about everyone finding sufficient evidence in the Bible for their arguments. The Bible was not the book of books but the book of many rationalities. What all could agree on, however, was that historically and textually, the Bible was full of "difficulties." The unresolved question was whether that impugned the Word, as Voltaire, Mme du Châtelet, David Hume, and many others believed, or whether it simply meant the truth of the biblical stories had to be read less literally.

On the subject of the Bible, Voltaire is best remembered for his witty condemnations of scripture.[51] His most famous purported bon mot came in 1776: "One hundred years from my day, there will not be a Bible on earth except one that is looked upon by an antiquarian curiosity-seeker." Such aspersions make it easy to overlook that Voltaire himself, who came from a pious family and received a Jesuit education, knew the Bible thoroughly. Despite early encounters with antireligious attitudes and the divisions among Christian communities, Voltaire devoted considerable attention to studying scripture. Among his friends were devout Catholic scholars and enlightened Calvinists such as Jacob Vernet. Famously, however, he turned against the Christian religion as oppressive. Above all, for Voltaire, that meant discrediting a Bible that fed a persecuting church.

For more than sixteen years the French philosophe poured forth a torrent of hostile publications in which he engaged with virtually every part of the Bible. His goal was twofold: to undermine the book while seeking to explain it in entirely human terms. In *La Bible enfin expliquée* of 1776, he offered almost three hundred pages of translation, summary, and commentary. Voltaire read the Bible carefully and profoundly critically. Although he was not always without sympathy for certain ideals, he rejected doctrinal formulations such as the Trinity or that Jesus was the Son of God. He was a man, never resurrected. Why, Voltaire asked, were there virtually no outside sources that attest to Jesus? The man, in his view, was clearly a well-meaning fanatic. Toward the end of his life, Voltaire softened somewhat, finding in Jesus some admirable qualities, although nothing supernatural, and the Frenchman died rejecting the teaching and ministrations of the church.

The eighteenth century marked a significant turning point in the life of the Bible in the West. Facing growing skepticism about its textual, linguistic, historical, and theological foundations, it did not slink from the stage. Quite the opposite. Scholars in England and Germany, far from abandoning the Bible, sought to recover its authority to keep religion alive and vital.[52] Enlightenment authors sought to rescue the Bible through the human sciences. The cost, however, was not insignificant: the Bible could no longer be regarded as a self-authenticating book of God's Word. Its future lay in authentication through its connection and relevance to human morality, aesthetics, and history. For these scholars, the renewed Bible was a book of human culture.[53] It was a radical solution with a radical outcome, a world of two Bibles: one for educated elites concerned with meeting the transformative intellectual climate of the eighteenth century, and one for the faithful masses seeking spiritual renewal in the great revivals of the age. Their approaches to the Bible differed, but their intentions converged—to preserve the Bible in a changing world.

While the Enlightenment is generally associated with great figures of philosophy, literature, music, and science, no picture of the Bible in the age of science and reason can hope to be accurate without engaging the question of what the book meant for the vast majority of men and women. After all, remarkable intellectuals and artists tend not to be very representative of society writ large.

Though it might seem like an unlikely source to convey the popular sentiment, one place to look is among the spiritualists in German and Eastern lands. From the middle of the seventeenth century, a religious and social movement within Protestantism known as Pietism espoused radical ideals of inner spiritual transformation. Many Pietists were women, and they were drawn to a practical devotion grounded in the study of the Bible and Christian living. They reacted against what they saw as the ossified world of the post-Reformation churches that had embraced hard-line theological positions and lost spiritual vigor and an inner sense of the divine presence. The Pietists emphasized personal responsibility for spiritual life, a conversion experience and direct encounters with God, and worship outside of churches. They were also enthusiastic missionaries whose influence spread across the Atlantic, and by the end of the eighteenth century, they made up over a quarter of the German congregations in the Americas.

Such people should not, however, be seen as an alternative to the Enlightenment but as very much part of it, as can be seen in two enormous works of the eighteenth century: the *Biblia Pentapla* and the Berleburg Bible. The *Pentapla* appeared from 1710 to 1712 and ran to a whopping 4,500 pages across three volumes. A polyglot text clearly not intended for worship or devotional use, it reflected some of the most profound Pietist beliefs. It brought together the principal German translations, Lutheran, Reformed, and Catholic, together with Dutch and Yiddish, in five parallel columns. The first full Yiddish translation of the Bible had appeared in Amsterdam in 1678. The editor, Johann Otto Glüsing (1675/76–1727), claimed to have compiled "the five most distinguished, best known, and most useful German translations of the whole Bible."[54]

In the tradition of polyglot Bibles, Glüsing's efforts brought together different versions to help the reader better understand scripture. Despite the size of his work, his audience was not just the learned but all the faithful, reflecting the editor's intention to foster a simple, biblical faith that imitated Christ. Glüsing's critics among the established Lutheran churches were savage. Believing that such information should be for the educated alone, they argued that providing the common faithful with such knowledge would only confuse them and undermine faith. Glüsing disagreed. Enlightenment ideas were for the churches.

In many respects, the *Biblia Pentapla* hearkened back to the ideals of Luther and Reformation by putting the Bible before the people, but it was also a creation of its age. In bringing together multiple German, Dutch, and Yiddish translations in one Bible, with notes and commentary, Glüsing embraced the Enlightenment principle of systematizing knowledge, believing that the critical study of the Bible fed, not threatened, faith. In this respect he stood in the tradition of Hugh Broughton and Puritan communities in England and

New England, where critical study of the Bible was consonant with fervent piety. Furthermore, another contemporary aspiration lay behind the gathering of the five versions. The dialogue of translations was a tool for religious toleration, another Enlightenment aspiration. Revealing the shared commitment to the faith, Glüsing believed, could help resolve tensions within the church. The Catholic translation sat alongside the Lutheran and Yiddish, displaying Pietist views of toleration.

Of even greater girth was the Berleburg Bible, which appeared in eight volumes between 1726 and 1742. It was the work of Johann Friedrich Haug (1680–1753) and a large team of researchers. A "veritable encyclopedia of biblical interpretation," the Berleburg included geographical, archaeological, theological, philological, and anthropological information.[55] On the page, short passages of scripture were engulfed in a sea of information. The Berleburg Bible offered a new translation together with a range of mystical and sometimes esoteric interpretations. Its purpose was to awaken Christians and fill them with love of scripture. In the commentary on the line from Revelation, "Take [the scroll] and eat it: it will be bitter to your stomach, but sweet as honey in your mouth" (10:9), we encounter the poem:

> *This book one should not read, but eat*
> *For the one who reads, to him it is easy to forget what he has*
> *   grasped;*
> *But the one who takes it into himself, into his flesh and blood,*
> *He obtains the power of the book, and has become one with it.*[56]

The commentary in the Berleburg Bible gathers some of the most radical thinkers of the Pietist tradition together, an unlikely grouping of Luther, heretical sects, and the Jewish Talmud. Such a miscellany is often perplexing to read with its wealth of contradictory information. Yet it is a compendium of knowledge and indebted to one of the great works of the Enlightenment, Pierre Bayle's *Historical and Critical Dictionary* (1697). Both draw together a vast body of knowledge according to set structural principles. What Bayle organizes by alphabet, the Berleburg does by the books of the Bible. In its expanse, Berleburg also shares much with Güsling's *Pentapula*, imparting biblical knowledge to the common people and rejecting the rigid divisions of the confessional churches. It was a child of the radical enlightenment.

Perhaps the most famous adherent to Pietism was Johann Sebastian Bach (1685–1750), in whose music is found the marriage of Enlightenment principles and deep devotion to the Bible that inspired so many of the age.[57] Bach certainly read widely in the devotional world of the Pietists and kept their works in his expansive library. Bach was a careful reader of the *Deutsche Bibel* (German Bible) prepared by Abraham Calov in the seventeenth century. The Calov Bible brims with commentary from Martin Luther, and Bach's careful notations survive.[58] They offer us a window on his deep faith. Bach followed in a rich tradition of Lutheran music dating to its founder, who spoke of the glories of praising God in song: "Music I have always loved. He who knows music has a good nature. Necessity demands that music be kept in the schools. A schoolmaster must know how to sing. Otherwise, I do not look at him. And before a youth is ordained into the ministry, he should practice music in school."[59]

In his music, Bach drew deeply on Lutheran theology, such as the distinction between Law and Gospel, which he wove through his cantatas. He did so as someone intimately familiar with the Bible and the tradition of Protestant and Catholic interpretations. As a cantor he was responsible for teaching elemental theology to those entering the church, and his music was written within the liturgical year of the Lutheran church, serving the various themes of the Christian seasons.

Pietism was far from the only movement of popular engagement with scripture in the age of reason, and perhaps no one embodied this ethos more than the transatlantic figure Jonathan Edwards (1703–1758).[60] Although he lived in New England and on the edge of the Enlightenment, Edwards was at the very heart of eighteenth-century thought, and there were few more influential preacher-scholars of the age. In his vast corpus of writing and preaching on the Bible, he drew together new developments of the Enlightenment with traditional views of scripture and doctrine. His brother-in-law gave him a "Blank Bible" in which the leaves of the King James Bible were sewn together with blank pages, onto which Edwards wrote an extensive commentary on the whole of the book. The Blank Bible is thus an invaluable source for Edwards's thinking on scripture from Genesis to Revelation.

Edwards grew up in a world in which reason was in ascendance. He held a deep-rooted belief in the rationality of all things, including the natural world and religion, and shared the aspiration to reconcile the Bible with rapid advances in natural science and Enlightenment thought. Drawn to the origins of the Bible, which he never doubted were divine, Edwards was acutely aware of the historical and linguistic problems that preoccupied some contemporary writers. For him, the Bible was the voice of God, but it arose out of the particular circumstances of an ancient world about which present scholars had imperfect knowledge. He acknowledged that many important pieces of the puzzle were missing but held that one could only speculate about what wasn't there.

Edwards accepted the historical nature of the Bible, that it was the work of many hands over a long period of time, which led to inconsistencies and redactions. As this chapter has shown, this view was by no means unique, but one of the most fascinating aspects of his work was his desire to soak up as much critical thinking about the Bible as possible while holding fast to its unquestionable authority. He did not shy away from entering the burning debates of his day: Did Moses write the Pentateuch? What was the relationship between biblical and pagan history? And were the miracles recorded in the Bible credible?

Yet Edwards never ceased to express his wonder: "Reading from Psalm 119, 'Open thou mine eyes, that I may behold wondrous things out of thy law,'" he enthused, "The word of God contains the most noble, and worthy, and entertaining objects of man's most noble faculty, viz. his understanding, the most excellent things that man can exercise his thoughts about."[61] The Bible, he believed, engaged the greatest of human capacities in a type of partnership, but it was so much more than any person could comprehend.

Edwards could interest himself in the historical peculiarities and contexts of the Bible without losing a sense that it transcended history because he believed in divine inspiration. The writers of the Bible were guided by God's penetrating inspiration, which also guided the hearts of those who receive in faith. Edwards also held to the Reformation principle that scripture interprets itself and is consistent when read in faith. In his vast notes on the Bible, he carefully recorded how both the Old and New Testaments reflected the truth of the history related in the Pentateuch. For Edwards, this certainty, against contemporary skeptics, confirmed that Moses was indeed the author. In maintaining his case for Moses, Edwards demonstrated his familiarity with contemporary historical scholarship that he marshaled to his cause. Of the Pentateuch, he wrote:

> It was impossible that this vast number of events, with so many circumstances, with names of persons, and places, and minute incidents, should be so particularly and exactly known, and the knowledge of 'em so fully, and distinctly, and without confusion or loss, kept up for so many ages, and be so often mentioned in so particular a manner, without error or inconsistence, through so many ages without a written record . . . and the comparing of the records of the Pentateuch with the innumerable citations and references, shows that this was in fact that record.[62]

Edwards also shared with fellow writers of the Enlightenment a fascination with other religions, and he read widely. In his notebooks he often toyed with comparisons between the Hebrew and Greek of the Bible, both of which he could read before entering Yale College, with languages and terms from other traditions.[63] He held to the long-standing belief that God had spoken Hebrew. Nevertheless, the Bible was uniquely authoritative. His efforts demonstrate the global reach of the Bible in the Enlightenment. Edwards maintained these notebooks even amid his missionary work among the Housatonic Native Americans. Living on the frontier of the European Enlightenment, Edwards saw himself as a unique figure called to make the faith accessible to Indigenous peoples while fully engaged with the newest learning from Europe. It was a new age.

The Bible of the age of science and reason proved supple and generative. There were challenges to its historical claims and linguistic legacy. At the same time, there were vigorous responses. Certainly philology, the scholarly study of languages, raised questions and put to the test traditional theological certainties of Catholicism and Protestantism. Moreover, during the Enlightenment, seeds of secularism were sown that would later germinate during the nineteenth century. In particular, historical-critical biblical interpretation, which flourished in German universities of the nineteenth century, had its roots in Enlightenment intellectual culture. Nevertheless, it would be a mistake to see this period as one of rejection or repudiation of religion. Transitions are generally slow and complex, and many of the most important Enlightenment thinkers, to say nothing of the common people, were resolute in their belief. The Bible retained center stage and, in most cases, was reconciled with what was being learned about science and history.

CHAPTER 7

THE KING JAMES BIBLE

During the seventeenth century, with the arrival of the age of science and reason, the Bible found itself in a world undergoing profound intellectual changes. Yet the Bible itself was no static object. Indeed, the very century that witnessed the scientific revolution also witnessed the birth of the most influential book in history: the King James Bible.[1]

The creators of the King James Version (KJV) could never have anticipated such a legacy, and neither was it their intention. Their Bible emerged at a particular moment of heated religious strife in England. Its form and language reflected the decisions of men hoping to address a crisis by putting the scriptures into the language of the people without notes or commentary. It was to be a Bible for all, but not forever. Those charged with the task were fully aware of the perils of translation, that rendering the Word into words was a never-ending task that each age must undertake anew. As the Bible itself says, "Of making many books there is no end" (Eccles. 12:12, NIV). They were not carving tablets but doing the best they could within the restraints placed on them. In widely consulting other translations, notably the Hebrew and Greek, as well as William Tyndale's, they strove not for innovation but to honor what had come before them by bringing to it the wisdom of their time. Their effort would prove more successful than they could have imagined. To this day, the King James Version (also known as the Authorized Version) remains the most widely read Bible around the globe, as well as one of the most printed books on earth. Nevertheless, like all previous efforts, this significant, sustained, and numerically successful effort would prove insufficient to bind the faithful together to a single interpretation of its meaning.

Despite the book's eventual renown, its beginnings were far from auspicious. Controversy dogged its every step, and the translation was afforded the reception of an unwelcome intruder. When first printed in 1611, the King James appeared in an England where the Geneva Bible prevailed everywhere. Produced in 1560 by a group of Protestant exiles in Switzerland, the Geneva had defined the Elizabethan Age. As discussed in chapter 5, it was read in the home, quoted by Shakespeare's characters, sung in madrigals, and preached from every pulpit in the land.

So why a new translation? The reasons for the appearance of this heavenly book were unmistakably worldly. It arose from an attempt to ease the religious strife that had beset England since its Reformation, pitting those who favored the compromises that retained traditional worship, bishops, and cathedrals against the more zealous, often Calvinist reformers determined to finish the work of reforming Christ's church throughout the land. The golden age of Elizabeth saw

Protestants set against Protestants in a nation where Catholic sympathies ran deep.

The Bible symbolized England's internal divisions. On church lecterns lay the handsomely produced Bishops' Bible, the official version sanctioned by the church for worship. The Bishops' reputation, however, was desultory on account of its error-filled, stilted translation, which pleased few. Despite its flaws, the Bishops' Bible still had the voice of Tyndale. But it suffered from inconsistent scholarship by a collection of writers who had used an amalgam of contemporary translations rather than the Hebrew and Greek.

The problems began with God. In the Old Testament the tetragrammaton, YHWH, is represented by "the Lord" and the Hebrew "Elohim" by "God." This was common practice in English Bibles. However, in the Psalms of the Bishops' Bible the practice was reversed, creating confusion. Further, the Bishops' Bible is known as the Treacle Bible on account of its rendering of Jeremiah 8:22 as "Is there not treacle at Gilead?" The use of the word "treacle" here makes little sense, as the prophet's meaning was that there was no healing physic. The translators of the King James replaced "treacle" with the less sticky "balm." Their "Is there no balm in Gilead?" is generally found in all modern English translations.

Outside the walls of the churches, in homes, villages, and cities, the Geneva reigned, but it, too, was controversial. Nevertheless, some of the translators of the Bishops' made extensive use of the Geneva, compounding the inconsistent tone of the church-sanctioned Bible. However, the Geneva was too Reformed for many of the church elite, the book of the "hotter" brethren. Most objectionable were the extensive and controversial notes that literally surrounded the biblical text on the page, offering unabashedly Calvinist instruction in the faith.

An opportunity for a resolution to the Bible controversy arose with Elizabeth's death and the accession of her successor, the Scottish king James VI, who as a young king had sanctioned the Geneva Bible in his native land. Baptized Catholic, James was brought up under stern Calvinist tutelage of his teachers. However, James's Reformed enthusiasm did not outlive his youth, and with his move to London came a distancing from his Scottish Calvinism. As James I, Supreme Head of the Church of England, he grew deeply distrustful of the Geneva Bible, in no small part because of its biblical glosses that sanctioned the legitimacy of resistance against a tyrannical monarch.

The possibility of rebellion chilled the heart of a ruler in such a fragile land, and James regarded the Geneva in the wrong hands as a seedbed of sedition. He desired a Bible more suited to a religiously divided England. When a group of moderate Puritans proposed a new version at a conference held at Hampton Court in 1604, James seized the opportunity to finally rid himself of the Geneva Bible, which he called the "worst of all."[2]

To draft the new Bible, the commissioning document created committees consisting of the "best scholars," who were to report to the bishops, who in turn answered to the Privy Council and, finally, to James himself. A communal interest in the well-being of King James's realm was to trump any individual's unique experience. While the king seems not to have played much of a role in the day-to-day decision-making, his hostility to the Geneva Bible was decisive, and it was declared that the defective Bishops' Bible would form the foundation for the revisions. Nevertheless, the Geneva Bible was extensively used.[3] Divided among Oxford, Cambridge, and Westminster, the six committees consisted of a broad range of men, from archbishops to country parsons.[4] In terms of theological loyalties, they combined high churchmen with Calvinist Puritans determined to push the English church closer to the stricter ideals of the Reformed faith. The choice of the Bishops' Bible set the agenda. The assorted company were not to draft a new translation but to improve the existing Bible.

Nevertheless, the scholars believed themselves to be translators and brought to the Bishops' Bible their impressive learning in biblical languages to create a much-enhanced version of the scriptures based on the latest scholarship.[5] They were fully aware of the complexities of the languages and the scholarly challenges they faced. Although the spirit of Tyndale was in the room, they went far beyond existing English translations. Even minor alterations to the English could signal significant changes in meaning.

Most of the men were highly trained scholars capable of reading Hebrew and Greek. In fact, they were much more university figures than poets or dramatists. In total, there were about fifty of them. The preface speaks modestly: "There were many chosen that were greater in other men's eyes than in their own, and that sought the truth rather than their own praise."[6] But spiritual humility could not hide that these men were among the greatest biblical scholars of their age. The mesmerizing beauty of the King James Bible was a creation of meticulous scholarship and deep reverence for the language that had come before.

The author of the preface, Miles Smith, elegantly memorialized the course followed: "Translation it is that openeth the window to let in the light; that breaketh the shell that we may eat the kernel; that putteth aside the curtain that we may look into the most holy place; that removeth the cover of the well that we may come by the water, even as Jacob rolled away the stone from the mouth of the well." While this opening language dramatically recalls the temple and rending of its curtain at Christ's crucifixion, Smith proceeded to confess tactfully the narrow horizon of the task: "We never sought to make a new translation, nor yet a bad one to make a good one, but to make a good one better; or out of many good ones, one principal good one."[7] We know, however, that the assembled scholars did much more than make a good translation better. Theirs was a new work of art.

The individual committees busied themselves with their assigned parts of the Old and New Testaments, and their suggested revisions were sent to Westminster for final adjudication. Revisions were based not only on biblical languages, Tyndale, the Bishops', and the Geneva, but also on the Greek Septuagint, the Latin Vulgate, and even Martin Luther's German translation.[8] Use of the Catholic Douay-Rheims Bible was implicitly forbidden for confessional reasons, but to little effect. It was clearly on the table. On some points, the guidance given to the authors was notably specific: popular forms of names for biblical authors, prophets, and apostles were to be retained and traditional English formulations employed, such as the use of "church" rather than "congregation." The 2015 discovery of the very first draft of the King James Bible, covered by newspapers around the world, has thrown light on the authors' precise work.[9]

Compared to the Geneva, the King James Bible had many fewer notes to accompany the text. In part, this was to free the new translation from the Calvinist interpretation, in particular on the right to resist a tyrant, prevalent in Elizabethan England and so hated and feared by some within the hierarchy of the church, including the king, its supreme head. The reduced number of notes reflected the mature views of Protestant leaders: the Bible was to be available to the people, but its interpretation rested in the hands of ordained clerical authorities. The distance from Rome proved not to be so great. Therein lay the hope for a Bible for the whole of a religiously riven kingdom.

The decision to reduce the notes, though it reflected James's hostility or insecurities, was also a dangerous gamble. The naked biblical text unaccompanied by notes to guide the reader exposed a long-standing anxiety of the Protestant Reformation. Martin Luther's call to "scripture alone" had gone hand in hand with the desire to put the Bible in reach of the faithful to allow women and men to encounter God's Word directly. Once this spirit was set free, however, fears arose about diverging or private interpretations of the Old and New Testaments. Who was to decide what scripture said? There clearly were differing claims, and subsequent disagreement was precisely what the Catholics predicted—the heretics would unleash chaos.

Pushed into a corner, Protestant reformers were forced to declare that it fell to the church (that was, themselves) to mediate the Bible. In other words, clergy educated in the study of biblical languages and theology and under the control of authorities retained the power to interpret scripture. In England, Archbishop Thomas Cranmer (1489–1556) captured the prevailing conviction of those in power that the gems of scripture were not for the hands of the common people. "The scriptures be the fat pastures of the soul," he wrote, "therein is no venomous meat, no unwholesome thing; they be the very dainty and pure feeding." Nevertheless, there were "idle babblers and talkers of the scripture" in "every marketplace, every alehouse and tavern, every feast house." Consequently, the church should be the arbiter of God's Word. Cranmer's chilling resolution could have been a mantra of the Protestant Reformation: "I forbid not to read, but I forbid to reason."[10] James wholly concurred. While Protestants and Catholics agreed that the church should interpret the Bible, they had very different views of what and who that church was.

Countering the Protestant anxiety of a cacophony of voices was the hope that the new Bible would win the acceptance of all groups in a land divided by religious faith. Surely all Protestants could concur that their faith rested on the Word of God. Reflecting this optimism, Miles Smith opened his letter to the readers with a paean of praise for scripture, one of the most famous and beautiful laudations of the Bible:

> But now what piety without truth? what truth, what saving truth, without the word of God? what word of God, whereof we may be sure, without the Scripture? The Scriptures we are commanded to search (John 5:39, Isa. 8:20). They are commended that searched and studied them (Acts 17:11 and 8:28–9). They are reproved that were unskilful in them, or slow to believe them (Matt. 22:29, Luke 24:25). They can make us wise unto salvation (2 Tim. 3:15). If we be ignorant, they will instruct us; if out of the way, they will bring us home; if out of order, they will reform us; if in heaviness, comfort us; if dull, quicken us; if cold, inflame us.[11]

As engraver Cornelis Boel's title page for the 1611 Bible conveyed, however, not every aspect of the book would be so ecumenical. Readers were presented with a powerful expression of the royal theology of the Church of England, rich in symbolism celebrating the priesthood of the clergy.[12] The copperplate engraving presented the "Holy Bible conteyning the Old and New newly translated out of the originall tongues and with the former translations diligently compared and revised by his maiestie's special commandment. Appointed to be Read in Churches." The name King James was nowhere to be found, but the force of his hand was evident. As the title made clear, this Bible issued from the crown, and its status as the official and preeminent Bible of England was unquestioned.

Moses and Aaron were prominently displayed on either side of the title, representing in the English context the king and archbishop. In the bottom corners, the evangelists Luke and John were seated flanking a pelican feeding her brood with her blood. In Christian tradition the bird signified Christ's passion and the Eucharist. Across the top of the page, the New Testament, represented by the apostles gathered around the Lamb of God, rested on the foundation of the Old Testament, symbolized by the twelve tribes of Israel. The prominence of the priest Aaron in this frontispiece was an arresting symbol of the English clergy, an implicit rebuke to the more radical Puritans.

James may have been missing from the title, but the new Bible was a reflection of his authority as monarch. The dedication described him as the "principal mover" and "author" of the translation. It was an intentional parallel with the divinity, long spoken of in Christian theology as the "first mover" and the "author of all things." No one would have missed the import of the dedication: Obedience to God was obedience to the king. James was king by divine right, and his word would prevail.[13]

The King James Bible would become best known, however, for the beauty of the words that lay beyond the title page.[14] The translators' task of bettering what had come before set them in a unique relationship to the tradition of the English Bible. Contrary to what one might assume, the language of the 1611 Bible did not mirror its age in the way Shakespeare had drawn on popular speech for his plays. Although the English language was in a period of rapid evolution, particularly in response to the advent of print, the translators embraced the past by making the Bible sound antiquated. To give one example, the translators retained "thee" and "thou," which by 1611 had passed from common usage. They artfully retained many of the words of William Tyndale from a century earlier to convey gravitas and elegance. The distance of time gave the King James an English that resonated with holiness and sanctity, and conjured wonder and reverence.

The choice had a profound impact on the English language. The sheer beauty of the words and deeply pleasing cadence of the phrasing endured for centuries on the lips of followers and unbelievers alike. Examples are legion: "bite the dust," "apple of my eye," "old as the hills," "wit's end," "the haves and have nots," "baptism of fire," "streets paved with gold," and "casting pearls before swine," to name a few, have endured. The brilliant legal scholar John Selden (1584–1654), whom the poet John Milton lauded as the most learned man in the realm, offered this brief assessment: "The English translation of the Bible, is the best translation in the world, and renders the sense of the original best."[15]

Given the appeal and widespread praise of the language, an intriguing but likely apocryphal possibility is that William Shakespeare played a role in the preparation of the psalms. Though there is no direct evidence to support the legend, many have decoded the psalms themselves as furnishing proof. Psalm 46 is the most frequently cited as revealing the poet's hand. In 1606 Shakespeare was forty-six years old, and if we count forty-six words from the start of the psalm we find the word "shake." If we then count forty-six words from the end—surprise, surprise!—we come to "spear." There is also a more complex calculation: if we add four and six to get ten and then move ten verses into the psalm and six words in, we arrive at "I am," which is followed four words later with "will." One final trick: if we reverse the sixth and fourth words it makes "William." While the cleverness of the conceit borders on a Dan Brown novel, it is likely a fantasy, or, as King James expert Gordon Campbell observes, an "absurd notion." Nevertheless, the internet is full of speculation. Campbell wryly adds, "Common sense is no impediment to such debate."[16] Yet, while the psalms are perhaps not from the hand of the great playwright, it is highly likely that the translators were influenced by his words, which were performed in London, Oxford, and Cambridge, where they worked.[17]

Purposeful antiquity, however, did not beget stasis. Almost from the moment of its creation the King James was repeatedly revised and improved following changing tastes. Of particular concern were its inconsistencies and errors. Consistency of language had not been an aim of the original translators, as it would be for their successors. In the 1611 edition, the same words were often spelled in different ways, suggesting that they might even have been variously pronounced. Influences on its original form came from divergent sources, and the use of longer words may have been a practice adopted from legal clerks, who were paid by the inch on the page. A common example was the addition of an *e* at the end of a word, such as "olde."[18] These were often removed in later revisions as printers sought to conserve space to cut costs.

Not all were beguiled by the new wonder. The most prominent critic of the King James was the enormously talented yet quarrelsome Puritan Hugh Broughton (1549–1612).[19] Although he was among the most brilliant linguists of his day and could translate the Hebrew prophets into Greek, Broughton had been excluded from the committees of the new Bible. His resentment proved powerful. By the time of the 1604 Hampton Court conference that initiated the King James, Broughton had been living in exile in Europe, from which he was an indefatigable controversialist, much to the annoyance of the king. The Puritan scholar advanced a broad range of schemes, from a new translation of the Bible to missions to convert the Jews in the Ottoman Empire. He was also a shameless self-promoter who believed himself unequaled in scholarly achievement. His exclusion from the committees owed more to his incendiary hotheadedness than oversight of his obvious mastery of Hebrew and Greek.

Broughton's criticisms of the King James might seem pedantic to our eyes, but they underscore that translation is a precise art and even small differences can have enormous consequences for meaning. Take, for example, Genesis 4:26, which the King James translators, following the English tradition, rendered, "Then began men to call upon the Name of the Lord." It has been read as marking the beginning of humanity's worship of God. Broughton, with good reason, believed this to be an error. He charged the translators with not taking into account Jewish exegesis, which understood the Hebrew "began" to mean "profaned." Broughton agreed with the Jews, and his version read, "Then was corrupted the calling upon the name of the Eternall." The outcome is two entirely different readings of the biblical text.[20] One (the KJV) speaks of the beginning of worship, while the other (Broughton's, following rabbinic scholarship) marks the beginning of the corruption of worship. Broughton would have given us a very different Bible.

Broughton is often portrayed as a crank who primarily objected to errors in the King James Bible, a sort of villain in the glorious creation story of a masterpiece. Such characterization minimizes the significance of his opposition. The prodigious scholar was not simply carping from the gallery but was well versed in the Jewish and Christian sources, which enabled him to offer penetrating and learned criticism. He harbored theological and personal objections to the project. At the same time, Broughton also passionately believed that the people were best served by an accessible translation crafted from the best scholarly labors. Such was his missionary zeal for a popular Bible that he prepared a large body of literature in English to instruct an eager group of lay followers in understanding scripture. His story is not merely of pique or a fetish for spotting errors; rather, it illuminates an alternative vision of what a new English Bible might have been. It reminds us that translations are not foreordained but arise from choices, circumstances, and contingency.

When the 1611 Bible appeared, there was little fanfare. It is not even known what King James thought of it. Up against the Geneva Bible so beloved by the people, the new translation stood little chance of success. Even major figures who had been significant supporters of King James, such as the bishop and scholar Lancelot Andrewes (1555–1626), continued to use the Geneva in their sermons. A Scottish edition of the King James Bible did not appear until 1633, the year of the coronation of Charles I as king of Scotland. Nevertheless, there was foreign interest as Dutch delegates at the 1618 Synod of Dort sought copies in preparation for their own national Bible.

As was often the case with new Bibles, the KJV's point of entrance was in church worship, where it was heard and seen by the people. This had to be done by fiat. First, printers stopped producing the Bishops' Bible, and the King James was introduced to be read from lecterns in services. To tackle the problem of the Geneva Bible, in 1616 James banned its publication in London, but that by no means brought about a quick demise. The Geneva continued to be printed in the Low Countries and imported into England.

It wasn't until 1640 that Archbishop William Laud forbade importation of the Geneva Bible into England, and even then, the flow and influence of the Geneva were not wholly stanched. Many readers missed the notes that had made the Calvinist Bible so accessible. Sensitive to the demand, the first foreign printing of the King James, produced in Amsterdam in 1642, included the notes from the Geneva Bible. The following year, the soldiers of Oliver Cromwell's army were issued the sixteen-page *Souldiers Pocket Bible*, made up of 150 passages from the Geneva Bible.

Throughout this period, the KJV continued to undergo a gradual evolution, and the version that ultimately emerged was the work of many hands. Already by 1629 numerous errors had been expunged and many of the antiquated spellings updated. In the Cambridge editions of the 1630s hundreds of changes were made, often by comparing the English to Hebrew and Greek. Whereas earlier revisions had focused on typos, efforts were now focused on improving the translation itself.

Not all went well. The most outrageous misfire came in 1631 with the so-called Wicked Bible, in which a crucial "not" was omitted from the seventh commandment, forbidding adultery. The error went undetected by the printers for nearly a year, and the government was not amused. The printers Robert Barker and Martin Lucas were summoned by King Charles I and given a tongue-lashing for the scandalous typo and their poor workmanship. Relieved of their printing license, they were fined the hefty sum of £300, although the punishment was never carried out. Most of the adulterous Bibles were destroyed, and only about twenty survive to this day, including one recently located in New Zealand.[21]

Mistakes, however, proved frustratingly difficult to avoid. John Baskett's 1717 elegant folio edition, so large that it was joked that it took a crane to lift it, was so full of misprints that it was commonly referred to as a "Baskettful of Errors." Famously, his edition of the King James was also known as the Vinegar Bible on account of the passage in Luke 20 known as the parable of the vineyard, which appears in Baskett's massive volume as the "parable of the vinegar." It is inviting to think what Jesus's vinegar teaching might have been. "One might expect," an outraged contemporary wrote to Baskett, "besides the dishonour done to religion by such careless editions of the Bible, the printer should have a little consulted his own reputation and the interest he has in the sale of the book, which we shall take all occasions to let the world know how unfit it is for public use."[22]

Despite these fits and starts, the King James Bible was well on its way to preeminence by 1660. It gained further popularity when the 1662 Prayer Book of the Church of England replaced scriptural texts from the Bishops' Bible with the King James. Over the next hundred-odd years, the King James would complete its ascent to become the Bible of English culture. Perhaps emblematic of this rising esteem was its place in the writing of the great poet John Milton (1608–1674). His personal Bible, now held in the British Library, was a 1612 edition of the King James. The heavily thumbed volume contains Milton's annotations and, on the flyleaf, his recording of births and deaths in his family, often in great detail. Milton was the most Bible-centric of the great English poets, and his *Paradise Lost* and

Paradise Regained contain more than two thousand allusions to the King James Bible.

The later seventeenth century saw the KJV become the only Bible in Britain. No longer challenged by the Geneva, it set down roots among the people and became their language of prayer and devotion. Its status was primarily due to the belief that it was the best possible translation, more than just a great piece of literature. In fact, literary fashion of the day held a contrary view. Among the educated elite the KJV was not at all regarded as a classic of literature. In England during the so-called Augustan Age of the early 1700s, there was a pronounced tendency to sneer at the KJV's antiquated and rather "rude" language, which was unfavorably compared to the Latinate English so admired by an age infatuated with Greece and Rome. For poets such as John Dryden (1631–1700), the King James was a relic of English that was crude and "Germanic," a pale imitation of the classical versions.

The Bible had noble company. Even Shakespeare did not escape Dryden's disdain. "It must be allowed," he wrote, "to the present age that the tongue in general is so much refined since Shakespeare's time that many of his words and more of his phrases are scarce intelligible. And of those which we understand, some are ungrammatical, others coarse, and his whole style is so pestered with figurative expressions that it is as affected as it is obscure."[23] Shakespeare has proven able to take the hit. In 1724, the English poet Leonard Welsted (1688–1747) made the same point in general terms: "We have laid aside our harsh antique words and retained only those of good sound and energy; the most beautiful polish is at length given to our tongue, and its Teutonic rust quite worn away."[24] The Augustans believed in the perfection of the English language, and they found the King James sorely wanting.

The tension between the educated elite and the widespread reception of the Bible can be seen most clearly in a rather obscure writer of the period. The Quaker Anthony Purver (1702–1777) was learned in Hebrew and Greek and prepared a translation of the scriptures intended to remedy the antiquated language of the King James. Yet, by his own admission, the times were changing. The King James was growing in popular affection during the eighteenth century, and there was increasing ease among the wider population with the idea that the elevated and distinctive language of the Bible rendered it special rather than flawed.

For most, in contrast with the tastes of the literary elite, the gravitas of the King James offered the voice of faith. Its words did not need to be brought into harmony with daily speech precisely because their strangeness conveyed the holy and transcendent. Purver was fully aware of the growing sentiment: "Yet the obsolete Words, and uncouth ungrammatical expressions in the Sacred Text, pass more unheeded as being oftener read and heard, especially when the mind is filled with an Imagination, that a Translation of the Scriptures must be so expressed."[25] Not surprisingly, Purver's effort sank with all hands on board.

For the vast majority of people, the KJV, as the sole Bible in England, framed not only religious experience but national identity. In 1712, responding to a remark that without the Bible and the Book of Common Prayer there would be no way of understanding the older forms of English, Jonathan Swift agreed and remarked on how formative these texts were for men and women, "for those books, being perpetually read in churches, have proved a kind of standard for language, especially to the common people."[26] As the only Bible in England, the KJV became the spiritual voice of the nation for children and adults alike. As the greatest modern scholar of the King James Bible, David Norton, reflected, "Its faith, its language, imagery, story and poetry, heard, read and quoted, was the highest common factor in the mental environment of millions over many generations."[27]

The KJV also found voice in music. At the time of its appearance in 1611, the new Bible was largely ignored by leading composers such as William Byrd (ca. 1540–1623), who used the Geneva Bible in his compositions. After the 1660 Restoration, attitudes began to change. Composers found the powerful language and rhythmic nature of the KJV translation conducive to high emotion, and the Bible began to appear in the works of composers such as Henry Purcell. New heights were achieved in the oratorios of George Frideric Handel (1685–1759), notably his *Israel in Egypt* and *Messiah*, which drew on direct quotations from the KJV. These oratorios brought sacred music into public performances, creating a new world for the Bible. The majesty of the Hallelujah Chorus (drawn from Revelation 19) greatly appealed to the Georgian love of pomp and ceremony.[28]

The KJV's newfound success did not slow its continual evolution. In fact, the version of the King James we know today appeared at the end of the eighteenth century, the work of an Oxford academic and clergyman, Benjamin Blayney (1728–1801), who has been described as the "single most important individual in the history of the KJV."[29] Oxford University Press engaged Blayney to revise the text, a Bible still thought to be riddled with errors and in need of rescue.

Drawing on the earlier editions of 1760 by Francis Sawyer Parris (1707–1760), Blayney made thousands of changes to the text, including spellings, tenses, and punctuation. He also revised the italicized words (used to indicate words not found in the original languages) through reference to Hebrew and Greek. In terms of modernizing language, he made such alterations as to render "fourscore" into "eightieth," "neesed" to "sneezed," and "crudled" to "curdled."

Parris and Blayney sought to remove from the 1611 and all subsequent editions the variations and errors introduced by printers. In the end, Blayney's 1769 version differed from 1611 in almost twenty-four thousand places. One enduring change that shaped the English language was his removal of the capitalization of nouns.[30] The practice of capitalizing nouns had been widespread in the eighteenth century, including in the American Constitution. The result of Blayney's numerous changes became the standard Oxford text, which remains largely unchanged.

By the nineteenth century, the King James articulated the spirituality of the nation, believers and unbelievers alike. Its forensic expression of the inner life of a people was best captured in the words of a critic. The Anglican hymnist Frederick William Faber (1814–1863) had converted to Catholicism, but in his dry-eyed account he witnessed the power of the Bible:

The power of all the griefs and trials of a man is hidden beneath its words. It is the representative of his best moments, and all that there has been about him of soft, and gentle, and pure, and penitent, and good, speaks to him forever out of his English Bible. It is his sacred thing which doubt never dimmed and controversy never soiled. It has been to him all along as the silent, but O how intelligible voice, of his guardian angel; and in the length and breadth of the land there is not a Protestant, with one spark of religiousness about him, whose spiritual biography is not in his Saxon Bible.[31]

From its genesis, the power of the King James resided in its words, read and heard. In the nineteenth century, however, it engaged the imagination in a new way that greatly enhanced its hold over the people. The Bible entered the imaginations of the English-speaking world of men, women, and children through pictures. With the exception of the Geneva, the Bible in English did not have a long tradition of illustrations, such as those commonly found in the German Luther Bible. Reading audiences of the nineteenth century, however, fired by an enthusiasm for travel literature and missionary accounts of distant lands, eagerly sought Bibles that exotically captured the worlds of the Old and New Testaments.

Illustrated Bibles spoke to a changing society and religious culture, a world of contrasts. Alongside the Evangelical fervor that had led to the establishment of Bible societies and missions and the abolition of slavery, the authority of scripture was being challenged on numerous fronts by science, archaeology, and historical scholarship. In the Victorian world, unbelief became a powerful force in a society that remained largely Christian. The faith was increasingly under siege, and older certainties were losing their hold. Church attendance began to decline, and an increasing number of prominent figures openly discussed their abandonment of Christianity.

Against this backdrop, the illustrated Bibles were an instant success. One of the most influential figures was John Kitto (1804–1854), the author of *The Pictorial Bible*. A devout Christian, Kitto, assisted by his wife, traveled through the Middle East and wrote accounts of his journeys for a popular magazine widely read in Britain and America. A scrupulous recorder of detail, he recounted how what he saw threw light on the world of the Bible and wrote a series of books on the culture of biblical peoples that helped Christians defend their faith against hostile secular assaults.

There was an enormous market for his illustrated works on every aspect of the Bible. Printed from 1836 to 1838 in London in three hefty quarto volumes, Kitto's *Pictorial Bible* ran to over two thousand pages and was filled with hundreds of images often copied from famous paintings. It soon became a fixture of the Victorian Protestant home. As a further aid to the reader, Kitto provided notes rich in detail about history, religion, architecture, and culture, making the Bible something of an encyclopedia for the family.

The Methodist publisher John Cassell (1817–1865) also produced a four-volume illustrated version of the King James Bible (still printed today), *Cassell's Illustrated Family Bible* (1859–1863). Cassell employed a range of engravers and artists to produce over nine hundred illustrations. Such were the profits from this edition that Cassell was able to purchase the rights to the most famous biblical illustrations of the century, Gustave Doré's drawings for the 1843 French translation of the Vulgate. It was of little consequence for pious Victorian Evangelicals that Doré (1832–1883) was a devout Catholic. The French Vulgate was widely praised as the preeminent illustrated Bible of the age. For his 1866 edition, Cassell brought together Doré's 243 engravings of the Old and New Testaments with the text of the King James Bible.

The Frenchman's illustrations would seem an unlikely fit for the typical Victorian family. Doré brought to life biblical characters in strikingly erotic ways. His most famous rendering, entitled *The Deluge*, is a scene from the flood in Genesis in which a father and mother desperately cling to a rock as the water rises. The four children seek refuge on the rock while a fifth is lifted on a shoulder, perhaps already drowned. The physicality of the scene is emphasized in the muscularity of the father and the suggestive pose of the youthful mother, who, like all the figures, is naked, her breast exposed. The overt sexuality of Doré's picture clearly shocked few readers at the time, as it appeared later in the Children's Bible of 1870 as a warning of divine wrath.[32]

Illustrated Bibles played several roles in a rapidly changing culture: they met a taste for greater historical knowledge, a fascination with foreign cultures, and a growing belief that the visual was integral to fostering faith. The winds of change brought many to turn to art as part of the defense of the book and religion. Bibles interpreted by images, it was believed, would reach a much broader audience. For the great Victorian writer John Ruskin, "all the histories of the Bible" were "yet waiting to be painted."[33]

Middle-class Victorian society was highly biblically literate, and reading scripture daily was a common practice, not only among Evangelicals. Attachment to the Bible held together the diverse culture of nineteenth-century Christianity.[34] The book lay at the heart of Victorian reverence for the family and household, and the family Bible was a treasure in which births, marriages, and deaths were carefully recorded and photographs and certificates stored. The Bible was the material expression of Victorian piety, a form of Christian devotion that placed increasing emphasis on family, children, the household, and the nearness of eternity. It was also symbolic of a distinctively nineteenth-century attitude, religious sentimentality.

Despite debates about the nature of the Bible among scholars and a growing chorus of secular critics, until the middle of the nineteenth century, the King James held its place among the people as the book of faith. In Samuel Butler's *The Way of All Flesh* (published in 1903 but written between 1873 and 1884), the weak-willed son Theobald Pontifex reflects the hold of traditional beliefs in a changing world: "In those days people believed with a simple downrightness which I do not observe among educated men and women now. It had never so much as crossed Theobald's mind to doubt the literal accuracy of any syllable in the Bible. He had never seen any book in which this was disputed, nor met with anyone who doubted it. True, there was just a little scare about geology, but there was nothing in it."[35]

But change did come. By the second half of the century, Victorian society was becoming increasingly aware of theories about the Bible that seriously questioned its status as a sacred book. Writing in 1874, one Roman Catholic critic pointed to the confessional difference: "'The [Catholic] Church existed before the New Testament' and could look to its doctrines and dogma to support and protect the faith of its members; Protestants had less to fall back on once the sacred texts were interrogated and found wanting."[36] Indeed, Protestants were forced on the back foot by a serious attack on their belief in the chronology of the Bible, its miraculous events, the divinity of Christ, and the relationship between the Old and New Testaments. Churchmen put up a spirited resistance, but skepticism about the Bible had moved from the universities into the wider public.

Belief in the literal truth of the Bible was under siege, and the King James Bible was center stage. Prominent writers, whether secularists or believers, waged their battles over religion with explicit references to the sacred text. Notably, the most prominent exponents of atheism in Britain were fully fixated on the Bible. Charles Bradlaugh, Annie Besant, Charles Watts, and G. W. Foote wrote extensively on the book in their efforts to expose it as not only fiction but extremely dangerous fiction.[37] The most famous and memorable secularist of the age was Bradlaugh (1833–1891), who spread his deep-rooted hatred of the Bible to audiences up and down Britain. In a pamphlet of 1861, writing under the pseudonym "Iconoclast," he offered the provocation that "perhaps there was a man who really lived and performed some special actions attracting popular attention, but beyond this Jesus Christ is a fiction."[38] Elsewhere, he wrote, "'I will demonstrate to any one that the 4 Gospels as we have them are a jumble of nonsense & contradiction."[39] And when Bradlaugh became the editor of the *Investigator* in 1858, he declared that its mission included the necessity of eradicating the Bible's malign influence.

Annie Besant (1847–1933), meanwhile, regarded the book as dangerous and despicable. In *My Path to Atheism* (1885), she wrote, "Most inquirers who begin to study by themselves, before they have read any heretical works, or heard controversies, will have been awakened to thought by the discrepancies and inconsistencies of the Bible itself. A thorough knowledge of the Bible is the groundwork of heresy." Decent parents, she argued, would not even allow their children to read the book: "Surely if any book be indictable for obscenity, the Bible should be the first to be prosecuted. I know of no other book in which is to be found such utterly unredeemed coarseness."[40]

Such objections, however, remained a minority viewpoint. More widespread convictions were grounded in a culture still centered on the Bible. As modern scholar Nathan MacDonald remarks, "It is difficult to remember just how suffused the culture of the Edwardian Era was in the language of the Bible. The Bible was hidden in plain sight. If you left school at 12 or 14 you probably knew the Bible better than many theology students now. Many people could quote it with ease."[41]

There was, however, a significant shift in attitudes toward the King James Bible among many. It was regarded less as a book of faith and instead was widely admired as a work of great literature, a jewel of the English language. This perspective continues to our time. The well-known Christian apologist C. S. Lewis (1898–1963) reacted with rage to this perceived secular view of the Bible:

> I could fulminate against the men of letters who have gone into ecstasies over "the Bible as literature," the Bible as "the noblest monument of English prose." Those who talk about the Bible as a "monument of English prose" are merely admiring it as a monument over the grave of Christianity.... The Bible has had a *literary* influence upon English literature *not* because it has been considered as literature, but because it has been considered as the report of the Word of God.[42]

Such was the success of the King James Bible. First regarded by most as unwelcome and unnecessary, it became a book of the broadest appeal because it was both unchanging and labile. It remains unrivaled among English Bibles in its ability to convey the divine in poetic gravity, prophetic justice, and spiritual euphoria. The King James was also a book of nostalgia, evoking a better age or a distant childhood. Its distance was a powerful attraction, like God's voice on a mountain. It was, and remains, a remarkably successful attempt to produce a Bible at once accessible to a large, diverse readership of individuals and bind them to a shared sense of a single, corporate church and state.

Yet, as we shall see in the chapters that follow, that voice for humans had diverging intonations: it was summoned to enslave, oppress, and missionize as well as to liberate. The story of the Bible, which has thus far focused primarily on its evolution in Europe, the Levant, and North Africa, will now take us around the world—across the Atlantic, on missions in every part of the world, to China, throughout Africa, and to the birth of a new global Pentecostalism. In each place, the history offered new iterations on a familiar story: the Bible made possible a closer, personal relationship with God while making impossible a single, doctrinally fixed faith.

CHAPTER 8

THE TRANSATLANTIC BIBLE

With each century that passed from the creation of the first identifiable Bible, the book's history pushed against and eventually shattered the usual constraints of time and place. Sovereigns and even entire nations came and went, but the Bible continued to adapt and thrive. By the early nineteenth century, with the reign of the King James Bible, a single translation of the sacred book had found its way into more hands than ever before. At no point, however, did it go uncontested or without criticism. And often these contestations and critiques were the thoughts, beliefs, and expressions of faith sought and experienced individually.

This internal, individual dialogue was perhaps most evident for the Puritans, for whom each moment offered a glimpse into eternity.[1] No event or thought, however seemingly mundane, escaped the eyes of men and women constantly examining themselves for signs of the

Spirit and the devil. They were in the midst of combat, as Christians had been since the devil tempted Christ in the desert. And as Christ had pleaded with his disciples in the garden, they endeavored to stay "awake." Nothing was to be overlooked or left unobserved. Anxiety and comfort were daily companions. Assurance was found through narrating their lives in the Bible.

Catholics and Protestants in the seventeenth century, notably women, felt compelled to examine and record their lives in journals in the spirit of ancient and medieval scribes, as an act of devotion.[2] Margaret Hoby (1571–1633), for instance, was a well-educated gentlewoman Puritan who wrote the first such diary for her kinsfolk: "After priuat praier I wrett notes in my testement and then eate my breakfast: after, I praied and then dined: after that I did sundrie beuse- nesses, and then I took a Lector and, after that, praied and examened myselfe: after that to supper, then to the Lector, and so to bed."[3] From waking to "and so to bed"—an expression later made famous by Samuel Pepys in his diary, but Hoby got there first—the diary covers everything, including breakfast. In reading the Bible, prayer, and meditation, no moment in life was too mundane not to be fraught with eternal consequences.[4]

Indeed, meditation on scripture and the earnestness or coldness of her prayers flowed together with Hoby's reflections on the household accounts, managing the estate in her husband's absence, and dealing with difficult tenants, like the ideal wife of Proverbs 31. Writing notes "in my testement" was no otherworldly indulgence. The whole day was a day lived in the Bible. Hoby spent time in private prayer but offered few private thoughts or opinions. In Puritan fashion, her story as recorded in her writing told of the turbulence of her spiritual life. The book she wrote was a physical manifestation of her inner self. Puritans regarded diary keeping as an imitation of God, who through Moses had written *the* book.

Hoby's book was also a product of her times. She was a businesswoman, and a shrewd one at that.[5] The diary forms a ledger, a daily accounting of her spiritual life that was not so different from the accounting she would have provided of the household and estate. Her book was covenantal, expressing a contractual relationship with God, and Hoby was keeping track of her end of the bargain. The world of the spiritual diary reflected the commerce of a growing mercantile society.

The Bible in the expanding transatlantic world of the seventeenth and eighteenth centuries prompted men and women to internalize and record their experiences of trying to lead the godly life. While thinkers from Galileo to Spinoza kept busy with debates about science, scholarship, and the Bible, for the common person this was an age in which the fervent biblical culture of Puritanism, Pietism, and Evangelicalism took hold and began to spread across the globe. Men and women found vibrant new ways of expressing an increasingly personal biblical faith and grew skeptical of traditional confessional identities. Yet again, this new biblical culture allowed individuals the opportunity to form their own personal, direct relationship with God, with the consequence that interpretations and religious practices proliferated well beyond any doctrinally fixed faith.

If there is one central character in this expanding global story, it is the Holy Spirit, whose presence was claimed on both sides of the Atlantic and across Asia to fire inward renewal and the spread of the gospel. This fervor expressed itself in missions, first to New England with the Puritans and Pilgrims, and then globally with the Moravians, a deeply devout sect committed to living the biblical message that emerged in Germany and established communities from Greenland to the Caribbean and Asia. These groups all stressed the intimacy of believers' relationship with God through Bible reading, prayer, and ethical living. The origins of these spiritual movements lay in a reaction against the seeming torpor among the European Protestant churches in the seventeenth century with their ossified theologies. Renewals took many forms in the name of the Spirit and spread like fire, notably with the awakenings in Europe, America, and Britain led by such figures as Charles and John Wesley, George Whitefield, and Jonathan Edwards. Preachers spoke in religious houses and fields for hours, their rhetorical flourishes bringing to life Paul speaking to the Athenians. For the revivals of the age, the Bible was theater in which the rekindled inner person was charged with transforming the world, of following Jesus's command to go to all nations.

Puritan fervor was grounded in the belief that the English Reformation had fallen short of the calling of the gospel. The church under the monarch, with its bishops, prayer books, liturgies, and cathedrals, was a pale imitation of what the Reformation had promised. The Puritans rejected the requirements of the English church establishment for worship and conformity. Adherence to the prayer book, with its repeated cycle of worship, and the requirement to kneel to receive Communion were among a host of outward acts that the Puritans rejected as unnecessary and, worse, unbiblical. They did not, however, break from the church. Quite the opposite: they sought to restore or purify it according to the principles of the Bible and the ideals of the Reformation. To do this, many had to leave their homeland.

One notable figure of this movement was Richard Sibbes (1577–1635), a Puritan who, unusually, did not marry, cultivated male relationships, and wore extravagant lace—characteristics that have earned him in modern times the speculative appellation "the gay Puritan." Sibbes was a prominent preacher and voice on the Bible. He shared with earlier reformers the conviction that the Bible interprets itself "by the powerful work of it in heart, by the experience of this blessed truth." However, one had to be receptive to this power of the Bible with a heart "suitable to divine truths" to create "answerable affections."[6] This meant growth of the person through the work of the Spirit. Sibbes shared the view of other Puritans that the Bible was essentially pure and simple, what John Milton called the "sober, plain, and unaffected style of the scriptures."[7]

Sibbes, with other Puritans, disdained what he saw as the mere intellectual study of the Bible. Those who studied the grammar and languages but lacked God's grace might achieve a level of knowledge but were unable to see "the things themselves." In the redeemed person reason prevailed over the depraved human will: "All grace comes in through the understanding enlightened." The deep well of God's grace was the Bible, for "the gospel breeds love in us to God."[8] There could be no relaxing, for growth in the Spirit fed by scripture was a daily challenge, and the lack of dynamism led to stagnation. Life was a constant battle of grace and nature, spirit and flesh, and the struggle against all human imperfections. Yet the ordered life was "sweet." The Puritan minister Richard Rogers opened his poem "A Sweet Meditation" with this:

> Oh, what a blessed thing it is
> with godly learned to talk,

By reading and by conference,
both as we sit and walk![9]

In sermons and instruction Puritans encouraged men and women to meditate on the Bible, to find themselves in the texts.[10] Meditation on scripture was essential to the journey through the world to the New Jerusalem. Church leader Richard Baxter assured the people that "God hath provided us a crown of glory, and promised to set it shortly on our heads"[11] One inevitable by-product of this approach was that not all Puritans read the Bible the same way, and variations of interpretation were found across the seventeenth century; nevertheless, there was a shared conviction that Spirit and Word acted in harmony.

But not all were satisfied with this alliance. Radical sects and Quakers, for example, questioned the primacy of scripture. Gerrard Winstanley (1609–1676), one of the founders of the Levelers, who argued for equality and communal possession of all goods, appalled many Puritans with his views on scripture, which he believed could be a tool in clerical hands for oppression. In one of the most striking passages of the age, Winstanley wrote: "The scriptures of the Bible were written by the experimentall hand of Shepherds, Husbandmen, Fishermen, and such inferiour men of the world. And the Universitie learned ones have got these mens writings; and flourishes their plaine language over with their darke interpretation, and glosses, as if it were too hard for ordinary men now to understand them; and thereby they deceive the simple, and makes a prey of the poore, and cosens them of the Earth, and of the tenth of their labors."[12]

The Quakers stressed an inner illumination not entirely dependent on scripture. George Fox, an English Dissenter and founder of the Quakers, referred to books, set prayers, and rituals as "empty forms." Revelation was not dependent on the Bible but parallel to it, and divine inspiration did not belong to the past but was ongoing. For Fox and his followers, scripture was thus the final test of neither belief nor conduct. The Bible was an account of Christ, the Word. The written record had no particular authority. The Bible itself was a book of words surpassed by the Word, God's son.[13]

In contrast, John Milton shared the Puritan belief in the simplicity of scripture, an argument he repeatedly used to attack the bishops of the established church. He rejected the way they "clothed" the Gospel in their rites, countering that "if the religion be pure, spirituall, simple, and lowly, as the Gospel most truly is, such must the face of the ministry be." Traditions of the church were dead, nothing compared to Christ's "hidden might." Scripture was living, constantly vivifying the faithful: "Truth is compar'd in Scripture to a streaming fountain; if her waters flow not in a perpetuall progression, they sick'n into a muddy pool of conformity and tradition."[14] For Milton, the Bible smashed the idolatries of human traditions and the corruptions of the church and its clergy.

This incredible sense of power also animated the conversion and life of John Bunyan (1628–1688), who had little of Milton's learning. For the author of *Pilgrim's Progress*, the force of the Bible guided individuals in a world of strife and conflict. Bunyan's encounter with malign spirits was deeply personal; the devil dogged him at every step. And experience was central to his conversion: through the teachings of the minister John Gifford in Bedford, Bunyan *felt* the presence of the Gospels: "He did . . . lead me into his words, yea . . . he did open them unto me, make them shine before me, and cause them to dwell with me and comfort me over and over."[15]

Throughout his writings, Bunyan took the images of the Old and New Testaments and wove them into his life. In *Pilgrim's Progress*, for instance, Christian accepts the absolute claims of scripture over the world he inhabits. The Bible and the world are in conflict, and through Christian's journey and tribulations, the Word constantly provides sustenance and comfort with the promise of the heavenly life to come. Throughout, the imagery and landscape, like a Brueghel painting, come from the Bible. More than any other writer of the era, Bunyan brought the words and world of the Bible into ordinary language, making them real for ordinary people.

The personal relationship with the Bible in Puritan culture was also evident in the practice of personal Bible reading. By the 1640s, Bibles with space for annotations were widely affordable and circulated in great number alongside a large body of devotional literature and aids to reading scripture. During the English Civil War, the price of Bibles was driven down by the bulk purchase of volumes by the Parliamentary army, which ordered around nine thousand copies. Cheap and transportable Bibles were available everywhere and lined the pockets of eager printers.

One of the leading lights of Puritan Bible culture was John Owen (1616–1683). Among his many achievements as theologian and preacher, he wrote what remains to this day the longest commentary ever on a New Testament letter (Hebrews). Though Owen was fully engaged with the intellectual currents of his day and learned in ancient languages, he resolutely believed himself a faithful student of scripture. In good Puritan fashion, he spoke of himself as a "simple reader." The Bible exposes "a thousand wiles . . . which cannot be counted," leaving every man and woman naked before God.[16]

Puritans were by no means the cheerless moralists imagined by their contemporaries and described in subsequent histories. They saw a simple, deep beauty in the Bible. They were also open-minded. John Owen, for instance, was raised on the Geneva Bible but preached from the King James. Owen spoke of the Bible as "the books of the Old, and the New Testament, given by inspiration from God, containing all things necessary to bee beleeved and done, that God may be worshipped and our soules saved."[17]

Laywomen and laymen were often taught by their ministers both to read the Bible and to write, fostering a culture of biblical writing that flourished in the post-Reformation of the seventeenth and eighteenth centuries. This distinctive biblical culture of writing "in divinity" took the form of an extraordinary amount of notes. For example, the biblical devotions of Lady Grace Mildmay (1552–1620), a devout Calvinist, ran to over nine hundred pages.[18] The handwritten notes were entirely personal engagements with the Bible, not intended for publication. These were the people for whom the vernacular translations of the Bible were created.

This form of engagement with the Bible had its roots in Elizabethan culture, when manuals appeared to guide the lay faithful on how to read their Bibles. For most people at the time, the whole point of learning to read was to be able to read the Bible. Men and women were instructed to note passages of particular value and to divide their Bibles in such a way as to facilitate a yearly reading of the whole book. They were also encouraged to connect particular verses with moments in their lives and their spiritual state. They were reading the Bible in the tradition of Augustine in his *Confessions*. Manuscript books were kept and often passed from parents to children. This form of Bible writing was among the most common literary forms in the seventeenth century; those who kept such works ranged from the nobility to more modest artisans and their wives and daughters. Those that were printed often became bestsellers.

Through poetry, journals, and life writing, there were varied ways in which a growing part of society could express its engagement with the Bible in their daily lives. These personal writings were often closely connected with what was heard from the pulpit, read in devotional tracts, and learned in catechism instruction. Bible reading was a strong tonic in the encouragement of writing among those who had previously been absent from literary culture, including women. Yet the price was dear. Devotional writing about the self was a constant spiritual battle to find imperfect words to express God's perfect Word. Writing about themselves was not intended to be what we would recognize as autobiography. It was about the lives of their souls.

Grace Mildmay's meditation on her own mortality offers us a sense of the genre. She translates the words of the Bible with her own voice:

> Every day of this life passed, present, and to come, forsake us
>   from our youth unto age
> We waxe old and wither, and from our age in the grave we con-
>   sume and turne to our dust and wee become as though we
>   had never been
> And all that knewe us, shall never knowe us more, all our
>   thoughtes perish and our years are spent and come to an end
>   even as a tale is told.
> Yet although we appeare as nothing in the sight of the world,
>   and in the world be cleane forgotten, we are registered in the
>   book of lyfe in perpetuall memory before our God forever.[19]

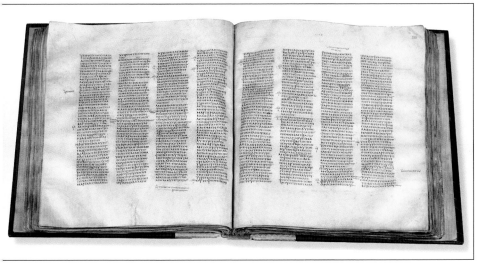

1. Codex Sinaiticus—Dating from the fourth or fifth century, the Codex Sinaiticus is one of the earliest complete Bibles. Written in Greek, its origins remain a mystery, but its importance is beyond doubt. Together with the Codex Vaticanus and Codex Alexandrinus, it is an invaluable witness to the oldest versions of the New Testament.

2. Syriac Gospels—A Syriac translation of the Gospels from the sixth century presents two figures who are not evangelists but embattled leaders of the early church, enclosed in a structure decorated with peacocks. The bishop and historian Eusebius (*left*) was a supporter of Emperor Constantine and a fierce opponent of heresy, while the Alexandrian monk Ammonius (*right*) was tortured to death after hitting the Roman governor with a stone.

3. Rossano Gospels—The physical form of the book increasingly reflected its sacredness. The purple vellum of the sixth-century Byzantine Rossano Gospels symbolized divine and human royalty. These Gospels are renowned for their images from the life of Christ, who is here portrayed entering Jerusalem.

4. Garima Gospels—Carbon dating has shown that the Garima Gospels from Ethiopia are among the earliest surviving illustrated Christian books. They are illustrations in a rich mixture of Byzantine, Syrian, and Ethiopian styles, reflected here in an image of Eusebius. Tradition holds that they were written in one day by Abba Garima, who Christianized the ancient Ethiopian kingdom of Aksum.

5. Moutier-Grandval Bible—The enormous Moutier-Grandval Bible is one of the treasures of the ninth century, the age of Charlemagne. It was prepared during the 840s at the monastery of St. Martin in Tours, previously led by the Englishman Alcuin, and was intended both to offer the best possible version of the Latin Bible and to reflect the glory of Charlemagne's empire. Here Moses receives the tablets of the Law.

6. Lindisfarne Gospels— Drawing on Arabic, Christian, and Celtic sources, scribes and artists in Britain and Ireland created the most sophisticated biblical illumination in the early Middle Ages. The eighth-century Lindisfarne Gospels, from Northumbria in England, open with a "carpet page," a full-page geometric pattern influenced by Eastern woven rugs, Celtic imagery, and Roman tiled floors.

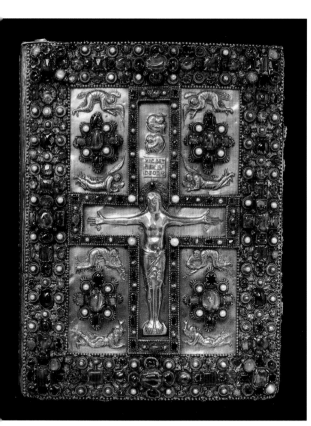

7. Lindau Gospels—One of the most magnificent examples of a jeweled cover belongs to the Lindau Gospels, from the late ninth century. Created for Emperor Charles the Bald, grandson of Charlemagne, the Gospels have binding that features the gold repoussé of Christ on a jeweled cross. The front cover of these Gospels for an emperor was likely created in France.

. Jahiris Byzantine Lectionary—Prepared for use in the Hagia Sophia in Constantinople around 1100, he Jaharis Gospel Lectionary dates from the height of the Byzantine Empire. Lectionaries were sacred books ontaining the arrangements of Gospel readings throughout the liturgical year of the Orthodox churches. hey were treated as sacred books, carried in the processional and read during worship.

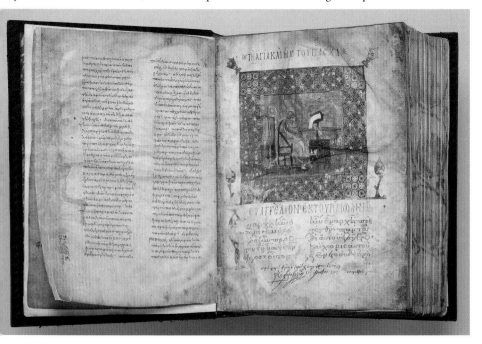

9. Chinese Syriac Gospel—The Bible traveled east along the Silk Road during the Middle Ages. There was long history of cultural contacts between China and the Eastern church. A Syriac Bible, dating from the Yuan dynasty (1279–1368), was recently found in a cave in China's Thousand Buddha Grottoes.

10. *Glossa Ordinaria*—A major achievement of the Western church was the *Glossa Ordinaria*, a collection of commentaries by the church fathers that accompanied the biblical text. The *Glossa* was the primary reference work for scholar in the medieval period, essential for all commentary on the Bible. Illuminated with two birds, this example of the *Glossa* accompanying the decretals (decrees of the church) is from thirteenth-century France.

11. Haghpat Gospels—The thirteenth-century Haghpat Gospels from Armenia open with the Eusebian canon tables widely found in African, Eastern, and Western biblical manuscripts. Framed by ornate architectural forms and decorated with images from nature, the canons provided a guide for the reader of the Gospels and were also an object of devotional contemplation.

2. Pantocrator, Chora Church—On entering the Chora Church in Istanbul, visitors encounter the mosaic of Christ as Pantocrator (ruler of the world). The inscription reads "Jesus Christ, the dwelling-place of the living." In his hand Christ holds a jeweled Gospel, representing the intimate bond between the Son of God and the book.

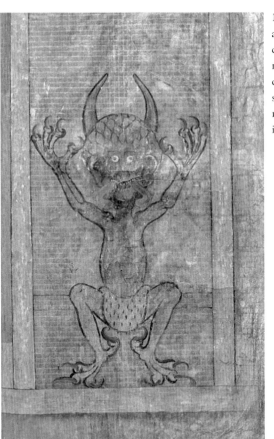

13. Gigas Bible—It's said that the devil had a hand in creating this Bible. The thirteenth-century Bohemian Latin Bible is the largest medieval codex, and legend holds that it was created in one night by a monk who sold his soul to the dark master. In return, the devil received a full-page portrait, rarely found in Bibles.

14. Armenian Gospel—The fourteenth-century Queen Mariun Gospel is named for a queen, who, following the fall of the Armenian kingdom, was first taken prisoner and then traveled across Asia as a pilgrim to Jerusalem, where she lived during a period of flourishing female spirituality in the city. This gorgeous depiction of the descent from the cross in the rich Armenian tradition was the work of the native artist Sargis Pidzak.

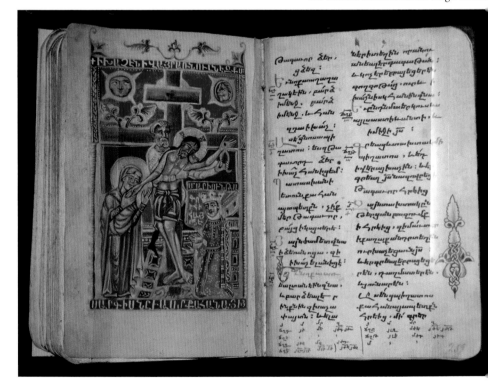

15. Book of hours—Books of hours contained scripture and the offices of the church in order that laypeople might engage in monastic prayer. Highly popular among the elite in the Middle Ages, they were exquisitely illustrated with biblical scenes and were treasured possessions. They represent a flourishing of lay biblical piety in the late Middle Ages. This sixteenth-century example from Bruges features the annunciation of Mary surrounded by gold and images of flowers and birds.

16. Bible moralisée—A creation of the thirteenth century were the Bibles moralisées, large parchment manuscripts that featured texts of the Bible with interpretive illustrations. The sins and evildoers of the Bible were often connected with contemporary events.

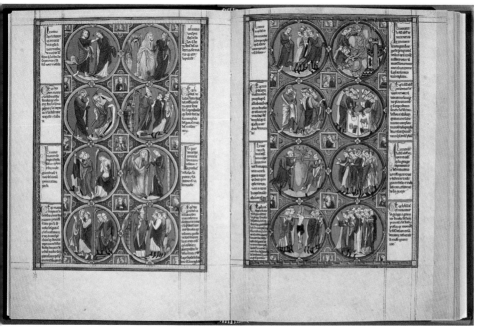

17. Gutenberg Bible—The printing revolution in the West began with a Latin Bible produced by Johannes Gutenberg in the 1450s. The ability to make one text available in thousands of copies helped the Bible spread across the Continent on a scale previously unknown. Within decades of Gutenberg's achievement, the Bible was the most widely printed book, a position it has never lost.

18. Moldovita Monastery, Romania—The painted walls of Moldovita Monastery in Romania are a masterpiece of late-medieval Byzantine art. As pilgrims approach the church, they encounter cycles of stories that bring them into the biblical world of the Orthodox faith, with its timeless liturgy.

19. Complutensian Polyglot—A vision of the union of piety and learning. The art of placing biblical texts and languages in parallel columns dates back to Origen in the third century, but with the advent of printing a new world dawned. The Complutensian Polyglot, printed in Spain from 1514 to 1517, sought to bring all the learning of the Renaissance world together in one six-volume Bible.

20. The Whore of Babylon—This 1524 colored woodcut in the Luther Bible of 1540 reflects the role of the Bible in religious polemic. The Whore of Babylon, from Revelation 17, here represents the papacy, following Luther's denunciation of the papal throne as the seat of the Antichrist.

21. Council of Trent—In the years of the Reformation, the Bible was not simply a Protestant matter. The Council of Trent, a Catholic reforming body, pictured here in an eighteenth-century print, took up the role of the Bible immediately. Scripture and the traditions of the church were declared the primary source of authority. The Latin Vulgate was affirmed as the Bible of the church.

22. Geneva—The Bible of Elizabethan England was prepared by a group of refugees in John Calvin's Geneva. Hugely popular for its language, explanatory notes, maps, and illustrations, the Geneva Bible was preached, read, and performed throughout the land. It provided the scriptural lines for the characters of Shakespeare, who understood which version of the Bible the people knew by heart.

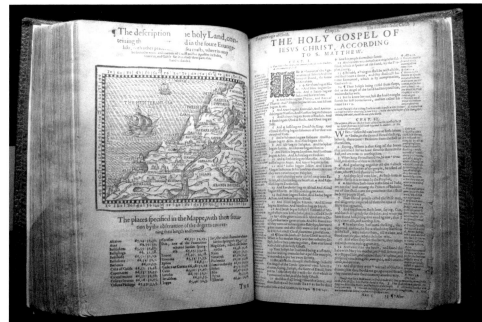

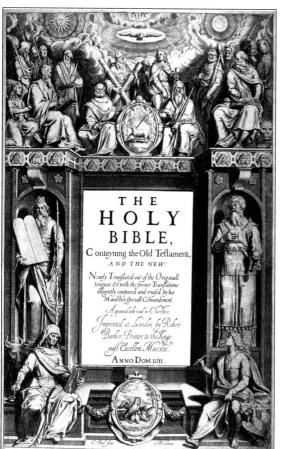

23. King James frontispiece—Although King James I/VI is not portrayed in the frontispiece of the 1611 translation he commissioned, the striking images tell us a great deal about the version that would become the most famous English-language Bible. In a vision of imposing architecture, the King James Bible begins with a representation of the Trinity, the apostles (including Paul), and prominent figures of Moses and Aaron, reflecting the authority of the English church in a religiously divided nation.

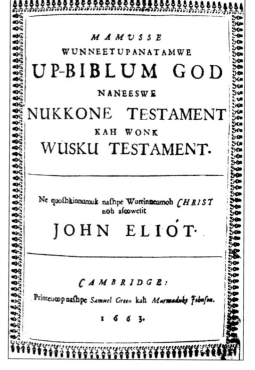

24. Eliot Bible—The 1663 Eliot Bible was the first Bible translated into an American Indigenous language. Prepared over fourteen years, the Bible is a written version of the spoken Algonquian language. It continued a long tradition of the Bible being translated into a language for which there was no written form.

THE DELUGE

25. Gustave Doré—The nineteenth century was the age of illustrated Bibles for mass audiences. Among the most prized images were the works of the French Catholic artist Gustave Doré. His drawings were found in many Protestant Bibles despite their often-erotic qualities, such as the muscular figures of the family struggling to escape the floodwaters.

26. Illustrated Bible, Nazareth— Beginning in the nineteenth century, illustrated Bibles and dictionaries were extremely popular among lay readers in the English-speaking world. Often sold by subscription, they contained vivid images of biblical stories together with interpretation of scripture and a wealth of historical and archaeological information. Pictured here is a drawing of the town of Nazareth from an 1893 Bible dictionary.

THE RIGHT REV. DR. CROWTHER.
MISSIONARY BISHOP OF THE NIGER REGION, AFRICA.

27. Bishop Samuel Crowther—A former slave who later became the first African bishop of the Anglican Church, Samuel Ajayi Crowther was a brilliant linguist. He was responsible for the enduring translation of the Bible into Yoruba, which became a model for other African versions.

28. Bible women—Indigenous female missionaries known as "Bible women" were active across Africa and Asia in the late nineteenth and twentieth centuries. They spoke local languages, had access to family homes, and reached locations far beyond the reach of Western missionaries. Frequently, they operated apart from the male clergy. This 1902 photograph shows the missionary Susan Emily Hartwell (*top left*) with Bible women in the Foochow Mission in China.

29. Korean board of translators—Many of the first translations of the Bible into non-European languages were begun by missionaries who, despite valiant efforts, frequently struggled to find the appropriate words and syntax in languages with no biblical vocabulary. The assistance of locals, who were often given little credit, was crucial. Nevertheless, these early efforts often laid the foundations for later, improved translations undertaken by native speakers. Shown here is the Korean Bible translation board of 1904.

30. General Feng—Known as the Christian General, Feng Yuxiang (1882–1948) was a Chinese warlord who became the Nationalist vice premier of the Republic of China. He was famous for his zeal in converting his soldiers to Christianity. Here they hold their Bibles to take an oath to follow Christian teachings.

1. Ethiopian priests—Two priests from the Ethiopian Orthodox Tewahedo Church read from the Gospels during worship in continuity with the ancient African faith that dates to the conversion of the Aksum empire in the fourth century. The Bible of the Ethiopian church has many more books than those of other Orthodox, Catholic, and Protestant traditions.

2. Football fan—The connection of the Bible with sports is worldwide. In Africa it is not uncommon to see Bibles at football (soccer) matches, with supporters calling out particular verses to aid their team. Here, at a semifinal match between Ghana and Cameroon in the 2017 Africa Cup of Nations, a Ghanaian supporter holds up a Bible. Unfortunately, Cameroon won, 2–0.

33. Kimbanguist church—The Kimbanguist movement, founded in the Belgian Congo in the 1920s, offered a powerful African and anticolonial interpretation of the Bible. Today the movement has over five million adherents worldwide. Here, a woman sings in a Kimbanguist church in Beni in the Democratic Republic of Congo.

34. Amity Printing Company—Today China is the largest producer of Bibles in the world. In Nanjing, Amity Printing currently produces about twelve million Bibles a year in hundreds of languages.

35. Annie Vallotton—Said to be the bestselling artist of all time, Annie Vallotton was a Swiss French Resistance fighter who went on to illustrate the Good News Bible, which has been printed over 225 million times. Her illustrations of the Bible are simple, without ethnicity, and deeply moving, such as this one of Job striking the ground.

36. Vallotton's Christ crucified—Using only eight lines, Annie Vallotton offered a powerful and unusual perspective on Christ's crucifixion to illustrate Luke 23.

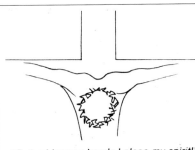

"Father! In your hands I place my spirit!"
(23.46)

The "book of lyfe," by engaging those previously excluded from intellectual pursuit, thus gave birth to a growing culture of lay expression on the page. In Milton's poetry, Bunyan's prose, the sermons of preachers, and the spiritual writings of women, Puritans cultivated and lived in an intense, sensuous, and emotional world of the Bible. Far from their stony reputation, their blood ran hot.

The transatlantic crossing offered many Puritans that which they believed was not possible at home in England: a pure church. Constantly professing their loyalty to the crown, they removed themselves from the oppressive rule of bishops and courts that imposed on them rituals they found abhorrent. While never separating from the church, the Puritans found in America the opportunity to read their Bible, preach, and worship according to their own ideals. It was the city on a hill, the New Jerusalem of Bunyan's vision, of the Gospel of Matthew (15:14). Not expecting a Bensalemite Bible to appear, they took with them the Geneva Bible with all its Calvinist notes. They were never to produce their own translation. Dependence on England for Bibles would remain the reality for American colonies for well over a century. In the middle of the seventeenth century, after the interregnum, the King James slowly displaced the Geneva at home and in the colonies. It soon became entrenched as the Bible of the settlers.

The challenge facing the Puritans in New England had been well known to Protestants since the 1520s. The Bible alone was authoritative, and each person could encounter and understand the Word of God. Maintaining the covenant, however, meant that interpretation of the Bible had to be strictly controlled. The Pilgrims of the Plymouth colony did not share the Puritans' call to covenant with God or their sense of mission. Yet they, too, struggled to reconcile free grace with order and the avoidance of multiple and conflicting interpretations.

The New England Puritan way was to insist on both individual salvation and the unified body of the covenantal community that was their colony, chosen by God. Grace was bestowed by God, but the covenant demanded the backbreaking work of holiness. The model was Israel, the literal story of the Old Testament brought to life in New England. It was a lived community of the Bible. Personal righteousness belonged to public submission to the will of God. For this end the New England Puritans saw themselves as uniquely suited. To ensure the purity of the biblical message, they had highly educated ministers preaching and teaching in the communities and overseeing the lives of the people. It was a heavily clerical faith. Literacy rates were remarkably high and a Bible, generally the King James, was to be found in most households. They saw themselves in the prophecies of the Hebrew Bible. They had fulfilled the Reformation. Although it was neither equivalent to the icons of Orthodox Eastern churches nor the liturgical book held aloft during the Catholic Mass, the Protestant Bible open on the Communion table, in the pulpit, or in the home remained a sacred object. For even the sternest Puritans, the physical Bible confirmed the presence of the Holy Spirit, transforming the profane into the holy.

Massachusetts Bay emerged as a new society based on biblical principles. America was a fertile but untamed land, and the Puritans' migration was an errand into the wilderness. The Word of God, as interpreted by God's ministers, was to govern every aspect of society. God spoke through the Bible and dissent was not allowed. The Bible was closely interwoven into the effort to mold a society across the New England colonies. The most famous expression of the "errand" was

John Winthrop's sermon aboard the *Arabella*, in which those making their way across the Atlantic were assured of their election by God to be a "modell of Christian charity."[20]

In words repeated in America across the following centuries, Winthrop (1588–1649) spoke of a "City upon a Hill" and a "model of Christian Charity." Such was God's covenant with his people, which they broke at their peril: "Soe that if wee shall deale falsely with our God in this worke wee have undertaken and soe cause him to withdrawe his present helpe from us, wee shall be made a story and a by-word through the world. . . . Wee [shall] be consumed out of the good land whether wee are goeing." The people of New England were a covenanted community in obedience to the Bible, which was "the articles of our Covenant with him."[21] Like the people of ancient Israel, they would be rewarded for faithfulness and punished for idolatry. To be a citizen in good standing was to be an active churchgoer.

Winthrop drew his biblical passages from both the Geneva and King James Bibles. The Geneva Bible so beloved by Puritans in the old country expressed most perfectly God's justification and the individual path to salvation. But in New England the Puritans faced a new task. No longer the opposition, they were charged with creating a new society over which they would govern. Personal redemption was inseparable from the sanctity of the community. The two could not be pulled apart, requiring strict discipline for individuals, families, and the community. As Winthrop put it, they would be "knitt together in this worke as one man . . . always having before our eyes our Commission and Community."[22]

The Puritan preachers expounded on the Bible, telling the people of their individual election and communal salvation. God's promise, the foundation of the covenant, would yield both rewards and punishments, and both were described in rich detail. In 1673, Urian Oakes (1631–1681), president of Harvard College, preached, "You have been as a city upon a hill (though in a remote and obscure wilderness) as a candle in the candlestick that gives light to the whole house. You have, to a considerable degree, enlightened the whole house (world I mean) as to the pattern of God's house." Lingering on the theme of election, he continued, "You have been through a handfull of people separated from the greatest part of the Christian world (as it is promised of Jacobs remnant that it should be in the midst of many people) . . . God hath privileged and honoured you greatly in this respect."[23] Those within the Massachusetts community who spoke against the covenant and stressed faith over any form of works were silenced and banished.

The foundation of Puritan reading was a distrust in human understanding and a reliance on the Bible as the expression of God's will.[24] The Bible was thus seen as an ongoing conversation between God and God's people, a view that resulted in a series of interpretive controversies. For instance, the controversial Anne Hutchinson (1591–1643), as she stood in court on charges of sedition, declared, "The Lord knows that I could not open scripture; he must by his prophetical office open it to me."[25] Hutchinson recognized that scripture was inspired, but she also claimed that her interpretation, which opposed the Puritan orthodoxy on election and grace, was from God. By declaring herself a true prophet, she simultaneously declared that the entire Puritan experiment was not only wrong but opposed to the spirit of God.

Though God was seen as the author and interpreter of scripture, the all-too-human New England Puritans produced a vast body of aids for reading the Bible. This created a certain tension: How much credit, they asked, was due to those people who diligently prepared materials for the better understanding of the Bible, and how much guidance was the direct guidance of the Holy Spirit? The question concerned how much each person was an active agent in the Christian life. Controversies arose as divisions of opinion emerged in the Antinomian Controversy, the Halfway Covenant, and the controversial figure of Roger Williams. The result was that Puritanism in New England was by no means uniform but rather included a wide range of interpretive possibilities. Against this reality, Puritans sought to preserve a sense of conformity.

The people were not passive in these interpretive multiplicities, and it would be a mistake to regard Puritans as anti-intellectual. They passionately believed in education and study. They took notes during sermons and discussed them in homes and gathering places. They read the Bible themselves, encountering the complexities of the texts and finding guidance from ministers and pastoral literature. They incorporated the Bible into letters and spiritual journals. And while many still relied on sermons for guidance, these were intended to go hand in hand with their own reading of the Bible. The preeminent minister John Cotton was bold in his encouragement of lay reading of the Bible: "If by reading these Epistles you might beleeve, and be humbled and comforted, and your joy might be full in reading, then truly you should not rest, till by reading you should find some measure of faith strengthened in you, to an holy feare of God."[26]

It was not merely their own personal relationship with God that the New England Puritans sought to develop in the wilderness of America. From its earliest days the Massachusetts Bay Colony was fired to bring Christianity to Indigenous peoples.[27] John Eliot arrived in

1651 and soon made his name as a missionary to Native Americans. Between 1647 and 1689 he founded an "Indian Library." During this time, he was aided by the Society for the Propagation of the Gospel in New England, which was established in 1649. Resources were sent across the Atlantic to enable Eliot to begin his missions to the Indigenous peoples. A Native American given the name John Printer also aided Eliot in his cause, and the result was the Eliot Indian Bible, the first complete Bible in the Americas. Over two thousand were printed, approximately one for every two Indigenous persons living in New England.

The Eliot Indian Bible was a translation into the Natick dialect of the Algonquin. Eliot's knowledge of the language was impressive, although he relied heavily on his Montaukett servant, Cockenoe, and a Narragansett man named Job Nesuton.[28] The translation was by no means exact but rather sought to convert place-names and stories of the Old and New Testaments into Algonquian. The Bible remained the primary Puritan tool for missionary work among the Indigenous until the American Revolution.[29]

The results were mixed. The Bible was made available in dialect so that many Indigenous people were able to read it. But the great conversions Eliot expected never materialized. Disappointment was expressed by one reader in the following marginal note: "I am forever a pitiful person in the world. I am not able to clearly read this, this book."[30] Eliot tried another approach. He wrote to a friend in England, John Baxter, to ask permission to translate one of his devotional works into Algonquian in order to encourage conversion. The effort was no more successful than the Bible.

The Eliot Bible was a casualty of the growing animosity that settlers had for the Indigenous communities, whether or not they seemed to have converted. Many of the books, Bibles, and tracts translated into local Native dialects were gathered up and destroyed by Native Americans and the English alike. When two Dutchmen came to John Eliot in 1679 and asked for an Indian Bible, Eliot told them that "in the late Indian War all the Bibles and Testaments were carried away and burned and destroyed."[31] He had not been able to save any. Only later printings would make the Eliot Bible available again.

Though firsthand accounts of conversion efforts, offered exclusively by European missionaries, often note little success, historians have more recently focused on the more nuanced interaction between colonists and Indigenous peoples, in which the latter often adopted the new faith slowly and on their own terms.[32] Through this cultural exchange of rituals, texts, and language, deeply personal and local religious cultures were gradually created. There was enormous diversity of meaning-making and beliefs among Native peoples that sometimes overlapped and sometimes did not.

There is no doubt, however, that there was an active culture of reading scripture among Native Americans, much of which has been documented by the historian Linford Fisher. Wunnanauhkomun, a Native American minister in Christiantown, Massachusetts, who died in 1676, "constantly read the Scriptures in his Family, and usually sang Part of a Psalm before Morning and Evening Prayer; and did very frequently and diligently instruct his Children and Household in the Things of God, and his Kingdom."[33] Abigail Sekitchahkomun, who made a "publick Profesion of Religion while she was but a young Maid," was taught to read when she was young and "made a good use of the Advantage, reading abundantly in the Bible, and such other good Books as our Indians have among them." Margaret Osooit, in reflecting on her sinfulness, "used to take her Bible, to which she was no stranger, and turn to and read such places in it as she apprehended to intimate what holiness was required to be in such as so drew nigh to God."[34]

One of our most illuminating sources for Indigenous reading of scripture comes from surviving copies of the Eliot Bible, which circulated in the Northeast. There are a considerable number of marginal notes left by readers that reflect close reading and decades of personal contact with the Bible. The names of some of the owners of the Bibles can be gleaned from information recorded. The last page in Malachi in one Bible reads, "In Boston the 17th of the 5th month, 1670," while on a page in the book of Romans the owner wrote: "I Mantooekit this is my hand." Across the title page of the New Testament in another Bible is written, "I Laben Hossuit own this Bible, June 11, 1747. Solomon Pinnon sold it to me. It cost four pounds."[35]

More than just personalization, however, the Bibles' marginalia demonstrate a range of interaction with the text: identification, alienation, and, at some points, expressions of sorrow, and mini-sermons of warning. On a blank page following the metrical psalms, an unknown Indigenous person wrote, "There is much of this word of God, this Bible, and the Lord Jesus Christ, and the one who believes in him shall find eternal life." In another Bible, the pages after the metrical psalms contain these words: "All this we believe in the name of Jesus Christ, who [is] our savior, whom you [possibly he] sent to me." Among the pages of the book of Isaiah is written, "Josiah Ned meditates about savior." The word "meditate," in fact, appears in the margin beside passages in Amos and several times in the Gospel according to Mark—indicating the adoption and use of another Christian practice with a long history.

At times those writing in the margins were speaking to future readers. The Bibles themselves thus became a veritable "cloud of witnesses"

(Heb. 12:1). The book of Acts contains the marginal exhortation "My brothers, remember love for God and all people, always." "Forever are happy all who believe, forever" comes a note in Exodus. "This truly is so among all of us. It was the truth in former times." Simon Papenau was particularly zealous with his Bible. In the book of Numbers he exhorted himself, "This is your book, you Papenau. Read it with c[on-centr]atrion. Your God [will] bless you." To his friends he wrote in Nahum, "I Simon Papen[au] say this to you, my f[ri]ends, all [of you] pray hard."[36]

There is plenty of evidence of Indigenous peoples taking up the Bible on their own terms and making the stories of the Israelites and first Christians their own. In the 1740s a group of Mohican converts were introduced to the Moravian leader Nikolaus Ludwig, Count von Zinzendorf (1700–1760). The Mohicans had traveled from New York to Pennsylvania, and on their arrival they were baptized. They adopted for themselves the names of the patriarchs Abraham, Isaac, and Jacob, and their wives were renamed Sarah, Rebecca, and Rachel. By claiming these Hebrew names, the Mohicans declared themselves "patriarchs of a new nation of believers." Another took the name of John to be a "Mohican John the Baptist paving the way for the emergence of a new Christian community."[37]

The Bible deeply influenced the first Native American literature published during the eighteenth century. Samson Occom (1723–1792) was a Mohegan minister who had converted to Christianity at the age of seventeen and became a missionary.[38] His *A Sermon Preached at the Execution of Moses Paul, an Indian* (1772) was the first printed book by a Native American. In his sermons Occom drew from the Bible to advocate holy living among Native Americans and to warn them against the dangers of alcohol. His love for his people is expressed throughout his writings, and he compared them to the Good Samaritan: "They are very Compassionate to one another, very Liberal among themselves, and also to Strangers, When there is Scarcity of Food amongst them, they will yet Divide what little they have. . . . This I take to be a Human Love or Being Neighbourly, according to our Text."[39]

Occom also employed the Bible to speak against colonial oppression of Indigenous peoples. Speaking against the greed of the colonialists, he cited the Great Commandment in the Gospel of Luke ("Thou shalt love the Lord thy God with all thy heart, and with all thy soul, and with all thy strength, and with all thy mind; and thy neighbour as thyself"; Luke 10:27, KJV) with biting words denouncing the absence of that love commanded by Christ, "These are a Covetous People, They Covet every thing that their Neighbours have, Yea This Sort of People I think are Monopolizers; don't you think so?"[40] He applied the same biblical text to his opposition to slavery: "I think I have made out by the Bible, that the poor Negroes are your Neighbours, and if you can prove it from the Bible that Negroes are not the Race of Adam, then you may keep them as Slaves, Otherwise you have no more right to keep them as slaves as they have to keep you as Slaves."[41]

During the eighteenth century, strong connections developed among German, British, and North American Protestant missionaries committed to taking the Bible to Indigenous communities. Most were Pietists and Evangelicals supported by the London-based Society for Promoting Christian Knowledge. German Pietists such as Henry Melchior Mühlenberg (1711–1787) arrived in Pennsylvania, while others accompanied Protestants who were expelled from Austria and arrived in Georgia in the 1730s. The missions in the Americas were part of a wider project in Europe and abroad to reach Jews, Catholics, and Muslims. Among the most remarkable were the Moravians, a radical group who by the end of the eighteenth century had established a global network of missions that spread to the Caribbean, America, Greenland, Africa, India, and Russia.

The hopes of this broad coalition of Pietists and Evangelicals extended to global conversion through scripture. There was great joy that a new age had dawned when the gospel would find fertile soil. This expectation laid on men and women the charge to spread scripture as quickly and as widely as possible. Some scholars now refer to these missionary groups as forming a "Protestant International."[42] Their inspiration was Christ's charge to "teach all nations" (Matt. 28:19, KJV), as action was required to be ready for Christ's imminent return. The Pietist leader Anton Wilhelm Böhme (1673–1722) looked to a new age in which God had roused Protestants "who do not only grieve" for the "Decay of True Piety, but do also contrive Means to repair it."[43] His views were shared by the Boston minister Cotton Mather, who believed that the Spirit would bring again the miraculous gifts of the apostolic age.

Apocalyptic hopes were a crucial part of the age of religious revivals and missions in the eighteenth century. The young Jonathan Edwards saw the growth of missions as a clear sign of God's working in history, which was now coming to a climax. He spoke of the "dawning, or at least a prelude, of that glorious work of God, so often foretold in Scripture, which in the progress and issue of it, shall renew the world of mankind."[44] From the Pietist missions in Europe and the Indies to the Moravians in Greenland and the Caribbean to the preaching among the Indigenous peoples of New England and abroad, all the signs of a new age were converging. The entire world would be saved. Edwards predicted that "many of the Negroes and Indians will be divines, and that excellent books will be published in Africa, in Ethiopia, in Turkey" to further the "light and knowledge" of God in the non-Christian world.[45]

The Pietists, Evangelicals, Moravians, and others were diverse in beliefs and practices but united in their belief that the sacred tool of their work was the Bible. It was their duty, they believed, to spread the Word through translation, printing, and education. In Halle, Germany, the Pietists built orphanages and public schools for all and a university. They also provided vocational training for young men and women. Over the course of the eighteenth century the Pietists in Germany produced more than two million Bibles. Missions were also served. Pietists in India produced a Tamil translation of both Testaments that was printed back in Halle along with translations of other religious literature. In India, native speakers were employed to teach the Bible to children and lead them through the catechism and prayers.

One of the key Pietist authors was Philipp Jakob Spener, whose *Spiritual Priesthood* and *Pia Desideria* inspired a fervent, deeply personal piety among their readers. In a work on the necessity of reading the Bible, Spener emphasized how scripture brings knowledge of Christ, God's Word: "He who has (who has gained the knowledge of the divine Word and has invested it according to his ability as a true servant), to him it will be given (by the power of further light of grace and wisdom to grasp more), and he will have the fullness (namely, more with which to serve others)."[46]

Responding to both the intellectual changes of the period and the rigid confessional fighting among Christian churches, Pietists believed that men and women should have access to the Bible, and their understanding of scripture formed a measure against which the male ordained clergy should be held. Naturally, the movement aroused the ire of the established clerical churches. Numerous women took to preaching and writing, such as Anna Catharina Scharschmidt, who declared that although she might be "a woman in regard to her gender," the "masculine power" of Christ spoke through her.[47] Scharschmidt believed herself a fully fledged member of the Pietist network of writers and preachers who sought the correct interpretation of the Bible.

The Pietist model of Bible-focused school was exported across Asia and the Americas, where it was widely adopted. Many Indigenous and enslaved people willingly came to the schools to learn to read and write and acquire knowledge of the Bible, which fostered their own religious expressions. However, the schools were closely involved with colonial interests, and although the desire to convert and educate was fervent, so too was the belief that a civilizing European influence was being brought to inferior peoples. The Pietist and Evangelical missions emphasized a culture of conversion that did not extend to social freedom or equality. Jonathan Edwards was a slaveholder, and the Moravians in the Caribbean adapted their Bible-based piety to convert, not liberate, enslaved peoples.

Several Indigenous Christians condemned this state of affairs. The Mohegan Samson Occom (1723–1792) from Connecticut, who became a Presbyterian cleric, drew a harsh comparison between Europeans and Indigenous peoples in his 1780 sermon on "Thou shalt love thy neighbour as thyself" (Matt. 22:39, KJV). The former were often "oppressors, over-reachers, Defrauders, Extortioners, with holders of corn." The "Savage Indians, as they are so often called, are very kind to one another, and they are kind to strangers." Slaveholders and those who supported slavery were "void of natural affection" and "not neighbors to anyone." Consequently, Occom concluded, they "are not lovers of God, they are no Christians, they are unbelievers, yea they are ungenteel and inhumane." He challenged the slaveholders to "prove it from the Bible that Negroes are not the Race of Adam."[48]

Evangelicals of the eighteenth century, a broad range of men and women committed to the good news of the gospel and individual conversion, were well aware of the challenges posed by scientific thought and deism, but their approach to scripture was shaped by their commitment to a spiritual reading. Although in various ways they were quite prepared to accept much of the learning of the age, the divine authorship of the Bible was never in doubt. Heart and mind were united in the Word.

Beyond their cooperative relationship in bringing the Bible to Indigenous communities, transatlantic Evangelicals were also deeply influenced by the Pietist tradition from German lands. Highly formative was the English translation of a devotional and instructional work by Anton Böhme (1673–1722) entitled *Plain Directions for Reading the Holy Scripture* (1708). The Bible was to be read with a spiritual, personal disposition in a disciplined manner in order to hear God's voice and be converted. Böhme spoke of bathing one's reading in prayer and meditation.[49] He guided his readers through a regimen of prayer, reading, and meditation.

Pietists and Evangelicals drew deeply from the tradition of Christian mysticism in their language of direct encounter with the divine through growth in holiness. Both sought to strip away all external things to reveal a purer heart inflamed by love. Repeatedly, the emphasis was on simplicity. "A true Simplicity of Heart," Böhme wrote, "that is, a sincere and unfeigned Desire to be made wise unto Salvation, through faith which is in Christ Jesus, is the best Preparation the reader can bring to so sacred a Study. If this be attested with unshaken Resolution, to order his whole Life and Conduct according to the Directions of the Word proposeth, he cannot fail of obtaining the End, for which the Scripture is given."[50]

This was the experience of many who heard the great preachers of the eighteenth century. Margaret Austin, who had been abused and abandoned by her husband, heard George Whitefield preach on the "Rich Man of the Gospel, how he had laid up treasures on earth but none in heaven." After the encounter, she recorded, "I was that person." She followed the preachers around in the conviction that she was to be found in the biblical stories and that they were personally addressing her. After one sermon, she wrote, "the Lord Saw fit to Let me See my Self."[51]

Scripture was internalized through various practices: reading alone and communally, preaching, singing, praying, and meditating. Often, Evangelicals brought the Bible into their daily lives through collections of individual verses they could immediately apply. In Scotland, Janet Jackson, following a revival meeting, wrote, "When I was kept from my nights rest, some sentences from Scriptures would come unto My Mind with sweetness; and I was frequently made to bless the Lord that such comforting and supporting words to people in trouble are in the Bible."[52] Ann Wylie in Glasgow recorded how, when she was dispirited, the words "Fear not, for thou shalt not be ashamed" came to mind. With her joy restored, she leaped up, kissed her Bible, and declared, "Now this is just all I want, I care for no more in the world."[53] The leader of the Methodist movement, Charles Wesley, although himself deeply learned, declared that he wished to read only one book. As Wesley believed, life was brief and the only purpose was to find one's way to heaven. The path was clear. "He hath written it down in a book. O give me that book! At any price give me the Book of God."[54]

In the face of the great intellectual and theological debates of the seventeenth and eighteenth centuries, the Pietists and Evangelicals restored an ancient tradition of spirituality. It was not mere nostalgia for a lost past. They took the tradition and infused new life, a passionate embodiment of the Christian life through the Bible. They lived in reading, prayer, and meditation, as had been done in the ancient and medieval worlds. They applied the Reformation principle of "scripture alone" and had learned much from the scientific and Enlightenment ideas. All were folded together into a spiritual world of encountering the Bible with sincere devotional intent.

In addition to the influence of Pietists and Evangelicals on the transatlantic spread of the Bible and particular practices of reading, perhaps nowhere was the missionary zeal more evident than in the work of the Moravians, who were among the most remarkable missionaries of the eighteenth century. The movement began in 1722 when a group of religious refugees from Moravia settled on the estate of the nobleman Nikolaus Ludwig, Count von Zinzendorf, and established the village of Herrnhut. The group, however, had roots in the late Middle Ages, dating back to Jan Hus (1369–1415) and his followers in Bohemia. Because of Zinzendorf's high-level connections to Danish royalty, the Moravians were able from an early stage to launch missions to Greenland and the Caribbean. By the 1740s, they were well established in Pennsylvania. They emphasized communal living, charity, and a deep, personal attachment to Jesus Christ.

Moravian missions were an expression of their reading of the Bible, which they approached through use of daily "watchwords." Beginning as a practice in 1722, watchwords were scriptural texts shared by households for common prayer and meditation. Initially transmitted orally, by 1731 they were printed in a book for the whole year, together with hymn verses. The Hebrew Bible texts were chosen by lot and then supplemented by a text from the New Testament.

The watchwords offered a running commentary on everyday events of life. Meditation and prayer on the texts were not so much a way of interpreting the Bible as a way of making sense of the world around them.[55] Each man and woman was asked to meditate on how God was speaking to them individually, and each day was to be lived under the guidance of Jesus.

In the Pennsylvania community, the watchwords were expounded at the end of the workday. The effects were powerful. One account from the community, from December 1743, notes, "We experienced rich grace today in the services, which dealt with the text and the watchword; blessed and ardent testimony was given to the blood from the wounds [of Christ]."[56] Typical of Moravian spirituality was the profound effect of Christ's presence in the heart. The aim of daily Bible readings was to move the inward person, as another account demonstrates: "Today, too, our watchword gave us unusual pleasure, as has generally been the case up to now. Our hearts have laid hold of the word of the Lord, which he gives us by his grace. There it shall remain. In all our brethren and sisters one encounters hearts filled with humble devotion because of all the grace which the Savior causes to flood through the congregation."[57]

The wide circulation of the Moravian watchwords in small books for devotion and worship was a central part of the transatlantic diffusion of the Bible in the eighteenth century. Editions flowed both ways across the Atlantic and were the lifeblood of the Moravian global community. People believed that through these watchwords Christ was speaking to them directly, showing them how to live in their particular circumstances.

As they had in England, women played a key role in the transatlantic Pietist, Moravian, and Evangelical biblical cultures of the seventeenth and eighteenth centuries. Despite being closed off from universities and other forms of education, they saw themselves as mentored by the Holy Spirit to mine the wisdom of the Bible, and they gave expression to their spiritual world in writing. Many Evangelical and Moravian women found in the Bible confirmation of their conversion experiences and the hard lives they lived, giving birth to and raising children and often enduring violence at the hands of men. The passion is expressed by Hannah Heaton in New England, whose conversion experience made her feel, she said, "as if I could not sleep while the heavens was fild with praises and singing. This night I was brought into the Lords prayr. Before I was afraid to say it but now it seemed sweet to call Godfather. Yeah my heart could say every word in it. Ah what sweet peace I felt while my mind was swallowed up in the scripture Matthew 5 from 9 to the 14."[58]

There were various ways in which women engaged with the Bible through communal reading, prayer, and instruction. Among Moravians, women gathered to meditate on the watchwords. While white women generally refrained from preaching, among African Americans the situation was somewhat different. After being told that it was not appropriate to preach, Jarena Lee (1783–1864) responded, "Did not Mary preach the risen Saviour, and is not the doctrine of the resurrection the very climax of Christianity—hangs not all our hope on this, as argued by St. Paul? Then did not Mary, a woman, preach the gospel? For she preached the resurrection of the crucified Son of God."[59] Another African American woman, Rebecca Protten (1718–1780), who had been converted by the Moravians, declared that "Christ had revealed his Word to her, and the visionary force of that inspiration was the only authority she needed."[60]

Like many before them, Pietist and Evangelical women found their lives in biblical figures. In addition to Mary Magdalene, they saw themselves in Jesus's mother Mary, Deborah, and the daughters of Philip. These biblical characters were not merely models of virtue but women who had suffered in ways contemporary readers could relate to directly. Such emotive and empathetic readings of the Bible filled the spiritual diaries of women.

Indeed, it was the experience of the Bible rather than theological ideas that seemed to be most compelling to many women. The guidance of the Holy Spirit opened the Bible to them. Sarah Pussimek, an Inuk woman living in Greenland who had been converted by Moravian missionaries, put it clearly: "The Holy Ghost was the best schoolmaster; if he rules in the heart, and makes the word of God to become true in one's soul, then a person can also speak without a book."[61]

Beyond communal prayer and the use of watchwords, the intensely biblical spirituality of the transatlantic world was also evident in an explosion of hymn writing and congregational singing. Brothers Charles and John Wesley, for instance, wrote a series of hymns entitled "Before Reading the Scriptures" that expressed the desire for a passionate encounter with the Word and were addressed to Father, Son, and Holy Spirit.

To the Father
Show us Thy Sire; for known to Thee
The Father's glories are:

The dread Paternal Majesty
Thou only canst declare.

To the Son
Open the Scriptures now; reveal
All which for us Thou art:
Talk with us, Lord, and let us feel
The Kindling in our Heart.

And to the Spirit,
Come Holy Spirit, (for mov'd by Thee,
Thy Prophets wrote and spoke;)
Unlock the Truth, Thyself the Key,
Unseal the Sacred Book.[62]

Charles Wesley's hymns on scripture were filled with the dramatic, personal encounters between the individual and Christ through the stories of the Bible. As the people sang, they found themselves in the story. When Jesus encountered the mute man, the singers declared, "Silent (alas Thou know'st how long) / My voice I cannot raise / . . . Thou shalt loose my Tongue." Through such songs, the words of the Bible become the words of one's own personal story. The Evangelical sense of transformation, for instance, remains best known from the hymn "Amazing Grace," by the repentant slave trader John Newton (1725–1807).

Amazing grace! (how sweet the sound)
That sav'd a wretch like me!
I once was lost, but now am found,
Was blind, but now I see.[63]

Newton organized his hymns according to various passages of scripture, emphasizing a deeply personal response to Christ and conversion of life. His hymns are rich in figural readings through which the biblical stories became immediate in the lives of those singing in church or at home. The language is emotional, physical, and touching, penetrating the heart by way of an immediate encounter with the divine. The Bible remains locked until opened by the Spirit. The sense of awe is palpable.

Another man who made the Bible sing during this period was Isaac Watts (1674–1748), who learned ancient and modern languages as a child and astonished many with his brilliance. It was assumed that a prestigious clerical education lay before him, but he remained a dissenter and stern Calvinist. A frail and sickly man, Watts's body contained a robust spirit that sought to infuse Christianity with song. In Calvinist tradition he set the psalms to music, but he desired to bring more of the New Testament into the sung worship of the people. He began to compose hymns that expressed the inner yearnings of the soul for Christ. In the preface to one of his hymn collections, he offered the following insight into his labors: "While we sing the praises of God in His church, we are employed in that part of worship which of all others is the nearest akin to heaven, and 'tis pity that this of all others should be performed the worst upon earth. That very action which should elevate us to the most delightful and divine sensations doth not only flat our devotion but too often awakens our regret and touches all the springs of uneasiness within us."[64]

Watts was controversial. Most Protestants sang psalms in worship, and there was considerable resistance to adopting hymns. In Philadelphia in 1789, the minister Adam Rankin addressed the general assembly of the Presbyterian church: "I have ridden horseback all the way from my home in Kentucky to ask this body to refuse the great and pernicious error of adopting the use of Isaac Watts' hymns in public worship in preference to the Psalms of David."[65]

Others were less scandalized by the prospect of new songs, and hymnals with Watts's over six hundred compositions sold quickly; soon even Presbyterians were singing. Perhaps no words can better capture the emotive, personal biblical world than the last two stanzas of one of Watts's most beloved hymns, "When I Survey the Wondrous Cross":

> *His dying Crimson,*
> *Like a Robe,*
> *Spreads o'er his Body on the Tree;*
> *Then I am dead to all the Globe,*
> *And all the Globe is dead to me.*
> *Were the whole Realm of Nature mine,*
> *That were a Present far too small;*
> *Love so amazing, so divine,*
> *Demands my Soul, my Life, my All.*

CHAPTER 9

THE AMERICAN BIBLE

Timothy Dwight (1752–1817) saw America's glory foretold in the book of Revelation. As a young student at Yale, he had become a fervent supporter of the American Revolution. For him, the prophet Elijah and the apostle Paul were models for the new republican leaders, men of their age born to transform the world. He tellingly referred to his grandfather, Jonathan Edwards, as the "second Paul." In 1785, while teaching at Yale, Dwight completed *The Conquest of Canaan*. This epic was inspired by John Milton's *Paradise Lost* and runs to an impressive three hundred pages. The allegorical poem captures his vision of a promised land for the new republic. Joshua, Moses's successor, guides the Israelites across the Jordan River:

> *Our sons, with prosperous course, shall stretch their sway,*
> *And claim an empire, spread from sea to sea*
> *In one great whole th' harmonious tribes combine,*
> *Trace Justice' path, to choose their chiefs divine;*

On Freedom's base erect the heavenly plan;
Teach laws to reign, and save the rights of man.[1]

After the bloodbath of the conquest, the Israelites triumph, as would the Americans over the British. It was God's will.

The Conquest of Canaan offered a vision of a godly, predestined people.[2] It was a view shared by the Founding Fathers, who framed their new nation in terms of the Bible, and by many regular Americans, who quickly took to the Bible.[3] In this new world, the Bible's promise of a personal relationship to God found a people who were characterized by their individualism and formed by the frontier. Without established churches and aristocracies, Americans embraced a distinctively individualistic Protestant approach, not only to the Bible, but to every aspect of life, from politics to commerce, as well as to the great moral issues of the age, above all slavery.[4] Catholics, constantly vilified in the American Protestant narrative as idolatrous, foreign, and subversive, likewise possessed a robust biblical culture that staked their claims against a Protestant vision of America. They rejected what had become a widespread assumption: that the Bible was a Protestant book.

The revivals that flourished throughout America in the eighteenth century placed the Bible at the center of a conversion-based spirituality that took its cue from John 3:3: "Except a man be born again, he cannot see the kingdom of God" (KJV).[5] It was a spirituality deeply based in human affections and individual piety, a powerful rejection of European-style state churches as well as Roman Catholicism. The revivalists believed that they lived the life of the Bible, whereas those who merely conformed to Christianity remained moribund. The Bible taught men and women that it was faith, not social status or hierarchical authority, that made them Christian. As Jonathan Edwards said of the disciples, they "attained to the knowledge of the truth; while the Scribes and Pharisees, men of vastly higher advantages, and greater knowledge and sagacity in other matters, remained in ignorance."[6] Essential was regeneration in Christ. Without it, hell awaited.

One of the most important voices of these revivals was the English preacher George Whitefield (1714–1770), who, during the Great Awakening of the 1730s and '40s, traveled up and down the Atlantic coast, preaching over 350 times.[7] A preacher of extraordinary drama, Whitefield could inhabit the characters of the Old and New Testaments. He described his devotion to the Bible as a "fire upon the altar of his soul."[8] He was deeply grieved by those of his day, including many men and women of the churches, for whom the Bible had become irrelevant.

The key verse in Whitefield's ministry was the King James rendering of John 3:7, "Ye must be born again." He recorded in his journal, "I began to read the Holy Scriptures upon my knees, laying aside all other books, and praying over, if possible every line and word."[9] When preaching on Genesis 5:24 ("And Enoch walked with God"), Whitefield offered one of his frequent exaltations of the Bible: "If we once get above our Bibles, and cease making the written word of God our sole rule both as to faith and practice, we shall soon lie open to all manner of delusion, and be in great danger of making shipwreck of faith and a good conscience."[10]

But white Protestants in early America did not hold a monopoly on Scripture—African Americans and Native Americans who converted to Christianity also claimed the Bible for themselves. The

African American Methodist minister John Marrant (1755–1791), one of the first Black preachers in America, learned Cherokee and chronicled his experiences among Indigenous peoples in *A Narrative of the Lord's Wonderful Dealings with John Marrant, A Black* (1785). During his missions, he preached wearing traditional Cherokee dress, which had been given him by a Cherokee chief. He returned to his family in Charleston with tomahawk and Bible in hand.

In his journal, Marrant describes a 1768 encounter with George Whitefield in Savannah, during which he was almost struck to the ground by Whitefield's preaching. During one of the sermons, Marrant reports, "just as Mr. Whitefield was naming his text, and looking round, and, as I thought, directly upon me, and pointing with his finger, he uttered these words, 'PREPARE TO MEET THY GOD, O ISRAEL.'"[11] Later, the Englishman prayed with Marrant and imparted a conviction of the personal illumination offered by the Bible. After this encounter, Marrant noted that he "now read the Scriptures very much."

This deeply individualistic approach to the Bible, in which devotion to scripture, rather than to any human authority, mattered most, would be a recurrent feature in American life. Nearly half a century after Whitefield traveled throughout the countryside, Thomas Campbell (1763–1854) and his son Alexander (1788–1866) left Scotland for America with a similar devotion to the Bible.[12] Both rejected the traditions of Presbyterianism as moribund and fixated on useless doctrinal debates. Thomas went first to America, settling in Pennsylvania after almost losing his life in a shipwreck off the coast of Scotland. Alexander studied for the ministry in Glasgow before departing from the Church of Scotland in disgust. When he arrived in America, he was surprised to find that his father had come to the same conclusions.

Both were convinced that the Bible, without doctrine, ought to be the Christian's only authority. Thomas declared, "Where the Scriptures speak, we speak. Where the Scriptures are silent, we are silent."[13]

Thomas was first drawn to the Baptists and rebaptized, but his views set him at odds with the church. He then decided to join with Barton Stone to form a loose collection of churches committed to the Bible alone and a return to earliest Christianity. The Restoration movement they launched proved integral to the Second Great Awakening, 1790–1840. Focused on the New Testament, members sought Christian unity based on biblical principles, stressing what is held in common and dispensing with divisive human doctrines. Both Thomas and Alexander were children of the Enlightenment and science. Thomas's desire for Christian unity was influenced by reading John Locke, while Alexander embraced science, for the study of both nature and the Bible.

The church, Alexander believed, had lost its way by embracing creeds and confessions and creating liturgies of worship. Salvation lay in recovering the simple faith taught by the Bible: "The union of Christians with the apostle's testimony is all-sufficient and alone sufficient to the conversion of the world."[14] The influence of the Campbells and Barton Stone was enormous. Thomas's journal, *The Millennial Harbinger*, was so popular that by the time of his death it had over two hundred thousand subscribers in a population of merely twenty-three million. An extensive chain of churches spread across the country, loosely connected but committed to a return to the New Testament and the simplicity of the first Christians. Soon the movement led to the formation of different churches, such as the Churches of Christ and the Disciples of Christ. Such convictions had a powerful effect on the spread of American Protestantism across the continent.

American Christianity in the early nineteenth century covered a vast expanse of religious territory, from Catholics and orthodox Presbyterians to Anglicans, Baptists, and Congregationalists.[15] The splintering of churches after American independence led to the formation of many sects, often following charismatic leaders. There was, however, some common ground across these divides. Prevalent was a powerful desire for the Bible and the belief that democracy had brought a new age of access to scripture. One result of this belief was that Bibles were produced in previously unimaginable numbers for homes and personal use.[16]

One of the most remarkable figures in this tidal wave of Bibles from the early nineteenth century was Mathew Carey (1760–1839), who produced both the Douay-Rheims Bible for Catholics and the King James for Protestants.[17] A veritable American Gutenberg, Carey would publish more than sixty editions of the KJV from 1801 through 1820. He did not, however, work alone. He was aided by the charismatic and gifted author Mason Locke Weems (1759–1825), who traveled through the country selling subscriptions for Carey's Bibles. Weems, who created the legend of the young George Washington and the cherry tree, was an enormously successful salesman. As he wrote on August 13, 1800, "Many things are not worth powder and shot. The Bible is a Galleon! Reserve your ammunition for that."[18]

Carey had a shrewd sense of his market. He printed Bibles in a variety of forms and sizes, some with extensive notes and illustrations, others on rough paper with text alone.[19] Carey was also able to embrace further advances in printing; with the creation of stereotype plates, pages of the Bible could be produced in vast quantities, making books available in vast numbers. With prices between three and twenty dollars, the Bible was available to Americans of both little and significant means. By virtue of his influence in spreading the Bible, Carey became a household name. Yet, like Gutenberg, he did not greatly profit financially, as getting the books to his customers was expensive and difficult. Weems relayed to his employer the difficulties of traveling on horseback on abominable roads with books, samples, and subscription lists to visit wealthy citizens, courthouses, and meetings, and then trying to make sure the books eventually arrived in the right place, undamaged, to be handled by local storekeepers, who often proved incompetent and thereby lost Carey and Weems business.[20]

Carey was not, however, the most influential force in Bible distribution in the nineteenth century, an honor reserved for the American Bible Society.[21] Founded in 1813 in New York in a building known as the Great Bible House, the society was quickly able to print over 360,000 Bibles in 1829 alone, a figure that would rise to over a million by 1860. The group's ambitious goal was a Bible in every house, though that proved beyond reach. Similar to Bible societies in Britain and across Europe, the society was not interested in theological interpretation or confessional differences but in making the book widely available, often in inexpensive formats. Above all, this meant the King James Bible, which by 1840 appeared in sixty editions.[22]

The American Bible Society initially followed a policy of providing editions that were not bound. This was the customary practice at the time and allowed readers to choose their own bindings, personalizing their Bibles. This changed at an early stage as the society became one of the first publishers to produce bound books, which were more economical. By 1818 readers could obtain bound Bibles with the text in two columns and no notes but section headings. At first, these Bibles were distributed by volunteer organizations, but by 1840 the society had a network of professional agents who sold the books door to door.

Because it produced them in such numbers, the society was able to outsell the competition, not least because they could make the Bibles so affordable, selling a New Testament for six cents and a complete Bible for forty-five.[23]

American publishers produced a steady stream of Douay-Rheims Bibles for Catholics, as well as Bibles in German, Greek, and Chippewa, but the mainstay was the King James.[24] In 1844 alone, nineteen publishers in six cities cumulatively produced twenty-seven editions of the KJV. From the time of the Puritans to the middle of the twentieth century, the King James dominated American culture, religious and secular. Sales dwarfed every other book, including the most popular novels of the nineteenth century: *Uncle Tom's Cabin*, *Little Women*, and *Ben-Hur*.

But toward the end of the century, there was an appetite for change and enormous excitement about the possibility of revision.[25] In 1881, a team of scholars in England produced a revised version of the KJV known as the English Revised Version, which was based on updated translations of the Hebrew and Greek and put into language more accessible for the people. In America, a committee worked with the English scholars to produce a version more suited to their market. Although there was transatlantic acrimony, both versions appeared in 1881 to great fanfare. In New York, the publishing firm Thomas Norton sold 250,000 copies of the Bible by 3 p.m. on the day of publication.

Highly effective marketing was at least partly responsible for its success. Every subscriber to the *Chicago Tribune* received a copy with their subscription, which amounted to almost 160,000 people in the Midwest. Stories about the English Revised Version ran repeatedly in the *New York Times*, including five editorials. The new Bible was hailed by all for its accurate translation and modern language, and in less than seven months, over three million copies were sold. The numbers, however, are deceptive. Despite all the attention and praise, the English Revised Version and its American counterpart failed to dislodge the traditional KJV, which continued to outsell the competition—fourfold. Devotion to the established translation ran deep.

While the mass production of Bibles in the first half of the nineteenth century largely took the form of accessible, unadorned versions affordable for all, technological and marketing innovations created possibilities for the production and distribution of more ornate versions. Illustrated Bibles were available from early in the century, but in the 1840s the publishing company Harper and Brothers in New York created a new phenomenon, a much-expanded and affordable illustrated Bible in fifty-four parts that readers could collect through subscription.[26] Each part sold for twenty-five cents, and the Bible could be collected in part or as a whole and bound according to the tastes and means of the public. For those with deeper pockets, color illustrations were available. Readers were treated to extensive notes, chronologies, and maps, as well as over 1,400 illustrations by Joseph Alexander Adams, who was influenced by the earlier work of John Gadsby Chapman, well known for his painting *Baptism of Pocahontas*, which hangs in the rotunda of the Capitol Building in Washington, DC.

When Harper and Brothers commissioned Adams and Chapman, they engaged two artists with a history of collaborating on projects for a wider public, and a particular aesthetic was imagined to make the Bible illustrations look more expensive. Copper was laid over woodcuts to give the illustrations the appearance of pen-and-ink drawings. In this process, Adams was greatly indebted to the new technology of electrotyping, which involved putting a wax mold into a copper solution with an electric charge. The result was a copper shell with metal type that offered much greater detail and quality than previously possible, and much faster. The result was regarded by the New York literary magazine the *Knickerbocker* "as not simply the most magnificent edition of the Word of God which has ever been offered to the American public, but as one of the most sumptuous productions of the typographic art, and as a most noteworthy monument of the high degree of perfection which the skill of artists and the enterprise of publishers have reached in this country."[27] Unlike the austere text-only Bibles distributed by the American Bible Society, the sacred book provided by Harper and Brothers invited readers to enter into the biblical world as imagined by Adams. As with medieval illustrated Bibles, the images took on a life of their own, in some ways rivaling the text and opening doors to changing perceptions.

Illustrated Bibles also afforded new possibilities for the portrayal of women. In contrast to traditional views of biblical women as temptresses (Eve, Delilah), the Harper and Brothers Bible placed a particular emphasis on maternal piety, reflecting the wider domestication of Christianity in Europe and America. Virtues such as wisdom, courage, and truth were often portrayed by female characters, emphasizing women's role in the cultivation of faith in the home. It was part of the Victorian sentimentalization of Christianity, the ideal of the home in which the family gathered to read from the Bible. This idea of the pious woman runs throughout the illustrations of the Harper Bible, with about eighty examples of women exemplifying Christian conduct, enhanced by the presence of children. For example, in Genesis 4 we find a joyous Eve elevating her infant, either Cain or Abel. She smiles maternally at her child, who in turn reaches out to her, the mother of all humanity.[28]

The idea that Christian women had a special role in the home was also present in stories from the American Tract Society (an evangelical organization founded in 1825), which repeatedly portrayed women, particularly mothers, as reading, writing, and praying with Bibles.[29] They were virtuous models for the unsaved. Often mothers were portrayed together with their children in a mutual bond of reading scripture. Sometimes roles were reversed, such as in the extensive literature for children. In *Little Mary*, for instance, the main character reads the Bible to her mother, in addition to visiting the poor and distributing tracts to women in her neighborhood. In another popular book, *Angel Lilly, or "Do You Love Jesus?,"* a young girl is rewarded for her saving influence with the ultimate gift: a Sunday school library built in her honor.

Children's Bibles were among the most influential religious publications of the nineteenth century.[30] Frequently illustrated, they often contained only a portion of the Bible. They employed a range of strategies, visual and written, to encourage children to learn the stories by heart. The surge of children's Bibles was a result of the great revivals of the eighteenth and nineteenth centuries, which emphasized conversion and a personal relationship with the Savior, Jesus Christ. Indeed, the Old Testament was presented to teach children that the stories of the Hebrew people, from Creation to the Exodus and the prophets, foretold the coming of Jesus. These Bibles, alongside a tidal wave of religious literature, had a profound influence on the piety of nineteenth-century Protestant children. They belonged, however, very much to the world of the white middle class. In the illustrations, the characters in both Testaments did not appear Middle Eastern but very European, linking the Bible to contemporary assumptions. Not surprisingly, children's Bibles had little place in African American churches.

With America awash in Bibles, it—unsurprising—featured prominently in the struggle over the most divisive moral issue of the young republic: slavery.[31] For African Americans, the Bible provided a call for freedom. For instance, in 1822, Denmark Vesey, a Charleston carpenter and freed slave deeply versed in the Bible, planned to lead a slave revolt. He described the plight of enslaved African Americans as akin to that of the Israelites in Egypt.[32] He found himself and his people in the Bible, in a story of liberation and salvation. He regarded Moses's words as a divine injunction: "He that stealeth a man, and selleth him, or if he be found in his hand, he shall surely be put to death" (Exod. 21:16, KJV).

The plans for the revolt were revealed, and Vesey along with four others was hanged, followed later by nearly thirty executions. The Charleston elite, who regarded their enslaved as little more than beasts of burden, were utterly persuaded that the Bible defended slavery.[33] In the aftermath of the foiled rebellion, the founder of the Charleston Bible Society, Charles Cotesworth Pinckney, wrote on behalf of the society to South Carolina governor Thomas Bennett with a request for a day of public thanksgiving that the revolt had been prevented. Pinckney, one of the original signers of the US Constitution, gave thanks for the protection of divine Providence and included in his letter numerous quotations from scripture in support of slavery.[34]

On this point, Pinckney had much from which to choose. In Genesis, there is the story of Ham, who, having exposed the nakedness of his father, Noah, is told that his son Canaan's descendants will be slaves of his brothers Japheth and Shem. In European and American interpretations of the story, Africans were held as standing under the curse of Ham.[35] Further on in Genesis, God is understood as sanctioning Abraham's enslaving of Canaanites. In Deuteronomy, God approves the enslavement of Israel's defeated enemies. The New Testament is equally problematic, not least because Jesus says nothing about slavery. The apostle Paul admonishes slaves to obey their masters, and the relationship between enslaved and their masters is never questioned. And in the Epistle of 1 Timothy, the Bible reports that a slave converting to the faith does not need to be emancipated by a Christian master.

Frederick Douglass put the case bluntly during the Civil War: "Nobody at the North, we think, would defend Slavery, even from the Bible, but for this color distinction. Color makes all the difference in the application of our American Christianity. . . . The same book which is full of the Gospel of Liberty to one race, is crowded with arguments in justification of the slavery of another."[36]

Opponents of slavery, particularly those in the North, often took a compromised position on the question of the Bible and the institution. Prominent men such as Moses Stuart of Andover Seminary and Charles Hodge of Princeton, along with others, regularly defended the right of enslaved peoples to be treated with dignity and denounced the numerous abuses by slaveowners. They stopped short, however, of calling slavery itself an evil condemned by the Bible. In this respect, they ceded the Bible to the proslavery advocates. This kind of equivocation is well represented by the Episcopal bishop of Vermont John Henry Hopkins, who in 1864 declared his opposition to slavery but then stood back, claiming that he needed to be circumspect. On the one hand, he declared that all "should be settled by the Bible," but on the other, he admitted that it did not condemn slavery.[37]

Much effort was exerted in trying to rescue the Bible in the debate over slavery. One common approach was to explain away the offending passages by claiming that they were historically contingent, reflecting the situation of ancient Israel and Mediterranean antiquity rather than the Word of God. Another was to claim that the abolition of slavery, while not directly in scripture, was a moral consequence of Christ's teaching. The Black antislavery advocate David Walker, in his 1829 *Appeal to the Coloured Citizens of the World*, turned the Bible on those who held that the curse of Cain was Blackness:

> Did they receive it from the Bible? I have searched the Bible as well as they, if I am not as well learned as they are, and have never seen a verse which testifies whether we are the seed of Cain or of Abel. Yet those men tell us that we are the seed of Cain, and that God put a dark stain upon us, that we might be known as their slaves!!! Now, I ask those avaricious and ignorant wretches, who act more like the seed of Cain, by murdering the whites or the Blacks How many vessel loads of human beings, have the Blacks thrown into the seas?[38]

A more radical solution favored by some was to set aside the Bible completely. The abolitionist and social reformer William Lloyd Garrison (1805–1879) echoed the beliefs of others that the matter simply could not be settled by the Bible. In their view, many contemporary issues, such as war and women's suffrage, were moral questions for which scripture had little to contribute. Garrison was mortified by the use of the Bible by prominent figures to defend political actions such as the Mexican War of 1846–1848, in which President Zachary Taylor had invoked scripture to justify "giving the Mexicans hell!"[39]

Passages encouraging war in the Bible, Garrison wrote, were not gospel. As for slavery, it was a moral blasphemy for which the Bible held some responsibility: "The God who, in America, is declared to sanction the impious system of slavery—the annihilation of the marriage institution and the sacrifice of all human rights—is my idea of the devil."[40] His supporter Henry C. Wright was even more inflammatory with a resolution condemning the Bible: "Resolved, That if the Bible sanctions slavery, and is thus opposed to the self-evident truth that 'all men are created equal, and have an inalienable right to liberty,' the Bible is a self-evident falsehood, and ought to be, and ere long be, regarded as the enemy of Nature and Nature's God, and the progress of the human race in liberty, justice and good."[41]

From the earliest days, the Bible shaped and was shaped by the African American experience in America. Among educated and illiterate, enslaved and free, the Bible was central to the narrative of bondage and liberation. James W. C. Pennington, the first Black student at Yale, attending the divinity school, demonstrated his deep knowledge of the Bible in his memoir *Fugitive Blacksmith* (1849). On the title page, he quoted the prophet Isaiah: "Let mine outcasts dwell with thee, Moab; be thou a covert to them from the face of the spoiler" (16:4, KJV). In a passage describing his escape from enslavement, Pennington wrote, "My reflections upon the events of that day, and upon the close of it, since I became acquainted with the Bible, have frequently brought to my mind that beautiful passage in the Book of Job, 'He holdeth back the face of His throne, and spreadeth a cloud before it' [Job 26:9]."[42] Despite his undeniable qualification, Pennington was not permitted to take a degree, an injustice rectified posthumously by Yale in 2023.

There was no one Black experience of the Bible and no single way of interpreting the book. Like the rest of America, African Americans read the Bible in strikingly different ways. Although many free Black people eagerly bought Bibles and sent them to enslaved men and women in the South, Frederick Douglass offered a different perspective based on his own experiences. For him, the Bible was the highest authority of slavery, the basis of slaveholding religion, and the justification for oppression and violence. It was the sacred basis for the Confederacy. He drew a distinction, however, between the Christianity of the South and the Christianity of Christ, and in his 1855 biography, for instance, Douglass recalled the role of the Bible in enabling him to read: "The frequent hearing of my mistress reading the bible—for she often read aloud when her husband was absent—soon awakened my curiosity in respect to this mystery of reading, and roused in me the desire to learn. . . . Indeed, she exultingly told him [her husband] of the aptness of her pupil, of her intention to persevere in teaching me, and of the duty she felt to teach me, at least to read the bible."[43] Later, Douglass likewise used the Bible to teach other slaves to read.

The Bible enabled Black men and women not only to read and write, which was itself an act of defiance, but also to find expressions of resistance within its pages. A common thread in the rich and varied experiences of African Americans involved the ways the Bible enabled them to express their experiences of enslavement and the struggle for freedom. Like Denmark Vesey, many African Americans identified with the ancient Israelites and the early Christians in facing oppression. Many had been converted by the Evangelical movements of the late eighteenth and early nineteenth centuries and were inspired by a powerful sense that Jesus was near.

In addition to reading the Bible, many African Americans related to it through song. Spirituals chronicled the biblical world of enslavement and freedom and became one of the largest and most significant parts of American folk music. The term "spiritual" itself derives from the King James translation of Ephesians 5:19: "Speaking to yourselves in psalms and hymns and spiritual songs, singing and making melody in your heart to the Lord." Originating in outdoor meetings often suppressed by slaveowners, the singing and dancing reflected a growing attachment to the figures of Daniel and Moses as embodying the African American experience. Many involve close identification with the suffering of Jesus.[44] The spirituals range from the sorrowful "Sometimes I Feel Like a Motherless Child" and "Nobody Knows the Trouble I've Seen" to those of assurance, such as "There is a Balm in Gilead":

> *Sometimes I feel discouraged*
> *and think my work's in vain,*
> *but then the Holy Spirit*
> *revives my soul again.*[45]

Spirituals have been spoken of as the voice of the "unwritten self," in which enslaved people, denied the opportunity to record their experiences in any written form, chronicled their biblical lives. Spirituals also expressed the biblical story of resistance, freedom, and wisdom. As W. E. B. Du Bois wrote in *The Souls of Black Folk* (1903), "Through all the sorrow of the Sorrow Songs there breathes a hope—a faith in the ultimate justice of things. The minor cadences of despair change often to triumph and calm confidence. Sometimes it is faith in life, sometimes a faith in death, sometimes assurance of boundless justice in some fair world beyond. But whichever it is, the meaning is always clear: that sometimes, somewhere, men will judge men by their souls and not by their skins. Is such a hope justified? Do the Sorrow Songs sing true?"[46]

The personal attachment to the Bible that flourished in the nineteenth century was often accompanied by spiritual visions and experiences that combined the scriptural and the personal. For many Black Christians, there was a powerful belief that divine revelation was not limited to the canonical scriptures. Consider, for instance, the story of Rebecca Cox Jackson (1795–1871), a free Black seamstress who wrote an autobiography called *Gifts of Power: The Writings of Rebecca Cox Jackson, Black Visionary, Shaker Eldress*.[47] She had a religious awakening during a thunderstorm at the age of thirty that led her to divorce her husband because he refused to teach her to read, declaring that "[If God] taught the first man to read, he can you." Jackson recalled, "I . . . prayed earnestly to Almighty God that if it was consistent with his holy will, to teach me to read, and when I found I was reading, I was frightened."[48] Miraculously, she began to read the Bible for herself.

She believed that her literacy was a gift from God, as was the power to hear his voice, prophesy, and heal. She later began writing her autobiography and continued writing it for over thirty years, describing the resistance and racism that she faced in her life, though the work was not discovered until 1981. Together with Rebecca Perrot, Jackson founded a Shaker community of women in Philadelphia, and went on preaching tours. She was absolutely clear about what God had enabled her to do:

For all these years I have been under the tuition of invisible Spirits, who communicate to me from day to day the will of

God concerning me and concerning various events that have taken place and those transpiring now and those that yet will occur in the earth. But this communication to me has been in words as clear and distinct as though a person was conversing with me. By this means I have been able to tell people's thoughts, and to tell them words they have spoken many miles distant from me. And also to tell them things they would do a year beforehand, when they had no thought of ever doing such things. I have had a gift: when the day was clear, to tell when it was agoing to thunder.[49]

Visions and the access to spiritual powers that enabled Jackson to preach the Bible and instruct others provided her with an authority denied to her as Black, female, and uneducated. Her evident gifts led to an enthusiastic following that she was able to address both in person and through her autobiography.

The gift of reading as the door to the spiritual life was also experienced by Henry McNeal Turner (1834–1915), the first Black chaplain in the US Army and who later became a bishop of the African Methodist Episcopal (AME) Church. After the Civil War, he founded many AME congregations in the South and was the first to ordain a woman as a deacon. Turner preached that God was Black:

We have as much right biblically and otherwise to believe that God is a Negro, as you buckra or white people have to believe that God is a fine looking, symmetrical and ornamented white man. For the bulk of you and all the fool Negroes of the country believe that God is white-skinned, blue eyed, straight-haired, projected nosed, compressed lipped and finely robed white gentleman, sitting upon a throne somewhere in the heavens. Every race of people who have attempted to describe their God by words, or by paintings, or by carvings, or any other form or figure, have conveyed the idea that the God who made them and shaped their destinies was symbolized in themselves, and why should not the Negros believe that he resembles God.[50]

Growing up, Turner was deeply troubled by not being able to read. Like Jackson and Douglass, the Bible transformed his life through literacy. Having prayed to God to understand what he could not read, he fell asleep, and, as he later wrote of the visits of God's messenger, "an angelic personage would appear with open book in hand and teach me how to pronounce every word that I failed in pronouncing while awake." That "angelic teacher . . . carried me through the old Websters spelling book and thus enabled me to read the Bible and hymnbook."[51] By the age of fifteen, Turner had read the Bible five times through and committed most of it to memory.

Harriet Tubman (ca. 1822–1913), the famed abolitionist who helped more than seventy people escape from slavery through the Underground Railroad, also had deeply personal religious experiences.[52] Badly mistreated by her slave masters, she received a wound to the head that would trouble her for the rest of her life. Soon afterward, she began to experience dreams that led to a powerful conversion experience. She became famous for expressing how God spoke to her soul, sharing her private revelations with others. Like many others, she looked to the stories of the deliverance of the Israelites in Exodus in speaking of the conditions of African Americans. Indeed, for her work and prophetic words she was called "Moses," the liberator of her people.[53]

For Jackson, Turner, and Tubman, it might seem that personal revelation put the Bible in the background of their Christianity, but none of them saw it that way. Belief that God spoke to them directly was always aligned with scripture. They saw themselves standing in the tradition of the prophets of Israel, continuing to bring God's salvation to the people.

The role of education for African Americans mirrored the wider nation. In nineteenth-century Protestant America, the Bible was firmly fixed in schools.[54] Fired by fierce anti-Catholicism, American educators placed the King James at the heart of the curriculum: the Bible was the foundation of civil society and good government. For the educator, politician, and abolitionist Horace Mann (1796–1859), the Bible spoke for itself as the source of moral and spiritual instruction. It was not to be taught with any particular confessional slant. The public school, he wrote, "welcomes the Bible, and therefore welcomes all the doctrines which the Bible really contains; . . . it listens to these doctrines so reverently, that . . . it will not suffer any rash mortal to thrust in his interpolations of their message, or overlay the text with any of the 'many inventions' which the heart of man has sought out."[55] For Mann, it "humanized" and "redeemed" children, especially those from homes without the Bible.

There was, however, a darker side to the promotion of the Protestant Bible in public schools: it served to define a particular conception of America and racial relations.[56] For many Americans, the greatest danger in the first half of the nineteenth century came from the arrival of Catholic immigrants and their "foreign" religion, antithetical to American ideals of freedom and republicanism. Textbooks were full of the evil deeds of Catholics throughout history.

Agitation between Protestants and Catholics led to violence in Philadelphia in May 1844, when riots broke out in response to Archbishop Francis Patrick Kenrick's demand that Bible reading be stopped in public schools.[57] Protestants, often of Irish background, attacked Irish Catholics. In the wake of the "Bible Riots," twenty people lay dead.[58] Six years earlier, Pennsylvania had mandated that the King James, with its pure language, be read in schools for moral instruction. In response to Kenrick's intervention, it was decided that the Douay-Rheims could be substituted for Catholics as long as it had no notes for instruction.[59] The Protestant authorities also faced objections from the Jewish community, but these were flatly ignored. The place of the Bible in the confessional wars over public education in the United States was crucial to the defense of a distinctly Protestant view of America: that the Bible alone provided the means by which the country integrated different traditions.

Virtually all Protestants in nineteenth-century America regarded Catholicism as an unbiblical religion and therefore an insidious enemy. Partisan polemic, however, blinds us to the truth that throughout the century, the Catholic Bible in the form of the revised Douay-Rheims continued to be published in great quantities, even if it did not match the scale of the King James.[60] Kenrick himself attempted to provide a contemporary Catholic translation that revised the Douay-Rheims and could challenge the dominance of the King James. His translation was impressive, taking note of scholarly developments in the field, but he died before completing it.[61]

In issues of doctrine and in worship, the Latin Vulgate remained the Bible of the Catholic Church, but private ownership of Bibles in Catholic households followed the rapid expansion among Protestants.

The Catholic hierarchy worked hard to disseminate Catholic Bibles.[62] Once more, education was key, and in 1884 the Third Plenary Council instructed all parish churches to establish schools for youth. As there was for Protestants, there was a broad range of Catholic tracts and devotional literature that engaged with scripture. Certainly, the church retained its authority in interpreting the Bible to guard against errant individual readings, and Catholics did not embrace what they saw as the Babel-like confusion of Protestant readings of scripture. Nor were they prepared to cede the stage to Protestants when it came to matters of the Bible.

One of the most powerful voices in the nineteenth century was Archbishop James Gibbons (1834–1921) in Baltimore, whose *The Faith of Our Fathers: Being a Plain Exposition and Vindication of the Church Founded by Our Lord Jesus Christ* went through 111 printings between its appearance in 1876 and 1980. It was the most popular book intended to instruct converts to the Catholic Church and is still thought of as one of the best introductions to the faith. Gibbons was a gifted and popular preacher, well known for his ability to apply Catholic doctrine to ordinary life.

Gibbons rejected the Protestant claim for sola scriptura, and in *Faith of Our Fathers* he made the case for the Bible in Catholicism. Throughout the book, he offered a hefty dose of scriptural quotations, all with the admonition that they cannot be heard and believed outside the Catholic Church. Gibbons fired a torpedo at the Protestant ship:

> With all due respect for my dissenting brethren, truth compels me to say that this unity of doctrine and government is not

to be found in the Protestant sects, taken collectively or separately. That the various Protestant denominations differ from one another not only in minor details, but in most essential principles of faith, is evident to every one conversant with the doctrines of the different Creeds. The multiplicity of sects in this country, with their mutual recriminations, is the scandal of Christianity, the greatest obstacle to the conversion of the heathen. Not only does sect differ from sect, but each particular denomination is divided into two or more independent or conflicting branches.[63]

Against the fragmentation of Protestantism, the Catholic Church offered unity. Gibbons leavened each part of his work with plenty of scripture and invoked the apostle Paul, so passionately claimed by Protestants, as the voice of Catholic unity:

St. Paul ranks schism and heresy with the crimes of murder and idolatry, and he declares that the authors of sects shall not possess the Kingdom of God. He also addresses a letter to the Ephesians from his prison in Rome, and if the words of the Apostle should always command our homage, with how much reverence are they to be received when he writes in chains from the Imperial City! In this Epistle he insists upon unity of faith in the following emphatic language: "Be careful to keep the unity of the Spirit in the bond of peace; one body and one Spirit, as you are called in one hope of your calling; one Lord, one faith, one baptism, one God and Father of all, who is above all, and through all, and in us all."[64]

Gibbons's command of the scriptures is evident throughout *Faith of Our Fathers*, and through use of the Catholic Douay-Rheims Bible, he demonstrated that Catholic scriptures could match the beloved King James stride for stride.

Beyond its pride of place in the disagreement between Protestants and Catholics, the Bible's intense hold on America can be seen in its frequent appearance in the literature of the time. Consider, for instance, Harriet Beecher Stowe's *Uncle Tom's Cabin*, which first appeared in serialized form in an abolitionist newspaper before being printed as a novel in 1851.[65] By the end of the century it was, after the Bible, the most popular book in America. The two were intimately connected, and several physical Bibles are central to the story. Unlike the Bibles of white characters, with their elaborate annotations, Tom's Bible is a New Testament that only he has marked. He keeps the Testament in his pocket, symbolizing his inner spirituality and its place as a living book. His interaction with the Bible throughout the novel is employed by Stowe to reflect his humanity and personhood, which slavery attempted to destroy. Stowe describes, for example, how he labors word by word through Christ's teaching in the Gospel of John.

The Bible also appears in one of the most striking moments in a nineteenth-century American novel, the stern Calvinist sermon delivered by Father Mapple toward the beginning of Herman Melville's *Moby-Dick* (1851).[66] Speaking from a pulpit shaped like the bow of a ship, preacher and readers were set upon the sea: "A brief pause ensued; the preacher slowly turned over the leaves of the Bible, and at last, folding his hand down upon the proper page, said: 'Beloved shipmates, clinch the last verse of the first chapter of Jonah—"And God had prepared a great fish to swallow up Jonah."'" The people were ready: "There was a low rumbling of heavy sea-boots among the benches, and a still slighter shuffling of women's shoes, and all was quiet again, and every eye on the preacher."[67] Taking the people through the story of Jonah, Father Mapple led them to his conclusion:

> He [Jonah] feels that his dreadful punishment is just. He leaves all his deliverance to God, contenting himself with this, that spite of all his pains and pangs, he will still look towards His holy temple. And here, shipmates, is true and faithful repentance; not clamorous for pardon, but grateful for punishment. And how pleasing to God was this conduct in Jonah, is shown in the eventual deliverance of him from the sea and the whale. Shipmates, I do not place Jonah before you to be copied for his sin but I do place him before you as a model for repentance. Sin not; but if you do, take heed to repent of it like Jonah.[68]

Ishmael, the principal character, entered the chapel whose very architecture anticipated many of the novel's main themes; he also left a memorable description of the pulpit in the Seaman's Chapel as an encomium to the significance of what was preached: "Its paneled front was in the likeness of a ship's bluff bows, and the Holy Bible rested on a projecting piece of scroll work.... Yes, the world's a ship on its passage out, and not a voyage complete; and the pulpit is its prow."[69]

Melville famously wrote to Nathaniel Hawthorne, "I have written a wicked book, and feel spotless as the lamb."[70] Many of his contemporaries agreed that *Moby-Dick*, which was much criticized in its day, was an attack on the Bible and the Christian faith.[71] Yet Melville had a much more intimate relationship to the Bible, in many respects creating a novel that was modeled on the Old and New Testaments. He was deeply interested in how the Bible's commandments, contradictions, and teachings related to modern America. The form of *Moby-Dick* reflects the multiple voices of scripture gathered in one book. The narrative moves freely between the first and third person so that it is not always clear who is speaking. The reader struggles to know with certainty how much trust to invest in any one character.

Melville mixed the sacred and profane in the story to achieve what he hoped would be an improvement on the Old and New Testaments. Nevertheless, by fictionalizing the Bible in an age when the biblical reading of most American Christians focused on repeating the words of the text, he created a work that many saw as blasphemous.

Another novel struck a more melodious chord. Lewis Wallace (1827–1905), who in addition to being a lawyer served as a Union general in the Civil War and later as governor of the New Mexico Territory, engaged in a conversation on a train with the noted atheist Robert G. Ingersoll (1833–1899) in 1876 about the truth of Christianity, which led Ingersoll to read the Bible and later convert to Christianity.[72] The encounter inspired Wallace to rewrite his short story into the novel *Ben-Hur: A Tale of the Christ*, which was published by Harper and Brothers in 1880. It tells of a young Jew from a good family who ends up following Jesus. Much of the dialogue comes out of the King James Bible. The novel was an enormous success, feeding an American Protestant public eager for biblical fiction. Its notoriety was heightened when President James A. Garfield told of how he stayed up all night to read it. He wrote an appreciative letter to Wallace that was printed in future editions. Capitalizing on American fascination with the Holy Land, Harper and Brothers produced an illustrated version with pictures of Palestine, Rome, and Egypt and notes on architecture, ancient cultures, and maps.[73]

Another book mirrored the Bible and its rapid dissemination in American culture: the Book of Mormon. Published by Joseph Smith in 1830, the Book of Mormon claims to include the revelations of ancient prophets who had lived in America from 600 BCE to the fifth century CE. Originally written in Egyptian on gold plates, the story goes, it was buried in New York State until 1827, when an angel revealed its location to the seventeen-year-old Joseph Smith in a vision and commanded him to translate it into English. Smith did so, preparing through dictation a text that was completed in 1829 and in many ways echoed the language of the King James Bible, from which a great deal of the book was taken.

The sources of the Book of Mormon are still much debated, but there is no question that Smith drew from a deep knowledge of the Bible to tell a story in which the liberation of the Israelites in Exodus and the messianic nature of Christ, who appeared in the Americas after his resurrection, pointed to the fulfillment of time. The Book of Mormon was never intended to replace the Bible but to augment it. In so doing, it fit well into the American Protestant culture of individual, emotional, and personal interpretation of scripture. Likewise, it shared with Protestantism the search for the literal sense of the Bible and the rejection of church authority and hierarchies in determining the meaning of God's Word. In this sense, the Book of Mormon shared a common desire to return to the pure faith of the primitive church.[74]

Nineteenth-century Americans had a broad vocabulary drawn from the Bible to describe themselves. Their intense patriotism was expressed in biblical terms such as "exodus," "chosen people," "promised land," and "New Israel." Even among the critical, the language of the Bible was ever present. The sense of a chosen identity was fiercely contested in the Civil War, when both sides claimed the Bible for their cause.[75] In Confederate states the Bible was taught to children as the moral foundation of the land. They were encouraged to read it, were taught "Bible morality," and recited the Ten Commandments in school, and mathematical books often made use of biblical stories. Reverend D. S. Doggett preached in Richmond that the war was a battle between "Bible believers" and Northern heretics and infidels.[76]

In his second inaugural address, in March 1865, Abraham Lincoln spoke of how North and South had "looked for an easier triumph, and a result less fundamental and astounding. Both read the same Bible and pray to the same God, and each invokes His aid against the other." Yet divine truth was elusive, as neither could fully claim the Bible: "The prayers of both could not be answered. That of neither has been answered fully. The Almighty has His own purposes."[77] Indeed, soldiers on both sides knew the Bible well, and preachers across the country drew radically different conclusions from the same biblical texts. That the Bible seemed not to confer on either side a clear moral victory caused much pain and anguish.

Despite this contested status, the Bible nevertheless shaped the narrative of the Civil War. Reports of soldiers' deaths were often accompanied by assurances that they had died well in the faith, hearing the Bible and accepting Christ. After the death of the Confederate soldier Randolf Fairfax, the minister Philip Slaughter spoke of his life as an ideal one molded by biblical truths. As a child he had played fairly, obeyed his mother, and asked for a Bible at the age of fourteen. He had carried into battle a copy of the New Testament. The minister assured the grieving that the young Fairfax had been saved.[78] Personalized or signed pocket Bibles found on dead soldiers also served a more worldly purpose: they were an important way of identifying bodies on the battlefield.

The America of the Civil War was overwhelmingly Protestant, and prevalent were the Evangelicals, who emphasized a personal relationship with God and the glory of the world to come. Yet faith in the Bible was being unsettled by wider questions regarding its literal truth. Skeptical voices were heard all over. In 1830 Ralph Waldo Emerson had declared in a lecture at Harvard that he no longer believed in the divinity of Christ. "I regard it as the irresistible effect of the Copernican astronomy," he stated, "to have made the theological scheme of redemption absolutely incredible."[79] Emerson was not alone in his skepticism. New lines of historical biblical criticism, emanating from Germany, argued that the first five books of the Bible were a composition of disparate literary traditions woven together at different times.

Many clergy and educated laity believed that the faith had to come to terms with the historical challenge posed by scholarship, principally by German universities that approached the Bible less as a book of faith and more as a historical document.[80] In short, there needed to be an answer to the question of "What is the Bible?" To take one example, Charles Augustus Briggs (1841–1913), a newly appointed professor of the Old Testament at Union Theological Seminary in New York, titled his inaugural lecture in 1891 "The Authority of Scripture."[81] Addressing the question of biblical criticism for the Presbyterian Church, Briggs did not intend to fan the flames but rather to douse them by arguing that full belief in the divine origins of the Bible did not conflict with the insights of biblical criticism. This approach, he argued, offered a way of saving the Bible from modern attitudes that threatened its status. Further, he was addressing the fears of the faithful that "the progress of criticism in our day has so undermined and destroyed the pillars of authority upon which earlier generations were wont to rest that agnosticism seems to many minds the inevitable result of scientific investigation."[82] He was right, as many Americans believed that science and biblical criticism were a grave threat to the foundation of Christianity, and they resisted fiercely. The Bible as divine revelation was at risk.

Briggs's arguments did not satisfy his audience, largely because for many he seemed to have gone over to the dark side. He argued that God and not the Bible should be venerated, and that scripture was one source of authority alongside others, such as tradition and the church. Further, he rejected ideas that the whole Bible was equally inspired. The texts, he pointed out, clearly showed evidence of the limitations of human authorship, and it would be foolish for modern readers not to accept that reality.

The issues that Briggs addressed ran far beyond the lecture hall. Across American Protestantism in the second half of the nineteenth century, there was deep anxiety about the threats faced by those Christians who sought to remain faithful to scripture as God's complete and true Word. As for Briggs, there was ultimately a heresy trial, and he was defrocked and excommunicated from the Presbyterian Church, leaving him to become an Episcopalian.

A towering figure in the controversy about the nature of the Bible was Benjamin Breckinridge (B. B.) Warfield (1851–1921), a professor at Princeton Theological Seminary and stern defender of Reformed Christianity. Warfield argued for "biblical inerrancy," the idea that the

Bible is without error in all its teaching and asserts nothing contrary to fact.[83] Against the winds blowing from Germany, Warfield held to the absolute authority of scripture as God's inspired word, sufficient for all believers. He took aim at the Modernism movement, which privileged human reason over traditional doctrine and welcomed the advances of modern science. Most dangerously, in Warfield's eyes, Modernists spoke of the Bible as authored by human hands and not by God. The Bible was certainly written by men, Warfield countered, and there is a clear human character to scripture. However, those men, in all their differences, faithfully recorded God's voice. Warfield held this position to be the teaching of John Calvin and the Reformed faith, which he resolutely defended.

The greatest threat to conventional wisdom was the rise of Darwinism, which put forward the case that the Bible was not even necessary to explain human origins. Writing a "spiritual autobiography" of Charles Darwin after his death, Warfield attributed the theory of evolution to the Englishman's loss of faith in the Bible: "As he more and more convinced himself that species, on the contrary originated according to natural law, and through a long course of gradual modification, he felt ever more and more that Genesis, 'must go.' But Genesis is an integral part of the Old Testament, and with the truth and authority of the Old Testament the truth and authority of Christianity itself is inseparably bound up."[84] Warfield referred to Darwin's thesis as an "unproved delusion" and quoted him as saying that "the Old Testament was no more to be trusted than the sacred books of the Hindoos."[85]

To preserve the Bible in the face of such an attack, many advocated embracing the spirit of scientific empiricism and adapting it to the critical study of the Bible. Newman Smyth at Andover Theological Seminary in Massachusetts advised theologians to "keep if possible open eyes for all the facts."[86] Briggs had made a similar point: criticism "tests" how the Bible is to be understood according to the "laws of thought and of history." As a result, it "eliminates the false, the uncertain, and the unsubstantial from the true, the certain, and the substantial."[87] America remained awash in the Bible during this new scientific age, but the struggle between Evangelical views and liberal thinkers marked a turning point in American Christianity. A new historical awareness had developed that would not go away.

The most powerful counter to the historical questions about the Bible came from a broad range of learned and popular figures who sought a faith-based reading of scripture. The first statement was *The Fundamentals*, a collection of ninety essays published between 1910 and 1915, first in twelve volumes and later in four. As the title suggested, it was an unequivocal statement of the foundations of the Christian faith and attacked a broad range of opponents, including historical critics, Modernists, and atheists. The Fundamentalists—a term coined by the Baptist editor Curtis Lee Laws—were alienated from the mainline liberal churches and the major institutions of higher education, leading them to form Bible colleges across the country.

The Fundamentalist-Modernist debate circled around how to interpret the Bible. Progressives embraced historical criticism and the need to speak to modern society, while Fundamentalists focused on retaining the coherence of scripture.[88] In 1920 influential Presbyterian writer David S. Kennedy articulated a view of American culture around which many Fundamentalists cohered:

It must be remembered that America was born of moral progenitors and founded on an eternally moral foundation. Her ancestors were Christians of a high order, purified by fire, and washed in blood. Her foundation is the Bible, the infallible Word of God. The decalogue written by the finger of God is her perfect guide in her religious and social life. There has been some weakening of this moral standard in the thought and life of America. This is the result of an age of luxury within and freedom from conflict from without. There is but one remedy: the nation must return to her standard of the Word of God. She must believe, love and live her Bible.[89]

The enemies to be faced came from without: German biblical criticism and the Communist threat. The believers faced a struggle to maintain a Bible society, and the answer was clear: "The Bible and the God of the Bible is our only hope. America is narrowed to a choice. She must restore the Bible to its historic place in the family, the day school, the college and university, the church and Sabbath-school, and thus through daily life and thought revive and build up her moral life and faith, or else she might collapse and fail the world in this crucial age."[90]

The battle for the Bible was a battle for civilization. The prominent Baptist preacher John Roach Straton (1875–1929), for instance, launched a fierce attack on what he saw as the moral degradation of New York City, with its theaters, dance halls, and other amusements. The Bible, he said, in the context of a typical attack on dancing, "is the foundation of all that is decent and right in our civilization."[91]

The most famous conflict was the Scopes trial in 1925, in which a mathematics teacher was charged with defying state law in Tennessee by teaching evolution, in contravention to the Bible.[92] Indeed, it has often been remarked that the Bible itself was on trial. The most dramatic moment in the courthouse occurred when the defense lawyer, Clarence Darrow, summoned prosecutor William Jennings Bryan to address the literal interpretation of the Bible. The questioning took place on the court lawn because of the number of spectators and the extreme heat. Darrow's cross-examination challenged Bryan on various biblical stories and their credibility when interpreted literally. Bryan responded that Darrow's sole intention was to denigrate the Bible.

Bryan's principal arguments were very much in line with Fundamentalist thought. Faith surpassed science: "It is better to trust the Rock of Ages, than to know the age of the rocks." Crucially, the Bible was scientific whereas Darwinism was not. "Science," he argued, "is classified knowledge; it is the explanation of facts." Darwinism was "guesses strung together," "a mere hypothesis." In the wake of the First World War, Bryan enumerated the catastrophe brought by Darwinism. Not only did it "destroy the faith of Christians," but it had "laid the foundation for the bloodiest war in history" by committing German culture to the philosophy of Nietzsche.[93]

By the first decades of the twentieth century, America's relationship to the Bible was complex and often contradictory. As the Fundamentalist-Modernist debate and diversification of denominations showed, there was little consensus, and more Americans than ever were openly prepared to reject the Bible altogether. Yet the sacred book was omnipresent. During World War I, the American Bible Society printed over five million "Army and Navy Editions" for servicemen and servicewomen. After the Immigration Act of 1917 required a literacy test for incoming residents, cards were made up as study aids, and most of them included Bible verses from the KJV.

Many travelers also began to find Bibles in the drawer beside their hotel beds. On September 14, 1898, a Bible distribution scheme was launched by two traveling salesmen, John Nicholson and Samuel E.

Hill, at the Central Hotel in Boscobel, Wisconsin, which was hosting a convention of raucous lumberjacks. Sharing a love of the Bible, Nicholson and Hill created the Christian Commercial Travelers Association, which they later renamed as Gideons International in honor of the Hebrew judge. The beginnings were modest, with the first order for twenty-five copies of the Bible to be placed in the Superior Hotel in Iron Mountain, Montana. From that small start, the Gideons, who are entirely lay run, have provided Bibles in a hundred languages to hotels, motels, schools, military installations, prisons, rescue missions, hospitals (in large print), airplanes, ships, and trains. The group has cumulatively placed over 2.5 billion complete or partial Bibles.[94]

From the Revolutionary period to the Second World War, the Bible formed the vision for a new society, a new world. Americans followed the centuries-old desire to create biblical communities, and despite its many divisions the expanding nation saw itself in the pages of the sacred book. The missionary impulses of American biblical culture, which built the country, raised the eyes of missionaries to distant hills and lands beyond the seas. The Bible should be the book of all peoples.

CHAPTER 10

MISSIONS
WORLDWIDE

In the early nineteenth century, Samuel J. Mills of the Andover Theological Seminary in Massachusetts had a vision for a missionary society that would take the Bible to the "heathen world." The organization he helped found to carry out these missions, the American Board of Commissioners for Foreign Missions, consisted of Congregationalists and Presbyterians. Their first target was none other than the Holy Land, which regrettably, in their view, lay in the hands of the Muslim Ottoman Empire. Beginning in 1820, American missionaries arrived in Palestine with the expectations of the ancient Israelites crossing the Jordan: the land of the Bible "was to be possessed."[1] These men and women were modern-day Joshuas, but instead of swords that put hapless kings to death, the American missionaries stepped ashore armed with the biblical injunction "Go ye into all the world, and preach the gospel to every creature" (Mark 16:15, KJV). Jesus's parting words, however, were given an added twist. The Bible not only brought the word of salvation, but it was also the means for what the board called "internationalizing morals," by which it meant inculcating benighted foreigners with the culture of Protestant America.

Fired by ideals of an international Evangelical Christianity, the board embodied the individualistic and conversion-focused principles of the Great Awakening in America. This exportable faith would feed a world hunger for the Bible, even if that world did not know it had an appetite. James L. Barton, the board's secretary, could not have been more explicit: "There was, in the hearts and minds of American Christians, not a little of the spirit of the crusaders of the middle ages. Why should the soil trodden by the feet of the prophets and apostles, yes, even by the Lord himself, remain a stranger to the voice of the preacher of righteousness and untouched by the feet of modern apostles?"[2]

Once in the Holy Land, the missionaries distributed Bibles and tracts for the conversion of local populations of Muslims, Jews, and ancient Christian sects. Converting Jews was a particular goal, as their conversion would herald Jesus's return. With their distinctive brand of American Evangelicalism, the missionaries had little understanding of what Eastern Christians valued in their ancient faith: liturgy, ritual, tradition, and mystery. For zealous Americans, such empty nonsense only confirmed that these churches were merely "Christian in name."

But this mission to the Holy Land was only the beginning. Europeans and Americans in large numbers answered the call to take their Bible-based faith to the world. They were to overcome ignorance, whether in the rituals of nominal Christians or traditional African customs, and face the complexities of Asian languages that seemingly could not express the divine mysteries of the faith. The vast majority acted from deep convictions to spread the gospel. At the same time, a powerful impulse for missionaries was their belief that conversion meant making those they reached more like them. Missionaries were persuaded that Europe and America were custodians of biblical Christianity and that they were called upon to carry out Christ's Great Commission. Christianity imparted Western civilization. In 1922 the Scotsman Donald Fraser published an account of his experiences in Malawi entitled *Winning a Primitive People*. Evangelical fervor had conquered the transatlantic world, and now it turned its sights to parts unknown. And in this undertaking, these new missionaries believed the Bible would serve as their most powerful agent.

Their emphasis on the Bible marked a sharp departure from earlier missions. Beginning in the sixteenth century, the Jesuits had taken the Catholic faith around the globe, first in Africa and soon thereafter to India, Japan, and China. The Bible, however, had not been their central focus. In Japan and China they had sought to spread the faith through adopting traditional forms of dress, studying the culture, and learning languages. They made use of ancient literary and philosophical forms of writing to communicate Christianity. They did not attempt to translate the Bible. In contrast, for the Evangelical Protestants who emerged from the Great Awakenings and abolitionist movement, the Bible was everything. Their labors led to the translation of scripture into vernacular languages around the world. Under their guidance, in the nineteenth and twentieth centuries millions converted to Christianity and churches were founded that laid the foundation for the explosion of the faith today in the Global South—gains that could not have been achieved without the utter conviction of thousands of women and men who left Europe and North America to commit themselves to the spread of the gospel. It was extremely perilous work, and many did not survive. Libraries are full of their memories and correspondence that recounts trials and adversities. Yet, contrary to the expectations of many missionaries, they sowed the seeds of vernacular Christianities that did not see themselves as European.

Without doubt, missionaries were often closely wedded to colonialism and imperialist interests, but the relationship was often fraught.[3] They imposed upon peoples across Africa, Asia, Oceania, and South and Central America an unshakable belief that the Bible would improve Indigenous peoples by making them "civilized." The Bible was used to defend and propagate oppression and the suppression of traditional cultures. It carried a wholly Western, white conception of Christianity deeply suspicious of what it saw as idolatry and immorality. For many in colonized lands, the Bible was the symbol of oppression, and resistance to European rule entailed rejection of its sacred book. Many others, however, took the book from missionaries and made it their own, finding themselves in the text, using the tools of education, and preaching a gospel message radically different from what the missionaries had delivered. The direct and personal relationship to God that the Bible enabled both made it the perfect tool for spreading God's message and thwarted attempts to impose control over how that message would ultimately be understood.

Emphasizing the colonial nature of European missions runs the risk of reducing Indigenous populations to merely passive recipients.[4] Theirs was not simply a story of domination and imposition: Indigenous leaders interacted with missionaries and accepted or rejected their teachings according to their own interests, whether religious or political. Often local leaders invited missionaries to preach, teach, and found schools, but usually on their own terms.[5] Placing too much emphasis on the colonialism of missions silences Indigenous agents and forgets that across Africa and Asia they translated the Bible into their own social realities in pursuit of their own ends. Further, much of the most effective evangelizing was carried out not by European missionaries but by Indigenous preachers, including women. They taught a biblical message that spoke more directly to the people, and their reach was much greater. These Indigenous preachers and teachers of the Bible laid the foundations for vernacular readings much more in harmony with traditional beliefs and cultures and distant from the message of white missionaries.[6]

One of the lasting legacies of the efforts to convert non-Christians during this period was the translation of the Bible into an extraordinary number of languages around the world. The Bible had always been the book of the vernacular, and now it created new communities. These translations, which are the direct ancestors of many versions of the global Bible today, often created written forms of languages and made scripture available to large populations. The results were mixed. The search for standardized written forms of languages that existed in numerous dialects frequently had the consequence of creating artificial versions that no one actually spoke. Yet in many locations, the written translations fed and sustained local cultures, allowing people to take hold of the Bible and make it their own. The story of missions is thus not only one of imposition but also one of creativity that spawned new cultures of the Bible.

The worldwide spread of the Bible in the early nineteenth century began with missionary-oriented societies springing up across Europe. The British and Foreign Bible Society, founded in 1804, ushered in a new age of the Bible as a global book. Its first general secretary, John Owen (1766–1822), gave voice to its vision: "A Society shall be formed, with this designation, The British and Foreign Bible Society; of which the sole object shall be to encourage a wider dispersion of the Holy Scriptures. This Society shall add its endeavours to those employed by other Societies for circulating the Scriptures through the British dominions, and shall also, according to its ability, extend its influence to other countries, whether Christian, Mahomedan, or Pagan."[7] The expressed intention of the society was to place the Bible in the hands of men and women so that they could read it for themselves. Its convictions were almost martial: Protestants without Bibles are soldiers without weapons and not ready for conquest or defense. Indeed, such was the focus on disseminating the Bible that it eclipsed any desire to teach particular Christian doctrines. The Bible would explain itself.

The society's approaches were sophisticated. To win public support, compelling stories were told to move hearts. One such emotive tale involved the sixteen-year-old Welsh girl Mary Jones, who out of her love of the Bible reportedly walked twenty-eight miles to find a copy.[8] When she arrived in the village of Bala, she was told there were no more copies to be had. A local minister, Thomas Charles, was stirred by her remarkable piety to give her his copy. Charles later recounted Mary's story to a meeting of the Religious Tract Society (a predecessor of the British and Foreign Bible Society), and its secretary was moved to reflect, "Surely a society might be formed for the purpose. But if for Wales, why not for the kingdom? Why not for the world?"[9]

In the spirit of the age, the British and Foreign Bible Society treated the dissemination of Bibles as a business. They had a laser focus on making the King James Bible available across the globe and little patience for the finer points of theological disagreement. The aforementioned John Owen drew a striking parallel with commercial London: "The line of business," he wrote, "is, with few exceptions, as direct at the Bible committee as it is at Lloyds; and there is little reason to expect the peculiar tenets of Calvin or Socinus to enter into a debate for dispersing an edition of the Scripture, as there would be if the same men met to underwrite a policy of insurance."[10]

The society's commercial spirit was matched only by its national devotion: it had no qualms about associating itself with nineteenth-century patriotism and Britain's sense of itself as a chosen nation and empire. The English, its members believed, were the inheritors of the mantle once conferred upon the Israelites as God's chosen people. As the Mission Register of 1813 put it, "You now are a favoured nation: your light is come: the glory of the Lord is risen upon you: all these heathen rites have ceased: the blood of the victim no longer flows: an established Christian Church lifts its venerable head: the pure Gospel is preached: ministers of the sanctuary, as heralds of salvation, proclaim mercy throughout the land while civil and religious liberty have grown up under the benign influence of the Gospel, that sacred tree, the leaves of which are for the healing of the nations."[11]

For all its sense of divine destiny, Britain was far from alone in its desire to spread the Bible. The first Bible missions, in fact, were undertaken by Danish Lutherans in India, who set themselves to learning Tamil and translating the Bible. Shortly after the appearance of the British and Foreign Bible Society, similar organizations sprang up across Europe and America, including the Basel Bible Society (1804), the Riga Bible Society (1812), the Finnish Bible Society (1812), the Hungarian Bible Institution (1812), the Russian Bible Society (1812), the Swedish Bible Society (1814), the Hanover Bible Society (1814), the Danish Bible Society (1814), the Netherlands Bible Society (1814), the American Bible Society (1816), and the Norwegian Bible Society (1817).

The results were astonishing. The British and Foreign Bible Society printed and distributed in the first three years of its existence an incredible 1,816,000 Bibles, Testaments, and Bible books in sixty-six different languages. By 1834, it had printed 8,549,000 editions in 157 different languages. Expansion, fueled by Evangelical fervor, was rapid, and by 1817 there were at least 117 missionary societies in Great Britain and its colonies.[12] Although largely Protestant, many of those committed to the cause of spreading the gospel across the world were frequently nondenominational and nonconfessional. Their work, however, often drew hostility or disdain from more established churches. In his letter of June 29, 1816, Pope Pius VII called Bible societies "a pestilence against which we must take all measures within reach of papal authority."[13] The spread of the Bible, which promised a direct and personal relationship to God, was seen by those who wielded religious power as having the potential to outrun their jurisdiction.

The Bible societies emerged from the revivalist and Evangelical movements of the late seventeenth and early eighteenth centuries, and their perspective was both local and global. Across Europe there was a movement away from the established churches created in the Reformation and toward more individualistic expressions of the faith rooted in the Bible. Such nonconfessional gatherings were held together by their shared devotion to the Bible, as John Owen wrote in celebration of the first anniversary of the British and Foreign Bible Society on May 1, 1805: "Persons of various communions, circumstances and stations; the Prelate and the Presbyterian, the Lutheran and the Calvinist, the Peer and the Quaker, here mingled in new and undissembling concord; and 'agreeing in the truth of God's holy word,' mutually professed their determination 'to live in unity and godly love.' Pride and contention, prejudice and bigotry fled before the genius of the Bible."[14]

The Bible, in their view, was essential to moral formulation, the creation of a polite, believing society. Bible missions took the form of bodies, or "societies," that were associations of choice, free individuals united by common Christian goals defined in nonconfessional and nondenominational terms. The politics of colonial expansion were explicit in the statements of many European Bible societies. In 1816 Gijsbert Karel van Hogendorp (1762–1834), the most influential and powerful Dutch politician of his day and president of the Netherlands Bible Society in The Hague, declared his desire that the Netherlands Bible Society expand its work in the Dutch East Indies with the purpose of translating the Bible into Indigenous languages. The arrival of the Bible, he held, would bring civilization to uncivilized peoples: "'Europe'—Napoleon said . . . —'has become civilized because of Christianity.' Everyone knows to what extent the Heathens are backward in terms of civilization. Also, for the operation of the State therefore it can be seen as important to distribute a means of civilization."[15]

When the Basel Mission was founded in 1815, the task of the missionaries was to be "spreaders of a beneficent civilization and messengers of the Gospel of peace to various areas of the pagan world."[16] The emphasis on the Bible as a book of civilization was very much part of the heritage of the previous century. The terms *verlichting* (enlightenment) and *beschaving* (civilization) were often used together by Dutch theologians, publicists, and preachers. One Dutch minister, in a synodal address in 1784, referred to Christianity as the way "to the true enlightenment and civilization of a Nation."[17]

Yet not all were uncritically beholden to the unquestioned imposition of European civilization. The first inspector of the Basel Mission, Christian G. Blumhardt, explained in 1827 that when the first missionaries were sent, they were to "knock at the door of Africa," in order to find out whether they were welcome.[18] They were to learn the languages and traditions of the local people in order to understand them better, as well as to teach them to labor in "field and garden work" in order to improve their living conditions and help them develop financial independence. He demanded from the missionaries a deep affection and love for both their work and the people. Quoting 1 Corinthians 13, Blumhardt counseled the missionaries to be "friendly, humble, patient . . . never boastful nor conceited, nor rude, never selfish, not quick to take offence."[19] The latent tension with colonial authorities was clear. Blumhardt went so far as to describe missionary work as "reparation for injustice committed by Europeans, so that to some extent the thousand bleeding wounds could be healed which were caused by the Europeans since centuries through their most dirty greediness and most cruel deceitfulness."[20] At the same time, missionaries quickly realized that the spread of the gospel depended on their flexibility toward traditional practices.[21]

A generation later, however, the noble objectives of the Basel Mission migrated toward closer cooperation with colonial interests. This change in attitude is evident from the first annual report of the Industry Commission of the Basel Mission in 1853–1854, which, while allowing that the gospel is "the origin, the well, the tree" of Western civilization, held that the economic aims of the mission were now "not only another form, not only a support of the mission, but they are mission in itself."[22] Missionary work was now fully aligned with the project of civilizing the peoples with the model of German culture. One later director of the Basel Mission, Otto Schott, would look back on this era with some regret. In 1884 he resigned as head of the Basel Mission in protest against the mixing of evangelism and trade. The mission had, he believed, "lost sight of the fact that the Mission Industries were created for the benefit of the Christian community" and now instead were "only looking for profit."[23]

Far from Europe, missionaries quickly discovered that their initial strategies and assumptions proved frustratingly ineffective. The belief that, once exposed to the Bible, people would be inspired to convert and that all that was necessary was to preach frequently often proved false. In 1907, Leslie Probyn, governor of Sierra Leone, rejected these naive assumptions: "It is thought by some that they [Africans] are always open to absorb what is good readily; that all you have to do if you want to make Christians is to export so many cases of Bibles, and on distributing the latter you obtain, with the quickness of a conjuring trick, a corresponding number of devout Christians. That is what is expected by many of the contributors to mission societies. It is not so." Africans, he continued, were a "cautious race" who would "not accept new ideas merely because they are presented to him by a white man." Missionary work, were it to succeed, could not "simply consist in distributing Bibles."[24]

Missionaries quickly came to realize that conversion required access to the Word of God in native languages.[25] The North German Missionary Society, like many other Protestant mission societies, saw language studies as essential to their work, which they understood as preaching of the gospel to the "heathens," who, although they might not know it, were beholden to Satan.[26] In the German missions in Togo and Ghana, where the Ewe language was spoken, competence in Ewe was required as a "weapon" in the "war" on "heathendom." Germans were often on the forefront of learning languages, preparing grammars, and translating the scriptures. During the First World War, when the

German missionaries were forced to abandon their missions in Togo and Ghana, they left behind a translation of the complete Bible into Ewe, which they recorded in their newsletter as the "greatest missionary of all time."[27]

The Germans' study of the Ewe language led them to perplexing questions familiar to all missionary translators. In order to learn languages in the standard European manner, grammars and dictionaries were required, but that involved imposing standardization foreign to the people they sought to reach. How to transform the diversity of primarily oral expression into standard written prose? Typical is an 1863 book that appeared in London and Berlin entitled *A Standard Alphabet for Reducing Unwritten Languages and Foreign Graphic Systems to a Uniform Orthography in European Letters*. Any resulting Bible would have to be a book of compromises and choices, drawing together different dialects of the tribes. The outcome was, all too often, a Bible in a somewhat artificial language for use in mission schools and churches. Locals had to adopt that language in order to read the Bible, sing, and understand sermons.[28]

Despite these formidable challenges, missionaries in the nineteenth century were convinced that all languages, however primitive, could reveal the divine. The devout Lutheran Friedrich Max Müller (1823–1900), who pioneered Western studies of the Indian subcontinent and of Eurasian language and who founded comparative linguistics, believed this divinity in languages was a gift of the Holy Spirit at Pentecost. His conviction also underpinned his belief in the universality of Christianity, for God had enabled the apostles to cross language boundaries to spread the gospel.

Many agreed. The Scots-Canadian missionary John Geddie (1815–1872), known as the father of Presbyterianism in the South

Seas following his work in the New Hebrides, regarded learning languages as an undertaking of "intense interest and delight." He believed himself "privileged indeed" to be enabled by God to "prepare the key" to "unlock the hidden treasure of divine truth."[29] John Inglis (1808–1891), his fellow missionary to the New Hebrides and the author of a dictionary of the Aneityum language, similarly believed in the sufficiency of local languages to reveal God's Word: "It is a matter for thankfulness to know that in the Aneityumese language God had provided a vehicle by means of which his whole inspired Word can be fully, clearly, intelligibly, and exactly communicated to the inhabitants of that remote and obscure island."[30]

For most Protestant missionaries, it was nothing less than a divine commission that languages be properly understood, for in their tradition the Bible must be read, which they held to be superior to hearing it spoken. Indeed, the insistence of the missionaries on the primacy of the written text put them at odds with cultures that were primarily oral. Europeans, notably Germans, threw themselves into compiling dictionaries of native languages as the essential first step toward spreading the Word. Indigenous languages were subjected to Western ideas of grammar and syntax.

Naturally, the Bible took pride of place in this work, but it appeared alongside a phalanx of supporting religious literature. In the English-speaking colonies, the most widely translated book, apart from the scriptures, was John Bunyan's *The Pilgrim's Progress*, omnipresent as devotional reading among Evangelical missionaries. But it was the Bible that served as the foundation for missionary schools, where it was the basis for education in European languages as well as for religious instruction. Missionaries taught girls and boys to read and write from the Bible and to commit long passages to memory.

The young German missionary Johann Ludwig Krapf (1810–1881) was enlisted by the Anglican Church Mission Society to undertake such work in East and Central Africa. Enduring enormous hardships, in 1837 he began traveling through Abyssinia, having learned Ge'ez, and arrived in East Africa in 1844.[31] A highly gifted linguist, Krapf compiled a four-column dictionary of English, Swahili, and Kikamba. Soon after followed a translation of the New Testament into Swahili.

Krapf's sense of purpose was visionary. He dreamed of creating missions that extended from Alexandria along the Nile, so that "Ethiopia shall soon stretch out her hands unto God."[32] Though Ethiopia was an ancient Christian country, Krapf's ambition concerned its conversion to Protestantism. He was a full-blooded believer that the Bible would bring not only salvation but material progress to Africans. To this end he prepared a translation of the Bible into Amharic, the most widely spoken language in Ethiopia. While he was in Ethiopia, the mother of the emperor inquired how Europeans obtained knowledge, and he replied that God's Word provided "not only spiritual but temporal rewards to those who obeyed His commandments." The English, Germans, and other Europeans, he observed, had "once been as rude and ignorant as the Gallas" (the Hamitic peoples of eastern Africa), but after their acceptance of the gospel, God had given them science and arts, wondrous blessings of an earthly kind.[33] Krapf saw his Swahili New Testament as part of a transformation of the world. The opening of the Suez Canal would bring Europeans to Africa, Islam would be pushed back, the slave trade would end, and great Christian nations would emerge.

By the end of the nineteenth century, missionaries in Kenya had made significant strides toward a translation of the Bible into Kikuyu, a Bantu language. In 1912 the United Kikuyu Language Committee was founded, drawing together several missionary societies. Speed was essential as the need was great, but the committee also wanted a uniform translation to be established and declared the only approved version. The translation was entirely in the hands of the missionary scholars, who felt themselves wholly entitled to mold the pluralities of linguistic expression into a standardized written form. No Africans were members of the translation committee, instead serving only as assistants. Yet, although they were excluded from decision-making, without their linguistic guidance the project would have been impossible.[34]

The homogenization of languages was a common missionary approach in making the Bible available to the people, but it also advanced the broader colonial purpose of centralizing authority. The committee proposed that Swahili should be the language for East Africa and others be subordinated. Therefore, missionary work and spreading the Word were to focus on Swahili, regardless of what other tongues were spoken. The Bible was a means by which regional differences and identities could be assimilated. Arthur Ruffell Barlow, who worked on the translation into Kikuyu, was clear about the benefits of speaking the local language: the "ability to converse with the people in their own tongue" was a means of "inducing sympathy and mutual understanding between the native and his white master which it becomes more and more necessary to foster as the tide of immigration of Europeans into the British East Africa rises."[35]

By permitting only Europeans to carry out translations, albeit with the significant assistance of native speakers, missionaries were able to make crucial decisions about what to include and what to exclude from their vernacular Bibles. Naturally, they took the languages very seriously and did not lightly decide which words and terms to prefer. All the while they imposed their standards of what a language should be, in particular a language of the Bible. Clarity (a Protestant virtue) was more desirable than diversity, so, if possible, single local words were to be found that directly conveyed Christian concepts.

As ever, the names for God were the most contentious. In Kenya, Barlow and his colleagues opted for the Agīkūyū name Ngai, although it was not felt to convey the full sense of the Hebrew divinity. The term "Ngai" was accompanied by a vigorous campaign to distinguish the Christian God from the Agīkūyū.[36] Equivalence of language was not to be confused with equivalence of religion.

A cautionary tale of missionary translation is the Igbo Union Bible, which appeared between 1906 and 1912, the work of Thomas Dennis (1869–1917) of the Church Missionary Society from the Church of England.[37] Produced in the Igbo lands of Nigeria, the Bible proved to be highly controversial and has been frequently described as ill-conceived, despite Dennis's undoubted brilliance. At the heart of the dispute and intense criticism, which continues to this day, was the claim that the translation was a damaging act of colonialism. Partially from ignorance and partially from intention, Dennis and his collaborators, including native assistants, flattened the wide diversity of Igbo languages into a standardized form. The Ibo Union Bible was a poorly chosen selection of dialects that, when combined, functioned as the language of no one. Without doubt, the Bible was central to an effort to impose uniformity on the Igbo people by reducing their languages to an artificial standard form and thereby making them easier to govern.

The Bible's reception was hostile, particularly among those Igbo whose language had been ignored. The influential Onitsha would not accept a Bible in the dialect of their rivals and refused to give up earlier translations into their tongue. The Church Missionary Society paid little heed to Indigenous opposition, however, believing that critics would come around if properly guided by the missionaries. Initial sales were promising, and by 1917, more than twenty-five thousand Bibles had been sold. This early success was driven primarily by a 1910 government declaration that "every mission should adopt the teaching of the vernacular in its day schools, and that no pupil should be passed onto the first standard in English, until he can read the Union Version of the New Testament."[38] Learning the Bible was also made a condition for baptism. Nevertheless, the Bible never garnered the respect of the people who were forced to use it. One Igbo critic said in 1925, "It is not a living language, and has no soul," while another argued that it was an outdated missionary effort.[39] In fact, many Igbo found the translation so foreign that they expressed the desire to read the English instead.

The miserable result was a stark contrast to the earlier Yoruba Bible prepared by Samuel Ajayi Crowther (1809–1891), a Nigerian linguist and clergyman. Captured by slave traders at age twelve and sold to the Portuguese, he was put on a ship to the Americas. At the last moment he was rescued and freed in British Sierra Leone, where he converted to Christianity and was educated in English, taking the anglicized name Crowther. A prodigious student, he studied languages and was ordained a cleric in England, obtaining a doctoral degree from Oxford. Crowther used his linguistic abilities to translate the Book of Common Prayer into Yoruba, for which he also wrote a grammar. Although Crowther had largely used Oyo dialect, he skillfully drew from other Yoruba languages in crafting his Bible. Crowther's Yoruba Bible was widely praised and well received among the Yoruba peoples. The translation, which was completed in 1889, has been credited with the flourishing of the language and is seen as an important part of cultural vitality and ethnic identity.[40]

The connection between colonialism and missionary work was also evident in India, where efforts to translate the Bible into Indian languages were part of a broader colonial effort to translate legal, literary, and religious texts.[41] Biblical translation was primarily seen as a means of conversion as well as improving the living conditions of the "natives." Consequently, it was not simply limited to language but reflected a complex set of attitudes toward Indian society, and the success of a Bible was determined not so much by linguistic accuracy as by its impact on audiences and ensuing conversions.[42]

The principal Bible organizations in India in the nineteenth century were the Baptist Society, from 1793, and the British and Foreign Bible Society (BFBS), from 1811. Immediately upon arrival in India, they began the work of translation. Up to that time, a complete Bible existed only in Tamil. The vast extension of the project created for the first time the ability to compare languages. The BFBS organized this work as a business, creating a financial model and establishing networks of translators, publishers, and distributors. The widespread view of missionaries was that translation into so many languages was essential to enable the Holy Spirit to do its work. The Bible alone, many optimistically believed, would win converts. The vision was of missionaries and Indian Christians presenting Bibles to lost but grateful Native people in the hope of creating in South Asia a Protestant literary culture and textual community.[43]

In India, one challenge missionaries faced was that the Christian Bible was a relatively late arrival: there were already cultures there with long traditions of written sacred texts, including Hindus, Buddhists, and Muslims. Missionaries in India had little conception of this rich tradition of sacred texts in the lands to which they came. They knew nothing of the character of Hindu writings and of their relationship to the communities. They generally assumed that the situation was similar to Christianity and there was one central book. The plurality of the sacred was bewildering.

The existence of these alternative religious texts also naturally created conflict. To Protestant missionaries, of course, Hindu and Islamic scriptures were simply false. Tract societies issued pamphlets arguing for the superiority of the Bible, describing Hindu scriptures as heathen superstitions and comparing the unity of the Bible with the many Hindu texts. The Qur'an was a different case. Closer in form to the Bible, it had to be denounced in another way: missionaries claimed it was full of deceit and was a degenerate imitation of the true Bible. Repeated efforts were made to draw distinctions between the "true" and "false" scriptures. Only the Christian Bible could reveal the truth. Not surprisingly, many educated Hindus and Muslims were deeply offended.

Interactions with other religions played a central role in the creation of Indian translations of the Bible. One stumbling block arose in finding the correct terminology for Christian biblical names and terms, such as for God. Indian languages had a wide vocabulary for the sacred, but missionary translators worried that adopting these terms would prove an impediment to conversion—that they would retain their traditional associations. At the same time, creating new terms risked depriving the work of meaning and emotional pull. In an 1899 tract, the problem was succinctly put: "Christian thoughts cannot buy ready-made clothes at Hindu stores."[44] Adopting the language of others was regarded as "unsafe." Nevertheless, there was a lively debate among missionaries about whether their cause was best served by making the Bible "familiar" or by rigorously keeping to the truth, even if that risked making it foreign to Hindus and Muslims.

Indian translations were rarely from Hebrew and Greek; instead, they were largely from the English King James Version, widely regarded as the best available version and the supreme symbol of English civilization. Colonial officials thought the Bible of the English church sufficient to resolve the problems thrown up by diverse Indian languages. In the nineteenth-century Tamil translation of the Bible, for instance, the King James was favored in dealing with difficult passages because the translation committee "believed that [their] safest and wisest course . . . was to follow the meaning adopted by the English."[45]

Tibet presented unique problems for the translation of the Bible. During the initial Moravian mission, German missionary Heinrich August Jäschke attempted the first translation.[46] However, as Tibetan was not a language but a broad range of dialects, not all mutually comprehensible, which was to be chosen? Jäschke chose Ladakhi (now often referred to as Lhasa Tibetan), the language of the learned elite, assuming that a more common dialect might breed contempt among those they sought to reach.[47] He also had assistance in the form of partial translations made by Catholic missionaries, who had offered options for word choice in conveying biblical stories.

Jäschke also decided to draw from traditional texts, which meant that his translation was heavily dependent on Buddhist vocabulary and phrases. For example, the phrase *rang grub dkon mchog* was used for "precious one" and was closely associated with precious jewels. Given this background, Jäschke made the following case for how to signify "God": "As to every Tibetan *dkon-mčog* suggests the idea of some supernatural power, the existence of which he feels in his heart and the nature and properties of which he attributes more or less to the three agents mentioned above, we are fully entitled to assign to the word *dkon-mčog* also the signification of God, though the sublime conception which the Bible connects with this word, viz that of a personal absolute, omnipotent being, will only with the spread of the Christian religion be gradually introduced and established."[48] For the cross, Jäschke rejected early Catholic efforts and alighted on *adapt brkyang shing*, which was a traditional instrument of torture: a person was tied to it and burning pitch or sealing wax was poured on them. Jäschke was a brilliant linguist but was also modest, repeatedly arguing that a European translation into Tibetan would always fall short not only because of language but because outsiders had a limited "spiritual horizon" to understand the culture.[49] At best, he believed, he was a pioneer laying the groundwork for Tibetan Christians to undertake their own version of the Bible.

Moravians were also active in Mongolia, which unlike Tibet had a tradition of Christianity. The first efforts for the Kalmyks, a Mongolic ethnic group that lived in Russian territory, were not full Bible translations but paraphrases of biblical stories. Old Sarepta, near Volgograd, was a Moravian community set up by Catherine the Great in 1765, but by the nineteenth century missionaries from the BFBS were present. So warm was the Kalmyks' reception of the Bible, reported Reverend C. F. Gregor in 1807, that the society approved the creation of printing type for Bibles in Kalmyk. Five years later, the Moravians had a translation of the Gospel of Matthew, and more were on their way.

Tension, even snobbery, arose between the English and the Moravians, with the former looking down on the simpler piety of the latter. One British missionary, writing from Tblisi in Georgia to an English colleague, could hardly disguise his contempt for Moravian efforts in preparing a Kalmyk Bible: "We were truly sorry to learn that this translation is so imperfect that it is scarcely fit to be put into the hands of the people. This is a source of great grief to Mr. Rahmn as well as to us. We are with him fully convinced that a new translation must be made and that by your own missionaries.... The Brethren's missionaries are good men but not men of learning. The same observations apply to the Mongolian."[50]

Farther south in the Pacific, the experience of the first missionaries to the Portuguese colony of Timor-Leste shows how certain challenges, such as presenting the concept of a monotheistic God in a polytheistic society, often required cultural flexibility and accommodation.[51] The first major translation of the Bible was the work of João Ferreira Annes d'Almeida (1628–1691), who at the prodigious age of fourteen undertook a Portuguese translation from Hebrew and Greek. Despite hailing from a Catholic country, Ferreira was born into a Dutch Reformed family and became a pastor. He worked in the Dutch East Indies, as well as in India (the Portuguese colony of Goa), before dying in Indonesia. His commitment to translation was enduring, and his Portuguese Bible had a long life, later serving as the foundation for twentieth-century Brazilian Bibles.

In attempting to reach the Timorese, the Portuguese had to come to terms with *lulik*, which resisted translation and was difficult to adapt to a Christian context. For the Timorese, *lulik* referred to religious objects and landscapes of special importance, not the Spirit in the traditional Christian sense. The concept was widespread across Southeast Asia and Polynesia: a sacred energy that animates while also limiting human activity—a source of power and morality. The Portuguese missionaries attempted to link *lulik* with idolatry using the Genesis story of the flood: "The flood dispersed, and the number of mankind increased. Soon they forgot the teachings of the ancestors, loved earthly things [rai nia saçán], did not follow Maromak's law, and worshiped empty things [buat let] and what they made lulik [ral-ulik]. After that, they did evil things to each other, engaged in war, and plundered each other: they only thought of doing evil to each other."[52] "Maromak" was the translation for "God," who could be worshipped properly, but also not. The issue was that in Timorese tradition, Maromak was the male god and was inferior to his wife, Mother Earth, Rai Inan. She was the supreme object of ritual worship. In translating the Bible, the missionaries sought to bring the natural world under the rule of Maromak as the all-powerful, male Christian God. Their efforts were hampered by their inability to understand traditional Timorese culture. The reconfiguration of the Tetum language and Timorese cosmology and the reorientation of their gods were closely connected to the Portuguese oppression of the colony and its traditional culture, which they regarded as inferior and barbaric.

Ferreira attempted to craft Bible stories that could be used in preaching by bringing the Timorese into scripture through association with the characters of the Hebrew Bible. In his Liurai Egypt (king of Egypt), the Timorese would have recognized their traditional *Ema bot* (governor). Echoing the story of the pharaoh and Joseph in Genesis, the king is disturbed by dreams and consults a local witch doctor, healer, and fortune-teller. In Ferreira's telling, the Joseph figure becomes ruler of the land after interpreting the pharaoh's dreams, which the others failed to do.

From the New Testament, in the passion scene of Christ's death, the priests are referred to as *sacerdote ulun sira*, which combines the Portuguese word for "priest" with the Timorese word for "head." Showing sympathy with the Timorese, as well as turning the Bible against the Portuguese colonialists, Ferreira represented the evil protagonist and persecutors of Christ as city-dwelling Europeans. Jesus is executed for claiming to be Maromak Oan, who is equal to Maromak Aman, God the Father, thus combining the Christian and Timorese gods to make Christ a Timorese prophet executed by European rulers and high priests.

A similar approach to cultural and spiritual integration was adopted in Indonesia, where Dutch Mennonites were active. The principal translator was an extraordinary missionary and engineer, Hillebrandus Cornelius Klinkert (1829–1913), who was able to work in a variety of Malay dialects to bring the Bible to the Javanese. Like Jäschke in Tibet, Klinkert argued that a translation could not be literal but should instead reflect meanings current in the wider culture, writing, "In passages where a literal translation into the Malay language would produce nonsense or would indicate an erroneous meaning, it is, I think, my duty to translate into Malay in such a way as I believe the sacred authors would have written had they been Malayans instead of Israelites."[53] He intentionally drew on Javanese expressions and aphorisms to convey the meaning of the Hebrew prophets, seeking "as much Malay flavor as possible."[54]

Bible translation had life beyond the intentions of European scholars and missionaries. Cultural mixing and integration, while primarily focused on the written text of the Bible, also involved integrating the book itself in ritual. In his *Among the Wild Ngoni*, the Scottish missionary Walter Angus Elmslie (1856–1935) describes setting up a mission among the Zulu in modern-day Malawi. He recounts a story of a young man who fell ill and whose father arranged for a dance to exorcise the virombo, spirits of dead men thought to occupy the bodies of the living.[55] When Elmslie refused to participate, the young man, Chitezi, sent Elmslie a request: in Elmslie's words, "to send him my Zulu

Bible, as, while he had to submit to his father, he desired to show he did not believe in what was going on. In the evening I went to see him and found his father, painted with red clay, in the midst of his divining instruments, and in a circle around him and his son, who sat reading the Bible, the drummers and dancers performed."[56]

In this remarkable scene, in which tradition was mixed with Bible reading, the missionaries' teaching had been appropriated and reworked: the Bible was accepted into a traditional dance and integrated into a healing ritual. Instead of seeing the Bible as an absolute authority, the Zulu gave it a place alongside their traditional rites. Rather than the Word of God, the Bible was a potential form of medicine. Elmslie admitted that he learned from the experience not to demonize traditional healing and to appreciate that it could be accommodated to Christian practices.

One of the most striking instances of the cultural flexibility of the Bible involves the Bible's reception in Korea in the nineteenth century, when missionaries from Europe began translating the Bible into the vernacular Hangul. As happened in other parts of Asia, in Korea the Christian sacred texts had to take their place alongside other traditions such as shamanism, Buddhism, Confucianism, and Daoism. The Bible was not untouched, and Korean translators and readers borrowed extensively to create distinctive local forms.

The first complete Hangul versions of the New Testament appeared in the late nineteenth century, the work of Scotsmen John Ross and John MacIntyre, along with unknown Korean colleagues.[57] Ross, educated in Glasgow, had worked as a missionary in Manchuria, where he had met Korean merchants and been inspired to visit the peninsula. He undertook to learn Korean with the aid of one of these traders, Lee Eung-Chan, whom Ross later baptized. A native

Gaelic speaker, Ross was an impressive linguist with his own approach to translation, which he outlined in a letter to a friend. He favored a literal translation from the Greek, not English, and resorted to paraphrase when required by cultural differences. Ross hit the familiar wall: How to render the biblical concepts of God, Jesus, Son of man, temple, and priest into Korean? Ross believed that the original Greek was most useful, but he was also able to draw on the work of the Chinese Delegates' Version of 1857. As with most translations of English, the shadow of the King James Bible also fell across his New Testament.

Because Korea was closed to foreigners at the time, Ross was forced to produce his New Testament outside of the country. Nevertheless, his efforts found a ready readership, and through the work of book peddlers, the Ross New Testament made its way across the Korean Peninsula. Access was aided by the support of the Scottish Bible Society in Japan. Indeed, it was in Japan that Ross's first efforts were advanced, by the Korean diplomat Lee Soo-jung, who transcribed the Chinese Delegates' Version into Idu script, which combined Korean phonology with Chinese characters. Since the fourth century, Idu had been the crucial means by which Koreans had learned Chinese. The Chinese-Idu Bible appeared in 1884, almost thirty years after Ross. This version had the advantage of being attractive to Korean elites, who, with their preference for Chinese, generally looked down on the vernacular Hangul. The first Western missionaries, such as the Presbyterian American Horace G. Underwood (1859–1916) and his colleagues, arrived in Korea in 1885 with Lee Soo-jung's translation in hand. Immediately, they took up the task of translating the complete Old and New Testaments, a new Hangul version to surpass the outdated Ross.

Underwood and his team searched for colloquial Korean in which to offer the Bible and were less beholden than Ross to Greek.

In contrast to Ross, who came up with literal terms that most Koreans would have found odd and difficult to pronounce, Underwood strove for a version more in sync with conversations in the home and marketplace. He was successful. The choice for Jesus Christ (*yeshu chrishudos*) remains the preferred use to this day. Underwood's team of American, British, and Korean scholars turned their hand to completing a full Bible. They chose a range of sources, including Hebrew and Greek, and the English Revised Version, while the Koreans studied the Chinese Delegates' Version and various Japanese translations. In addition, a plethora of commentaries and tracts on translation techniques were consulted, all with the intention of producing a literal translation. The result was the Korean Bible of 1911.

Unlike Ross's version, the Korean Bible was printed in Korea and was intended for both a learned and popular readership. It sought to combine the elegance of earlier Chinese-based translations with widespread use of the vernacular, and the 1911 version remains much appreciated for its literary and idiomatic qualities. The work on the Bible in Korean was enormously stimulated by the Great Pyongyang Revival of 1907, led by Kil Sun-joo (or Gil Seon-ju), whose preaching and public confession of sins inspired thousands to convert. The resulting thirst for the Bible led to the production of over six hundred thousand copies. At the same time, the Korean version of the Bible embodied the will of independence movements to liberate the country from Japanese colonial rule.

This chapter, like most histories of nineteenth-century missions, has focused primarily on missionary translation work carried out by men. It is imperative, however, to acknowledge that much of the daily missionary work was undertaken by women. Barred from ordained ministry, women worked as teachers and cultivated extensive networks of contacts crucial to the spread of the Bible. At home and abroad, women were crucial organizers of missions and frequently wrote tracts and accounts of their experiences. Their role was well appreciated within the patriarchal missionary world. It was widely recognized that success in missions often hung on the ability to reach women in the native communities. Rose Greenfield, a Scottish nurse who taught health care to Christian girls in Punjab, spoke for many in her address to the missionary conference in Calcutta in 1882:

> For I believe that the heart of Hinduism is not in the mystic teaching of the Vedas or Sharsters [*sic*], not in the finer spun philosophy of its modern exponents, not even in the bigoted devotion of its religious leaders; but enshrined in its homes, in the family life and hereditary customs of the people; fed, preserved, and perpetuated by the wives and mothers of India. . . . Let us in our Master's name lay our hand on the hand that rocks the cradle, and tune the lips that sing the lullabies. Let us win the mothers of India for Christ, and the day will not be long deferred when India's sons also shall be brought to the Redeemer's feet.[58]

The challenge of reaching women was formidable. A set of practices known as purdah strictly separated women from men, so Indian women were not easily accessible to missionaries. To overcome this obstacle, missionaries relied on what were known as "Bible women," women trained by missionaries to reach places in communities inaccessible to European and American men. Often having a deep knowledge of the book that enabled them to employ scriptural passages with great dexterity, Bible women became essential on account of their place between the Western missionaries and the Indigenous culture. In the deepest sense of the word, they were the translators of the Bible into vernacular cultures. They could adapt the Bible to local experiences. In India, for example, they explained that the blood of Jesus was more effective in washing away sins than water from sacred Hindu sites.[59]

Certainly, Bible women reflected nineteenth-century ideas of gender and class. Missionary societies long believed that women were best suited to reach other women and that they would develop sisterhoods, and, further, that the Bible would instruct Indigenous women in proper and respectable gender roles. The Bible women would visit the locals, distribute Christian literature, teach Bible and Sunday school classes, lead prayer, and often provide medical care. They also enabled other Western women to have greater contact with the locals. They were strongly supported by women's missionary societies, and their number grew significantly during the late nineteenth and early twentieth centuries. The goal was captured by one missionary in the Philippines, who remarked, "We need to reach the women of the islands very specially in order to make the work count most."[60] To which the Baptist missionary Charles Briggs in the Philippines added: "Single women can do effective work in the Philippines [because] there is little of the social prejudice against their sex, or of false ideas about womanhood that will hinder [them]."[61]

In nineteenth-century Syria, Protestant Bible women significantly outnumbered ordained male clergy. Many of them came from lower classes and were responsible for reaching poor villages on the margins of society, which were not usually visited by missions.[62] They represented a Victorian ideal of "women for women's work," educating both adults and girls, often among the very poor. They were charged with reading the Bible and not interpreting it, but as one account of a Syrian woman in Beirut demonstrates, the distinction was impossible.

In 1860 a Syrian Protestant in Beirut, known as one of the Bible women, became the first woman preacher in her land. This role for women had been founded only three years earlier by the London Bible and Domestic Female Mission. The woman's name was unknown at the time, and the British missionaries recorded her identity as Umm Yusif ("mother of Yusif"), a Syrian convention. Only later did we learn from an official record that her name was Taqla Yazbek Sabunji. First married to a Greek Orthodox man who died, she was converted to Protestantism by reading the Bible with her second husband, who belonged to the Evangelical Syrian church. This experience inspired her to share scripture with other women. The work was not easy. As she would later write:

> I went up to the second story of the khan.... Five women asked me to read to them. While I was reading, one of them asked me, "What was your first religion?" I told her I was Greek. She said, "Why have you become a Protestant?" I told her I had read the New Testament; and now I felt I should like to show my sisters the way the New Testament teaches; for whatever it teaches us we ought to do. Then one woman asked, "Is it wrong to tell lies?" I said, "Yes, it is"; and read to them the fifth chapter of Acts, and they were afraid. After which I left them, and went to another place.[63]

Despite the challenges of such conversations with Muslim and Orthodox women troubled by scripture, Taqla continued to work with British missionaries and defended her right as a woman to spread the Bible. When challenged by a Maronite monk about her work as a woman, she appealed to the view shared by the Bible women: "Is the Testament for *men*, and not for women? Jesus died for *all*, not only for the men; and we ought to teach the truth that God teaches us, and to beware of false doctrine."[64]

Reading and sharing were not separate from missionary work and the spread of the gospel. Arab Bible women followed the work of British missionaries and became interpreters of the Bible. Their efforts were described as *mubashira*, Arab for "preacher" and a term they shared with men. They were received by Muslim women as the equivalent of women who read to them the Qur'an. This recognition provided an important point of access.

Despite their importance to missionary work, because the Bible women were often themselves working-class and served on the margins of society, they left few written records. Hostility from male clergy also served to keep them from the written accounts. Nevertheless, in villages with no Protestant pastors, women often carried out spiritual direction and pastoral care. And like their male counterparts, Bible women saw the Bible as their most powerful agent in bringing Christianity to new lands. Their work thus helped bring the Bible to new souls and allowed a stunning array of people from different cultures to develop their own relationship with God.

CHAPTER 11

SHANGDI AND SHEN
IN CHINA

Missionaries around the world were often viewed as an unwelcome presence, and the Bible as a dangerous book. Nowhere, however, was this more the case than in China. Until well into the twentieth century, the Old and New Testaments in China remained powerful symbols of a foreign religion. But the tension dates back much further. From the earliest centuries of Christianity, missionaries arriving in China struggled to negotiate vast cultural differences and sophisticated, ancient languages. The cultures of Confucianism, Daoism, and Buddhism, together with innumerable forms of popular beliefs, demanded that the worth of the Bible be demonstrated, not just asserted. Even where the Bible found acceptance, it was usually alongside and not in place of traditional sources of wisdom.[1]

Over the centuries, the Chinese had every reason to be mistrustful. Until the end of the weak Qing dynasty in 1911, the Bible, for the

335

Chinese who knew about it, was Western and alien, a symbol of their humiliation at the hands of foreigners, such as in the Boxer Rebellion of 1900, which ended with the Chinese forced to pay reparations to European governments. The rebellion was in part fueled by resentment of foreign missionaries in the country.[2] That is not to say there were not many conversions during the period of missions, but the Bible was slow to acquire a Chinese voice. However, as happened in every new context, the Bible's promise of a personal relationship with God outstripped the authority of those who carried it into new lands. Ultimately, through cultural blending, reinterpretation, and rebellion, Chinese Christians claimed the Bible as their own.

Although the Chinese Bible is relatively recent, appearing only in the past few centuries, the presence of scripture in China dates to the spread of Christianity in the East during its early centuries, possibly from the age of the apostles. In the early 1930s, three bas-relief sculptures were discovered in the city of Lianyungang (in present-day Jiangsu province). These sculptures are believed to belong to the reign of the Mingdi emperor (r. 57–75 CE) in the Later Han dynasty (25–220 CE). Originally, it was thought that these sculptures depicted Buddhist figures and dated from the entry of Buddhism into China. Recently, however, a radical interpretation has been put forward.[3] The figures might be Christian, depicting the faces of the apostle Thomas and Mary, mother of Jesus, with various possible candidates for the third. Could these images bear witness to the journey of the apostle Thomas from India to China? Although some churches have never doubted the veracity of this claim, most scholars remain skeptical. Nevertheless, it is hard not to be intrigued that some of the earliest Christian communities may have existed in China.

Less contested is the arrival of the faith with the Church of the East in the seventh and eighth centuries.[4] Also called the Nestorian Church, after Nestorius (ca. 386–ca. 451), archbishop of Constantinople, the Church of the East was identified by its disputed understanding of the nature of Jesus Christ. In particular, although the Nestorians did not reject the idea that the Son of God was equally divine and human, they did not accept the formula adopted at the Council of Chalcedon (451 CE) that pronounced him one person with distinct divine and human natures. Instead, Nestorians held to a less clear separation of the two. The point might seem esoteric, but the controversy and division were very real.

Scattered evidence over the following millennium offers few glimpses of the Bible's encounter with Chinese culture. The most significant witness is the Italian Franciscan missionary Giovanni da Montecorvino (1247–1328), who lived in Beijing for the last thirty years of his life. Appointed by the Byzantine emperor to papal Rome in an effort to negotiate the reconciliation of the Eastern and Western churches, Montecorvino ended up in Persia and India, where he wrote an influential account of the region. In 1294 he arrived in Beijing and wrote letters describing the hostility he encountered from Nestorian Christians. Pope Clement V appointed him archbishop of Beijing and patriarch of the East in 1307, and four years later Montecorvino baptized Khaishan Külüg, the third great khan (1307–1311), and his mother. The Franciscan also translated the whole New Testament and Psalms into Old Uyghur at the Mongolian Yuan court. The work was reportedly well received and prepared with the best of Chinese or Mongolian calligraphy.[5] However, if that Bible ever existed, it does not now.

The first European missionaries to enter China during the early modern period were the Jesuits Michele Ruggieri (1543–1607) and Matteo Ricci (1552–1610). Having established contacts with Confucian scholars, they wrote and translated Western texts into Chinese, principally concerning mathematics, astronomy, cartography, and technology. Success was achieved through mastery of the language, the cultivation of elite contacts, and adoption of Confucian practices. Recognizing the cultural and linguistic challenges of translating the Bible directly into Chinese and how poorly many of the first Christian texts were received, Ruggieri and Ricci made the canny choice to embrace the style of traditional Chinese literary forms. Their successors produced catechisms and translations of the Ten Commandments alongside literary works drawn from the Bible. Examples include *The Life of Jesus According to the Gospels* (*Tianzhu Jiangsheng Yanxing Jilüe*) by the distinguished Italian Jesuit mathematician and theologian Giulio Aleni (1582–1649), who taught widely in China and wrote prolifically. Aleni's *Life of Jesus*, the first biography of Christ in Chinese, attracted a widespread readership, and its enduring legacy was its influence on later Catholic and Protestant missionaries. Aleni's fellow Jesuit Manuel Dias the Younger (1574–1659), who adopted the name Yang Manuo, was the author of another effort to explain the Bible in Chinese with his *Explanation of the Holy Scripture* (*Shengjing Zhijie*). Dias was also the first to introduce the telescope into China, and he wrote a text on astronomy that was translated into Chinese.

With their rigorous training in mathematics, the Jesuits were admired by the Chinese, who greatly prized their knowledge, and science and technology served as bridges to religious dialogue with Confucian scholars. But the Bible was another matter. The task of translating the two Testaments, with their uniquely Jewish and Christian language and concepts, was deemed virtually impossible. Even if one had sufficient grasp of the language, Chinese culture had no equivalence of the Hebrew God or the Christian Trinity. Even when Pope Paul V (1550–1621) issued a decree in 1615 permitting translations of holy scripture into the classical Chinese language, the Jesuits did not take up the cause, though efforts were made to provide Chinese translations of liturgical texts for worship.[6]

The Jesuits preferred accommodating the Bible to Chinese scholars through creative texts such as philosophical dialogues. This approach was known as "transwriting" (*yishu* in Chinese), and the intention was not so much to literally render the Latin into Chinese but, rather, to convey biblical messages in culturally sensitive terms. It was, without doubt, a shrewd and effective choice, creating fruitful dialogues with Chinese scholars and winning converts to the Catholic faith. From Europe, however, there was suspicion and even hostility. Those unfamiliar with the world in which the Jesuits were living in China saw accommodation as watering down or even distorting the Bible and Catholic doctrine. Conflict between the Jesuits and the highest circles in Rome began a centuries-long debate on how to deal with Chinese culture.

The thorniest problem the Jesuits confronted was God—that is, how to speak about God. Matteo Ricci concluded that the God whom the ancient Chinese worshipped as Shangdi ("Sovereign on High") was the same as the one named Tianzhu ("Lord of Heaven") by the Jesuits.[7] This, he determined, should be the Chinese name for the Christian God, thereby linking Christian and Confucian moral teachings. Ricci's resolution stirred a storm of controversy. "What does it matter to our mission," responded the Franciscan Antonio de St. Marie, "whether the ancient Chinese knew God or did not know him? Whether they named him in one way or another? The question is completely indifferent. We have come here to announce the Holy Gospel and not to be apostles of Confucius."[8]

So visceral was the hostility that the Bible remained untranslated until the following century. The earliest surviving translation into classical Chinese was prepared by Jean Basset (ca. 1662–1707), a French priest who arrived in China in 1689.[9] Originally from Lyons, Basset belonged to the Missions Étrangères de Paris and was engaged in evangelical activity in the Jiangxi region.[10] From 1702 until his death in 1707, he worked in Sichuan, and he planned to translate the New Testament into Chinese with his assistant and Confucian convert John Xu (or Johan Su, d. 1734). He began his work in 1704, basing his Chinese translation on the Latin Vulgate. Basset died in Canton having managed to translate the four Gospels, the Acts of the Apostles, and the Epistles of Paul.

Basset's unfinished version bore the Latin title *Novum Testamentum in Lingua Sinica*. Although it was neither accorded official status nor ever printed, the Basset-Su translation became a milestone in the efforts to create a Chinese Bible. With its careful attention to finding appropriate classical Chinese words for the Latin, Basset was successful in opening scripture to Confucian, Buddhist, and Daoist converts in ways the Jesuits could not. His unfinished work garnered such praise that, even unprinted, it became a crucial source for later efforts, including those by Protestants.

Basset was fiercely critical of those Jesuit priests who had thrown themselves into the translation of Western scientific and literary texts into Chinese and neglected the Bible. "I am surprised," he wrote, "that they took trouble to produce many translations, yet they did not translate the Bible, or at least some scriptures like the Four Gospels into Chinese. . . . As a result, the Chinese in the [imperial] court are now better trained in mathematics than in [the Christian] religion. Once the Europeans are expelled, their mathematics may remain with the books that they have prepared, but the [Christian] religion will perish for lack of any similar kind of support [from biblical works]."[11]

Nevertheless, Basset's work was taken forward by a Jesuit. The Frenchman Louis Antoine de Poirot (1735–1813), later known as He Qingtai, was a painter and linguist who worked in the court of the Qianlong emperor. Uniquely skilled in languages, he had numerous duties, including translating diplomatic documents from Latin and Manchu, one of the official languages of the Qing dynasty. In the 1790s, he prepared the first Guanhua (imperial Mandarin) translation of both the New Testament and Old Testament—although the latter was not complete. Despite applause from Rome, the Curia was not yet prepared to sanction a Chinese Bible on the grounds of continuing translation controversies and an ongoing debate over the use of Chinese rituals in worship. They forbade the printing of Poirot's translation, and it remained in manuscript, of which only two copies are known to have survived, one in Hong Kong and the other in Shanghai.[12]

Despite Catholics' notable head start on the task, the first complete Chinese Bible was the child of Protestant missions. The first printed versions appeared in the early nineteenth century, the work of a pair of Protestant missionaries who were both rivals and somewhat collaborative: Joshua Marshman (1768–1837) and Robert Morrison (1782–1834). Marshman, a poor Baptist who had studied in Bristol, made his way to Calcutta with his wife in 1799. There he met another Baptist missionary, William Cary, with whom he translated classics of Indian literature into English.

Marshman then moved to the West Bengal city of Serampore, where he began studying Chinese with a Macao-born Armenian, Hovhannes Ghazarian (1781–1856), better known as Johannes Lassar. Ghazarian, who was fluent in Chinese and had two Chinese assistants, was busy with his own translations of the Gospels but allowed Marshman to study with him for five years. The Englishman's first achievement was to produce an English translation of *The Analects of Confucius*, a classic collection of the sayings of the philosopher and one of the most studied books in China for over two thousand years. In the same year (1809), he also published a series of works on the Chinese language, as well as a grammar. Together with Ghazarian, Marshman completed the Chinese New Testament in 1811, with a complete Bible following in 1822. This version, which appeared from a press in Serampore in India, circulated primarily among Chinese living outside China. Nevertheless, it was the first printed Chinese Bible.

Morrison, Marshman's contemporary, actually lived in China, working in Guangzhou. Morrison, a Presbyterian pastor with the London Missionary Society, studied Basset's unpublished translation in the British Library, which inspired him to write a tract on the need for a Chinese Bible. Many of the leading figures of the English church were skeptical that such a daunting task was even possible, and Morrison received little encouragement. However, he did find one mentor, Dr. David Bogue, the head of Hoxton Academy (a seminary for missionaries) and a zealous advocate for missions to China. Although Morrison was planning to head to Africa, Bogue persuaded him that China was the place for his missionary work. Morrison wrote to a friend encouraging him to join him in China and urging him to "take into account the 350 million souls in China who have not the means of knowing Jesus Christ as Saviour."[13]

Morrison arrived in China in 1807, when there was considerable hostility toward the English and missionaries in particular. Living largely in seclusion, he studied Mandarin with some Chinese converts to Catholicism. Morrison was eager to learn the common speech of the people and began an ill-advised effort to adopt Chinese customs and dress. The effort went badly wrong, and much of his time in China was miserable. Nevertheless, he devoted himself to translation and missionary work. After he published a Chinese translation of the book of Acts and Gospel of Luke in 1812, a full New Testament followed in 1813. Together with a colleague, Morrison produced a complete Chinese Bible in 1819. Morrison's efforts were made possible by the work of native speakers who aided him in his translation work. Morrison's missionary efforts were not particularly successful; he spoke of baptizing only ten people, but he referred to his assistants as "Chinese helpers who were potential converts."[14]

Despite their pioneering efforts, both Marshman's and Morrison's translations were criticized for their deficiencies, largely on account of their decision to forgo elegance in favor of highly literal translations. Neither produced—or intended—Bibles that were literary landmarks; Marshman and Morrison were focused on conversions and the needs of common people. The larger problem, as they would soon discover, was that their translations were into literary, classical Chinese, which virtually no one spoke. Their Bibles were simply not sufficient to the task of missionizing the continent.

Marshman and Morrison were not the only translators to make this mistake. The same fate befell the efforts of Karl Friedrich August

Gützlaff (1803–1851), a Lutheran in the service of the British government who had an extraordinary career as a missionary and Bible translator. One of the first missionaries in Korea and Siam, Gützlaff began—although did not finish—translations into Thai and Cambodian. The gifted linguist was committed to reaching Indigenous cultures and, like Morrison, revived earlier Jesuits' controversial practice of dressing in Buddhist clothing. His ill-advised decision both affronted many Chinese and drew derision from Westerners. Undaunted, Gützlaff was willing to court danger on several fronts: he sailed on ships smuggling opium along the coast of China and distributed missionary literature by throwing it overboard and hoping for the best—the approach was both haphazard and illegal. He was also a popular author, penning vivid accounts of his feats in the East for an eager reading public in Europe.

For a time, Gützlaff also served as the Chinese secretary for the British colonial authority in Hong Kong. He edited a Christian magazine in Chinese and founded a school to train Chinese as missionaries. The latter project was his undoing. The venture went sour because Gützlaff was scammed by his Chinese students: some of them grossly inflated the number of converts, while others simply never traveled to the places they were sent. Mission reports were fabricated, and Gützlaff was utterly fooled. The missionaries even took the New Testaments Gützlaff gave them and sold them back to the printer, who then resold them to the unwitting Gützlaff.

Complete humiliation came when Gützlaff was in Europe raising funds for his mission and reports of the swindle were widely reported. Though there was no direct evidence that Gützlaff was involved in the fraud, it made little difference to the public, as his speeches and articles had falsely presented an extremely rosy picture of missionary work in China. The scandal was a personal disaster, and Gützlaff died a broken man.

Despite this, Gützlaff's achievements in the East were enduring. Together with Walter Henry Medhurst and the American missionary Elijah Coleman Bridgman, he produced a translation of the complete Bible in 1847 (with help from colonial administrator John Robert Morrison, who died in 1843 before their translation was finished). It became known as the Gützlaff-Medhurst. They worked together, although Gützlaff was largely responsible for the Hebrew Bible. The result was a triumph, but like the Bibles produced by Marshman and Morrison, its usefulness was severely limited by the decision of the four men to translate the Bible into a form of classical Chinese called High Wen-li. The consequence, naturally, was that the Bible was of little use for missionaries engaging with people in their various dialects.

Shortly after the Gützlaff-Medhurst Bible appeared, Medhurst played a key role in the next rendition, which took a different approach. Rather than relying on the work of a few scholars and their Chinese assistants, a more collaborative endeavor was envisaged by a group of British and American missionaries. A series of local committees were to be formed to work on the Bible and make recommendations, while an overarching body, which met in Hong Kong in daily sessions from 10 a.m. to 2 p.m., was to be responsible for the final text. The first meeting of the missionaries was held in 1847, and a team of Chinese teachers was assembled, although their role was hardly acknowledged in the final version of 1850.

All did not go well with this democratic approach: division arose between the Americans and British over the name for God. How do you make the language of a nonmonotheistic culture express the God of the Bible? Opinions varied. As discussed earlier, since the seventeenth century, Catholics had preferred "Tian-zhu," meaning "Heavenly Lord" or "Lord of Heaven." The Catholic faith therefore identified itself as Tian-zhu Jiao, the "religion of the Heavenly Lord."[15] Marshman, who often translated "God" in the Bible as "Shen," which means "spirit," also used "Tian-zhu." For "Holy Spirit," he adopted "Shen Hun," which is one of the two types of spirits or souls that leave or remain in the body after death. Later, in his 1822 edition of the Chinese Bible, Marshman settled on "Shen" for "God" and, for "Holy Spirit," "Sheng-shen-feng" (Holy god wind or Holy Ghost wind). No one knew how to resolve the question.

In the 1840s, the so-called term question dominated and deeply divided Protestant missionaries.[16] Every option presented problems. The primary candidates for God's name were "Shen" and "Shangdi," but each had different connotations. "Shangdi" (Sovereign on High) was favored as the name for the Christian God by Medhurst, the leader of the 1843 commission, as the best approximation of Chinese understanding. He and his supporters saw "Shangdi" as more Chinese, but their view did not find favor with many of the Americans, who desired to stick with "Shen." The disagreement, which became known as the "term question," led to a rancorous divide of the translation teams in 1851, eventually resulting in the creation of two versions of the Bible. The Delegates' Version, as the British version became known, was published during the 1850s, beginning with the New Testament in 1852, followed by the Old in 1854. A complete Bible appeared in 1858. The alternative, American version was published in 1863.

There was, however, a familiar problem. Once more, the translators had opted for classical Chinese, which made the Bible inaccessible to most people. Medhurst and his colleague John Stronach attempted to broaden the reach of their Bible by preparing a translation into Nanjing

Mandarin, which was published by the British and Foreign Bible Society in 1856. It was the first translation not to use literary Chinese. Still, this was a language that was not spoken by many who lived throughout the country.

To overcome the distance between the classical Chinese of the Protestant translations and the language of the villages, missionaries threw themselves into preparing translations of scripture into local dialects. In their attempts to reach remote areas, they were greatly aided by Chinese colporteurs.[17] Protestants in the nineteenth century translated the Bible into several local Chinese dialects: Ningbo, Hangzhou, and Cantonese. They romanized local dialects and were also crucial in the development of an easy-to-read, novelistic Chinese, one that more closely approximated the spoken language around Beijing. Missionaries' use of *ouhua Baihua*, or Europeanized vernacular, in their nineteenth-century writings played a key role in the acceptance of vernacular as the national written language in 1919.

The translation of biblical texts for ordinary people would not have been possible without the assistance of local Chinese "helpers," as they were often called, who were often enthusiastically praised in letters home and memoirs. Most of these translated biblical texts were small portions of the Bible or smaller tracts produced locally on aging lithographic presses. The Shanghai mission of the American Board of Commissioners for Foreign Missions was a center for the production of biblical texts. Missionaries would then journey across the country distributing the printed materials.[18]

Western Europeans were not alone in their missionary zeal to reach the Chinese through translations of the Bible. From the late eighteenth century, the Russian Ecclesiastical Mission sought to propagate the Orthodox Bible in China, particularly among the Manchu and Mongol peoples.[19] Once again, the problem was translation and the great distance between Chinese and the Greek and Old Slavonic of the Russian Orthodox churches. As with the Europeans, progress was possible through the leadership of a few individuals. Nikita Yakovlevich Bichurin (1777–1853) was a monk (his monastic name was Iankinf) who became head of the Russian Orthodox Mission in Beijing, rising to the office of archimandrite. Facing serious problems of cultural difference, he devoted himself to the study of Chinese society, history, rituals, language, and geography. After fourteen years as head of the Orthodox mission, Iankinf returned to Russia, where his religious views landed him in controversy and then exile. Among his extensive works was a Russian-Chinese dictionary that was the foundation for the first Orthodox Chinese Bible.

In China, Iankinf's successor, Archimandrite Peter Kamensky (1765–1845), encouraged missions and the translation of Orthodox liturgical and biblical writings into Chinese, Manchurian, and Mongolian. Great care was taken to distinguish the Orthodox faith from the teachings of Protestant and Catholic missionaries. Nevertheless, boundaries were porous. The first Chinese Orthodox Bible was a New Testament by Stepan Vaciliyevich Lipovtsov (1770–1841), a member of the Russian Ecclesiastical Mission in Beijing. The translation was highly influential among the Orthodox in China, but it had actually been commissioned by the British and Foreign Bible Society.

Lipovtsov's New Testament augured a rich age of translations into Chinese of biblical books and classics of Russian Orthodox writings, such as books on the life of Christ and prayer books. The Orthodox missionaries reached large numbers across Manchuria and Mongolia, and great effort was made to integrate Christian writings with traditional literary forms, including the formats in which they were printed.

Familiar difficulties arose. Orthodox scholars struggled to find the appropriate Chinese vocabulary for the Greek and Old Slavonic names for God, Christ, and the Holy Spirit.

Though the Gützlaff-Medhurst Bible from 1847 was inaccessible to many ordinary Chinese, it nevertheless exerted a considerable influence on Chinese history through its role in a catastrophe known as the Taiping Rebellion (1850–1864), which nearly toppled the Qing dynasty.[20] Hong Xiuquan (1814–1864) was a Hakka Chinese who converted to Christianity through reading the tract "Good Words to Admonish the Age," written by Liang Fa (1789–1855), an assistant to John Robert Morrison. Liang's text, which was full of quotations from the Bible, particularly from Genesis, Isaiah, Matthew, and Romans, spoke powerfully to Hong. His career had not started promisingly, as he had trained for a position in the imperial government but failed to master the required Confucian texts. Hong then drifted toward studying the Bible in Hong Kong in 1847 with an American Baptist missionary named Issachar Jacox Roberts.

The Bible presented Hong with a symbolic universe that enabled him to make sense of a series of visions he had experienced during illness. It was revealed to him that he was a savior figure as spoken of in the Old and New Testaments. Indeed, he was no less than the second son of God, brother of Jesus, and was commanded to overturn the corrupt Qing dynasty and rule over a heavenly kingdom with its capital in Nanjing. Though Hong declared the 1847 version of Gützlaff-Medhurst to be the official version of his apocalyptic movement, his relationship to the text was elastic, and he felt empowered by his revelations to rewrite the Bible according to his own strict moral code. Distasteful stories, such as Lot's daughters getting their father drunk and procreating with him to ensure the family line (Gen. 38), were removed on account of their scandalous content. He also excised any mention of wine from both Testaments.

Hong's movement coalesced around the idea of restoring a true Chinese religion that had been corrupted by emperors and Confucian scholars, and he spoke of a warrior God who would unite the divided Chinese. Hong's preaching started among his family and fellow Hakka, creating a group in 1845 that became known as the God Worshippers' Society. The circle quickly widened to include displaced and disaffected peasants, miners, traders, pirates, gentry, and military deserters. The attractive promise was of "myriads of years of eternal happiness and glory in heaven."[21] Life in the society was radically ascetic and involved the segregation of sexes, as well as bans on smoking, gambling, and prostitution.

In 1851 Hong declared the founding of the Taiping Heavenly Kingdom in the mountains of South Guangxi. Within two years, the Taipings had advanced through central China and captured the Ming capital of Nanjing. The Qing dynasty was in grave danger of being overthrown. The brutality was unimaginable. In Nanjing, on his march to found "God's Little Kingdom," Hong's army slaughtered forty thousand Manchus, whom he believed to be "devils."

Hong's vision came from the book of Revelation: "I saw the Holy City, the new Jerusalem, coming down out of heaven from God, prepared as a bride beautifully dressed for her husband" (Rev. 21:2, NIV). Blood and conquest would bring about this apocalypse. "Our Heavenly King," one Taiping wrote, "having personally received God's mandate, shall eternally rule over mountains and rivers . . . thousands and thousands of generations of boundless happiness should be founded for eternity."[22]

Initially, Western missionaries, far from being horrified by what was being done in the name of the Bible, welcomed the rebellion and its goal of establishing a Christian ruler in China. However, they wholly misunderstood Hong's intentions, his hatred of the Western presence in China, and his vision for the Bible. Hong, in fact, had written his own version of the Ten Commandments and was determined to rewrite the Bible to make it more compatible with Confucian moral teachings, which he regarded as authentically Chinese.

The missionaries cooled quickly on the Taipings, particularly as the Qing dynasty was prepared to negotiate with Western powers to give the missionaries what they wanted: unfettered access to the country. Hong and his followers thus presented a serious problem for Europeans and Americans. Who exactly were the Chinese Christians? The violence, the rewriting of the Bible, and the unpredictable conduct of the Taipings persuaded many Westerners that they were not really Christians. Accordingly, the rebellion stirred efforts in the West toward the evangelization of China. The British and Foreign Bible Society, on hearing of the revolt, immediately assumed that it fell to the organization to lead these semi-Christian Chinese to become true believers. A plan for a million copies of the Bible was launched. The society raised a good deal of money and hired Chinese agents in Shanghai, Hong Kong, Ningbo, Fuzhou, Xiamen, and Guangzhou, where foreigners were allowed, to distribute Bibles. The effort proved less than successful. According to statistics from 1860, of the more than 250,000 Bibles printed, fewer than 30,000 were sold.[23]

Hong's movement marked a decisive change in the Bible's relationship to China. It was no longer firmly in the hands of Western missionaries and scholars, and the Taiping Rebellion had made the Bible about a China purged of foreign intervention and renewed in character to pursue its own destiny. It was at that moment that the Bible became Chinese, understood on different terms and envisioning a religion of freedom, not colonial and economic subordination. Although his reading of the Bible was followed by few influential Chinese after the collapse of the revolt, Hong created an enduring image of the liberating warrior guided by God's Word.

The situation for Christian missions in the mid-nineteenth century was precarious. The Taiping Rebellion had revealed an attraction to a Christianity that rejected Westerners, the efforts to translate the Bible into Chinese were struggling, and Chinese rulers had greatly restricted the movement of missionaries. Reaching the people required creative approaches, and during the nineteenth century Protestants adopted the earlier Jesuit tactic of making contact through the adoption of traditional artistic forms.

In the nineteenth and twentieth centuries, stories of the Bible and the interpretations propagated by the missionaries were made available to Chinese audiences in a range of genres, such as paraphrases, sermons, hymns, and worship songs.[24] Men, women, and children were also taught to recite catechisms. Yet greater imagination was required for a culture that so prized reading and books. Many missionaries sought to connect with the Chinese tradition of public storytelling and love for vernacular novels. This led to the advent of Christian novels that were generally retellings of biblical stories.

Missionaries recognized that fiction might prove an effective way of surmounting cultural differences, and efforts were made to tailor the stories to Chinese cultural norms.[25] Many of these novels became extremely popular and were generally more welcome than plain translations of the Bible.

The Scotsman James Legge (1815–1897), linguist and author, was among those who believed that literature offered rich opportunities to spread the word. In his *Brief Biography of Joseph*, he wrote, "This work, albeit in the form of a novel, neither fabricates information nor supplies 'branches and leaves' as one pleases. In conformity with the historical accounts of the Bible, the novel refrains from making any addition or deletion."[26] Yet Legge and others were not simply writing tracts but using Chinese literary forms to tell biblical stories.

One of the first tracts by a Westerner in Chinese was from the translator William Milne, whose *Zhang Yuan liang you xianglun* (*Two Friends*) told the story of Zhang and Yuan. Zhang was a Christian and Yuan was not, and their discussions ranged over the central teachings of faiths, including sin, resurrection, and reincarnation, bringing together Confucianism, Buddhism, Daoism, and folk religions.

Both Legge and Milne, who had prepared translations of classical Chinese texts, carefully modeled their writing on traditional styles. Legge consciously shaped his life of Joseph around Confucian ideals, such as an ordered and harmonious family. Jacob was presented as having mismanaged his role as father. Joseph, in turn, was a Confucian sage, a moral paragon through his rejection of the sexual advances of Potiphar's wife. Indeed, his chastity placed Joseph very much within the Chinese world, with the consequence that he would be honored "with a good reputation for thousands of generations."[27] Legge also made frequent allusions to classical Confucian works.

Alongside these novels, Western Protestant classics were translated into Chinese, most notably John Bunyan's *The Pilgrim's Progress*.[28] First introduced in China by William Muirhead in 1851, it was translated by Western missionaries into more than ten Chinese dialects. Like the works of Legge and Milne, these translations made use of Confucian forms and imagery and Chinese narrative features to convey the pilgrim's journey, with the first version of the work entitled, in Chinese, *Progress on the Path to Heaven*.

There were also picture books, as popular in China as they were in Europe and America, that contained a mixture of Bible sections and biblical literature. Many were exquisite in quality, such as the *Illustration to the Life of Jesus Christ* (1887), *The Colorful Illustration to the Old Testament* (1892), and *The Colorful Illustration to the New Testament* (1892).[29] Some of the earlier works included *The Illustration to the Typology of the Savior* and *The Illustration to the Savior's Deeds*, which appeared in 1869 from the Nanjing Catholic Church. These works served several functions. They presented the Bible in graphic form for Chinese Christians and others who did not have access to the Old and New Testaments. But there was a more intriguing aspect. Like the literary works, the picture books enhanced their attractiveness to the Chinese people by incorporating Buddhist and folkloric images in biblical stories, emphasizing the harmony of the Bible with traditional culture.

Though Christian missionaries went to great lengths to adapt the Bible to preexisting spiritual and cultural beliefs, there were still significant differences that limited its uptake. Confucians were unable to accept the Bible as canon because the Confucian "canon" referred merely to an imperial selection of examination texts. There was no immutable text in the sense of a Christian Bible. Further, Confucians did not speak of divine origins of their texts as Christians did about the Bible. Instead, Confucian writings received their authority from humans. This attitude fostered skepticism toward Christian claims for divine origins for their scripture.[30]

Daoism also played a role in the formation of the Chinese Bible, in particular through its classic sixth-century BCE text *Tao Te Ching*, often attributed to Laozi.[31] Like Confucian writings, significant Daoist philosophical and religious conceptions made their way into Chinese Bibles. The Chinese Union Version of 1919 has the Daoist *kongxu hundun* for the biblical "chaos" in Genesis 1:2. *Hundun* refers to the traditional Chinese sense of primordial chaos before heaven and earth separated. It is unintelligible, chaotic, and messy.[32] This usage was first adopted in Karl Gützlaff's 1838 Old Testament, and nearly every Bible since has followed suit. There are also clear links made in the translation works of the nineteenth and twentieth centuries between Daoist and Christian cosmogony, that is, the origins of the universe. For instance, the Spirit or Breath of God spoken of in Genesis found contact with Daoist ideas of a primordial wind and a dark void. Other Protestants were prepared to go further. The Protestant missionary Theos Walter believed that he found in Daoist language a term for "Logos," the Word, leading to his extraordinary statement, "Our missionaries have used this word *Tao* to represent *logos* in their translation of the New Testament, and the first five verses of St. John's Gospel are nearly as much Taoist as Christian in the Chinese text."[33]

Despite the popularity of novels and picture books, by the end of the nineteenth century there was widespread acknowledgment that the missions lacked a usable Chinese Bible. The response was the General

Conference of Protestant Missionaries, which met in Shanghai in 1890. The representatives were of one mind that a Bible in the languages of the people was a must, launching the drive toward the Chinese Union Version.[34] The intention was for three forms: traditional classical Chinese, an easier form of classical Chinese akin to the language most novels and fiction used, and Mandarin. Accordingly, three translation committees were appointed to prepare three versions for the whole of China, with expenses covered by the British and Foreign Bible Society, the American Bible Society, and the National Bible Society of Scotland. First to appear, in 1897, were the Gospels of Matthew and Mark, leading to a revised New Testament in 1904. The original languages of Hebrew and Greek were consulted when necessary but were not regarded as foundational for the translation. With Chinese translators working as partners rather than as assistants, the final version of the Chinese Union Bible appeared in 1919, almost thirty years after the Shanghai conference.[35]

In fact, as with the effort nearly three quarters of a century prior, there were two versions, known as the Shen and the Shangdi, based on their choice of names for God. The new Chinese Bible was not without criticism, and numerous errors in the translation were made by both Chinese and foreign commentators. Nevertheless, it was widely embraced by Chinese communities domestically and abroad, and it played a key role in the establishment of Mandarin as the primary spoken language of China. By 1929 over a million Mandarin Union New Testaments had been sold in China and half a million complete Bibles had been printed. That number would rise significantly during the Second Sino-Japanese War.

The Union Bible appeared in China during a period of conflicting attitudes. During the first two decades of the twentieth century, charismatic and fundamentalist revival movements and American influence sprang up across the country under evangelists who claimed prophetic powers.[36] It was a time of mass conversions and baptisms and enormous hunger for the Bible. Pentecostal influences grew quickly, and leaders of these charismatic movements focused on the literal reading of the Bible. One of the most remarkable communities to emerge out of the early Republican period was the True Jesus Church, founded by Wei Enbo (ca. 1876–1919).[37] (Today, the True Jesus Church is one of the largest churches in China and Taiwan, and its Chinese interpretations of the Bible are spread by mission churches in the United States, United Kingdom, and Bolivia.) The church had both Pentecostal and Adventist influences but was distinctively Indigenous in origin. Wei was a poor farmer from Rongcheng who arrived in Beijing to trade silk and foreign merchandise. One day, having been involved in a street fight, he was helped by a member of the London Missionary Society, and he soon became involved with the church. Eventually Wei was tossed out of the society because, in his own words, he had broken the seventh commandment (adultery).

Toward the end of his life, Wei had a profound religious experience when Pentecostal missionaries laid hands on him to cure his tuberculosis. Although he was not healed—he would die of the illness three years later—he received the baptism of the Holy Spirit and began to speak in tongues. Wei gave a remarkable account of his conversion. He was led to a river by the Holy Spirit, and a voice from heaven instructed him to be baptized "face down" in the cold water on his own, unassisted by clergy or missionaries. He remarked that he felt wholly cleansed in body and spirit. According to a contemporary account of the event, "After a thirty-nine day fast—discreetly one day shy of Jesus's record—Wei had sightings of Jesus, Moses, and Elijah, and the twelve disciples, at which point the Lord commanded him . . . [to] correct the [Christian] Church."[38] Jesus also gave him a new name, Wei Baulo (Paul Wei), marking him out as an end-time apostle charged with preaching the return of Christ. After this experience, he began to distribute a pamphlet entitled "Articles of the Correction" in which he detailed his revelations and vision of a reformed church.

Wei quickly attracted followers and founded the True Jesus Church. Its central tenets reflected the experiences of its founder: face-down baptism, strict observance of the Sabbath, and the ritual of foot washing in imitation of Christ's washing of the feet of his disciples (John 13:5). The terms were rigorous and exclusive: there was no salvation outside the True Church. To this day, the members of the church date the fourth and final age of the faith from 1917 and Wei's baptism, marking a blessed time when God had "sent down the Holy Spirit to establish the True Jesus Church as the end-time refuge" so that those who joined the True Jesus Church, according to Wei, "would be spared the catastrophe of the Last Days and enter into the Heavenly Kingdom of eternity."[39]

The Bible was at the heart of the claim made by the True Jesus Church that it was the only path to salvation. After Wei's death in 1919, leaders of the church began to place strong emphasis on theological education and the study of scripture, as they were concerned about pernicious influence of too much emphasis on miraculous signs. In the early 1920s Wei's son, Wei Yisa, founded the first seminary, to educate students in the Bible as the full truth. By 1947 the church had seminaries in eight provinces in China. Included among the "twelve fundamental doctrines" of the church are that "the Bible, including the Old Testament and the New Testament is the only scripture to testify to the truth," and that "neither other religious scriptures nor writings are sufficient to substantiate truth."[40] Guo Ziyan, a leader of the church in the 1940s, further stressed the importance of the Bible in his writings: "We must respect the authority of the Bible, which is the inerrant standard of the truth when we read it. It cannot be interpreted in a private way or explained arbitrarily. . . . All the sermons of other denominations or individuals should be examined through the lens of Scripture in order to tell whether they are true or not."[41]

At the same time, many Chinese people continued to view the Bible and Christianity as Western symbols of imperialism. The Christian Bible, they believed, was not a source of liberation for the Chinese but a relic of the premodern world. During the 1930s, the pursuit of an authentically Chinese Bible flourished in Republican China with the founding in 1937 of the Bible society the China Bible House, which was committed to enhancing the Chineseness of Protestantism.[42] There was also considerable debate in the universities, where many professors sought to replace traditional Confucian sources with a new emphasis on science. The old Confucian canon was cast aside by the examination revolution of 1905, which abolished the study of classic Chinese literature as preparation for government service. It was believed to favor the traditional elites. Educational reform took place alongside the reorganization of the military. The Bible's reputation as an object of imperialism was further exacerbated by growing anti-Western sentiments, which peaked in the May Fourth movement from 1917 to 1921. The movement protested the Chinese government's weak response to the Treaty of Versailles, which transferred Shandong province from German to Japanese control without consulting the Chinese. Speaking broadly, the period between the 1911 revolution and the Communist victory in 1949 was one of competing impulses, and the Bible was held to be both the source of a new China and a significant obstacle.

Efforts were made to find a middle way. Wu Leichuan (1870–1944), a leading theologian of the interwar period who had been trained in the imperial system of Confucian classics and who had converted to Christianity in 1915, sought to harmonize the ancient works with Christianity. He emphasized the comparable ethical teachings of the Bible and the *Zhongyong*, a central book of Confucianism that advocates balance and harmony. Following the influence of Western Protestantism, he downplayed the miraculous events in the Bible and instead emphasized its social message.

For Wu, imitating Jesus was the way forward to the moral recovery of Chinese society and salvation from both Western colonialism and its destructive civil wars.[43] To this end he sought to explain the Bible in terms of traditional Chinese culture. Jesus Christ was the "Holy Son of Heaven" (Shengtianzi), the sage-king of Shujing, the wise one who was both beginning and end. Wu also interpreted the work of the Holy Spirit as equivalent to the Confucian concept of *ren*, a quality of altruistic and benevolent conduct. It reflects the willingness to sacrifice for the well-being of the community, even to the point of death.[44] Wu was part of a tradition of writers who sought a genuinely Chinese reading of the Bible.

Tensions between Christian and anti-Christian sentiments in China during the 1920s and '40s took place against the backdrop of a flourishing Chinese literary culture, in which the Bible played a significant and at times controversial role. One of the leading figures of the age was Zhu Weizhi (1905–1999), theologian and author.[45] A noted biblical scholar, Zhu introduced into China Western ideas of the Bible as literature. A Christian and nationalist, he wrote the book *Christianity and*

Literature in 1941, which examined closely the relationship between the poetry of the Hebrew Bible and Chinese literary traditions. He responded to the Chinese anti-Christian critics of the Bible by offering a fresh interpretation of its character, as remarkable sacred literature. He quoted a famous line of Matthew Arnold's, "To understand that the language of the Bible is fluid, passing, and literary, not rigid, fixed, and scientific, is the first step towards a right understanding of the Bible."[46]

The movement toward a more authentically Chinese interpretation of the Bible was not limited to liberal-minded writers who thought in terms of social and political renewal. More conservative voices had similar interests. Take, for instance, Ni Tuosheng (1903–1972), better known as Watchman Nee. An influential church leader, Ni adamantly declared that Christ, more than a mere social reformer and moral example, was the savior who died on the cross to save the faithful from perdition. In his well-known books, such as *The Spiritual Man* and *Normal Christian Life*, Ni developed a distinctively Chinese approach to sanctified living in which the person is saved in spirit, soul, and body.[47]

Several remarkable Chinese leaders emerged during the interwar period who declared the Bible the salvation of their nation. Guo Ziying (1865–1927), the first ordained Chinese minister of the Seventh-day Adventists, led the evangelization of the southeastern provinces of Guangdong and Fujian. Educated by Scottish Presbyterian missionaries, Guo became principal of Presbyterian College in Xiamen. He later recounted his conversion, which began with the story of a young Adventist student named Timothy Tay who went to the market to buy vegetables on Sunday. He was brought before Guo to explain why he had shopped on the Sabbath. He cheerily said, "Sir, your student did not buy on a Sabbath. Today is the first day of the week." Stunned by the response, Guo took to his Bible and became convinced that Saturday, not Sunday, was the Sabbath.[48]

Following numerous missions with Timothy Tay, Guo connected with other Chinese groups drawn to Adventist teachings, and in 1907 he founded an Adventist church in Chaozhou that still exists today. Although he had some contact with foreign missionaries, Guo worked largely with Chinese people. He extended his influence through his extensive publishing, which included a book outlining the tenets of Adventism and expositions of biblical prophecies. His close contact with the publishing world made him one of the leading Chinese interpreters of the Bible during the first two decades of the century.

Another distinctively Chinese voice on the Bible came from the striking figure of Feng Yuxiang (1882–1948), known as the Christian General. Of humble origins, Feng first encountered Christians in Beijing in 1906 and was deeply impressed by their conduct of living: they did not visit prostitutes, nor did they smoke opium. He awoke to the conviction that this religion might offer the way forward for Chinese society. Feng was also impressed that Jesus was nailed to the cross by his enemies and that he spent time with carpenters, fishermen, and poor unfortunates (*qiongxiaozi*) like himself. His adoption of the faith put him in some danger because many Chinese people viewed Christianity as a foreign, imperialist religion at odds with their culture.

As Feng rose through the army from major to general, he was open about his faith and his conviction that Christianity would save China. At one point, he came into contact with a Canadian Presbyterian missionary, Jonathan Goforth (1859–1936), who had been prominent in a series of revivals across Manchuria, and he invited Goforth to lead a revival among his troops. During the revival, the general broke into prayer in front of the men. Reportedly more than a thousand soldiers were baptized. Later, it was claimed that half the army (over ten thousand soldiers) was baptized.[49]

Feng's soldiers were to live the Bible, with officers responsible for scripture studies with the troops. Goforth recorded that "every night the army is a busy hive of Christian activity. . . . It is not unusual to find officers conducting open-air meetings on the streets."[50] The Bible was interpreted as setting the standard of conduct for both the soldiers and the people under their control. Smoking, drinking, and brothels were forbidden. Each officer was expected to have his New Testament on hand. As one Westerner observed, "Just as a father gathers his family about him for Bible reading and prayers, so the captains and corporals of the army conduct the service for those committed to their care."[51]

One missionary friend recalled how Feng's "tall stature reminded [him] of Saul, his ruddy countenance of David."[52] The general combined Christian faith with a robust nationalism and hostility to imperialism. He claimed that "China's greatest need was for Jesus" because "all national greatness is really due to the presence of spirit of God."[53] As his army grew, his ardor for Christianity slowly cooled and his relationship with missionaries became more strained, in part because of his antagonism toward foreigners. He continued to maintain that he was a Christian, but over time, his army came to include many Buddhists and Muslims.

Having incited rebellion against Chiang Kai-shek's government, Feng saw his military career end in 1930 with a defeat by Nationalist forces, which forced him to retire from service and move abroad. After spending a couple of years in America, he died in a fire on board a Soviet ship that was taking him back to China. In many respects, Feng followed in the path of Hong, believing that a powerful Christian warrior would free China from imperialism and establish a new society on biblical grounds. The close connection between religion and nationalism was carried forward by General Chiang Kai-shek (1887–1975), who supported a translation of the Psalms by the Catholic scholar Wu Jingxiong (John Ching Hsiung Wu) as part of a vision of national reform.

With the preeminence of the Union Version of 1919, the story of the Bible in China may appear to be a mostly Protestant affair, but in the first half of the century Catholics likewise made significant advances.[54] In 1922 the Jesuit Joseph Hsiao Ching-shan (Xiao Jing-shan, 1855–1925) published a translation of the Latin Vulgate New Testament in Mandarin, which appeared just after the Protestant Chinese Union Version. Two years later, at the Plenary Council of Shanghai, Catholic leaders regretted that there was no complete Chinese Bible or translation of the Old Testament. Plans were begun for a Catholic Mandarin Bible, but they foundered on the lack of qualified scholars.

The task was also pursued by Ma Xiangbo (1840–1939), who was born into a prominent Chinese Catholic family and studied under French Jesuits, becoming a priest in 1870. Following French aggression toward China he left the priesthood, married, and devoted himself to founding Catholic institutions of higher education. Ma was deeply rooted in the classics of Greek, Latin, and Chinese literature and was committed to a vision of education that drew them together. He was also deeply learned in science and mathematics, in which he saw no conflict with religion. In many respects the culmination of his labors in education and politics was his translation of the New Testament into classical Chinese, which he completed in 1937, two years before his death. The translation and his notes spoke to his search to find the resonances among Jewish, Christian, and Confucian thought.[55]

Also devoted to reconciling Christian and Chinese thought was the remarkable figure of Wu Jingxiong (1899–1986), who would eventually translate many of the psalms. Born in Ningbo in Zhejiang province, the son of a banker, Wu studied the Confucian, Daoist, and Buddhist classics before taking up law in Shanghai. The law school, which was part of a Methodist mission, introduced him to the Bible, and as a young student he demonstrated extraordinary gifts for both legal and biblical studies, earning him a place at the University of Michigan Law School. In America, Wu was quickly disabused of his idealistic views of the Christian land, and his faith faltered. He devoted his scholarly writing to comparing American and Chinese legal traditions. One of his writings brought the approbation of Supreme Court justice Oliver Wendell Holmes, and the two became friends. After returning to China, Wu became an eminent judge and legal scholar, and he wrote a draft of the Republican constitution in 1933. His books and articles were read around the world.

Wu's deep spirituality was wedded to his love of Chinese classics, and for him the two could not be uncoupled. His approach to translation was less systematic than ethereal. He would translate whichever psalm captured his imagination on any given day and was particularly drawn to Hebrew poetry that expressed characteristically Chinese wisdom, such as love of nature or the philosophy of retributive justice.[56] His goal was to make the psalms speak to the Chinese people as if they had been written in their language. His translations of the Psalms and the New Testament were carried out in *wenyan*, the literary language, and are widely regarded as a treasure of Chinese literature.

While Ma Xiangbo and Wu Jingxiong demonstrated the Indigenous interest in a Chinese Catholic Bible, the task of translating a complete modern Catholic Bible would fall to an Italian from Catania. Giovanni Stefano Allegra (1907–1976) was studying with the Franciscans in Rome when, in 1928, he attended the celebration of another Franciscan, Giovanni da Montecorvino, the fourteenth-century Franciscan who had translated the Bible into Chinese while living in Beijing.[57] The young Allegra was inspired to follow the same path, a journey that would last forty years. After being ordained a priest in 1930, he traveled to China and began to study the language with a native speaker. By 1937 his draft of the New Testament was completed. Exhausted by his efforts, he returned to Italy for several years before returning in 1940 to China, which was at war with Japan. In 1941 and 1942 he was interned by the occupiers and lost most of his translation manuscript. As he was moved from camp to camp, Allegra worked for the release of other missionaries while at the same time resuming work on his Bible translation.

After the war, Allegra formed a college of Franciscan friars in Beijing to complete the translation of the Bible, but they were forced to flee with the victory of the Communists in 1949. By that point the first three volumes of the Old Testament were finished, but it would take another twelve years to complete the rest, including the New Testament. Together with four Chinese friars, Allegra lived in Jerusalem and then in Hong Kong, where he remained for the rest of his life. The culmination of his work came in 1968 with the publication of the one-volume Chinese Catholic Bible known as the Sigao Shengjing. The translation was widely praised for its elegance and accuracy. Printed in Hong Kong, the Sigao Bible would not be permitted in mainland China for another two decades. It remains today the pre-ferred Bible of the Chinese Catholic Church.

The victory of Mao and the Communists in 1949 led to the virtual disappearance of the Bible in public in China for almost thirty years. Indeed, possessing it was forbidden and punishable. With the end of the chaotic Cultural Revolution in 1976, Christianity slowly began to reemerge into the light. The Bible was restored in the churches that suddenly sprang up around the country, but there were sharp differences in attitudes toward the book.[58] The Union Version remained the most widely used, but its place in the government-regulated, officially sanctioned churches—known as the Three-Self Patriotic Movement (TSPM)—differed radically from its place in the more conservative, evangelical churches.

For the TSPM, the Bible was a historical document inspired by God but written by human hands.[59] That meant it was to be read historically and contextually in order to determine what it said about contemporary contexts and issues. The Bible's role was seen less as conveying the absolute Word of God and more as establishing contacts between the churches and the Communist Party, emphasizing the churches' patriotic and nationalist sympathies. Christ, for these churches, was much less a savior than a cosmic figure who embodied principles of love. Ideas such as justification through faith and personal salvation found little resonance, as they were seen as offensive to nonbelievers.

While the rapidly growing autonomous churches in China today have extremely diverse congregations, they share a very high view of the Bible, quite distinct from the TSPM's. For the most part, they reject the cultural compromises of the sanctioned church and the need to cater to nonbelievers or the party. They also reject Western liberal theology and are much more inclined to read the Bible with an eye to the miraculous. Shaped by their experiences of persecution by the Communist regime, they emphasize the place of suffering and commitment, as well as missionary work. Their members include both the rural poor and urban elites, and many churches, such as Beijing Ark Church, boldly resist government pressure.

One of the Ark Church's founding members, Yu Jie, speaks of robust commitment to the Bible and criticism of the government. Thoroughly grounded in a conservative reading of scriptures on questions of sin and salvation, Yu has been placed under police surveillance and imprisoned, and he was forbidden to go anywhere near the Olympic sites in 2008. In the *Chicago Tribune* he wrote, "Beijing shouldn't be host of the Olympic Games anyway. At the moment, China should invest the money in the country's education and public health systems, rather than building gigantic and glamorous stadiums to show off its status and save face."[60] He called for prayer for the two thousand Christians of the autonomous churches who were imprisoned for not yielding to the government. Above all, he sought prayers that Chinese Christians would be able to follow the Bible.

In 1998 several of the leading, larger autonomous churches issued a statement on the nature of the Bible in which they declared it not only inspired by God but the whole truth and without error. "In seeking to understand scripture," they wrote, "one must seek the leading of the Holy Spirit and follow the principle of interpreting Scripture by Scripture, and not taking anything out of context. In interpreting Scripture, one ought to consult the traditions of orthodox belief led by the church throughout her history. We are opposed to interpreting Scripture by one's own will, or by subjective spiritualization."[61]

A different attitude toward the Bible is found at Chinese universities, where there has been robust engagement with it as a work of Western literature and philosophy that can be studied in comparison with Chinese literary traditions. There has also been considerable interest in the Old Testament as a record of the Jewish people from antiquity through to the time of modern Israel.

Women form the majority of church members in China across the theological spectrum, roughly 70 percent, but because most of the churches are evangelical, their roles have been limited. Many churches not registered with the government do not permit women to be ordained to the ministry or to administer the sacraments. Yet, as in Africa and South America, recent voices in China have emerged that speak to new ways of looking at the Bible from feminist perspectives. Reverend Cao Shengjie, president of the China Christian Council and a distinguished church leader in international gatherings, is deeply committed to the Bible and has frequently remarked that China has its distinctive approaches. "If we proceed from a literal interpretation," she wrote, "then there are things in the Bible that are not helpful to women's position.... Feminist theology has always stressed hermeneutics, not only for passages that value women, but have called for close study of those passages that have been seen as belittling to women.... Reading the Bible from a woman's perspective frequently brings women new light."[62]

From its earliest days in China, the Bible has existed in fecund relationship with traditional cultures. One strikingly beautiful modern expression of this marriage of ancient art with contemporary design is the work of the artist Fan Pu, who practices the ancient art of paper cutting.[63] Drawing inspiration from Confucian and Western sources, such as the medieval *Biblia pauperum* we encountered earlier, she demonstrates how traditional folk art can be transformed through the use of modern techniques and materials. Like others before her, she finds harmony between Confucian and biblical wisdom. In her delicate paper triptychs we find biblical narratives together with ancient sayings. Drawing primarily from the Gospels, she frequently portrays women of the Bible. She said of her approach: "I start with talking to the Old Testament characters, then with those from the New Testament, and finally I converse with Jesus Christ. . . . I would comprehend an excerpt from the Bible through meditation, and move on to configuring a composition."[64] A member of a house church, Fan Pu embraces the dialogue of Christian and traditional and contemporary Chinese culture through meditation, images, and calligraphy to express contemporary identities. Her work reaches a wide audience through its accessibility in form and expression. "I think people are naturally proud of themselves," she said. "Even toddlers like to strike a heroic prose and claim that they have super strength, no one likes to admit poverty." She added, "The real poor people are those who are poor in spirit."

Today, freedom of religion in China is limited, extended only to men and women over the age of eighteen who join churches sanctioned by the government. Autonomous churches exist and flourish, but under a heavy hand. Restrictions, however, are no deterrent for the state in turning a profit through the commodification of a sacred book. In 2018 Communist China became the largest Bible-printing nation in the world. The numbers are staggering. The Nanjing Amity Printing Company alone has produced more than 186 million Bibles for readers in 110 countries. Such was its influence in providing Bibles for American Christians that when President Donald Trump imposed tariffs on China in 2018, the Bible was exempted. Despite their value, however, Bibles do not circulate freely in China.[65] Since the 1950s, they have only been available through government-run agencies and registered churches.

More recently, in November 2021, Apple was forced to remove the Bible and Qur'an from its Chinese app store. President Xi Jinping has also shut down many of the autonomous churches and announced plans to have the Bible rewritten to harmonize more favorably with Communist tenets. Profit and proscription, alongside deep devotion, characterize the Bible in contemporary China a century after the appearance of its most enduring translation, the 1919 Chinese (or Mandarin) Union Version.

CHAPTER 12

AFRICAN VOICES

When the white man came to our country, he had the Bible and we had the land. The white man said to us, 'Let us pray.' After the prayer, the white man had the land, and we had the Bible."[1] Archbishop Desmond Tutu's mordant remark is often retold across Africa and repeated in the West, but what is less familiar is what he has occasionally added: "And we got the better deal!" The late archbishop's humor is poignant in telling the long story of the Bible's arrival on the continent and of its role in colonization, liberation, and the rapid proliferation and vibrancy of Christianity across sub-Saharan Africa.

In many regions of the world, the tension at the center of the Bible's global history, between its promise to individuals of a personal, immediate relationship with God and a common, corporate worship of God, has been somewhat resolved by a general rise in religious individualism and a general weakening of established churches. However, Africa has traveled a different path. Alongside incidences of Africans finding in the Bible encouragement for highly individualized experiences with God, African churches have experienced tremendous growth and success. Indeed, as a corporate body of worship, by number of adherents, it has come to eclipse the churches in England and America. Catholicism has also enjoyed remarkable growth on the African continent. While the Bible arrived long after Christian faith, in Africa it has occasioned a visible strengthening of corporate forms of worship and practice.

The Bible is the beating heart of Christianity in Africa, where intense religiosity contrasts sharply with the continuing decline of religion in Europe and North America, which now receive missions from Africa. Today, there are more Anglicans in Nigeria than in the United Kingdom and the United States combined. Among Catholics, the twentieth century saw a rise in Africa from approximately two million to two hundred million adherents, making African Catholics about a quarter of the world's Catholic believers. From Egypt to South Africa, there exists a broad spectrum that includes Orthodoxy, Catholicism, mainline Protestantism, and Pentecostalism. The boundaries between these denominations are constantly shifting, and they share a strong charismatic character alongside the ancient traditions of the Orthodox churches in Egypt and Ethiopia.

As the title of Nigerian writer Dipo Faloyin's book argues, Africa is not a country. From Coptic Egypt to the Pentecostal churches of South Africa and Nigeria, the continent has an enormous range of diverse Christian cultures. Its religious diversity and enthusiasm are nowhere more evident than in its biblical culture. At least portions of the Bible have been translated into approximately 650 of Africa's 2,000 languages, and full translations exist in roughly 150 languages. In the history of the Bible in Africa, the legacy of colonialism looms large, but not uniformly. In many respects the Bible was empire, the most important arrival from Europe and America. The seeds of missionaries fell on fertile and stony ground alike, largely dependent on the extent to which those bearing the message engaged with local African cultures. Overall, however, the impact of the missions was enormous, converting millions to Christianity and spreading the Bible throughout the continent.

The missions, however, could not control the harvest. The more they came to know the Bible, the more Africans found their voice in the two Testaments. New readings, preaching, and forms of worship proved clarion calls for liberation. The book became the source of widespread hopes for a genuine African faith that spoke in the languages of the people and reflected their place in the stories of salvation. There was no one path, and African Christian cultures, with their intense focus on the Bible, emerged out of complex relations with colonial missions and their own traditional cultures. One result was the rising success of organized forms of worship that, for all their debts to their European Catholic and Protestant origins, were made distinctively African.

Africa was in the Bible long before the Bible was in Africa, even long before Christianity. Joseph, the son of Jacob, was sold into slavery in Egypt, explaining how the Israelites came into Africa. Moses led God's people out of Egypt and into forty years of wandering in the Sinai Desert. After being warned in a dream of Herod I's vindictive decree to execute all male children under the age of two, Joseph and Mary fled with their infant son, Jesus, into Egypt. An Ethiopian eunuch read Isaiah and sought baptism from the disciple Philip.

When the sacred book did arrive, in the early centuries after Christ, it spread through Coptic Egypt and south along the Nile to

Ethiopia, where Ethiopian Christians believe the Ark of the Covenant was brought and remains. Across North Africa, Latin translations of scriptures circulated widely, read and heard in the churches of the fathers Tertullian, Cyprian, and Augustine of Hippo. Long before the missionaries arrived, the Bible was found from the Sinai to modern-day Morocco, and its earliest manifestations as a physical book may well have come from Alexandria in Egypt. With the Muslim conquests in the seventh century much of that Christian North African world vanished, but the survival of Bibles from the era bears enduring witness to its vitality. As discussed in chapter 3, the Garima Gospels from Ethiopia may be the oldest surviving illustrated Bible.

The Bible returned to sub-Saharan Africa in full force beginning in the sixteenth century, with the dawn of European imperialism. In the eighteenth and nineteenth centuries, the Evangelical fervor that swept across Europe, from Britain to Scandinavia, inspired missions to "rescue" Africa. Stories of missionaries in Africa often emphasize the role of men and women from Europe and America, but they were always small in number, and their mortality rates from illness were very high. The rapid spread of Christianity in the nineteenth and twentieth centuries was much the work of Africans themselves.[2] For instance, according to the statistics of the 1910 World Missionary Conference in Edinburgh, in sub-Saharan Africa there were 7,650 "foreign missionaries" and 26,747 "native workers."[3] Most Africans never saw a foreigner. The unglamorous work of evangelizing was carried out by African agents, many of whom were trained at missionary colleges in Europe and returned to found churches that were locally led.

Churches and schools were established in which the Bible not only offered religious sustenance but often was used to teach reading and writing. Learning to read and write, as well as to recite the Bible from memory, was understood by many Africans as a divine gift. Indeed, the ability to read was regarded by many as magical, a source of power that conveyed on spiritual leaders an aura of divinity. The South African prophet Isaiah Shembe (1865–1935) was an itinerant preacher, healer, and prophet who founded in 1911 the Nazareth Baptist Church (Ibandla IamaNazaretha), which was based on Zulu traditions. He recounted the miraculous manner in which he came to read the Bible: "No, I have not been taught to read and write, but I am able to read the Bible a little, and that came to me by revelation and not by learning. It came to me by miracle. . . . God sent Shembe, a child, so that he may speak like the wise and educated."[4]

Yet, for many Africans, the colonial Bible yielded a bitter harvest.[5] Rather than gospel as good news, what was heard were injunctions to obedience, even servitude. Missionaries presented the Bible as offering an image of what Africans should be, faithful and obedient Christians who had renounced their pagan heritage. Through preaching, religious instruction, education, and medicine, missionaries cultivated an ideal of the African Christian, who both served in the propagation of the gospel and sustained colonial economics and administration. For the Kenyan novelist Ngugi wa Thiong'o (b. 1938), the Bible was "the propagation of ideologies which naturalize the hierarchical oppositions of slave and master, native and colonizer, pagan and Christian, savage and European, Black and white, etc. upon which colonial and imperial rule were predicated."[6] As another African writer observed, "We were taught to read the Bible, but we ourselves never did what the people of the Bible used to do."[7]

In order to translate the Bible out of its colonial context, Africans needed to find a place for it in their own imaginations and cultures. This reappropriation of the missionaries' Bible occurred in many different contexts and through a wide range of stories and practices. Consider one sermon Isaiah Shembe preached in a rural community in the KwaZulu-Natal region of South Africa in 1933.[8] He told of a pope who possessed a secret book that the conquered people were not allowed to see. While away, the pope forgot to lock away his Bible, and it was found by some boys sweeping his apartment. When they read it, they found a story of how their land had been devastated by conquest and would not be restored without this book. They immediately transcribed the text before returning the Bible to its place. When the pope returned and saw that he hadn't locked it away, he asked the boys whether they had opened his secret book, which they denied. The pope dismissed them, and they went out and preached what they had read.

Shembe's sermon story has many arresting aspects. After covertly acting against the ruling authorities, the boys were able to gain access to the forbidden book. Empowered by the ability to read, they found a prophecy about their people that revealed how the book was not to be concealed but was, in fact, the very source of their freedom. They fooled the pope, who was less capable than his position would suggest. Their response was to return to school and continue their education, suggesting that their liberation would come from acquiring tools from the system imposed on them. In educating them, the colonialists were unwittingly sowing the seeds of a new, liberating faith.

Shembe's tale of conquest and resistance, preached in the 1930s, had deep roots in African culture. The boys' act of transcription is a reminder that the Bible was constantly being translated, in terms of both language and culture. The first translations into African languages appeared from Portuguese missionaries at the end of the fifteenth century, and the first reported publication in a Bantu language was a Kikongo catechism prepared by Cornelio Gomez and published in Lisbon around 1548. These early works were scriptural passages intended to instruct the people in the recently arrived religion. Many Europeans, however, were skeptical that translation was even possible. At the end of the fifteenth century, Berthold, archbishop of Mainz, questioned whether any African language could possibly express the Greek and Latin mysteries of the great authors of the Christian faith, a view that would be shared by many later missionaries of the nineteenth and twentieth centuries.

The arrival of European missionaries in Africa in the late eighteenth and early nineteenth centuries was fueled by both Enlightenment ideals of reform of religious life and Evangelical, revivalist fervor. Most missionaries from Europe came from more conservative and Evangelical churches fired by the biblical commission at the conclusion of the Gospel of Matthew: "Therefore go and make disciples of all nations, baptizing them in the name of the Father and of the Son and of the Holy Spirit" (Matt. 28:19, NIV).

As a result, from the beginning Africans were generally taught more conservative interpretations of the Bible that included powerful beliefs in the reality of spiritual battles, as Paul spoke of in his letter to the Ephesians: "For our struggle is not against flesh and blood, but against the rulers, against the authorities, against the powers of this dark world and against the spiritual forces of evil in the heavenly realms" (Eph. 6:12, NIV). The churches the missionaries founded and the converts they baptized were largely drawn to Evangelical tendencies toward apocalyptic expectations and more literal readings of the Bible.[9]

These evangelizing efforts were often accompanied by coercion and threat. The power of the gun enabled trade and religion, and the possession of weapons signified strength and authority for both Europeans and their African allies. But the Bible itself was also used as a tool of control. Its symbolic force was evident from an account by the early explorer and naturalist William Burchell (1781–1863), who made ritual use of the book to punish a seemingly disobedient African. From the first encounters, the talismanic power of the Bible embodied the claims of explorers, merchants, and missionaries, and the message was clear. The Bible, like those who wielded it, was all-powerful, controlling every aspect of life and demanding full submission to those who possessed it. John Campbell (1766–1840), the Scottish director of the London Missionary Society, told of how he was visited by the senior wife of Chief Mothibi in South Africa: "The Bible being on the table gave occasion to explain the nature and use of a book, particularly of that book—how it informed us of God, who made all things; and of the beginning of all things, which seemed to astonish her, and many a look was directed towards the Bible."[10]

The Bible also served as a tool of control by providing support for European views of Africans, or "dark-skinned peoples," as inferior. As discussed previously, the most pernicious and enduring use of the Bible in justifying the subjugation of Africans and the slave trade came from the book of Genesis. Africans were thought by many Europeans to be the descendants of Ham, the second son of Noah. According to the legend, Noah's cursing of Ham, who saw his father's nakedness, implicated those with dark skin, although the reference is found nowhere in the Bible.[11]

Even though this claim rested on a deeply flawed and tendentious reading of the text, the use of the curse of Ham to distinguish colonialists from Africans was widespread. A songbook used in missionary schools, published in 1911 in the Belgian Congo by the Order of the Missionary Sisters of the Precious Blood, includes three songs in Lingala written by Sister Arnoldine Falter that directly invoke the curse of Ham. One is entitled "Esisezelo ea Kam" (Punishment of Ham):

> *O Father Ham, what did you do?*
> *We are suffering so much*
> *By God we are punished*
> *Harshly without pity*
> *The punishment that He inflicted on you.*
> *Is inherited by us all.*[12]

Racist accounts of Christianization drawn from the Bible remained a staple part of how Africans were told their own history. A Dominican schoolbook prepared in the Belgian Congo in 1951 could not be more explicit. According to this history, first the "Arabs" had mistreated Black people, especially women and children, whom they sold. The "great chief of Europe," King Leopold II of Belgium, sent soldiers to defeat the Arabs. Africans, in this account, were pagans without knowledge of God and, reflecting colonial prejudices, were described as "lazy, distrustful, and envious." When Leopold heard of their miserable situation, he sent priests and nuns, who missionized and built hospitals. The fruits of their labors were rich: "Nowadays, animosity and jealousy no longer exist among blacks, for the Kingdom of God has already come to the Congo. Glory to the King."[13]

Missionary efforts, however, did not take place in a vacuum, and Africans were not mere recipients of the Bible. The successes and failures of missions depended on local circumstances and the ability of Europeans and Americans to adapt to cultures and appeal to audiences. That they would be successful was far from given, and once exposed to the Bible, particularly in their own languages, many Africans saw new possibilities for reading and hearing that led away from the missionaries.

Until the nineteenth century, only a few sporadic efforts were made to translate the Bible into vernacular languages. That changed with the missionaries of the nineteenth century, who viewed Bible translation as essential to spreading the gospel. Over the course of the century, efforts were begun that often took decades to complete. These are stories of remarkable achievement and abject failure. The missionaries were learning the languages, constantly discovering previously unknown dialects and nuances of expression. They often fumbled, but the overall success of their efforts can hardly be overstated. By sowing the seeds of vernacular versions, the harvest of local, Indigenous Christian communities in Africa was prepared.

The first translation into an African language was the Gospel of Matthew in the Bullom languages of Sierra Leone, printed in 1816 by the German G. R. Nylander. The first complete Bible, however, was translated into Gã, spoken around Accra in Ghana, and did not appear until 1866. Johannes Gottlieb Christaller (1827–1895) from the Basel Mission followed shortly thereafter with the Akuapem Twi Bible, which remains in use to this day. A similar case is the Ewe Bible from Ghana, which first appeared in 1913 and is still read today. These missionary translations have served the faithful for centuries, although in the past few decades there have been movements across Africa to produce more modern versions that reflect contemporary language. The Bible Society of Ghana, for instance, has prepared an updated revision of the Akuapem Twi.

In Nigeria the situation is even more complex. The African nation is dominated by four main languages: Hausa in the north, Yoruba in the west, Igbo in the east, and Nigerian Pidgin, a version of English, in the urban areas and in the oil fields. However, one of the earliest translations of the New Testament in the county was into Efik, the work of Scottish missionaries in 1862. Curiously, the Gospels, Epistles, and Acts appeared with Genesis attached. Its publication was financed by Black Jamaicans who claimed ancestry from the region.

The Yoruba Bible, however, was not the work of missionaries but was carried out by a native speaker, Bishop Samuel Ajayi Crowther (ca. 1807–1891). As a young boy he was sold to Portuguese slave traders and placed on a ship to be sent across the Atlantic. The slave ship on which he was being transported was intercepted by antislavery forces, and he was released in 1822. He settled in Sierra Leone, where he learned English and commenced reading the Bible. Ajayi was sent to England, where he converted to Christianity and took the name Samuel Crowther. He returned to Freetown in 1827 and continued his studies of languages, including Greek and Latin as well as Teme, spoken in Sierra Leone. In 1841 Crowther was asked by the British Society for the Extinction of the Slave Trade and the Civilization of Africa to take part in a mission up the Niger River to promote antislavery and preach Christianity. His detailed journal of the mission won Crowther a wide public and considerable prominence. Two years later, in 1843, he was called back to England for further studies and to be ordained as a clergyman. Returning to Africa, he led missions during the 1840s and 1850s. He was instrumental in the founding of self-governing African churches and engaged in dialogue with Muslims. In 1864 he was consecrated "Bishop of the Countries of Western Africa Beyond the Queen's Dominions," the first African bishop in the Anglican Church.

A brilliant linguist, Crowther worked on a vocabulary of the Yoruba language and a translation of the Book of Common Prayer into Yoruba. It was his work on the Bible, however, that proved foundational. It was the first by a native African, and Crowther committed himself to capturing the language spoken by the people. He was known to join meetings of tribal leaders to learn words and phrases commonly used. His translations of Romans and Luke appeared in 1850 and the complete Bible thirty-four years later. Crowther's work remains the "King James Bible" of the Yoruba-speaking peoples.[14] At the end of his life, he reflected, "The 'Sword of the Spirit' [the Bible], placed in the hands of the congregations, in their own tongue, will do more to convince and convert them than all our preaching, teaching and meetings of so many years put together."[15]

In neighboring Cameroon, there are likewise many languages and dialects with which missionaries struggled. A New Testament in Duala appeared in 1848, followed by a complete Bible in 1872, the work of Alfred Saker (1814–1880) from the Baptist Missionary Society. Like other Victorian missionaries, Saker included with his Bible translation a Duala version of John Bunyan's *The Pilgrim's Progress*.

In colonial Central Africa, Protestant missionary activity began in the 1860s and 1870s, but Bibles did not appear until about twenty years later. In Congo, a Belgian colony after 1908, more than two hundred languages were spoken, prominently Lingala, Swahili, Otetela, Ciluba and Kikongo, and translations by Catholics were not available until the early twentieth century. William Holman Bentley, an English missionary, and a Bakongo deacon named Nlemvo translated the first New Testament into the dialect of Kikongo spoken in M'banza-Kongo, in December 1893.[16] The complete Kikongo Bible in the same dialect did not follow until 1916, eleven years after Bentley's death. Other Bibles had to wait: the Ciluba version was published in 1927 and the Otetela and Swahili versions in the 1960s.

One of the most influential African translations was the Luganda Bible of 1896. The first translation of biblical books into this Bantu language had appeared in 1887, nine years earlier, but the complete Bible became a model for other versions. Following the Kiunguja Swahili Bible, it was the second full Bible of East and Central Africa, and the first to appear in one volume. Its influence is due in part to the fact that Luganda is the most widely spoken language in Uganda, as well as across parts of Tanzania and western Kenya.

Used by missionaries and African evangelists, the Luganda Bible was deeply influential because it was translated into a series of dialects. Today, this Bible is still used in regions where Luganda is not the native language but where reverence for the book runs deep and the people are willing to retain it. In its early form in the 1890s, the Luganda Bible was known as the Biscuit-Tin Bible because it was the right size to be stored in tin boxes, along with other valuables.[17] Such was its popularity that between 1888 and 1913 16,000 full copies and 6,400 New Testaments were printed and distributed.

The origins of the Luganda Bible were closely connected to the expansion of British authority in Uganda, where a translation was deemed essential for the spread of Christianity. A romanized orthography was designed for the language, and reading houses were established where new converts gathered to learn to read the Bible. Large numbers sought baptism, reportedly fifty thousand in the Anglican Church in Buganda. The speed with which Christianity was spreading only enhanced the urgency for a translation.

Catholics in Uganda were not inclined to accept the work of Protestants and set about creating their own translations, although they never produced a complete Bible. Between 1891 and 1913, translations of the Gospels and scripture narratives into Luganda were printed in France, the work of missionaries. But it was not until the 1930s that New Testaments, whole or in parts, were printed in Kampala, the work of the White Fathers mission. Ugandan Catholic scholars revised the New Testament in the 1960s, and in the following decade ecumenical efforts began among Catholics, Protestants, and Orthodox that culminated in a new Luganda translation in 1979.

Once more, the most formidable obstacle to translation was God—that is, how to name God. Christians were not alone in struggling with this. On the east coast of Africa, the conundrum had already been encountered by Muslims, who labored to render the full nature of Allah into Indigenous languages. Christian missionaries adopted a number of strategies, although frustration and a troubling sense of compromise often resulted. Were the names of African deities transferable?

Some missionaries found reason for optimism in the Bantu name "Mulungu" (later "Mungu"), which was used by both Christians and Muslims.[18] In Bantu culture, shared with others such as the Kikuyu, Mulungu was a distant creator. Jesus Christ, as the son of God, later became *mwana wa Mulungu* (child of Mulungu), and the name "Mulungu" for the Christian God is today found in more than thirty African languages.

In northern Tanzania, Christians preferred the name of the Iraqw deity Looah for the name of God.[19] The parallels seemed propitious. Looah was creator and sustainer of the universe and was understood as benevolent, a god of justice and order. The problem was that for the Iraqw, Looah was female and mother, the giver of light and children, which conflicted with traditional Christian patriarchal conceptions of God. Iraqw culture saw mothers as creators, loving and caring. Men, in contrast, were compared to the evil one, Neetlangw, who for Christians was Satan.

Some encouraged the Iraqw to use a borrowed Swahili name for God, but they strongly preferred their own. The matter went far beyond semantics. For Africans, to lose the name Looah was to deny a significant part of their understanding of the divine. Supporters of the term pointed to maternal language in the Bible, such as in Psalm 131, when God says, "I have calmed and quieted my soul, like a weaned child with its mother" (ESV). One proposed way forward was through the adoption of the Swahili/Bantu name "Mungu," who was also not gender specific but was designated male by the translators. However, the matter remains far from resolved. During discussions in the 1990s concerning an Iraqw translation of the Old Testament, Iraqw Christian leaders pleaded for the restoration of the name Looah. A female Christian leader and teacher at the Waama Bible College in Mbulu spoke of how she found it extremely difficult to evangelize God's name in Swahili. In contrast, it was much easier to evangelize and discuss religious matters with non-Christian Iraqw when God's name in Iraqw was used.[20]

A similar problem appeared in South Africa, dating to the first early Christian missionaries. Englishman John Colenso (1814–1883), who became the first Anglican bishop of Natal in South Africa and a significant defender of African traditions against the views of most colonial administrators and missionaries, took up the cause of the Zulus against what he saw as the oppression by the Boers. Among his goals was creating the best possible translation of the Bible into the Zulu language. Despite the sincerity of his intentions, Colenso's colonial condescension was never far below the surface. "We have had the greatest difficulty," he wrote in 1855, "in fixing on a proper name for God. I cannot bear the mean and meaningless name of uTixo [*sic*], with its disagreeable click and poverty of sound."[21]

After finding the alternatives insufficient, Colenso despaired: "No one, who has not tried, can conceive how hard, and almost impossible it is, to give correct representations in another, and that a barbarous tongue, of the refined and expressive language of some parts of the Bible and Prayer Book."[22] Indeed, despite Colenso's objections, "uThixo" became the Zulu word for the Christian God in the complete Bible of 1883 and remained so until a retranslation in 1924 replaced it with "uNkulunkulu." But the matter was not settled. In the 1970s, a team of South African scholars opted for another traditional name for God, "uSimakade" (He who stood since long ago), commonly used by Zulu Christians. They also adopted "uMvelinquangi" (He who appeared first) with the following explanation: "Therefore in Zulu we say he is Simakade. In the New Testament we use this name of the Lord in passages quoted from the Old Testament. Umvelinquangi, this name of God is an original word. It is used where he is revealed as Creator, the One who was from the beginning, the Lord of the whole world."[23] A few years later, in the early 1980s, the proposal met with fierce resistance from scholars from the Dutch Reformed Church, who claimed that the name uMvelinquangi "refers to the first ancestral spirit, and not the God of the Bible."[24]

The spread of the Bible was by no means by foreign missionaries alone. One of the most extraordinary stories is of the Liberian prophet William Wadé Harris (1860–1929), whose charismatic preaching led to a wave of conversions across West Africa. His crusades attracted tens of thousands, but his attitudes to colonial Christianity were complex. Above all, Wadé Harris advocated for his fellow Africans to make the Bible their own.

The price was high. The people, Wadé Harris held, needed to renounce much of their Indigenous culture, which was inimical to the gospel (though only to an extent: he was and remained a polygamist). Wadé Harris's teachings demanded a distinctive form of accommodation with white missionaries, whose churches and schools he believed offered a way forward to an authentically African Christianity. Africans, he felt, needed to learn the religion of the colonialists and acquire the tools necessary to find their voice. For his part, he zealously translated scripture into his native Grebo in the hope that the people might understand the Bible in terms of their African experiences.[25]

The Ghanaian theologian Kwame Bediako (1945–2008) regarded Wadé Harris as "a trail-blazer and a new kind of religious personage on the African scene, the first independent African Christian prophet," who was not so much concerned with belief in the Bible as with actually living the Bible.[26] Rather than worry about what the Bible reported Moses saw, or Elijah did, or Jesus experienced, Wadé Harris cared about spiritual involvement with these figures in one's life. For Bediako, Wadé Harris was a paradigm of a non-Western and essentially Indigenous apprehension of the gospel. He was an African Christian "uncluttered" by Western missionary controls.

Wadé Harris's complex relationship with his own culture speaks to a burning and enduring question for Africans: Where are the boundaries between Christianity and traditional beliefs and rites? For the Liberian, the reply was unequivocal: to accept the Word, the people had to abandon traditions of witchcraft and magic and adopt a more European approach, embracing education and rejecting superstition.

The colonialists, he argued, were God's necessary punishment for African idolatry, and freedom would only flow from the pure Word of God. To one of his followers he wrote, "Read the Bible, it is the word of God. I am sending you one in which I have marked the verses that you should read. Seek the light in the Bible. It will be your guide."[27] European schooling would liberate Africans to find their own culture in Christianity. White missionaries offered the tools of reading and writing, which enabled them to impart the secrets of the Bible to Africans.[28] Those skills would ultimately enable the people to find their own way, apart from the colonialists, a properly "de-paganized" African Christianity grounded in the Bible.

Wadé Harris's strategy of limited accommodation contrasts with one of the most dynamic and controversial religious phenomena to emerge out of colonialism in Africa. The Kimbanguist movement was begun by the eponymous and charismatic Simon Kimbangu (1887–1951), a Baptist catechist who belonged to the Cingombe ethnic group, part of the Kongo ethnic group. He was born in the village of Nkamba, near Matadi in the southwestern part of the Belgian Congo (now the Democratic Republic of Congo). Kimbangu placed the Bible at the heart of his advocacy of a Christianity that did not accept the God of the missionaries, although it was deeply focused on Christ. As he extolled his followers, "You must believe in Him and put His teachings into practice. You must no longer continue considering Him as the White man's God, but really as the son of the Eternal."[29]

Kimbangu's account of how he received the Bible involved its direct transmission from God to Africa, rather than through missionaries. In a dream, he was told by a mysterious figure, "This is a good book. You must read it and proclaim its contents." Certainly, his understanding of the scriptures, to the consternation of the Catholic Church, was firmly in the Protestant tradition of putting them in the hands of the people. Before his arrest by Belgian colonial police, he told his followers, "The Spirit has revealed to me that the time has come now for me to surrender myself to the authorities. I will leave you nothing but the Bible. Read it at all times and in all places, and put God's Commandments into practice unfailingly."[30] Kimbanguists referred to the Bible as *mokanda ya bomoyi*, a Lingala phrase meaning "the book of life." The Kimbanguists experienced and lived the realities of the peoples of the Old and New Testaments, whose lives they understand as being as real today as millennia ago.

In the Kimbanguist churches, music brought the Bible to the people, who sang of ancient figures as present in their lives, instructing and admonishing them.

Chorus: *Noah, Noah, Noah,*
Noah, Father Noah,
Noah, open the ark,
The children are drowning!

Alto: *Impossible, impossible*
My children, that's impossible.
Impossible, impossible
Children, that's impossible.
Look for another refuge.

Mezzo: *In the world we used to live in,*
I was the one who prophesied.
When I was building the ark,
You refused to listen to me!

Tenor: *Look at these herds, Noah!*
Look at these works, Noah!
Open the ark,
Our children are drowning![31]

Kimbangu embodied that biblical narrative, and there was much about him that seemed mythical. He carried a staff in the tradition of Moses, with which he was said to perform miracles of healing. Such was the reverence for him that one of his supporters was reported to declare, "God has promised us to pour His Holy Spirit over our land. We have implored Him and He has sent us a savior for the Black race—Simon Kimbangou [*sic*]."[32] The enthusiastic supporter declared him to be the chief and savior of all Black people, to be compared to the savior figures of Moses, Jesus Christ, Mohammad, and Buddha. "God did not want us to hear His Word without giving us any proof," he explained, "so He gave us Simon Kimbangou, who is for us like the Moses of the Jews, the Christ of the foreigners, and the Mohammad of the Arabs."[33]

Kimbangu was not alone in turning to the Bible for resistance to colonialism and finding African voices. Unease and hostility toward the Bible were often expressed as nations were gaining their independence. At a 1960 conference in Kinshasa on the nature of African theology in the postcolonial period, the participants widely acknowledged that many Africans were deeply suspicious of the Bible, given the prominent place of the book in European efforts to "civilize" and rule them.

The Congolese theological student Tharcisse Tshibangu proposed that a truly African biblical culture must free itself from "Western rationalism," a philosophy of doubt that seeks certainty. Africans should instead favor their own traditions of reading the Bible with intuition and synthesis. Tshibangu advocated that Africans place "spontaneous trust" in the senses and experience and remain open to the spiritual.[34] The dialogue between African culture and the Bible, he believed, should begin with the revelation of the Bible in terms of the African mindset, enabling the identification of specific values in Black culture that could be promoted through education.[35]

For many in Africa, the Bible, and more specifically the Epistle of James, with its condemnation of social injustice and political abuse, played a key role in the development of liberation theologies. Take, for instance, the 1915 revolt led by John Chilembwe (1871–1915) in Nyasaland (Malawi), which was a crucial moment in the development of religiously grounded resistance to colonialism.[36] Chilembwe protested against the miserable conditions for African workers on colonial plantations, and in the violent revolt the leaders quoted the fifth chapter of the Epistle of James as the inspiration for their actions: "Now listen, you rich people, weep and wail because of the misery that is coming on you. Your wealth has rotted, and moths have eaten your clothes" (James 5:1–2, NIV). Chilembwe was hunted down and killed by a police patrol, but he is considered a hero of Malawian liberation; he is celebrated every year on January 15, and his face appears on Malawian currency. Chilembwe encouraged African self-respect and advancement through education, hard work, and personal responsibility, as advocated by Booker T. Washington, whose writings he came to know during a missionary tour in America.

The Namibian political leader and writer Zephania Kameeta (b. 1945) likewise invoked scriptural texts in the struggle against white South African occupation. He took, for example, Psalm 1 ("Blessed is the man that walketh not in the counsel of the ungodly, nor standeth in the way of sinners, nor sitteth in the seat of the scornful," KJV) and adapted it to "Happy are those who reject the evil advice of tyrants / Who do not follow the example of sellouts / And are not resigned to live as slaves."[37] Similarly, in his translation of Psalm 23, Chilembwe revised the familiar King James verse "The LORD is my shepherd; I shall not want. He maketh me to lie down in green pastures: he leadeth me beside the still waters" to a much more activist "The Lord is my shepherd; I have everything I need / He lets me see a country of justice and peace / And directs my steps towards his land."[38]

In South Africa, the Bible stood on both sides of the racial divide. Long cited by the Dutch Reformed Church as the foundation for separation, the book also fired defiance. Following the end of apartheid, Deputy President Thabo Mbeki (b. 1942) declared the Reconstruction and Development Programme to have an "almost biblical character," referring to its prophetic force. Classically educated and well versed in the King James Bible, Mbeki loved to draw on the wisdom literature in his prophetic reading of past and present. "The book of Proverbs," he asserted, "contains some injunctions that capture a number of elements of what I believe constitute important features of the Spirit of Ubuntu" (the South African term for "humanness" espoused by Archbishop Desmond Tutu).[39] In the fourth Nelson Mandela Annual Lecture, Mbeki so often referenced the book that he joked to appreciative laughter that he was "about to become a priest."[40] In a later speech he attacked the racist use of the Bible by white rulers who interpreted the Bible to justify segregation.[41]

Canaan S. Banana (1936–2003), the African liberation theologian and first president of Zimbabwe from 1980 to 1987, argued that Africans in postcolonial societies needed to rewrite the Bible. Certain texts in the Bible, he said, continued to be used to justify oppression—it served to maintain the status quo rather than fully liberate all people.[42] More controversial was Banana's view of the Bible itself. He believed that Revelation was not limited to the sacred book: "The material contained in the Bible is but a small part of the gamut of God's revelation to humankind. . . . The voices of the people of the 'third' world are voices of God's revelation, inspired by God's Spirit. Why are they not reflected in the Bible, directly testifying to God's presence in their lives, in their time?"[43] Against narratives of colonialism, Banana argued for the full compatibility of the Bible with socialism, which he described as "the legitimate child of Christianity." In his view, one could "return to the Bible, mainly the New Testament, to prove that Christianity is nothing else but socialism and therefore Christianity can only be fully realized in socialism."[44]

Banana also saw the Bible as containing the views of some peoples and not others, which meant it required further enhancement through the collection of sacred texts from around the world.[45] Restricting revelation of the divine to a certain people at a certain time in history could not embrace all people through the centuries; many people, such as Africans, had no voice in the Bible. A closed canon of the Bible only perpetuated abuse. Essentially, he recommended that the canon of the Bible be reopened and inappropriate texts that supported oppression be removed so as to prevent racism, sexism, and exploitation. Banana wanted to create a supra-Bible that would speak to all human conditions.[46] "A Bible liberated from its oppressive limitations," he wrote, "would, I believe, enable humanity to more adequately fulfill our responsibility as a people of God."[47]

Black theology in Africa, influenced by American writers such as James Cone, recognizes that the Bible alone is not a sufficient foundation for raising up the voices of the marginalized and silenced. To do so requires breaking from orthodox or classical theology. The Bible must be read in light of Black experiences of oppression. The two cannot be separated. It is in light of their history and culture that many Africans can read passages in the Bible where they find Black heroes and heroines who inspire and sustain.

Part of the effort to reclaim the Bible in Africa has involved taking seriously the perspectives of ordinary people and making the contexts of their lives central to reading the Bible.[48] African cultures, in these approaches, are both the source and subject of reading the Bible. The book is received not only individually but in terms of the concerns of wider communities and societies, both religious and secular.[49] For many Africans, the power of the book crucially resides in its promises of healing. The stories of William Wadé Harris and Simon Kimbangu speak to the widespread conviction that the Bible, in its words and as a physical object, is a source of transformative power. Among the Yoruba peoples of West Africa, notably Nigeria, Benin, and Togo, there is vivid evidence for the use of the Bible in healing and the battle against malign spirits. The psalms, for instance, are thought to provide protection and are often recited over amulets or engraved on objects intended to stave off evil and ensure prosperity. In one well-known instance, a chief placed Psalm 7 ("O Lord my God, in thee do I put my trust: save me from all them that persecute me, and deliver me," KJV) under his pillow with this accompanying prayer:

> O merciful Father, Almighty and everlasting King, I beseech Thee in the holy name of Eel Elijon to deliver me from all secret enemies and evil spirits that plan my destruction always. Protect me from their onslaught and let their evil forces be turned back upon them. Let their expectation come to naught and let them fail in their bid to injure me. Let their ways be dark and slippery and let Thy holy angels disperse them so that they may not come nigh unto my dwelling place. Hear my prayer now for the sake of holy Eel Elijon. Amen.[50]

The power of the Bible to overcome evil is sometimes presented more directly, with the Bible serving as a weapon for combat. According to one Zulu song, for instance, "Aka na mandla uSathane / S'omshaya nge vhesi": "Satan has no power / we will clobber him with a [biblical] verse."[51] In other cases, the Bible is understood more as a charm. This view is common even among highly educated Africans. For instance, Mercy Amba Oduyoye from Ghana relates the story of her sister:

> I was completely puzzled when I arrived at a sister's house and saw an open Bible in the cot of her newborn babe. "You have left your Bible here," I called. "No, it is deliberate; it will keep away evil influences." I was dumbfounded: the daughter of a Methodist pastor, with a doctorate in a discipline of the natural sciences, earned in a reputable U.S. university, using the Bible as a talisman! When I told this story in the course of a

social occasion in Nigeria, a discussion ensued that revealed many more such uses of the Bible.[52]

But the power of the Bible is not only found within homes. At soccer matches in Africa, Bibles are frequently held, both opened and closed, to influence the result.[53] Particular verses are believed to be especially helpful in scoring goals.

The curative forces of the Bible in the right hands have converted millions. When the hugely popular and controversial Nigerian televangelist TB Joshua died in 2021, the prominent young artist Victor AD, who attributes his rise to fame to his faith in God, left a moving Instagram message in which he recalled, "God used you to heal me of a skin disease as a little boy, after moving from one hospital to another but all to no avail."[54]

The ministries of Bible-based healing continue to arouse incomprehension and even derision, particularly in the West. A November 2016 report on the BBC News website investigating controversial healing ministries in Africa tried to maintain some critical distance, but with evident skepticism. It spoke of a South African pastor who was spraying insecticide on his church members in a healing ritual that shocked many. The report was at pains to stress that this was no mere isolated incident: "Cities and towns across the continent are plastered with signs and posters advertising churches, usually with apocalyptic names, promising instant cures and salvation from every intractable situation or sickness."[55]

More controversially, TB Joshua's YouTube channel, which with almost six million subscribers was one of the most popular Christian channels, was blocked by YouTube after Joshua claimed he could "cure" homosexuality and after reports of abusive videos on the channel. In one video, with 1.5 million views, Joshua is said to slap a woman sixteen times, while in another he required a man to cut off his dreadlocks to cure him of his attraction to men. After being blocked, Joshua's church, the Synagogue Church of All Nations, started its Emmanuel TV platform, which gained twenty-five thousand subscribers inside twenty-four hours.[56]

Despite Western suspicions, healing is, of course, central to Christ's ministry. In Luke's Gospel, Jesus asks who has touched his garment. His followers are perplexed, but he does not relent. When a trembling woman comes forward to admit that she had sought healing for twelve years of the issue of blood, Jesus does not reproach but cures: "And he said unto her, Daughter, be of good comfort: thy faith hath made thee whole; go in peace" (Luke 8:48, KJV). Tales of dramatic healings underscore how, for many Africans, the Bible confirms the reality of evil and the demonic in ways foreign to many Western Christians.

Similarly, passages in the Bible that are often read metaphorically by Western readers are often read by African women and men as speaking to the very real spiritual struggles between good and evil. As one African Catholic writer has put it: "[Jesus] is superior to the angels and spirits and to any ancestor one might think of; he surpasses in dignity and efficacy all soothsayers and sacrificers."[57] Particularly resonant are the New Testament stories of the Gadarene swine and the healing of Jairus's daughter.[58]

Take, for instance, the view of one Tanzanian author, who wrote that "what happened to the demoniac in Mark 1:21–28 happens to many demoniacs in Tanzania as it once happened to Esther in 1982."[59] The story of Esther involved demonic possession over several years that kept her from school. In response, an exorcism was carried out: "After singing three songs, three texts which narrate demon possession and exorcism, we read one text from each of the first three Gospels. The fourth text on which the sermon was based was Mark 1:21–28." The witness heard the screams of the demons issue from Esther's mouth: "We are being burned! We are being burned!" Finally: "We are going out!" Esther was wholly cured. The author concluded that "exorcism brings both spiritual and bodily or material blessings to the individuals and society. Due to such blessings, the church should see to it that exorcism is done whenever the need arises."[60]

African readings of the Bible often emphasize aspects of the Hebrew Bible and New Testament that speak of spiritual powers, healing, and miracles more directly than many churches and Christians in the West. When Paul speaks of "principalities and powers," he is taken to be evoking the powerful spiritual world and the struggle between good and evil.[61] The kinship Jesus spoke of, for example in the Gospel of Mark ("Whoever does God's will is my brother and sister and mother," Mark 3:35, NIV), has powerful resonances with the Akan of Ghana, who share a similar way of speaking about family and community. Examples are legion. The traditional "Grand Ancestor," recognizable to many Africans, becomes a way of speaking about the Son of God. Further, Jesus as a miracle worker defeating evil forces is highly relatable in a culture where the spiritual and physical struggles against spirits, disease, and death are daily realities.

Wisdom literature of the Bible found in Proverbs also has considerable resonance for many Africans, who easily relate it to their own traditions of sayings. Ghanaian theologian Mercy Oduyoye (b. 1934), for instance, reports that during her student years in a Methodist girls' boarding school, the girls would come together for assembly each day, and it was expected that they recite a text from the Bible: "It was our tradition to quote from the book of Proverbs, Ecclesiastes or the Sermon on the Mount; Proverbs was our favorite. Proverbs were already a part of our culture and we schoolgirls could easily get away with converting Akan proverbs into King James language and then simply inventing chapter and verse numbers."[62]

Sister Catherine Gaynor, an Irish nun who served in Nigeria during the Biafran War, offered in 1969 a perspective on how the people engaged the Bible in a manner different from her Western background: "Later I came to realize how close our Nigerian people are in their thinking and in their sense of community to biblical man and to the early Christians, open to God, ready to receive his word and to make it part and parcel of their lives. In a way it is probably easier for them to reach the meaning behind the inspired word than it is for us."[63]

This openness to the Bible is, in part, a product of education. Young people are often taught the Bible through stories, songs, proverbs, and other traditional texts. Oral literature is greatly treasured, with its vast inheritance of stories and legends. Across Africa, proverbs and riddles are highly esteemed; there is a love of rhetoric and verbal games that serve both education and entertainment. Among the Kikuyu in Kenya, such ways of learning the Bible are not only spiritual practices but essential to communal socialization.[64]

The emergence of African Christianity as a global religion is very much a story of the Bible. Pastors, teachers, and artists draw from the book through the lens of Indigenous and local appropriations and interpretations. Through song, drama, storytelling, and repetition the Bible creates community and participation.[65] The distinctive methods of interpretation, such as spontaneous song during worship in response to the reading of the Bible, encourage young and old to involve themselves in the book. The Bible in Africa often falls between tradition and the modern world, a position that has spawned distinctive practices and cultures that foster diverse African identities. For example, the South African artist Azaria Mbatha (b. 1941) creates works in which the centrality of Africa (Egypt) is represented in the Joseph story from Genesis. It presents the true African context as permeating the well-known tale of Egypt. Symbols and ideas are drawn from Zulu culture. In one panel, the family reunion in Genesis 46 is portrayed in terms of the African ideal of *ubuntu*, or humanness, and the story ends with prophetic hope.

African Christianity was seeded by the missions of the nineteenth and twentieth centuries, but in our time these roles have reversed. Africa is part of the "new sending countries," which also include countries in Asia and Latin America, that are sending missionaries around the globe, notably to Europe and America. African missionary activity is committed to taking the Bible to the European continent and around the world. Its focus is not only the African diaspora but also non-Africans. Some of the largest churches in Europe are African led. In London, the Kingsway International Christian Centre was founded in 1992 with two hundred people and now draws twelve thousand each Sunday, led by the Nigerian pastors Matthew Ashimolowo and Yemisi Ashimolowo. In a recent interview with news website *Evangelical Focus*, Nigerian Baptist minister Israel Olofinjana, head of the One People Commission, a community of Evangelical leaders in the UK dedicated to diversity and unity, spoke about the influence of African Christianity in Europe: "I strongly believe that European Christians, because we grew up in this culture, sometimes we need an outsider to help us elucidate the problem and to find a better and holistic solution, as you think together. Because

Africans have not been shaped by that Enlightenment thinking, there is something about their faith that believes that God is robust and can do the impossible. That sense of optimism and faith that God can change things is one that I think African Christians have really brought in."[66]

In his view, Africa can lead the way in reviving Christianity. It is no surprise, he argues, that African churches are the fastest growing, for "they have not been tempted by the rationalistic worldview that reduces our world to the natural. They still believe in the supernatural. That infuses optimism and challenges the secular worldview. It says there is not only narrative: yes, there is the natural but what about the supernatural?"[67] In turning from a history to a future of the Bible, there is every reason to believe that African voices will be central to the story.

CHAPTER 13

GLOBAL
PENTECOSTALISM

Pentecostals are on fire. Filled with the Spirit, they are not satisfied with mere assent to a verbal confession of faith but are baptized into an utterly transformed existence in which all promises of the Bible are possible, including exuberant speaking in tongues, the healing of terminal illnesses and addiction, and social and political liberation.[1] Men and women await Christ's imminent return by preparing biblical communities in which the Holy Spirit enlightens, cleanses, and fills with rapture. Pentecostals read and hear the Bible with absolute certainty, confident that what they do not understand will be revealed by the all-providing Spirit.[2] This is a revelation available to all who seek it in the Word of God as found in his book. With their optimistic belief in recovery and renewal, Pentecostal churches have been remarkably successful in attracting those seeking to turn their lives around and leave behind alcohol, political corruption, and prostitution. Women play a leading role.[3] In a world beset by darkness and demons, they have turned to the Bible and God so that a purging fire can be kindled.[4]

In contrast to earlier missionizing Western churches, which derided or sought to erase older customs, Pentecostalism has embraced an openness to traditional and Indigenous expressions of religion.[5] As a result, it has given millions a Bible in which they can see themselves and which they read and listen to in gatherings that range from small villages to urban megachurches. By furnishing this enthusiasm for and personal connection to the Bible, the movement has flourished among Blacks, whites, and Native Americans in North America and Europe, and spectacularly in South America, Africa, and Asia.[6] Pentecostalism is presently second only to Catholicism as the largest form of Christianity, numbering almost a quarter of the religion's adherents. In China alone, there are roughly eighty million Pentecostals, and the largest congregation in the world is the Yoido Full Gospel Church in Seoul, Korea, with eight hundred thousand members and four hundred clergy.[7]

Denominational boundaries, however, are porous. Indeed, many Pentecostal faithful, largely known as charismatics, remain inside Catholic and traditional Protestant churches and may not self-identify as Pentecostals. Pentecostalism is therefore better understood as a large-tent movement, covering an enormous range of groups, denominations, beliefs, and practices; it cannot be limited to a single set of doctrines, rites, or institutions. Nevertheless, commonly shared convictions are evident, such as Spirit baptism, belief in miracles, and the emphasis on a personal relationship with Jesus. Most Pentecostals are adamant that their beliefs accord with the traditional teachings of the church, such as God as Trinity and the unique saving work of

Christ. Most prominently, they share an absolute commitment to the Bible as the literal Word of God.

Beyond growing rapidly in absolute numbers, Pentecostalism is most notable for its truly global nature. Through immigration Pentecostals are frequently on the move, creating communities and building churches.[8] In the 1960s in Central and South America, Pentecostals made up less than 30 percent of the region's Protestant believers and between 10 and 20 percent of the whole population. By the end of the first decade of the twenty-first century, the Pentecostal percentage of Protestants had risen to around 75 percent. Although its roots were among the rural poor, there has been a notable emergence of Pentecostal communities in major urban centers. In Asia the numbers are smaller but the rates of growth are similar, leading one scholar to estimate that "at least a third" of Asia's Christian population is now charismatic or Pentecostal, and the proportion is "steadily rising."[9] Even in Muslim-majority Indonesia, the major Pentecostal church has over two million members, and megachurches have been established in Jakarta and Surabaya. Primarily in Central and South America, but also in Asia, Pentecostals have been heavily involved in politics, forming political parties in Brazil, Chile, Nicaragua, and Nigeria with considerable influence and with growing numbers of elected members.[10] Guatemala has had two Pentecostal presidents.

Such unfettered enthusiasm, though a boon to membership, also carries dangers that are realities of many charismatic churches: the conflation of spiritual gifts with worldly wealth, exclusion through insistence on single interpretations and purity of moral standards, and bitter divisions over the message of the Holy Spirit. The growing influence of Pentecostalism in the political worlds of South America and Africa has also divided many of the faithful. As the nearly two-thousand-year history of the Bible has frequently revealed, the possibility of a close personal relationship to God often challenges the stability of any single, doctrinally fixed faith. With its focus on local practices and traditions, as well as literal, sometimes radical interpretations of the Bible, Pentecostalism shows the power and versatility of this sacred book to meet the spiritual needs of people in the twenty-first century. But it also shows that Christianity will always, as it has since the time of Christ, remain in motion. As the Nigerian theologian Ogbu Kalu (1942–2009) noted about Pentecostals, they "believe that they have a message for contemporary communities, a message that contests the interpretations of the canon by the older mainline churches."[11]

Pentecostal and charismatic churches emerged from Catholic and Protestant churches during the 1960s, although they have deep roots in nineteenth-century America, when many Christians separated from established churches to form communities visibly filled with the New Testament's supernatural powers.[12] These breakaway groups went by a range of names, including the pejorative tag "Holy Rollers," but they shared the conviction of the fourfold gospel of personal salvation, Holy Ghost baptism, divine healing, and the Lord's impending return.[13] Baptism in the Spirit was directly connected to speaking in tongues, which for some North American Pentecostals was the true mark of a believer. Those who did not speak in tongues were second-class Christians.

The rise of Pentecostalism in America in the late nineteenth century was related to a renewed interest in methods of healing through the Spirit in both churches and the secular world. Ministers such as John Alexander Dowie and Maria Woodworth-Etter traveled around the country in the 1880s and '90s holding "spectacular healing revivals."[14] Beyond these tent meetings, their ideas and practices, along with others, began to spread through conferences, summer camps, books, and magazines. Among the most important of these ideas was a distinctive understanding of the human encounter with the divine, which enabled them "to capture lightning in a bottle and, more important, to keep it there decade after decade, without stilling the fire or cracking the vessel."[15]

This distinctive understanding of Christianity is heavily indebted to enslaved African Americans who blended African traditions to create a "slave religion" that embraced older traditions of dreams, visions, healing, trances, and belief in spirits. This borrowing was most explicit in the Wesleyan Holiness movement, one of the most powerful forms of American Christianity in the late nineteenth century. The Holiness movement, holding to African practices, John Wesley's views of perfectionism, and powerful belief in a second, postsalvation blessing, emerged as one of the main voices of a multiracial spirituality during the Reconstruction age.

The Azusa Street Revival in 1906 Los Angeles under William J. Seymour also demonstrated that the roots of Pentecostalism lay in the Black church.[16] Seymour preached "baptism of the Spirit" and racial integration. It was not a vision that would endure as American white Pentecostalism fell back into segregation and racism.

Over the next half century, Pentecostals moved from the fringes to the heart of America's religion, and by the end of World War II, they could be found in all the leading Protestant and Catholic churches. Parachurch groups, such as Women's Aglow and Full Gospel Business Men's Fellowship International, emerged alongside the YMCA and allowed men and women to express their commitment to the biblical supernatural. More recently, such leading figures as Admiral Vern Clark, chief of naval operations, and John Ashcroft, US attorney general, both publicly identified as Pentecostals. In the 1990s, the magazine *Christian History* named Azusa Street pioneer William J. Seymour one of the ten most influential religious leaders in America. And beyond America, as briefly indicated at the outset of this chapter, Pentecostalism has experienced even more widespread growth.

This success is due in no small part to the Pentecostal Bible, a vast energy source that bears witness to God's ongoing revelation in the world, affirms that the miracles recounted in scripture are as real today as in the days of Christ and his disciples, and extols scripture as an inexhaustible font of power transforming lives through the indwelling Spirit. The Bible, in their view, is a conduit of intense spiritual force, and reading, whether silently or aloud, and hearing it can be redemptive—and solitary—experiences. Individuals and communities become the characters of the Bible in worship, music, praise, and healing. As one Guatemalan pastor puts it, "We believe in the word of God; personally, the Holy Spirit is my teacher; without him there is no correct interpretation of the scriptures."[17] A Nigerian Pentecostal pastor similarly observes that "the Bible contains nothing else but the Word of God, and so, whatever is found in that Scripture must be taken as impeccable truth. Thus, the biblical authority is viewed as binding, with particular reference to believers or faithful Christians that the Pentecostals are aspiring to be."[18]

Supernaturalism, long regarded by mainline Protestants and Catholics as having ended with the age of the apostles, very much fills the experiential world of believers. Alongside the miracles of Jesus recounted in the Gospels, Pentecostals have an especial attachment to the book of Acts, which is the foundation of their baptism in the Spirit and speaking in tongues (see Acts 2:1–16, 10:44–48, 19:1–6).[19] Further, the biblical book shapes their view of the world around them, which is suffused with spiritual forces, benign and malign. Acts and Paul's letters show how the disciples continued Jesus's miracles and healing ministry and how the Spirit acted through them (see 1 Cor. 12–14). Perhaps in more ways than in other traditions, the Bible is, for Pentecostals, a powerful identification with the earliest Christians and offers hope that the contemporary world experiences the spiritual revolution of first-century Palestine.

For Pentecostals, the words of the Bible were recorded to be actualized in this life, here and now. The Bible constantly speaks to the present. In the English-speaking world, the favored version has remained the King James Version, which, with its sonorous voice, emphasizes the actualization of the Word in the lives of men and women, children and adults, and the gifts of the Spirit, notably speaking in tongues and healing. God pours forth the Holy Spirit on believers in tangible ways. As one witness says, "Pentecostalism requires a God on the loose, involving himself with the fine details of our earthly existence and actively transformed lives."[20]

The Christian life is thus lived through an intense encounter with the Bible that is neither intellective nor distant: the book is not merely an authority in the churches but their lifeblood, as the worldviews of the biblical writers and the worldviews of Pentecostals converge in the shared belief that God remains an active and primary agent in the biblical stories.[21] Pentecostals are often falsely thought to supplant the Bible with their exuberant experiences of the Spirit, but that is a misapprehension; faithful men and women live with the book daily, often not reading anything else and committing passages to memory.[22] Indeed, in their view, everything that happens in life has long been set out in the Bible, which provides the essential guide to daily life with all its struggles. Adoption of the lives of biblical characters is far more important than theoretical ethical principles or doctrinal understanding. Christ, the apostles, and the holy men and women of the Hebrew Bible are not merely shining examples: they are spiritually present, and their lives are to be embodied and reenacted by those filled with the Spirit.

For Pentecostals, the Bible is a book of constant and progressive revelation, which leads them to place great stock in the past as fully informing the present. The origins of the holy book are indisputable: it was dictated by the Holy Spirit. Unlike other Protestants, most Pentecostals view the Bible as both a fixed foundation of the church and the means by which God continues to speak to each generation, revealing new experiences and insights into God's will. What distinguishes them from Evangelicals is their emphasis on prophecy, words of knowledge, and discernment of the Spirit. Therefore, as we head toward the end of time and God's fulfillment, each generation acquires insights not wholly grasped by those who came before.

Central to this unfolding of revelation is an intense focus on the person of Christ, who is to be found throughout the Old and New Testaments. He is the savior, and the redeemed have been washed in his blood. The Bible exhorts Christians to the active imitation of him. Never static, the book is, as one believer describes it, like "an athlete's instruction video, showing how to execute a back flip, spike a volleyball, or dance a pirouette."[23] Another puts the point clearly: "We Pentecostals have always considered ourselves to have something of a special relationship with the sacred page, almost as if we have a unique affinity with the Bible and hold a significant position among the guardians of its truth."[24]

Pentecostals approach the Bible with a literalist sensibility, but it is not helpful to think of them as fundamentalists, for many favor a more intuitive reading of scripture that has a special interest in the supernatural elements of scripture, such as miracles, magic, visions, healings, and prophecies.[25] Facing the challenges of daily life in an uncertain world, many Christians on Native American reservations and in developing nations in Asia, Africa, and Latin America identify with parts of the Bible often ignored by Western liberals, particularly passages about healing and spiritual warfare, as well as apocalyptic expectations and readings that generate a palpable suspicion of the secular world.[26] The Bible is a lens through which to view pressing social and economic realities, and both Testaments are seen as fresh, encouraging, and authoritative.

In contrast to most Protestants, from fundamentalists to liberals, Pentecostals do not see themselves as "interpreting" the Bible so much as listening to God. The Word of God is both the Word and present truth. The Word of God enters the person to be "ingested," as the biblical words come to constitute the person.[27] The sacred book is nutritive, feeding the faithful in body and spirit. They also speak of the Bible as reproductive—God's Word is a seed that penetrates to impregnate with the truth. The physicality of the Pentecostal encounter with the Bible is intimate, a full transformation of the whole person into life in the Spirit. Each person lives in a dynamic and ever-growing relationship with the Bible, and they experience revelation through seemingly ordinary daily events. A newspaper article, a blog post, a television program, or an incidental conversation could be the means through which God speaks to them. Every moment is suffused with divine possibilities.

Central to the biblical drama is the pastor who leads the congregation. Pentecostals do not hold to hierarchical authority, but ministers enjoy enormous, often revered status. They are the primary means through which God speaks and are interpreters of the Bible. They are singled out for divine favor, receiving gifts of the Spirit, and are able to discern biblical wisdom for others. In both America and the Global South, clericalism has had more controversial associations, such as God's apparent blessings with material wealth. The pastor's income, house, car, and even private jet symbolize the material benefits of the Spirit. In short, they have what the people desire and can achieve with sufficient faith. While such seeming excesses are often derided by wider society, that risks missing how inspirational such blessings are for many who struggle with poverty and exclusion.

The power of pastors lies in the Word, as found in the Bible, both spoken and performed. Discerning the divine in the world is central to preaching, as is strongly evident in Black Pentecostal sermons. Past and present are interwoven as the people are led to see themselves in the lives of biblical characters and charged by the experience to renew their lives. The results in Black churches can be astonishing and mesmerizing: sermons are sung and chanted, enabling the people to overcome their tribulations through a dynamic interplay of preacher and congregation as they experience both lamentation and joy. Pentecostals often stress how God emphasizes certain parts of his Word at certain moments, which are known as "present truths."[28] In a sermon, Georgia senator Raphael D. Warnock, senior pastor of Ebenezer Baptist Church and the son of two Pentecostal preachers, amusingly recalled the life of the Bible in his family:

My parents had so much faith. You know they used to just live in the world of the Bible. They were Pentecostal preachers and so they spoke to us in King James English. "Thou shalt wash the dishes [laughter], lest I smite thee with my rod and my staff. . . ." When I went to Morehouse on a full-faith scholarship, I turned to my parents as they were getting ready to drop me off as a young freshman and I just wanted a few dollars, you know, to make it. And my dad—a veteran of World War II, a strong man, loving father—looked at me. True story, spoke to me in King James English. He said, "Silver and gold hath I none [laughter]. But such as I have, I give unto thee. The grace of the Lord Jesus Christ go with you."[29]

As mentioned above, and as is evident from Senator Warnock's humorous experience, Pentecostal approaches eagerly interpret God's Word but with a focus on the experiences of believers, offering readings both elaborate and creative. The Bible is taken literally and seriously. "I believe in the plenary inspiration of the Scriptures," trumpeted B. H. Irwin, founder of the Fire-Baptized Holiness Church. "I detest and despise . . . this higher criticism, rationalism, and this seeking on the part of ungodly professors to do away with objectionable parts of the Word of God, and as fire-baptized people we stand on the whole Book, hallelujah!"[30]

For Pentecostals, the Bible is more experiential; it is life in the Spirit. Indeed, traditional education in the Bible is often viewed more as an impediment than a spiritual gift. Knowledge is subordinated to the necessity of a "clean heart." Doctrine has only served to obscure God's voice, as Charles Parham told his followers: "There are a thousand contradictions, if you read the Scriptures through the creed's spectacles, but cleansed by the blood from false doctrines and traditions . . . the Bible stands out clear and bold, without a possible contradiction."[31]

In encountering the Bible, the Pentecostal approach is not to seek any systematic theology but, rather, to meet God in the text.[32] In Bolivia, Pentecostal writer Pedro Moreno noted a missionary's surprise when asked why the curriculum at the local ministry training center did not include courses on church history: "We are training Christians to evangelize the people now. We do not need to study church history."[33] Pentecostal statements of faith thus tend to be short and little interested in details of theology; rather, they cohere around such terms as "rule of faith," "spirit of the Bible," "heart of the message," and "tenor of Scripture."[34]

Education is nevertheless seen as crucial.[35] From the early twentieth century in America, Bible schools were established and members encouraged to join. In these schools, which were often small, consisting of fewer than forty members, they would learn the "full Gospel."[36] The schools spread rapidly across the country and became the foundation for the largest Pentecostal educational institution, Oral Roberts University. Roberts's influence was so widespread that in 1978, *Christian Century* judged him to be one of the ten most influential religious leaders in America. Today, there are hundreds of Pentecostal Bible schools across the globe. The centrality of the Bible in education reinforces the core discipline of the faith, which is not mere subjective following of the Spirit but life drawn from the continuous reading of scripture and the kerygmatic gifts of preaching, teaching, and daily living.

To these gifts we must add worship. In addition to preaching and prayer, music is central to this Spirit-filled praise. Many Pentecostals see themselves as warriors battling malign spiritual forces in the struggle to lead the Christian life, and they afford a special place to David, whose psalms encourage constant worship and song.[37] Indeed, David's psalms have been inspirational for modern forms of Pentecostal music and worship in renewal movements, such as the Toronto Blessing of the 1990s. There is no more arresting example of this phenomenon than the massive success of Bethel Church in Redding, California, which has eleven thousand members and its own music label and music publishing house. Its songs have topped the charts and have been widely streamed on Spotify and Apple Music.

Lively Spirit-led music is also important in Africa among Pentecostals, where vivifying faith is not primarily channeled through speaking in tongues but rather in untrammeled exuberance and participation.[38] Music is combined with lengthy sermons in which the people are fully engaged and by no means mere spectators. In the fervent atmosphere of worship, themes of success, victory, and prosperity, sometimes in material ways, prevail as worshippers are actively encouraged to find their story in the Bible.

Pentecostalism has enjoyed a significant advantage over traditional Protestant churches through its adeptness in connecting with traditional language, customs, and rituals. While both Catholicism and Protestantism encountered constraints in their efforts to ensure more doctrinal readings of the Bible in China and Africa, Pentecostals did not. Among the Cree in Alberta there is a powerful connection between Pentecostal preaching from the Bible and traditional animist beliefs. Shamanism and animistic practices flourish within Cree Pentecostalism. The radical change of life demanded by biblical living is not seen in opposition to the preservation of traditional medicine, rituals, and communal living. It is a meeting of the Bible with a way of life away from Euro-Canadian influence.[39]

Take, for instance, the members of some neoprophetic churches in Latin America and Africa who believe that if the Word of God is sharper than a sword, then the Bible could sometimes serve as a literal, physical weapon against the enemy.[40] By pointing a physical Bible at a foe, such as a witch, one might mediate the power of the Spirit and overcome evil. This ritual act in neoprophetic churches in Africa is by no means uncommon in spiritual battles, and preachers are expected to use the Bible in ways familiar to African religious traditions and attitudes toward malign spirits. Indeed, it is crucial to demonstrate that the Bible is more effective than older, non-Christian rituals. The role of the Bible as a weapon against possession plays an important role in attracting men and women to Pentecostal churches, but the talismanic nature of the book extends to disease, barrenness, curses, and setbacks in life: the churches hold out the prospect of much-needed relief. The appeal is evident in the long queues of both members and nonmembers outside of advertised healing sessions in neoprophetic churches, where people are fully persuaded that help is to be found in the Bible.[41]

Pentecostalism in Latin America is often divided between those who are very poor, who often live an oral faith, and the more literate middle classes. But despite differences of class and economic standing, certain aspects are widely shared, notably the call to action. The strong eschatological urgency of Pentecostals in their expectations of the end-times has led to a heavy emphasis on fulfilling the Great Commission of Matthew 28. One study has shown that three-quarters of Pentecostals in Brazil, Chile, and Guatemala believe that it is the duty of each person to evangelize.[42] The reflections of one man in Mexico engaged in evangelizing are illuminating:

Never in all my years as a missionary had I participated in such fearless and aggressive evangelism. Several times that day I wondered if I would get home alive, but I stopped wondering what made their church grow so fast. These people took seriously Jesus' words about going to the highways and byways and compelling folks to come in. Furthermore, they depended on local pastors and evangelists like my son-in-law, whose level of training did not alienate them from the common people. Whatever they lacked in theological sophistication was made up for in other ways.[43]

The Pentecostal Bible in the Global South is largely the Bible of the poor, read in the cultural contexts of agrarian, tribal, animistic, and economically impoverished peoples.[44] The economic depredations of biblical characters of the ancient Near East are existentially much closer to those of the poor in South America and Asia than to the comfortable lives of most Europeans and North Americans. This experiential reality makes understandings of the Bible in the Global South very different from those found in the Global North.[45] This affinity is deepened by the fact that Pentecostals often pioneered a strategic alliance with local religions. Many Pentecostal Africans, for instance, came to see that the Bible was more sympathetic to many of their traditional practices than were the European and North American missionaries, who had admonished them with hostility toward what were seen as pagan rituals and beliefs. The genealogies of the Old and New Testaments, for example, provide clear and positive support for ancestor veneration.

Engagement with traditional beliefs and customs can also be found in Korea, which was heavily influenced by American missionaries but soon developed its own character.[46] In the case of South Korea, this has meant engagement with traditional religions such as shamanism and Buddhism. At the Yoido Full Gospel Church in Seoul, for instance, there is the prayer mountain, a place of prayer and fasting where mystical revelations and other wonders frequently occur. Mountains and hills have been places of spiritual retreat and pilgrimage in Korean spiritual practices for centuries. Buddhist temples are generally found on the sides of mountains, as are cemeteries, and mountains are traditionally associated with the good spirits from whom both shamans and pilgrims receive power and blessings. Such beliefs fit well with the sacred place of mountains in the Old Testament, leading to a robust mixture of Christian and traditional spirituality. In addition, notable among Korean and Chinese Pentecostals is the strict moral code evident in societies influenced by Confucianism.

In other places, the connection between Pentecostalism and local culture can be found in the importance attached to the spoken Word. For instance, in Chinese Pentecostal churches, biblical words are most forceful when uttered. Protestants in the Three-Self church in Huanghaicheng place stronger emphasis on individuals' testimonies than on the prophetic roles of pastors. The more well versed in the Bible the speaker is, the more readily they can select the passages most appropriate to, for example, illness or demonic possession. In the case of exorcism, a combination of prayer, speaking in tongues, singing, and reading from the Bible will be employed.[47] Among Chinese Pentecostals, the essential term is *ling'en*, which broadly means "charismatic." Neither scripture nor teaching is regarded as exhaustive, and they can be augmented by individual insights or revelations. A leader of a group might ask, "Does any brother or sister have an insight?" And spiritual gifts might include the learning of languages or aptitude in business.

These gifts are not seen as learned but as directly offered by the Spirit. Testimonies of healing and other extraordinary events are given in the groups.

Pentecostalism is most controversial when the question of prosperity through the Spirit arises. Many traditional Christians dismiss Pentecostalism for its alleged emphasis on the prosperity gospel, viewing this as crassly selling the Bible and faith for material rewards.[48] Although generalizations can be misleading, aspects of this criticism are certainly true. Arising in America, preachers of the prosperity gospel were beamed into homes and public places in Latin America and Africa with their promises of material benefits accruing from belief. American preachers such as E. W. Kenyon, Oral Roberts, and Kenneth Copeland led the way for a vast array of proponents whose US-based programs were often broadcast in Africa and Latin America. Their message was and remains focused on the Bible as fulfilling all human needs and offering an invitation to the faithful to share the victory of Christ over sin, poverty, and illness.[49]

Selected passages from the Bible are accorded especial significance and interpreted as saying that God blesses through material wealth, such as Deuteronomy 8:18ff (God gives power to become wealthy), Malachi 3:10ff (God opens windows of blessings to those who tithe), John 10:10 (God gives abundant life characterized by wealth), and others.[50] A positive confession of faith leads to health and well-being, as expressed by the Nigerian singer Uche in a song popularly known as "Double Double." The lyrics speak of God as a good God and say that when you believe in him, God doubles your money, houses, cars, and everything you have.

Such emphasis on biblical prosperity marks one point of distinction between traditional Pentecostalism and so-called Neo-Pentecostals.

Traditional Pentecostals adhere to a long-standing embrace of ascetically moral living and reject material wealth. They read and hear a different voice of the Bible than the message of the prosperity preachers, who link the Holy Spirit with health and wealth. Traditional Pentecostalists look more to Paul's words in 1 Timothy about the love of money, or mammon, being the "root of all evil" (1 Tim. 6:10, KJV). They focus on living lives of godliness and service and not on getting a promotion or buying a Mercedes-Benz. Neo-Pentecostalism, in contrast, more readily advocates a mentality in which life is a battlefield and obstacles to prosperity are overcome through Spirit-led efforts. The heroes are not to be self-denying but rather are equated with the warriors of the Bible.[51]

This focus on prosperity has occasionally led to financial scandal. In South Korea, for instance, the most prominent figure in Korean Pentecostalism, David Yonggi Cho, based his preaching of prosperity on the following verse: "Beloved, I wish above all things that thou mayest prosper and be in health, even as thy soul prospereth" (3 John 2, KJV). Toward the end of his life, he was charged with embezzlement. Nevertheless, his influence reached around the globe and was especially notable in Africa, where he enjoyed a devoted following. His gospel of great expectations of the Spirit resonated with those suffering spiritual, financial, and bodily ills, and his message was unequivocal: "Religion is useless if religion can't give hope."[52]

The gospel of prosperity was also promoted by William Mwangangi of Nairobi's Jesus Manifestation Church. In a sermon broadcast on January 3, 2006, he used 1 Samuel 16, about Samuel's finding (or locating) David and anointing him. The time of anointing of favor had come, Mwangangi said, for it was the year of God's favor. Money,

Mwangangi promised his listeners, will find you. "You have struggled for years," but

> that [has] now come to an end and now the rewards will flow out of God's abundant grace: You just believe the prophetic word from God. This will be manifest in your life. Don't ask how; that is not your [business]. . . . You don't deserve a car, but because of God's favour you will find yourself driving a Mercedes Benz. You don't deserve to buy a bungalow, but because of God's favour you will buy a bungalow; you don't deserve to work in a bank, but because of God's favour you will be working in a bank. The favour of God gives you what you don't deserve to have.[53]

Martin Ssuna, also from Nairobi, was even more emphatic in his 2006 sermon on Luke 6:8, where Jesus tells the man with a withered hand to stand up and heals him. "Jesus is coming right now," Ssuna promised. He continued,

> Tonight, Jesus is saying stand on your feet. Jesus said, "What are you doing, drunkard, jobless, murderer?" Redemption is present for all who turn from sin: Get up! Get up! You have been down, a nobody. Somebody shout, "Get up!" Shout "Up! Up! Up!" [By now the whole congregation is shouting.] Whoever told you you are down, supposed to die, have HIV, cancer . . . Jesus said: "Get up!" Lift your hands: I'm up! Jesus said: "Get up!" Get up from rape, child abuse. . . . He's calling your house, your business: Get up! Are you ready? Your anointing, your favour, your breakthrough is coming![54]

Ssuna's sermon conveys the transformative power of the biblical message. What Jesus has done for the man with the withered hand he will also do for those who live in poverty or are addicted to pornography. They will be not only healed but lifted out of their nothingness to become prosperous leaders. The pastor himself, he says, is a living example of the blessings: the Spirit is alive in him, and his material circumstances reflect its blessings. In the words of Kenyan preacher Wilfred Lai on May 28, 2006: "I am your Moses. God has sent me to deliver you from everything that has been binding you."[55]

The Holy Spirit manifests in visions, dreams, and healing. Pentecostals have a deep personal relationship with the Holy Spirit, who is always referred to as a person. The blessings of miracles are closely connected to expectations of the imminent return of Christ. The abundant blessings are both interior and exterior, with an emphasis on healthy living. David Yonggi Cho, for instance, based his preaching of prosperity on the following verse: "Beloved, I wish above all things that thou mayest prosper and be in health, even as thy soul prospereth" (3 John 2, KJV). The King James translation captures the sense of God's enriching benevolence.

When it comes to the prosperity gospel, nothing rivals the Universal Church of the Kingdom of God in São Paulo, Brazil, where Pentecostal pastors dressed like rabbis preach in a ten-thousand-seat venue intended to resemble the Temple of Solomon. The seven million members of the UCKG make it the second-largest group of Protestants, after the Assemblies of God in the United States. Its controversial leader is Edir Macedo (b. 1945), whose preaching not only drives out demons but offers a message of great wealth to the country's millions of poor. Macedo is proof of what he preaches: he's a former street preacher and lottery worker who over the course of four decades has built the UCKG into a billion-dollar church-media empire. His influence is far from limited to the spiritual realm; in 2019 Macedo and his supporters played a key role in the election of Brazil's first Evangelical president, the far-right ex–army captain Jair Bolsonaro.

Macedo is known to preach for hours, and his style is not flamboyant but deeply personal. He often quietly asks, "Do you love your wife? Yes or no? Of course you do. Amen." Winning over the masses of faithful is the first step toward addressing more controversial subjects, such as the "well-known" danger that Satanists kidnap children and sacrifice them. Men and women are faced with the unbearable consequences of what the devil will do if they do not offer up their money to the church through their tithes. Macedo never raises his voice, but he speaks in a persuasive, sonorous manner.

UCKG's membership is largely female and comes from Brazil's African-descended, Indigenous, and mestizo communities. Each person is requested to donate 10 percent of their earnings, as well as anything extra they can offer. The "request" is more than direct, and intimidation is evident. The tithing process can consume one-third of the service. The line from UCKG's promises to its adherents and the centrality of the Bible is immediate. Pastors, for example, may use an open Bible as a kind of fetish, carrying the book and exhorting the faithful to place money, checks, watches, and jewelry on it. In the São Paulo headquarters, a conveyor belt behind the pulpit carries the gifts of the people directly past a gilded ark to a safe room offstage.

The show business culture of the UCKG is an extreme form of how Pentecostals have made extraordinary use of all forms of media to spread their message. Global Pentecostal churches have been at the forefront of making the Bible and supporting material available through modern technology. The distribution of resources serves both large churches and more modest gatherings. In Nigeria groups of men and women who gather to read the Bible and pray, known as "cell groups," are crucial to reinforcing extended families and communities in the face of urban growth, and it is within these gatherings that intensive study of the Bible takes place, usually weekly and under the guidance of a teacher.[56] Bible Life Ministries and other organizations in Botswana and Zimbabwe distribute Bible materials at the end of Sunday services.

Beyond personal contact, the other media frequently used are radio, television, and the internet, which are deployed in the spirit of Acts 1:8: "But you shall receive power when the Holy Spirit has come upon you; and you shall be my witnesses in Jerusalem and in all Judea and Samar'ia and to the end of the earth" (RSV). The goal is to ensure the communication of messages from the Bible in both private and public spaces.[57] In Zimbabwe, it's common to encounter bumper stickers with such claims as "This car is covered by the blood of Jesus. Yours too can be covered." The bumper sticker includes the name and address of the car's owner in case someone who sees it wants to contact them for further information. When inflation was ravaging the Zimbabwe economy from 2000 to 2008, preachers shifted tactics and adopted economic language to spread the gospel: "God knows no inflation" bumper stickers on cars accompanied the playing of taped sermons on buses.

One writer, traveling by bus through Zimbabwe, recounts that the riders listened to the sermons of P. D. Chiweshe for four hundred kilometers.[58] The bus became a church, a sacred space for the propagation of the Bible. Gospel CDs and pamphlets in Nigeria and Zambia, respectively, are understood as essential tools of the Bible as a "living text," and recorded music becomes alive when it reaches the listener. So, for many Pentecostal Christians, there is a strong bond between printed, recorded, and spoken forms of the Bible. The book has been commodified in many ways, through a range of multimedia forms, blurring if not obliterating the distinction between a dead letter and the spoken Word.[59]

Perhaps most dramatic is the role of multimedia in attending to the ill, enabling a distant pastor to enter homes and hospitals. Many Pentecostals believe that blessings can be transmitted through radio, television, and the internet, and there are many testimonies of healing during these broadcast religious programs. Indeed, special healing messages are often recorded for distribution. Some are certain that even touching the radio, television, computer, or cell phone during these broadcasts can be a means of receiving healing, similar to Paul's handkerchiefs and aprons in Acts 19:12.[60]

It is not uncommon throughout Pentecostal communities for listeners to keep bottles of oil at home for use with the pastors' message. In Mexico, for example, pastors often equate illness with demons and instruct the people on the wiles of malign spirits, which are intelligent and can turn a person's mind against itself.[61] Bible verses are crucial to the deliverance from a demon, which can involve freeing the person from anger, resentment, and bitterness, which are sources of sin. Proverbs 17:22 is commonly cited: "A cheerful heart is good medicine, but a crushed spirit dries up the bones" (NIV). The expulsion of an angry disposition and the adoption of joy open the person to the healing of the Spirit.

This focus on healing is a major appeal of Pentecostalism in Latin America, Africa, and Asia, and it has embraced Indigenous beliefs and practices in a far more positive manner than other Western-oriented Christian churches. The focus on miraculous healing is not, however, uncommon in American Pentecostalism: the practices of handling poisonous snakes, drinking poison, or holding hot coals, which persisted for many years among Pentecostal groups in the southern Appalachians, arose from a literal understanding of Mark 16:18.[62]

Across the globe, Pentecostals have succeeded by encouraging an immediate, personal relationship between believer and God, a relationship mediated and explained by the Bible. Even when this connection seems the most remote—miracles delivered by radio, promises of material rewards, the sale of bumper stickers and oils—it is in fact the opposite. Only because of the promise of an immediate, personal, and intimate experience with God through the read, heard, and lived Word of his Bible are these interventions of faith possible.

CHAPTER 14

"WORLD WITHOUT END"

H ow do we take leave? When I was an undergraduate, a professor
memorably remarked that "how we end things says a great deal
about who we are." In the New Testament, Jesus's departure is reve-
latory. This global history of the Bible aspires to something far hum-
bler. Its conclusion is simply this: the Bible's global history is reason for
hope. Most books published do not have histories worth remembering,
global or otherwise. That the Bible emphatically does is evidence of its
unique worth. Fittingly, a parable of its qualities is offered up by a short
work of fiction, *The Book of Sand* by Jorge Luis Borges.

In the story, the narrator, alone in his Buenos Aires apartment,
receives an unexpected visit from a man selling Bibles. European
in appearance, the salesman explains that he has a number of Bibles
on offer, to which the surprised, unnamed narrator responds that he
already has a collection, including a Latin Vulgate, a Wycliffe Bible,

Cipriano de Valera's reformed Spanish Bible, and the Luther Bible, which he does not much like. But there is a twist. The man offers to sell him not a Bible but a "holy book." What is it, if not a Bible? That is the question that prompts the narrator's curiosity. Taking it in hand, he notices the spine reads "Holy Writ" and "Bombay." The visitor explains that he bought it from an illiterate man in India for some rupees and a Bible. Although he could not read, the Indian man referred to it as the "Book of Books" and regarded it as talismanic.

The mysterious salesman, who turns out to be from Orkney in Scotland, says it is really a "Book of Sand" because "neither the book nor sand has any beginning or end." Indeed, when the narrator attempts to open it to the first and last pages, the book will not allow him to see them—there are always more pages to turn. Once the book is opened, incomprehension reigns. The page numbers are Arabic numerals, but the text seems to be in an Indian language. The narrator leafs through the book and spots illustrations, yet when he attempts to return to them, they are not to be seen. Indeed, words that are found disappear. Sensing his frustration, the salesman says, "The number of pages in this book is no more or less than infinite." The salesman demands a high price, and at first the narrator balks. Ultimately, however, he produces money from his pension and parts with his black-letter Wycliffe in exchange for the Book of Sand.

The narrator soon becomes obsessed with the book, but his efforts to explore it only lead to further mystification. He cannot orient himself in the volume, which seems to keep changing. Exasperated, he places it on the shelf behind his set of *The Thousand and One Nights*, another book that he could not finish. But it won't leave him alone, and in a disturbed sleep he dreams of it. More accurately, he is haunted. Getting up in the night, he pulls the book off the shelf. Although driven to distraction, he has grown possessive and secretive in a Faustian manner. No one must know he has this book, no one is to see it—perhaps he should not have it at all. The thrill of the book soon gives way to paranoia and panic: "To the luck of owning it was added the fear of having it stolen, and then the misgiving that it might not truly be infinite." He has become enslaved to something he believes might be "monstrous."[1]

How to destroy it? Burning it conjures thoughts of a censorious past, of irreparable loss, and terrifying consequences: "I thought of fire, but I feared that the burning of an infinite book might likewise prove infinite and suffocate the planet with smoke."[2] He decides that the only thing to do is to lose it. Let it go. He alights on a plan, sneaks into Argentina's National Library, and goes downstairs, where he "lost the Book of Sand on one of the basement's musty shelves."[3]

Borges's Book of Sand is not the Bible, yet it is. It is the book of books, with a mysterious beginning and end. Its origins are unclear, and its physicality has generated both reverence and anxiety. It is infinite and inexhaustible, like the Bible, and appears in one moment to be specific to a particular time and place and then in another moment its eternality is revealed. Again, like the Bible. The Gospel of John tells us that the Bible knows its own inexhaustible nature: "And there are also many other things which Jesus did, the which, if they should be written every one, I suppose that even the world itself could not contain the books that should be written" (John 21:25, KJV). Yet we have only a single book, the Bible.

Unlike the Book of Sand, the Bible has resisted being lost. In fact, it is constantly being rediscovered. As its global history demonstrates, year after year it becomes more accessible, more available, more global. Today, the largest producer of Bibles in the world is no longer

Europe or North America but Communist China. The Amity Printing Company in Nanjing has state-of-the-art technology that has to date reached over two hundred million copies at a rate of about seventy a minute. The Russian Bible Society, restored in 1990 after the collapse of the Soviet Union, annually prints one million Bibles and is currently translating it into over eighty languages for ethic groups across the country. The world's most popular Bible app, YouVersion, exists on over five hundred million smartphones, tablets, and internet pages in over 1,800 languages. And YouVersion has recently released Bible App Lite, which, once downloaded, can be used entirely offline, a response to concerns in sub-Saharan Africa and Southeast Asia, where internet access is limited. The Lite version is the top ten in the Google Play store in seventeen African countries and number one in Kenya. It was recently announced that the most popular Bible verse is Philippians 4:6: "Don't worry about anything; instead, pray about everything. Tell God what you need, and thank him for all he has done" (NLT).

The Bible's global ubiquity doesn't imply global familiarity. By certain metrics, Western society today is much less biblically literate than in previous generations. There are plenty of studies to chart the decline. Recently, a study showed that 15 to 17 percent of American millennials read the Bible once or twice a month. Among those who attend church once or twice a month, the report found, almost 50 percent read the Bible either once or twice a month or a few times a year.[4] As with church attendance, the decline seems to have accelerated with the COVID-19 pandemic. But predictions of doom lack a broader view. Despite these declines, the Bible has also made inroads with new communities by keeping pace with developing senses of identity and contemporary concerns. There is the Africana Bible, feminist Bibles, queer Bibles, eco Bibles, and a wide variety of Bibles for Indigenous peoples.

And in secular societies, the Bible is still frequently encountered in movies and in gospel music, such as the hugely popular productions of Bethel, a charismatic church in Redding, California, whose music has found a large audience both in Christian communities and the wider public.

Our history of the Bible has reached an end, arriving at the Bible's global ubiquity. But the Bible dictates its own history, which is without end. The Gospels offer us a range of perspectives, mostly positive, although also somewhat terrifying about this matter. The disputed ending of Mark tells us, "And they went forth, and preached everywhere, the Lord working with them, and confirming the word with signs following" (Mark 16:20, KJV). John, we know, speaks of how all the books in the world could not contain the deeds and words of Jesus (John 21:25). Matthew provides the words that have inspired Christian missions from their earliest days: "Go ye therefore, and teach all nations, baptizing them in the name of the Father, and of the Son, and of the Holy Ghost: Teaching them to observe all things whatsoever I have commanded you: and, lo, I am with you always, even unto the end of the world" (Matt. 28:19–20, KJV). Luke records that Jesus blessed his disciples and ascended to heaven, leaving them full of joy and returning to Jerusalem to worship in the temple (Luke 24:50–51).

Even though Jesus's command to go unto the whole world has been fulfilled in astonishing ways, our world remains closely connected to those early Christians who heard parts of diverse scriptures in their communities. Individuals and communities seek to hear God speak to their particular experiences and cultures. The strength of the Bible has always been in its locality: translations into the languages of communities enabling them to find themselves in its stories. Each Bible is a revolution, a product of its culture and moment. Every translation, every illuminated Bible, every app expresses a longing for the infinite. The global book remains deeply personal and local, often creating tensions between individual and corporate reception. It defines and shapes those who seek to actualize its words in their lives, to capture its model of holy living. Yet it will not be owned by anyone and continues to defy all efforts to anchor it in fixed institutions. It inspires striving but rejects possession and exclusivity. Every claim to the clarity of the Bible, from Augustine and Martin Luther to Billy Graham, has been immediately challenged.

Just as the apostles Paul and Peter fiercely disagreed in Jerusalem, the cloud of witnesses who have since read the Bible have never gone forth with a single mission. Those who claim the message of the Bible do so with an urgent need to get it right. Justice is established in this world and eternity in the next. For Christians there is no greater fear than getting the Bible wrong, an anxiety that has inspired great faith and inflicted devastating damage.

Like the world in which it is read, heard, seen, and sung, the Bible is a book of many parts. True to its name, it is a book of books. And each book of the Bible, from the Pentateuch and Psalms to the Gospels, possesses a unique identity and vision of God and humanity. For two thousand years different parts of the Bible have exerted allure for different individuals and communities. Exodus offers inspiring stories of liberation, while the conquest of Canaan speaks of loss of land and violence. The prophets, with their different characters, give voice to repentance and the consequences of idolatry along with the assurance of God's certain promises. The Psalms contain the whole of human experience, from deep despair to exuberant joy. The early Christians of the book of Acts have inspired innumerable attempts to live the authentic biblical life and die in the faith. From the moment it came together as a codex, the Bible has been read richly and selectively to assorted ends. But its own end remains visible only through a glass darkly.

It is as a work of prophecy that the Bible gives us some purchase on its own end. Let's take the last book of the Bible, Revelation. Rarely read, even by most Christians, John of Patmos's vision is bewildering, full of seemingly impenetrable signs and symbols. Enthusiasts of the book have always claimed that it is a map of our future. The book opens with an explanation that appears misleading: "The Revelation of Jesus Christ, which God gave unto him, to shew unto his servants things which must shortly come to pass; and he sent and signified it by his angel unto his servant John" (Rev. 1:1, KJV). But they have not yet come to pass. The word "shortly" reminds us once again that, from the mythological beginnings in Genesis to the extravagant visions of Revelation, the Bible dwells in time and yet is timeless.

Revelation is a book of prophecy. John is taken up to heaven, where the angels show him what will soon take place. His visions include the four horsemen who presage disaster and ravage for the world. Jesus will return with his army of angels and destroy evil, but John sees nothing of the present world surviving. Written after the suppression of the Jewish revolt and the destruction of the temple in Jerusalem in 70 CE, Revelation reflects the world John knew. It is a book of war that arose in a context of brutality and suffering.

Prophecy is a distinctive mark of contemporary global Christianity. The widespread thirst for prophecy based on the Bible, particularly in Pentecostalism and charismatic Christianity, has been controversial. Prophetic figures have become leading voices in Africa, often displacing untrusted politicians in the public mind. The growth of prophecy owes much to cultures of uncertainty in Africa about immigration and emigration, the absence of the state in social affairs, and economic uncertainties. Prophecy has also become embedded in Western capitalistic culture, expressed in music and business approaches toward churches; even the Bible reflects a global attitude of commodifying religion.

But prophecies also play a crucial role in offering hope, and none more than the prophesied return of Jesus. Yet almost two thousand years after his ascension into heaven, Jesus has not returned. A myth, perhaps, or maybe a reminder that the Bible has its own sense of time. Recall the image of Christ holding the Gospels that greets the visitor or worshipper at the Chora Church in Istanbul, where human time is caught up into holy time. The Bible and Christ are one. The book, like the Son of God, was and is and shall be.

One of the most arresting aspects of John's revelation is how at the end of time all humanity shall stand together, and from a book, we shall all be judged: "And I saw the dead, small and great, stand before God; and the books were opened: and another book was opened, which is the book of life: and the dead were judged out of those things which were written in the books, according to their works" (Rev. 20:12, KJV). The sense of impending judgment on the whole of humanity contrasts with optimistic views of unity in this world. On this side of eternity, the Bible has been read in judgment of the greatest phenomenon of our time, globalization. Many Christians argue that the Bible anticipates globalization in its declaration that the faith should go unto the whole world. It is present in God's command in Genesis to "replenish the earth, and subdue it" (1:28, KJV) as well as in Jesus's departing words in the Gospel of Matthew. And with the technological revolution of our time, the Bible has spread throughout the world with speed previously unimaginable.

Debates, as the writer of Ecclesiastes says about books, are without end. For two thousand years the Bible has been discussed, interpreted, and lived for what it says. But crucially, it is also frequently silent, like Jesus before Pilate. Was there silence before God said, "Let there be light"? The Israelites were enslaved in Egypt for four hundred years, and the Bible says nothing about that time. There were no prophets, and God was silent. The psalmist cries out, "Unto thee will I cry, O LORD my rock; be not silent to me: lest, if thou be silent to me, I become like them that go down into the pit" (Ps. 28, KJV). Yet the book of Revelation speaks of everything ending with silence: when the seventh seal is opened "there was silence in heaven about the space of half an hour" (Rev. 8:1, KJV).

In grasping to understand its words and its silences, for over two millennia the Bible's readers have found hope. To borrow the title of a 1965 film, the Bible tells the greatest story ever told. Its words have comforted, inspired, sickened, and haunted humanity. Its text belongs to the global world of sacred texts, with which, today more than ever, it is in conversation. At its end, it holds a warning that safeguards its own future, and humanity's:

> If any man shall take away from the words of the book of this prophecy, God shall take away his part out of the book of life, and out of the holy city, and from the things which are written in this book. (Rev. 22:19, KJV)

The Bible remains inexhaustible.

ACKNOWLEDGMENTS

During the writing of this book I have been the fortunate recipient of generosity and wisdom that I cannot repay.

The origins of this venture date to a discussion in a café in New Haven, Connecticut, when, pencil in hand, Brian Distelberg of Basic Books invited me to say what I would like to write a book about. He did not flinch when I replied, "The Bible." Brian has been unfailingly supportive, and his guidance was essential. I was also fortunate to work with Alex Cullina at Basic Books and my marvelous copyeditor, Erin Granville. My agent, Don Fehr, likewise encouraged this unlikely project, and his enthusiasm heartened me. I had the great fortune to work with Thomas LeBien, Amanda Moon, and James Brandt at Moon and Company, who offered expert guidance in the preparation of the final manuscript.

Writing a story that stretches over two thousand years is a gargantuan task. Will Tarnasky and Nate Antiel were invaluable conversation partners and advisers who offered reflections, suggestions, and feedback. I was also able to work with wonderful research assistants: Alexander Batson, Teddy Delwiche, and Sam Young. Micah Oosterhoff masterfully fact-checked the manuscript. Colleagues at Yale and the wider academic community generously read drafts and put me straight on a good number of points. I am grateful to Euan Cameron, Volker Leppin, Mark Letteney (who graciously allowed me to see his excellent book prepublication), Kirsten Macfarlane, Vasileios Marinis, Jeffrey A. Miller, Ken Minkema, Kyama Mugambi, and Chloe Starr. I have taught several courses on the Bible at Yale and have benefited from rich exchanges with students and fellow teachers, in particular my colleagues Joel Baden (with whom I ran a seminar in the Beinecke Library on medieval and early modern Bibles), Harry Attridge, Howard Bloch, Carlos Eire, Chris Kraus, Larry Manley, David Quint, and Jane Tylus. My graduate students, past and present, have taught me a great deal, and I thank Alexander Batson, Elizabeth Buckheit, Flynn Cratty, Colin Hoch, Pranav Jain, Dan Jones, Max Scholz, Serena Strecker, and Justine Walden. At Yale Divinity School, Isaiah Cruz, Mike Gordon, and I'noli Hall shared their experiences and insights on Pentecostalism. Justin Hawkins organized evening gatherings at which first iterations of chapters were read. It was then that I learned that I was still too academic. I wish to thank the Yale librarians and staff for enabling me to use their rich collections, including the Gutenberg Bible. In particular, Kathryn James, formerly curator for early modern books at the Beinecke, played a key role. From my home university I have received generous and consistent support. Dean Greg Sterling of Yale Divinity School, himself a distinguished scholar of the Bible, has from the start been unflaggingly encouraging.

My intensive work on the Bible at the University of St. Andrews, Scotland, began with a four-year major grant from the Arts and Humanities Research Council of the United Kingdom for my project on the Protestant Latin Bible. It was a pleasure to work with Matthew McLean. Over the years I have given papers and workshops at the

Acknowledgments

British Academy, Oxford University, the University of St. Andrews, Cambridge University, Wheaton College, Clemson University, Baylor University, Union Theological Seminary, McGill University, the University of King's College in Halifax, Canada, the University of Zurich, the University of Geneva, the Gotha Library in Germany, and the Israel Institute for Advanced Studies in Jerusalem. The comments and conversations on every occasion were provocative and invaluable. In 2022–2023 I was a Whitney Humanities Fellow at Yale and had the chance to discuss my work with colleagues from disciplines across the university. During the spring semester of 2023 I was a guest at the Institut d'Histoire de la Réformation in Geneva, which was a most agreeable setting in which to complete the first draft. I am grateful to my hosts, Christophe Chalamet and Ueli Zahnd, as well as to my generous sponsor, Pierre Keller. In the Institut I was made very welcome, and I thank in particular the director, Daniela Solfaroli Camillocci, and Hadrien Dami, Nicolas Fornerod, and Giovanni Gellera.

Away from the classrooms, conferences, lecture halls, and libraries, I had the great fortune to discuss the Bible with wonderful friends. I want in particular to mention Jérôme Castan, Ross Douthat, Carlos Eire, Thomas Fulton, Bill Goettler, Clifton Granby, Pierrick Hildebrand, Ward Holder, Maria LaSala, Kathryn Lofton, Samuel Loncar, Francisco Marcos, Yaakov Mascetti, Joyce Mercer, Matt Miller, Victoria Morrow, Mark Peterson (often on the golf course), and Melanie Ross, and also Camil Abdelmoula, who enabled me to talk about the Bible in French and is a relative of Annie Vallotton, with whom the book opens. My friend and former colleague Andrew Pettegree, whom I have thanked in every book I have written, happily shared his wisdom on writing a trade book.

My family encouraged and sustained me with their love. My daughter, Charlie, who never ceases to amaze me, taught me the power of curiosity leavened with humor. Our dogs, Dougal and Freya, took me on many walks through the Vermont countryside during which much of this book was plotted.

Finally, this book is dedicated to my partner for life, Rona Johnston. In 2024 we celebrate our thirtieth wedding anniversary. I feel as lucky today as I did that day three decades ago in St. Leonard's Chapel in St. Andrews, Scotland. Nothing I can write here can fully express my admiration and love.

ILLUSTRATION CREDITS

1. Codex Sinaiticus: Zev Radovan/Alamy Stock Photo
2. Syriac Gospels: Photo by Sergio Anelli/Electa/Mondadori Portfolio/Getty Images
3. Rossano Gospels: Photo by De Agostini/Getty Images
4. Garima Gospels: Wikimedia Commons/Public Domain
5. Moutier-Grandval Bible: Photo by Fine Art Images/Heritage Images/Getty Images
6. Lindisfarne Gospels: travelib history/Alamy Stock Photo
7. Lindau Gospels: The Morgan Library & Museum. MS M.1. Purchased by J. Pierpont Morgan (1837–1913) in 1901.
8. Jahiris Byzantine Lectionary: Photo by Heritage Art/Heritage Images/Getty Images
9. Chinese Syriac Gospel: CFOTO/Future Publishing/Getty Images
10. *Glossa Ordinaria*: British Library/Alamy Stock Photo
11. Haghpat Gospels: Wikimedia Commons/Public Domain
12. Pantocrator, Chora Church: Photo by Dilara Acikgoz/INA Photo Agency/Universal Images Group/Getty Images
13. Gigas Bible: Wikimedia Commons/CC0
14. Armenian Gospel: Eddie Gerald/Alamy Stock Photo
15. Book of hours: Photo by Sepia Times/Universal Images Group/Getty Images
16. Bible moralisée: Photo by Fine Art Images/Heritage Images/Getty Images

17. Gutenberg Bible: Ian Dagnall Computing/Alamy Stock Photo
18. Moldovita Monastery: Photo by DeAgostini/Getty Images
19. Complutensian Polyglot: Wikimedia Commons/Public Domain
20. The Whore of Babylon: Penta Springs Limited/Alamy Stock Photo
21. Council of Trent: Heritage Image Partnership Ltd/Alamy Stock Photo
22. Geneva: Photo by Hi540/Wikimedia Commons/CC BY-SA 4.0 DEED
23. King James frontispiece: Wikimedia Commons/Public Domain
24. Eliot Bible: Photo by Culture Club/Getty Images
25. Gustave Doré: Alex Ramsay/Alamy Stock Photo
26. Illustrated Bible, Nazareth: Publishers: Matthew George Easton. John Bartholomew & Co. (1893). Wikimedia Commons/Public Domain
27. Bishop Samuel Crowther: Photo by © Historical Picture Archive/CORBIS/Corbis/Getty Images
28. Bible Women: Wikimedia Commons/Public Domain
29. Korean board of translators: Photo by Pictures from History/Universal Images Group/Getty Images
30. General Feng: OMF International UK
31. Ethiopian priests: Pascal Boegli/Alamy Stock Photo
32. Football fan: Issouf Sanogo /AFP/Getty Images
33. Kimbanguist church: Eduardo Soteras/AFP/Getty Images
34. Amity Printing Company: Imaginechina Limited/Alamy Stock Photo
35. Annie Vallotton: Illustrations by Swiss artist and storyteller Annie Vallotton, as taken from the Good News Translation © 1976, 1992, 2015 American Bible Society. Used by permission.
36. Annie Vallotton: Illustrations by Swiss artist and storyteller Annie Vallotton, as taken from the Good News Translation © 1976, 1992, 2015 American Bible Society. Used by permission.

NOTES

Introduction

1. Stephen Tompkins, "The Best Selling Artist of All Time," BBC News, March 11, 2004, http://news.bbc.co.uk/2/hi/uk_news/magazine/3501430.stm.

2. Gregory the Great, *Morals on the Book of Job*, vol. 1, Library of the Fathers of the Holy Catholic Church [...] (Oxford, UK: John Henry Parker, 1844), 9.

Chapter 1: Becoming a Book

1. Chris Keith, *Jesus Against the Scribal Elite: The Origins of the Conflict*, rev. ed. (New York: Bloomsbury T&T Clark, 2020), 47–65.

2. Crucial reading is John Barton, *A History of the Bible: The Book and Its Faiths* (London: Allen Lane, 2019). See also Michael L. Satlow, *How the Bible Became Holy* (New Haven, CT: Yale University Press, 2014).

3. Extremely helpful is Lee Martin McDonald, *The Formation of the Biblical Canon*, 4th ed. (New York: Bloomsbury T&T Clark, 2018).

4. See Lee Martin McDonald, *Formation of the Christian Biblical Canon*, 2 vols. (1988; New York: Bloomsbury T&T Clark, 2018).

5. See Bart D. Ehrman, *The Orthodox Corruption of Scripture: The Effect of Early Christological Controversies on the Text of the New Testament*, updated ed. (New York: Oxford University Press, 2011).

6. Matthew D. C. Larsen and Mark Letteney, "Christians and the Codex: Generic Materiality and Early Gospel Traditions," *Journal of Early Christian Studies* 27, no. 3 (2019): 383–415.

7. Edward Ullendorff, *Ethiopia and the Bible* (London: Oxford University Press, 1968); Bruk A. Asale, "The Ethiopian Orthodox Tewahedo Church Canon of the Scriptures: Neither Open nor Closed," *Bible Translator* 67, no. 2 (2016): 202–222.

8. Konrad Schmid and Jens Schröter, *The Making of the Bible: From the First Fragments to Sacred Scripture*, trans. Peter Lewis (Cambridge, MA: Harvard University Press, 2021), 256–264.

9. Schmid and Schröter, *Making of the Bible*, 275–276.

10. On early literature, Schmid and Schröter, *The Making of the Bible*, 237–240.

11. Steve Mason, "Josephus and His Twenty-Two Book Canon," in *The Canon Debate*, ed. Lee Martin McDonald and James A. Sanders (Grand Rapids, MI: Baker Academic, 2002), 110–127; John Barton, "The Old Testament Canons," in *The New Cambridge History of the Bible*, vol. 1, *From the Beginnings to 600*, ed. James Carleton Paget and Joachim Schaper (Cambridge, UK: Cambridge University Press, 2013), 145–164, https://doi.org/10.1017/CBO9781139033671.011.

12. Tobias Nicklas, "Christian Apocrypha and the Development of the Christian Canon," *Early Christianity* 5 (2014): 220–240.

13. Natalio Fernández Marcos, *The Septuagint in Context: Introduction to the Greek Versions of the Bible*, trans. Wilfred G. E. Watson (Leiden, the Netherlands: Brill, 2000); Timothy Michael Law, *When God Spoke Greek: The Septuagint and the Making of the Christian Bible* (New York: Oxford University Press, 2013).

14. David Brakke, "Canon Formation and Social Conflict in Fourth-Century Egypt: Athanasius of Alexandria's Thirty-Ninth 'Festal Letter,'" *Harvard Theological Review* 87, no. 4 (1994): 395–419.

15. Nicholas Thompson, "Mighty in the Word: Athanasius's Doctrine of Scripture in His War on Arianism," *Puritan Reformed Journal* 10, no. 1 (2018): 91–105.

16. Philip Schaff, ed., *A Select Library of the Nicene and Post-Nicene Fathers of the Christian Church* (Buffalo, NY: Christian Literature Company, 1887), 4:550–555, quoted in "Athanasius on the Canon," Bible Research (website), accessed December 1, 2023, https://www.bible-researcher.com/athanasius.html.

17. "Athanasius on the Canon," Bible Research (website), accessed February 10, 2024, https://www.bible-researcher.com/athanasius.html.

18. Edmon L. Gallagher and John D. Meade, *The Biblical Canon Lists from Early Christianity: Texts and Analysis* (New York: Oxford University Press, 2018). See also Juan Chapa, "The Earliest Christian Manuscripts and Their Contribution to the History of the Canon," *Annales Theologici* 35, no. 2 (2021): 429–445.

19. See Robert Bartlett, *Why Can the Dead Do Such Great Things? Saints and Worshippers from the Martyrs to the Reformation* (Princeton, NJ: Princeton University Press, 2013), 3–7.

20. Cyril Hovorun, *Eastern Christianity and Its Texts* (New York: Bloomsbury T&T Clark, 2022); James W. Barker, *Tatian's Diatessaron: Composition, Redaction, Recension, and Reception* (New York: Oxford University Press, 2021).

21. See the essays in Charles A. Bobertz and David Brakke, eds., *Reading in Christian Communities: Essays on Interpretation in the Early Church* (Notre Dame, IN: University of Notre Dame Press, 2002).

22. David Brakke, "Scriptural Practices in Early Christianity: Towards a New History of the New Testament Canon," in *Invention, Rewriting, Usurpation: Discursive Fights over Religious Traditions in Antiquity*, ed. Jörg Ulrich, Anders-Christian Jacobson, and David Brakke (Bern: Peter Lang, 2011), 263–280.

23. Timothy Stanley, "The Early Codex Book: Recovering Its Cosmopolitan Consequences," *Biblical Interpretation* 23, no. 3 (2015): 369–398.

24. Tertullian, "The Apology," NewAdvent.org, accessed December 1, 2023, https://www.newadvent.org/fathers/0301.htm.

25. St. Justin Martyr, "First Apology," NewAdvent.org, accessed December 1, 2023, https://www.newadvent.org/fathers/0126.htm.

26. AnneMarie Luijendijk, "Books and Private Readers in Early Christian Oxyrhynchus: 'A Spiritual Meadow and a Garden of Delight,'" in *Books and Readers in the Premodern World: Essays in Honor of Harry Gamble*, ed. Karl Shuve (Atlanta: Society of Biblical Literature, 2018), 121.

27. Quoted in Luijendijk, "Books and Private Readers," 121.

28. Essential reading is Harry Y. Gamble, *Books and Readers in the Early Church: A History of Early Christian Texts* (New Haven, CT: Yale University Press, 1997); see also Roger S. Bagnall, *Early Christian Books in Egypt* (Princeton, NJ: Princeton University Press, 2009); and Timothy N. Mitchell, "Christian Papyri and the Ancient Church," *Bibliotheca Sacra* 173 (2016): 182–202.

29. Gamble, *Books and Readers*, 237.

30. Maureen A. Tilley, *The Bible in Christian North Africa: The Donatist World* (Minneapolis, MN: Fortress, 1997).

31. Quoted in Karl Shuve, "Unreliable Books: Debates over Falsified Scriptures at the Frontier Between Judaism and Christianity," in Shuve, *Books and Readers in the Premodern World*, 172.

32. Quoted in Shuve, "Unreliable Books," 182.

33. Quoted in Bart Ehrman, "A Letter from Peter to James . . . Against Paul!," *The Bart Ehrman Blog: The History and Literature of Early Christianity*, August 3, 2022, https://ehrmanblog.org/a-letter-from-peter-to-james-against-paul/.

34. Shuve, "Unreliable Books," 183–184.

35. Lee Martin McDonald, "Fluidity in the Early Formation of the Hebrew Bible," *Hebrew Studies* 61 (2020): 73–95.

36. Crucial on early Christian writing are the following: Bart D. Ehrman, *Misquoting Jesus: The Story Behind Who Changed the Bible and Why* (New York: HarperOne, 2005); Kim Haines-Eitzen, *Guardians of Letters: Literacy, Power, and the Transmitters of Early Christian Literature* (New York: Oxford University Press, 2000); Lincoln H. Blumell, "Scripture as Artefact," in *The Oxford Handbook of Early Christian Biblical Interpretation*, ed. Paul M. Blowers and Peter W. Martens (New York: Oxford University Press, 2019), 7–32; Larry W. Hurtado, *The Earliest Christian Artifacts: Manuscripts and Christian Origins* (Grand Rapids, MI: William B. Eerdmans, 2006); and Theodore de Bruyn, *Making Amulets Christian: Artefacts, Scribes, and Contexts* (New York: Oxford University Press, 2017). See also Alan Mugridge, *Copying Early Christian Texts: A Study of Scribal Practice* (Tübingen, Germany: Mohr Siebeck, 2016).

37. Hugo Lundhaug and Lance Jenott, *The Monastic Origins of the Nag Hammadi Codices* (Tübingen, Germany: Mohr Siebeck, 2015).

38. Kim Haines-Eitzen, "The Social History of Early Christian Scribes," in *The Text of the New Testament in Contemporary Research: Essays on the Status Quaestionis*, 2nd ed., ed. Bart D. Ehrman and Michael W. Holmes (Leiden, the Netherlands: Brill, 2013), 479–495.

39. Michelle Brown, "Spreading the Word," in *In the Beginning: Bibles Before the Year 1000*, ed. Michelle Brown (Washington, DC: Freer Gallery of Art and Arthur M. Sackler Gallery, Smithsonian Institution, 2006), 69.

40. Michelle P. Brown, *The Lindisfarne Gospels: Society, Spirituality, and the Scribe* (Toronto: University of Toronto Press, 2003), 398.

41. Brown, *Lindisfarne Gospels*, 398.

42. Kim Haines-Eitzen, *The Gendered Palimpsest: Women, Writing, and Representation in Early Christianity* (New York: Oxford University Press, 2012).

43. Quoted in Brown, "Spreading the Word," 67.

44. Quoted in Stephan Füssel, "Bible Production in Medieval Monasteries," in *The Book of Bibles: The Most Beautiful Illuminated Bibles of the Middle Ages*, ed. Andreas Fingernagel and Christian Gastgeber (Cologne, Germany: Taschen, 2016), 14.

45. Quoted in Larry W. Hurtado and Christ Keith, "Writing and Book Production in the Hellenistic and Roman Periods," in *The New Cambridge History of the Bible*, vol. 1, *From the Beginnings to 600*, ed. James Carleton Paget and Joachim Schaper (Cambridge, UK: Cambridge University Press, 2013), 80.

46. William E. Klingshirn and Linda Safran, eds., *The Early Christian Book* (Washington, DC: Catholic University of America Press, 2007).

47. Barton, *History of the Bible*, 243–252.

48. D. C. Parker, *An Introduction to the New Testament Manuscripts and Their Texts* (Cambridge, UK: Cambridge University Press, 2008), 14.

49. Brent Nongbri, *God's Library: The Archaeology of the Earliest Christian Manuscripts* (New Haven, CT: Yale University Press, 2018), 26.

50. Nongbri, *God's Library*, 26–27.

51. Nongbri, *God's Library*, 37.

52. Gary Frost, "Adoption of the Codex Book: Parable of a New Reading Mode," *Book and Paper Group Annual* 17 (1998), https://cool.culturalheritage.org/coolaic/sg/bpg/annual/v17/bp17-10.html.

53. Thanks to Dr. Mark Letteney for the analogy.

54. J. Neville Birdsall, "The Codex Vaticanus: Its History and Significance," in *The Bible as Book: The Transmission of the Greek Text*, ed. Scot McKendrick and Orlaith O'Sullivan (London: British Library and Oak Knoll Press, 2003), 39; Nongbri, *God's Library*, 134–135.

55. Nongbri, *God's Library*, 134–135.

56. Daniel M. Gurtner, *Exodus: A Commentary on the Greek Text of Codex Vaticanus* (Leiden, the Netherlands: Brill, 2013), 7.

57. See the discussion of codex and canon in Mark Letteney, *The Christianization of Knowledge in Late Antiquity: Intellectual and Material Transformations* (New York: Cambridge University Press, 2023), chapter 5.

58. Jesse R. Grenz, "The Scribes and Correctors of Codex Vaticanus: A Study on the Codicology, Paleography, and Text of B(03)," *Tyndale Bulletin* 73 (2022): 221–224.

59. T. C. Skeat, "The Codex Sinaiticus, the Codex Vaticanus, and Constantine," *Journal of Theological Studies* 50, no. 2 (1999), 583–625; Gregory Robbins, "'Fifty Copies of the Sacred Writings' (*VC* 4:36): Entire Bibles or Gospel Books?," in *Studia Patristica*, vol. 19, *Papers Presented to the Tenth International Conference on Patristic Studies Held in Oxford 1987*, ed. Elizabeth A. Livingstone (Leuven, Belgium: Peeters, 1989), 91–99. The dating is by Anthony Grafton and Megan Williams in *Christianity and the Transformation of the Book: Origen, Eusebius, and the Library of Caesarea* (Cambridge, MA: Belknap Press of Harvard University Press, 2008), 215–221.

60. H. J. M. Milne and T. C. Skeat, ed., *The Codex Sinaiticus and the Codex Alexandrinus* (London: British Museum, 1938), 21.

61. Brent Nongbri, "The Date of Codex Sinaiticus," *Journal of Theological Studies* 73, no. 2 (2022), 516–534.

62. Stanley E. Porter, "Hero or Thief? Constantine Tischendorf Turns Two Hundred," *Biblical Archaeology Review*, September/October 2015, 45–53. See also Stanley E. Porter, *Constantine Tischendorf: The Life and Work of a 19th Century Bible Hunter* (New York: Bloomsbury T&T Clark, 2015).

63. D. C. Parker, *Codex Sinaiticus: The Story of the World's Oldest Bible* (London: British Library, 2010), 129.

64. Parker, *Codex Sinaiticus*, 131.

65. Eva Mroczek, "True Stories and the Poetics of Textual Discovery," *Bulletin for the Study of Religion* 45, no. 2 (2016): 21–31; and Nicola Denzey Lewis and Justine Ariel Blount, "Rethinking the Origins of the Nag Hammadi Codices," *Journal of Biblical Literature* 133, no. 2 (2014): 398–419.

66. Parker, *Codex Sinaiticus*, 133.

67. Quoted in Porter, "Hero or Thief?," 49.

68. See the rich detailed information on Codex Sinaiticus on the website Codex Sinaiticus, hosted by the Codex Sinaiticus Project, accessed December 2, 2023, https://codexsinaiticus.org/en/codex/history.aspx.

69. James Keith Elliott, *Codex Sinaiticus and the Simonides Affair* (Thessaloniki, Greece: Patriarchal Institute for Patristic Studies, 1982).

70. Quoted in Parker, *Codex Sinaiticus*, 160.

71. T. C Skeat, "The Codex Vaticanus in the Fifteenth Century," *Journal of Theological Studies* 35, no. 2 (1984): 454–465.

72. S. P. Tregelles, *A Lecture on the Historic Evidence of the Authorship and Transmission of the Books of the New Testament* (London: Samuel Bagster and Sons, 1852), 83–85.

73. Thomas Law Montefiore, *Catechesis Evangelica: Being Questions and Answers Based on the "Textus Receptus" [. . .] Part I, St. Matthew* (London: Longman, Green, Longman, and Roberts, 1862), 272.

74. See DigiVatLib, the Vatican Library website, shelfmark Vat.gr.1209, https://digi.vatlib.it/view/MSS_Vat.gr.1209.

75. Quoted in Hermit of Saint Bruno, "Who Were the Desert Fathers, and Why Are They Still Important Today?," St. Mary's Hermitage, August 16, 2021, https://celtichermit.com/2021/08/16/who-were-the-desert-fathers-and-why-are-they-still-important-today/.

Chapter 2: Tongues of Fire

1. Ignatius Aphram Barsoum, *History of Syriac Literature and Sciences*, ed. and trans. Matti Moosa (Pueblo, CO: Passeggiata, 2000).

2. Peter Williams, "The Syriac Versions of the Bible," in *The New Cambridge History of the Bible*, vol. 1, *From the Beginnings to 600*, ed. James Carleton Paget and Joachim Schaper (Cambridge, UK: Cambridge University Press, 2013), 528.

3. Georgi R. Parpulov, "The Bibles of the Christian East," in *The New Cambridge History of the Bible*, vol. 2, *From 600 to 1450*, ed. Richard Marsden and E. Ann Matter (Cambridge, UK: Cambridge University Press, 2012), 309.

4. Edward Ullendorff, *Ethiopia and the Bible* (London: British Academy, 1968), 31–72; Ephraim Isaac, "The Bible in Ethiopic," in *New Cambridge History*, 2: 110–122.

5. See G. A. Mikre-Sellassie, "The Early Translation of the Bible into Ethiopic/Geez," in *Bible Translation and African Languages*, ed. Gosnell L. O. R. Yorke and Peter M. Renju (Nairobi, Kenya: Acton, 2004), 303.

6. Judith S. McKenzie and Francis Watson, eds., *The Garima Gospels: Early Illuminated Gospel Books from Ethiopia* (Oxford, UK: Manar al-Athar, University of Oxford, 2016), 17.

7. Bruk A. Asale, "The Ethiopian Orthodox Tewahedo Church Canon of the Scriptures: Neither Open nor Closed," *Bible Translator* 67, no. 2 (2016): 207.

8. Sidney H. Griffith, "The Bible in Arabic," in *New Cambridge History*, 2:123–142; Sidney H. Griffith, "The Gospel in Arabic: An Inquiry into Its Appearance in the First Abbasid Century," in *Arabic Christianity in the Monasteries of Ninth-Century Palestine* (Burlington, VT: Ashgate, 1992); D. Thomas, ed., *The Bible in Arab Christianity*, The History of Christian–Muslim Relations 6 (Leiden, the Netherlands: Brill, 2007); Theresia Hainthaler, *Christliche Araber vor dem Islam*, Eastern Christian Studies 7 (Leuven, Belgium: Peeters, 2007); S. H. Griffith, "From Aramaic to Arabic: The Languages of the Monasteries of Palestine in the Byzantine and Early Islamic Periods," *Dumbarton Oaks Papers* 51 (1997): 11–31.

9. Quoted in Griffith, "Bible in Arabic," 127.

10. Quoted in Griffith, "Bible in Arabic," 129.

11. Griffith, "Bible in Arabic," 130.

12. Otto F. A. Meinardus, *Two Thousand Years of Coptic Christianity* (Cairo: American University in Cairo Press, 1999); Jill Kamil, *Christianity in the Land of the Pharaohs: The Coptic Orthodox Church* (London: Routledge, 2002).

13. Nicola Denzey Lewis, *Introduction to Gnosticism: Ancient Voices, Christian Worlds* (New York: Oxford University Press, 2013); Elaine Pagels, *The Gnostic Gospels* (New York: Random House, 1979).

14. See Bentley Layton and David Brakke, eds., *The Gnostic Scriptures*, trans. Bentley Layton, 2nd ed. (New Haven, CT: Yale University Press, 2021).

15. J. R. Russell, "On the Origins and Invention of the Armenian Script," *Le Muséon* 107 (1994): 317–333; Thomas V. Gamkrelidze, "Typology of Writing, Greek Alphabet, and the Origin of Alphabetic Scripts of the Christian Orient," in *Current Trends in Caucasian, East European and Inner Asian Linguistics*, ed. Dee Ann Holiskey and Kevin Tuite (Amsterdam: John Benjamins, 2003), 85–96.

16. Vrej Nersessian, *The Bible in Armenian Tradition* (New York: J. Paul Getty Museum, 2001), 14; Levon Ter Petrosian, *Ancient Armenian Translations* (New York: St. Vartan, 1992); J. M. Alexanian, "The Armenian Gospel Text from the Fifth Through the Fourteenth Centuries," in *Medieval Armenian Culture*, ed. Thomas J. Samuelian and Michael E. Stone (Chico, CA: Scholars Press, 1984), 381–394; S. P. Cowe, "Tendentious Translation and the Evangelical Imperative: Religious Polemic in the Early Armenian Church," *Revue des Études Arméniennes* 22 (1990–1991): 97–114; Claude E. Cox, "The Armenian Version and the Text of the Old Greek Psalter," in *Der Septuaginta-Psalter und seine Tochterübersetzüngen*, ed. A. Aejmelaeus (Göttingen: Vandenhoeck and Ruprecht, 2000), 174–247.

17. Siméon Vailhé, "Isaac of Armenia," in *The Catholic Encyclopedia*, ed. Charles G. Herbermann et al., vol. 8 (New York: Encyclopedia Press, 1910), http://www.newadvent.org/cathen/08175b.htm.

18. Gabriele Winkler, *Koriwns Biographie des Mesrop Maštoc: Übersetzung und Kommentar* (Rome: Pontificio Istituto Orientale, 1994); Sergio Laporta, "Koriwn," in *The Oxford Dictionary of Late Antiquity*, ed. Oliver Nicholson (Oxford, UK: Oxford University Press, 2018).

19. Quoted in Nersessian, *Bible in Armenian Tradition*, 14.

20. Quoted in Moses Khorenats'i, *History of Armenians*, trans. Robert W. Thomson (Cambridge, MA: Harvard University Press, 1991); Nersessian, *Bible in Armenian Tradition*, 22.

21. Bruce M. Metzger, *The Bible in Translation: Ancient and English Versions* (Grand Rapids, MI: Baker Academic, 2001), 41–42.

22. Stephan H. Rapp Jr., "Georgian Christianity," in *The Blackwell Companion to Eastern Christianity*, ed. Ken Parry (Malden, MA: Blackwell, 2007), 139; Malkhaz V. Songulashvili, "The Translation of the Bible into Georgian," *Bible Translator* 41, no. 1 (1990), 131–134; G. Garitte, *L'ancienne version géorgienne des Actes des Apôtres d'après deux manuscrits du Sinaï* (Leuven, Belgium: Peeters, 1955); Helmut Koester, *Ancient Christian Gospels: Their History and Development* (Philadelphia, PA: Trinity Press International, 1990), 403–430.

23. Rapp, "Georgian Christianity," 139.

24. David Marshall Lang, "Recent Work on the Georgian New Testament," *Bulletin of the School of Oriental and African Studies* 19, no. 1 (1957): 82–93.

25. Robert P. Blake, *The Old Georgian Version of the Gospel of Matthew from the Adysh Gospels with the Variants of the Opiza and Tbet' Gospels* (Turnhout, Belgium: Brepols, 1976).

Notes for Chapter 2

26. Michael Tarchnisvili, *Geschichte der kirchlichen georgsischen Literatur* (Vatican: Città del Vaticano, Biblioteca Apostolica Vaticana, 1955), 314–315; E. Khintibidze, *Georgian-Byzantine Literary Contacts* (Amsterdam: Hakkert, 1996).

27. A. A. Alekseev, *Textgeschichte der slavischen Bibel, Bausteine zur Slavischen Philologie und Kulturgeschichte*, ser. A: Slavistische Forschungen (Cologne: Böhlau, 1999); A. A. Alexeev, "The Slavonic Bible and Modern Scholarship," *Jews and Slavs* 3 (1995): 25–39.

28. Francis Dvornik, "The Significance of the Missions of Cyril and Methodius," *Slavic Review* 23, no. 2 (1964): 195–211; Dimitri Obolensky, "The Heritage of Cyril and Methodius in Russia," *Dumbarton Oaks Papers* 19 (1965): 45–65; George C. Soulis, "The Legacy of Cyril and Methodius to the Southern Slavs," *Dumbarton Oaks Papers* 19 (1965): 19–43.

29. Quoted in Henry R. Cooper Jr., "The Bible in Slavonic," in *New Cambridge History*, 2:184.

30. I. Ševčenko, "Three Paradoxes of the Cyrillo-Methodian Mission," *Slavic Review* 23, no. 2 (1964): 220–236.

31. W. K. Matthews, "Sources of Old Church Slavonic," *Slavonic and East European Review* 28, no. 71 (1950): 466–485.

32. Cooper, "Bible in Slavonic," 62–63.

33. Augustine to Jerome, 403 CE, NewAdvent.org, accessed December 6, 2023, https://www.newadvent.org/fathers/1102071.htm.

34. Catherine Brown Tkacz, "'Labor Tam Utilis': The Creation of the Vulgate," *Vigiliae Christianae* 50, no. 1 (1996): 42–72.

35. For a comprehensive examination of Old Latin scriptures, see H. A. G. Houghton, "The Earliest Latin Translations of the Bible," in *Oxford Handbook of the Latin Bible*, ed. H. A. G. Houghton (New York: Oxford University Press, 2023), 1–18; Philip Burton, *The Old Latin Gospels: A Study of Their Texts and Language* (New York: Oxford University Press, 2000); Bonifatius Fischer, *Die lateinischen Evangelien bis zum 10. Jahrhundert*, 4 vols., VLB 13 (Freiburg: Herder, 1988).

36. Quoted in Metzger, *Bible in Translation*, 31.

37. On Augustine and Jerome, see Stuart Squires, "Jerome's Animosity Against Augustine," *Augustiniana* 58, no. 3/4 (2008): 181–199.

38. The literature on Jerome is enormous. Recommended are J. N. D. Kelly, *Jerome: His Life, Writings, and Controversies* (London: Duckworth, 1975); Megan Hale Williams, *The Monk and the Book: Jerome and the Making of Christian Scholarship* (Chicago: University of Chicago Press, 2006); Andrew Cain, *The Letters of Jerome: Asceticism, Biblical Exegesis, and the Construction of Christian Authority in Late Antiquity* (New York: Oxford University Press, 2009); Pierre Nautin, "L'activité litteraire de Jerome de 387 à 392," *Revue de Théologie et de Philosophie* 115 (1983): 247–259; W. H. Semple, "St. Jerome as a Biblical Translator," *Bulletin of the John Rylands Library, Manchester* 48, no. 1 (1965): 227–243.

39. Adam Kamesar, "Jerome and the Hebrew Scriptures," in Houghton, *Oxford Handbook of the Latin Bible*, 49–64; E. Burstein, "La compétence de Jerome en hebreu," *Revue des etu niennes* 21 (1975): 3–12.

40. Stefan Rebenich, "Jerome: The 'Vir Trilinguis' and the 'Hebraica Veritas,'" *Vigiliae Christianae* 47, no. 1 (1993): 50–77; Paul B. Decock, "Jerome's Turn to the Hebraica Veritas and His Rejection of the Traditional View of the Septuagint," *Neotestamentica* 42, no. 2 (2008): 205–222.

41. Elizabeth A. Clark, "Theory and Practice in Late Ancient Asceticism: Jerome, Chrysostom, and Augustine," *Journal of Feminist Studies in Religion* 5, no. 2 (1989): 25–46.

42. Quoted in Williams, *Monk and the Book*, 203.

43. St. Jerome, "Letter 53," NewAdvent.org, accessed December 7, 2023, https://www.newadvent.org/fathers/3001053.htm.

44. St. Jerome, "Letter 53."

45. Cornelia Linde, *How to Correct the "Sacra Scriptura"? Textual Criticism of the Latin Bible Between the Twelfth and Fifteenth Century* (Oxford, UK: Society for the Study of Medieval Languages and Literature, 2012), 33–35.

46. John Moorhead, *Gregory the Great* (London: Routledge, 2005), 49–68.

47. Paul Meyvaert, "Bede, Cassiodorus, and the Codex Amiatinus," *Speculum* 71, no. 4 (1996): 827–883.

48. Shari Boodts, "The Bible in the Carolingian Age," in Houghton, *Oxford Handbook of the Latin Bible*, 169–186; Rosamond McKitterick, *The Carolingians and the Written Word* (Cambridge, UK: Cambridge University Press, 1989).

49. H. H. Glunz, *History of the Vulgate in England from Alcuin to Roger Bacon* (Cambridge, UK: Cambridge University Press, 1933); François L. Ganshof, "Le révision de la Bible par Alcuin," *Bibliothèque d'Humanisme et Renaissance* 9 (1947): 7–20.

50. Quoted in Justin A. Smith, "Alcuin's Bible," *Journal of Religion* 2, no. 10 (1883): 323.

51. Herbert Kessler, *The Illustrated Bibles from Tours*, Studies in Manuscript Illumination 7 (Princeton, NJ: Princeton University Press, 1977), 5, 14, plates 1, 44, 48, 87, 107.

52. David Ganz, "Mass Production of Early Medieval Manuscripts: The Carolingian Bibles from Tours," in *The Early Medieval Bible: Its Production, Decoration and Use*, ed. Richard Gameson (Cambridge, UK: Cambridge University Press, 2009), 53.

53. J. Duft, *Die Bibel von Moutier-Grandval*, British Museum Add. Ms. 10546 (Bern: Verein Schweizerischer Lithographiebesitzer, 1971).

54. Christopher de Hamel, *The Book: A History of the Bible* (London: Phaidon, 2005), 37.

55. Rosamond McKitterick, "Carolingian Bible Production: The Tours' Anomaly," in Gameson, *Early Medieval Bible*, 68.

56. "Lindau Gospels," Morgan Library and Museum, accessed February 11, 2024, https://www.themorgan.org/manuscript/76874.

57. Lawrence Nees, "Problems of Form and Function in Early Medieval Illustrated Bibles from Northern Europe," in Gameson, *Early Medieval Bible*, 139.

58. Lynne Long, *Translating the Bible: From the 7th to the 17th Century* (Burlington, VT: Ashgate, 2001), 26.

Chapter 3: Manifestation of the Savior

1. Anne Karahan, *Byzantine Holy Images: Transcendence and Immanence; The Theological Background of the Iconography and Aesthetics of the Chora Church* (Leuven, Belgium: Peeters, 2010); Neslihan Asutay-Effenberger and Arne Effenberger, *Byzanz: Weltreich der Kunst* (Munich: Verlag C. H. Beck, 2017).

2. Karin Krause, *Divine Inspiration in Byzantium: Notions of Authenticity in Art and Theology* (New York: Cambridge University Press, 2022), especially 87–144.

3. Herbert L. Kessler, "The Word Made Flesh in Early Decorated Bibles," in *Picturing the Bible: The Earliest Christian Art*, ed. Jeffrey Spier (New Haven, CT: Yale University Press, 2007), 141–143.

4. Quoted in Lawrence Nees, "Problems of Form and Function in Early Medieval Illustrated Bibles from Northwest Europe," in *Imaging the Early Medieval Bible*, ed. John Williams (University Park: Pennsylvania State University Press, 1999), 133.

5. See the essays in Susan Ashbrook Harvey and Margaret Mullett, eds., *Knowing Bodies, Passionate Souls: Sense Perceptions in Byzantium* (Washington, DC: Dumbarton Oaks Research Library and Collection, 2017).

6. Michael W. McLellan, *Monasticism in Egypt: Images and Words of the Desert Fathers* (Cairo: American University in Cairo Press, 1998); Malcolm Choat, Maria Chiara Giorda, eds., *Writing and Communication in Early Egyptian Monasticism* (Leiden, the Netherlands: Brill, 2017); Gawdat Gabra and Hany N. Takla, eds., *Christianity and Monasticism in Middle Egypt* (Cairo: American University in Cairo Press, 2015); Gawdat Gabra and Hany N. Takla, eds., *Christianity and Monasticism in Alexandria and the Egyptian Deserts* (Cairo: American University in Cairo Press, 2020).

7. See Stephen J. Davis, *Coptic Christology in Practice: Incarnation and Divine Participation in Late Antique and Medieval Egypt* (New York: Oxford University Press, 2008).

8. Davis, *Coptic Christology*, 120–121.

9. Davis, *Coptic Christology*, 119.

10. Isabelle Cochelin, "When Monks Were the Book: The Bible and Monasticism (6th–11th Centuries)," in *The Practice of the Bible in the Middle Ages: Production, Reception, and Performance in Western Christianity*, ed. Susan Boynton and Diane J. Reilly (New York: Columbia University Press, 2011), 61–62.

11. Richard Gyug, "Bibles, Biblical Books, and the Monastic Liturgy in the Early Middle Ages," in Boynton and Reilly, *Practice of the Bible*, 34–35.

12. Cochelin, "When Monks Were the Book," 68.

13. Charles Barber, "Contemplating the Life of Christ in the Icons of the Twelve Feasts of Our Lord," in *New Testament in Byzantium*, ed. Derek Krueger and Robert S. Nelson (Washington, DC: Dumbarton Oaks Research Library and Collection, 2016), 221–237.

14. S. M. Roye, *The Inner Cohesion Between the Bible and the Fathers in Byzantine*

Tradition: Towards a Codico-Liturgical Approach to the Byzantine Biblical and Patristic Manuscripts (Tilburg, the Netherlands: Orthodox Logos, 2007), 85.

15. Quoted in Hans-Joachim Schulz, *The Byzantine Liturgy: Symbolic Structure and Faith Expression*, trans. Matthew J. O'Connell (New York: Pueblo, 1986), 128.

16. Martha Roy, ed., *The Coptic Orthodox Liturgy of St. Basil: With Complete Musical Transcription* (Cairo: American University in Cairo, 1998); Abraham Azmy, *The Coptic Liturgy of St. Basil in Pictures* (Hamden, CT: Virgin Mary and Archangel Michael Coptic Orthodox Church of Connecticut, 2000); Institute of Coptic Studies Choir, *The Divine Liturgy of St. Basil with Its Hymns*, sound recording, 1967, American Folklife Center, Library of Congress, https://www.loc.gov/item/2009655441/.

17. "4—Liturgy of the Word," Heritage of the Coptic Orthodox Church (website), accessed February 11, 2024, https://copticheritage.org/library/contemplations/4-the -liturgy-of-the-word/.

18. Until the 2015 canonization of the victims of the Armenian massacre of 1915–1917, Gregory was the last Armenian to be made a saint.

19. Hugh Wybrew, *The Orthodox Liturgy: The Development of the Eucharistic Liturgy in the Byzantine Rite* (London: SPCK Publishing, 2013), 39–49.

20. Elisabeth Yota, "The Lectionary," trans. Saskia Caroline Dirkse, in *A Companion to Byzantine Illustrated Manuscripts*, ed. Vasiliki Tsamakda (Leiden, the Netherlands: Brill, 2017), 287–299.

21. On the development of biblical iconography, see Anne-Orange Poilpré, *Maiestas Domini: Une Image de l'Eglise en Occident, Ve–IXe siècle* (Paris: Cerf, 2005).

22. Eugen J. Pentiuc, *The Old Testament in Eastern Orthodox Tradition* (New York: Oxford University Press, 2014), 320.

23. Eusebius Pamhili, *The Life of the Blessed Emperor Constantine*, book IV, chap. XXIV, in *A Select Library of the Nicene and Post-Nicene Fathers of the Christian Church*, Second Series, ed. Henry Wace and Philip Schaff (New York: Christian Literature Company, 1890), 1:546.

24. Jaroslav Pelikan, *Imago Dei: The Byzantine Apologia for Icons* (Princeton, NJ: Princeton University Press, 1990), 22.

25. Mary B. Cunningham and Elizabeth Theokritoff, "Who Are the Orthodox Christians? A Historical Introduction," in *The Cambridge Companion to Orthodox Christian Theology*, ed. Mary B. Cunningham and Elizabeth Theokritoff (Cambridge, UK: Cambridge University Press, 2009), 17–18.

26. Kathleen Maxwell, *Between Constantinople and Rome: An Illuminated Byzantine Gospel Book (Paris gr. 54) and the Union of Churches* (Burlington, VT: Ashgate, 2014), 270–271.

27. Cunningham and Theokritoff, "Who Are the Orthodox Christians?," 22.

28. Sergei L. Loiko, "Russia Bible Museum Sees the Books as National Treasures," *Los Angeles Times*, July 22, 2012, https://www.latimes.com/world/la-xpm-2012-jul -22-la-fg-russia-bible-museum-20120723-story.html.

29. Charles Barber, *Figure and Likeness: On the Limits of Representation in Byzantine Iconoclasm* (Princeton, NJ: Princeton University Press, 2002); Kenneth

Parry, *Depicting the Word: Byzantine Iconophile Thought of the Eighth and Ninth Centuries* (Leiden, the Netherlands: Brill, 1996).

30. See Lawrence Duggan, "Was Art Really the 'Book of the Illiterate'?," *Word and Image* 5, no. 3 (1989): 227–251; and Celia M. Chazelle, "Pictures, Books, and the Illiterate: Pope Gregory I's Letters to Serenus of Marseilles," *Word and Image* 6, no. 2 (1990): 138–153.

31. Quoted in Susan Ashbrook Harvey, "Bearing Witness: New Testament Women in Early Byzantine Hymnography," in Krueger and Nelson, *New Testament in Byzantium*, 211.

32. Carolinne White, ed. and trans., *Gregory of Nazianzus: Autobiographical Poems* (Cambridge, UK: Cambridge University Press, 1996), 3.

33. R. J. Schork, *Sacred Song from the Byzantine Pulpit: Romanos the Melodist* (Gainesville: University Press of Florida, 1995).

34. John A. McGuckin, "Christian Spirituality in Byzantium," in *Collected Studies of John A. McGuckin*, vol. 3, *Illumined in the Spirit: Studies in Orthodox Spirituality* (New York: St. Vladimir's Seminary Press, 2017), 157.

35. Quoted in Benedict XVI, "Romanus the Melodist," speech, Vatican City, May 21, 2008, EWTN.com, accessed December 7, 2023, https://www.ewtn.com/catholicism/library/romanus-the-melodist-6364.

36. On the creation of illuminated manuscripts, see the essays in Stella Panayotova and Paola Ricciardi, eds., *Manuscripts in the Making: Art and Science*, 2 vols. (London: Harvey Miller, 2017–2018).

37. Matthew R. Crawford, *The Eusebian Canon Tables: Ordering Textual Knowledge in Late Antiquity* (Oxford, UK: Oxford University Press, 2019); Alessandro Bausi, Bruno Reudenbach, and Hanna Wimmer, eds., *Canones: The Art of Harmony—The Canon Tables of the Four Gospels* (Berlin: De Gruyter, 2020).

38. Judith S. McKenzie and Francis Watson, *The Garima Gospels: Early Illuminated Gospel Books from Ethiopia* (Oxford, UK: Manar al-Athar, University of Oxford, 2016), 41.

39. Carl Nordenfalk, "Canon Tables on Papyrus," *Dumbarton Oaks Papers* 36 (1982): 30–31.

40. Guglielmo Cavallo, *Codex purpureus Rossanensis* (Roma: Salerno Editrice, 1992); Gianni Morelli, *L'arte nella età dello spirito: Il Codice purpureo rossanense* (Reggio Calabria: Laruffa, 2005).

41. See Kathleen P. Whitley, *The Gilded Page: The History and Technique of Manuscript Gilding* (New Castle, DE: Oak Knoll, 2000), 28–35.

42. Ingo F. Walther and Norbert Wolf, *Codices Illustres: The World's Most Famous Illuminated Manuscripts, 400 to 1600* (Cologne: Taschen, 2001), 62.

43. William C. Loerke, "The Miniatures of the Trial in the Rossano Gospels," *Art Bulletin* 43, no. 3 (1961): 171–174.

44. Paul Needham, *Twelve Centuries of Bookbindings, 400–1600* (New York: Pierpont Morgan Library, 1979), 21.

45. John Lowden, "The Beginnings of Biblical Illustration," in Williams, *Imaging the Early Medieval Bible*, 58.

46. Peter Darby, "The Codex Amiatinus Maiestas Domini and the Gospel Prefaces of Jerome," *Speculum* 92, no. 2 (2017): 344.

47. Rachel Moss, Felicity O'Mahony, and Jane Maxwell, eds., *An Insular Odyssey: Manuscript Culture in Early Christian Ireland and Beyond* (Dublin, Ireland: Four Courts, 2017); George Henderson, *From Durrow to Kells: The Insular Gospel-books, 650–800* (New York: Thames and Hudson, 1987); Jennifer O'Reilly, *Early Medieval Text and Image 1: The Insular Gospels*, ed. Carol A. Farr and Elizabeth Mullins (New York: Routledge, 2019); Marina Smyth, "Monastic Culture in Seventh-Century Ireland," *Eolas: The Journal of the American Society of Irish Medieval Studies* 12 (2019): 64–101; James E. Doan, "Mediterranean Influences on Insular Manuscript Illumination," *Proceedings of the Harvard Celtic Colloquium* 2 (1982): 31–38.

48. Walther and Wolf, *Codices Illustres*, 19.

49. Walther and Wolf, *Codices Illustres*, 68.

50. Robert G. Calkins, *Illuminated Books of the Middle Ages* (Ithaca, NY: Cornell University Press, 1983), 46–62.

51. Walther and Wolf, *Codices Illustres*, 128.

52. Christopher de Hamel, *A History of Illuminated Manuscripts* (London: Phaidon, 1997), 32.

53. Michelle P. Brown, *"In the Beginning Was the Word": Books and Faith in the Age of Bede*, Jarrow Lecture 2000 (Jarrow, UK: St. Paul's Church, 2000).

54. Darby, "Codex Amiatinus Maiestas," 343; Celia Chazelle, *The Codex Amiatinus and Its "Sister" Bibles: Scripture, Liturgy, and Art in the Milieu of the Venerable Bede* (Leiden, the Netherlands: Brill, 2019).

55. Darby, "Codex Amiatinus Maiestas," 354.

56. Nees, "Problems of Form and Function," 165.

57. Nees, "Problems of Form and Function," 175.

58. Michelle P. Brown, *Painted Labyrinth: The World of the Lindisfarne Gospels*, rev. ed. (London: British Library, 2004); Michelle P. Brown, *The Lindisfarne Gospels: Society, Spirituality, and the Scribe* (London: British Library, 2003).

59. Quoted in Richard Gameson, *From Holy Island to Durham: The Contexts and Meanings of the Lindisfarne Gospels* (London: Third Millennium, 2013), 93.

60. Walther and Wolf, *Codices Illustres*, 70.

61. Paul Meyvaert, "The Book of Kells and Iona," *Art Bulletin* 71, no. 1 (1989): 6–19.

62. Walther and Wolf, *Codices Illustres*, 84.

63. Quoted in Albrecht Classen, "The Book of Kells—The Wonders of Early Medieval Christian Manuscript Illuminations Within a Pagan World," *Mediaevistik* 32 (2019): 60.

64. Eginhard, *Life of Charlemagne*, trans. Samuel Epes Turner (New York: Harper & Brothers, 1880), 62.

65. Chantry Westwell, "Medieval Manuscripts Blog: Gold Galore in the Harley Gospels," *Medieval Manuscripts Blog*, British Library, August 14, 2022, https://blogs.bl.uk/digitisedmanuscripts/2022/08/the-harley-golden-gospels.html.

66. Matthias M. Tischler, "Towers of Faith: Views on the Biblical Landscape of the Tenth-Century Iberian World," After Empire: Using and Not Using the Past in the Crisis of the Carolingian World, c. 900–1500 (website), November 14, 2017, https://arts.st-andrews.ac.uk/after-empire/2017/11/14/towers-of-faith/.

67. John Williams, "The Bible in Spain," in Williams, *Imaging the Early Medieval Bible*, 180.

68. Williams, "Bible in Spain," 185.

69. Williams, "Bible in Spain," 182–183.

70. Quoted in Williams, "Bible in Spain," 186.

Chapter 4: Book of Life: Medieval Worlds

1. Quoted in Ian Christopher Levy, "Nicholas of Lyra (and Paul of Burgos) on the Pauline Epistles," in *A Companion to St. Paul in the Middle Ages*, ed. Steven Cartwright (Leiden, the Netherlands: Brill, 2012), 266.

2. Quoted in John F. Boyle, "St. Thomas Aquinas and Sacred Scripture," *Pro Ecclesia: A Journal of Catholic and Evangelical Theology* 4, no. 1 (1995): 92–104, https://www3.nd.edu/~afreddos/papers/Taqandss.htm.

3. Henri de Lubac, *Medieval Exegesis: Theology, Scripture, and the Fourfold Sense*, trans. Mark Sebanc and E. M. Macierowski (Grand Rapids, MI: W. B. Eerdmans, 1998).

4. Klaus Schreiner, "Volkstümliche Bibelmagie und volksprachliche Bibellektüre: Theologische und soziale Probleme mittelalterlicher Laienfrömmigkeit," in *Volksreligion im hohen und späten Mittelalter*, ed. Dieter Bauer and Peter Dinzelbacher (Paderborn, Germany: Degruyter, 1990), 358.

5. Cornelia Linde, *How to Correct the "Sacra Scriptura"? Textual Criticism of the Latin Bible Between the Twelfth and Fifteenth Century* (Oxford, UK: Society for the Study of Medieval Languages and Literature, 2012), 1–6.

6. Frans van Liere, "Andrew of St. Victor, Jerome, and the Jews: Biblical Scholarship in the Twelfth-Century Renaissance," in *Scripture and Pluralism: Reading the Bible in the Religiously Plural Worlds of the Middle Ages and Renaissance*, ed. Thomas J. Heffernan and Thomas E. Burman (Leiden, the Netherlands: Brill, 2005), 59–75; Frans van Liere, "Following in the Footsteps of Hugh: Exegesis at Saint Victor, 1142–1242," in *A Companion to the Abbey of Saint Victor in Paris: Brill's Companions to the Christian Tradition*, ed. Hugh Feiss and Juliet Mousseau (Leiden, the Netherlands: Brill, 2018), 223–243; Constant J. Mews and Micha J. Perry, "Peter Abelard, Heloise and Jewish Biblical Exegesis in the Twelfth Century," *Journal of Ecclesiastical History* 62, no. 1 (2011): 3–19.

7. For more on Bacon, see Amanda Power, *Roger Bacon and the Defence of Christendom* (Cambridge, UK: Cambridge University Press, 2013).

8. Frans van Liere, *An Introduction to the Medieval Bible* (New York: Cambridge University Press, 2014), 99.

9. G. A. Mikre-Sellassie, "The Early Translation of the Bible into Ethiopic/Geez," *The Bible Translator* 51 (2000), 308.

10. Sellassie, "The Early Translation of the Bible into Ethiopic/Geez," 312.

11. Cristian Ispir, "Glossed Bibles, Hypertexts and Hyperlinks," *Medieval Manuscripts*

Blog, British Library, January 29, 2018, https://blogs.bl.uk/digitisedmanuscripts/2018/01/glossed-bibles-hypertexts-and-hyperlinks.html.

12. See Lesley Smith, *The "Glossa Ordinaria": The Making of a Medieval Bible Commentary* (Leiden, the Netherlands: Brill, 2009).

13. Andrew Kraebel, *Biblical Commentary and Translation in Later Medieval England: Experiments in Interpretation* (Cambridge, UK: Cambridge University Press, 2020), 482.

14. See the essays in Jane Dammen McAuliffe, Barry D. Walfish, and Joseph W. Goering, eds., *With Reverence for the Word: Medieval Scriptural Exegesis in Judaism, Christianity, and Islam* (New York: Oxford University Press, 2010).

15. See Eric Lawee, *Rashi's "Commentary on the Torah": Canonization and Resistance in the Reception of a Jewish Classic* (New York: Oxford University Press, 2019).

16. Daniel Berger, "A Generation of Scholarship on Jewish-Christian Interaction in the Medieval World," *Tradition: A Journal of Orthodox Jewish Thought* 38, no. 2 (2004): 4–14; Daniel Stein Kokin, "Polemical Language: Hebrew and Latin in Medieval and Early Modern Jewish-Christian Debate," *Jewish History* 29, no. 1 (2015): 1–38; George Y. Kohler, "'Scholasticism Is a Daughter of Judaism': The Discovery of Jewish Influence on Medieval Christian Thought," *Journal of the History of Ideas* 78, no. 3 (2017): 319–340.

17. Hannah W. Matis, "Early-Medieval Exegesis of the Song of Songs and the Maternal Language of Clerical Authority," *Speculum* 89, no. 2 (2014): 358–381; Mary Dove, "Sex, Allegory and Censorship: A Reconsideration of Medieval Commentaries on the Song of Songs," *Literature and Theology* 10, no. 4 (1996): 317–328.

18. See Kenneth R. Stow, "The Church and the Jews," in *The New Cambridge Medieval History*, vol. 5, *c.1198–c.1300*, ed. David Abulafia (Cambridge, UK: Cambridge University Press, 2008), 204–219.

19. See Deeana Copeland Klepper, *The Insight of Unbelievers: Nicholas of Lyra and Christian Reading of Jewish Text in the Later Middle Ages* (Philadelphia: University of Pennsylvania Press, 2007), 1–3; and Philip D. W. Krey and Lesley Smith, eds., *Nicholas of Lyra: The Senses of Scripture* (Leiden, the Netherlands: Brill, 2000).

20. Quoted in Devorah Schoenfeld, "One Song or Many: The Unity of the Song of Songs in Jewish and Christian Exegesis," *Hebrew Studies* 61 (2020): 138.

21. Levy, "Nicholas of Lyra," 265–291.

22. The literature on the Crusades is vast. See Jonathan Riley-Smith and Susanna A. Throop, *The Crusades: A History*, 4th ed. (London: Bloomsbury Academic, 2023); Helen J. Nicholson, *Women and the Crusades* (Oxford, UK: Oxford University Press, 2023); Jonathan Riley-Smith, *The First Crusade and the Idea of Crusading* (London: Continuum, 2003); Carl Erdmann, *The Origin of the Idea of Crusade*, trans. Marshall W. Baldwin and Walter Goffart (Princeton, NJ: Princeton University Press, 1977); and Connor Christopher Wilson, *The Battle Rhetoric of Crusade and Holy War, c. 1099–c. 1222* (New York: Routledge, 2022).

23. See the essays in Elizabeth Lapina and Nicholas Morton, eds., *The Uses of the Bible in Crusader Sources* (Leiden, the Netherlands: Brill, 2017).

24. Philippe Buc, *L'ambigüité du Livre: Prince, pouvoir, et peuple dans les commentaires de la Bible au Moyen Age* (Paris: Editions Beauchesne, 1994). See also Paul Alphandéry, "Les citations biblique chez les historiens de la première croisade," *Revue de l'histoire des religions* 99 (1929): 139–157.

25. Quoted in Joseph Michaud, *Michaud's History of the Crusades*, trans. W. Robson, vol. 1 (London: George Routledge & Co., 1852), 364. See also Christoph T. Maier, *Preaching the Crusades: Mendicant Friars and the Cross in the Thirteenth Century* (Cambridge, UK: Cambridge University Press, 1994), 4, 161.

26. See Helen Gittos and Sarah Hamilton, eds., *Understanding Medieval Liturgy: Essays in Interpretation* (New York: Routledge, 2016); Matthew Cheung Salisbury, ed., *Medieval Latin Liturgy in English Translation* (Kalamazoo, MI: Medieval Institute Publications, 2017); and James Monti, *A Sense of the Sacred: Roman Catholic Worship in the Middle Ages* (San Francisco: Ignatius, 2012).

27. Cyrille Vogel, *Medieval Liturgy: An Introduction to the Sources*, ed. and trans. William Storey and Niels Rasmussen (Washington, DC: Pastoral, 1986), 314–355.

28. Uwe Michael Lang, "Kissing the Image of Christ in the Medieval Mass," *Antiphon: A Journal for Liturgical Renewal* 22, no. 3 (2018): 264.

29. "Vani Gospels: Ancient Manuscript to Be Exhibited in Tblisi," Agenda.ge, March 23, 2015, https://agenda.ge/en/news/2015/634.

30. Nancy P. Sevcenko, "Wild Animals in the Byzantine Park," in *Byzantine Garden Culture*, ed. Anthony Littlewood, Henry Maguire, and Joachim Wolschke-Bulmahn (Washington, DC: Dumbarton Oaks Research Library and Collection, 2002), 81.

31. Dante Alighieri, *Purgatory*, Canto XXIX, in *The Divine Comedy*, trans. A. S. Kline, Poetry in Translation (website), 2000, https://www.poetryintranslation.com/PITBR/Italian/DantPurg29to33.php.

32. Quoted in Virginia Reinburg, "Liturgy and the Laity in Late Medieval and Reformation France," *Sixteenth Century Journal* 23, no. 3 (1992): 530.

33. Quoted in Reinburg, "Liturgy and the Laity," 530–531.

34. James H. Morey, "Peter Comestor, Biblical Paraphrase, and the Medieval Popular Bible," *Speculum* 68, no. 1 (1993): 35.

35. This point is effectively made in Kraebel, *Biblical Commentary*, 1–20.

36. R. Howard Bloch, *Paris and Her Cathedrals* (New York: Liveright, 2022), 132–133.

37. Mark Cartwright, "The Stained Glass Windows of Chartres Cathedral," World History Encyclopedia (website), October 16, 2018, https://www.worldhistory.org/article/1277/the-stained-glass-windows-of-chartres-cathedral/.

38. Dante, *Purgatory*, Canto XXII.

39. Andrew Kraebel, "Chaucer's Bibles: Late Medieval Biblicism and Compilational Form," *Journal of Medieval and Early Modern Studies* 47, no. 3 (2017): 437–460; Craig T. Fehrman, "Did Chaucer Read the Wycliffite Bible?," *Chaucer Review* 42, no. 2 (2007): 111–138.

40. Geoffrey Chaucer, "The Pardoner's Tale," in *The Works of Geoffrey Chaucer*, ed. Alfred W. Pollard (London: Macmillan, 1910), 153.

41. The classic study of forms of memory in the Middle Ages is Mary Carruthers, *The Book of Memory: A Study of Memory in Medieval Culture*, 2nd ed. (New York: Cambridge University Press, 2008), 18–55.

42. Annie Sutherland, "Biblical Text and Spiritual Experience in the English Epistles of Richard Rolle," *Review of English Studies* 56, no. 227 (2005): 695–711.

43. Volker Leppin, *Ruhen in Gott: Eine Geschichte der christlichen Mystik* (Munich: C. H. Beck, 2021); Barbara Newman, "What Did It Mean to Say 'I Saw'? The Clash Between Theory and Practice in Medieval Visionary Culture," *Speculum* 80, no. 1 (2005): 1–43.

44. Corina Nicolescu, *Moldovita*, trans. Elisa Madolciu (Bucharest: Editura Sport-Turism, 1978); Adela Văetiși, *Monasteries and Churches of Romania* (Bucharest: Noi Media Print, 2009).

45. Walther and Wolf, *Codices Illustres*, 142.

46. Gregory of Sinai, *Most Beneficial Chapters in Acrostic* 99 (PG 150:1272), quoted in Georgi R. Parpulov, "Psalters and Personal Piety in Byzantium," in *The Old Testament in Byzantium*, ed. Paul Magdalino and Robert Nelson (Washington, DC: Dumbarton Oaks Research Library and Collection, 2010), 79.

47. Quoted in Parpulov, "Psalters and Personal Piety," 81.

48. Quoted in Parpulov, "Psalters and Personal Piety," 80.

49. Schreiner, "Volkstümliche Bibelmagie," 348.

50. Schreiner, "Volkstümliche Bibelmagie," 351.

51. Thomas of Celano, *The First Life of St Francis*, chap. 2, in M. L. Cameron, *The Inquiring Pilgrim's Guide to Assisi*, trans. A. G. Ferrers Howell (London, 1926), online at https://dmdhist.sitehost.iu.edu/francis.htm.

52. Walther and Wolf, *Codices Illustres*, 169.

53. "The Codex Gigas," National Library of Sweden, accessed December 8, 2023, https://www.kb.se/in-english/the-codex-gigas.html.

54. John Lowden, *The Making of the Bibles Moralisées* (University Park: Pennsylvania State University Press, 2000), 12.

55. Katherine H. Tachau, "God's Compass and *Vana Curiositas*: Scientific Study in the Old French *Bible Moralisée*," *Art Bulletin* 80, no. 1 (1998): 7–33.

56. Lowden, *Making of the Bibles Moralisées*, 9.

57. John Lowden, "The *Bible Moralisées* in the Fifteenth Century and the Challenge of the *Bible Historiale*," *Journal of the Warburg and Courtauld Institutes* 68 (2005): 73–176.

58. Christopher de Hamel, *The Book: A History of the Bible* (London: Phaidon, 2005), 150.

59. Nancy Ross, "Bible Moralisée (Moralized Bibles)," Smarthistory (website), Center for Public Art History, January 21, 2016, https://smarthistory.org/bible-moralisee-moralized-bibles/.

60. Avril Henry, ed., *Biblia Pauperum: A Facsimile and Edition* (Ithaca, NY: Cornell University Press, 1987).

61. De Hamel, *Book*, 159.

62. Christopher de Hamel, "Books of Hours: Imaging the Word," in *The Bible as Book: The Manuscript Tradition*, ed. John L. Sharpe and Kimberly Van Kampen (London: British Library, 1998), 137–143.

63. Wendy A. Stein, "The Book of Hours: A Medieval Bestseller," Heilbrunn Timeline of Art History, Metropolitan Museum of Art website, June 2017, http://www.metmuseum.org/toah/hd/hour/hd_hour.htm.

64. Virginia Reinburg, *French Books of Hours: Making an Archive of Prayer, c. 1400–1600* (New York: Cambridge University Press, 2012), 3.

65. Charlotte Steenbrugge, *Drama and Sermon in Late Medieval England: Performance, Authority, Devotion* (Kalamazoo, MI: Medieval Institute Publications, 2017); Carolyn Muessig, ed., *Preacher, Sermon, and Audience in the Middle Ages* (Leiden, the Netherlands: Brill, 2002); Siegfried Wenzel, *The Art of Preaching: Five Medieval Texts and Translations* (Washington, DC: Catholic University of America Press, 2013).

66. Siegfried Wenzel, *Medieval "Artes Praedicandi": A Synthesis of Scholastic Sermon Structure*, Medieval Academy Books 114 (Toronto: University of Toronto Press, 2015).

67. Quoted in Siegfried Wenzel, "The Use of the Bible in Preaching," in *The New Cambridge History of the Bible*, vol. 2, *From 600 to 1450*, ed. Richard Marsden and E. Ann Matter (Cambridge, UK: Cambridge University Press, 2012), 686.

68. Wim Francois, "Vernacular Bible Reading in Late Medieval and Early Modern Europe: The 'Catholic' Position Revisited," *Catholic Historical Review* 104, no. 1 (2018): 37.

69. Andrew Gow, "Challenging the Protestant Paradigm: Bible Reading in Lay and Urban Contexts of the Later Middle Ages," in *Scripture and Pluralism: Reading the Bible in the Religiously Plural Worlds of the Middle Ages and Renaissance*, ed. Thomas J. Heffernan and Thomas Burman, Studies in the History of Christian Traditions, 123 (Leiden, the Netherlands: Brill, 2005), 161–191.

70. Quoted in "Why Wycliffe Translated the Bible into English," *Christian History Magazine*, issue 3 (1983), https://christianhistoryinstitute.org/magazine/article/archives-why-wycliffe-translated.

71. Quoted in "Why Wycliffe Translated."

72. Su Fang Ng, "Translation, Interpretation, and Heresy: The Wycliffite Bible, Tyndale's Bible, and the Contested Origin," *Studies in Philology* 98, no. 3 (2001): 315–338.

73. Mart van Duijn, "Printing, Public, and Power: Shaping the First Printed Bible in Dutch (1477)," *Church and Religious Culture* 93, no. 2 (2013): 279; Suzan Folkerts, "Reading the Bible Lessons at Home: Holy Writ and Lay Readers in the Low Countries," *Church History and Religious Culture* 93, no. 2 (2013): 217–237.

74. Andrew Colin Gow, "The Bible in Germanic," in Marsden and Matter, *New Cambridge History*, 2:198–216.

75. Wim François, "Vernacular Bible Reading in Late Medieval and Early Modern Europe: The 'Catholic' Position Revisited," *Catholic Historical Review* 104, no. 1 (2018): 51.

76. Gemma Avenoza, "The Bible in Spanish and Catalan," in Marsden and Matter, *New Cambridge History*, 2:288–306.

77. Jesse D. Mann, "Reading the Bible in the Fifteenth Century: The Case of Juan de Segovia," *Journal of Medieval Religious Cultures* 43, no. 1 (2017): 115–134.

78. Margriet Hoogvliet, "Encouraging Lay People to Read the Bible in the French Vernaculars: New Groups of Readers and Textual Communities," *Church History and Religious Culture* 93, no. 2 (2013): 259.

79. Hoogvliet, "Encouraging Lay People to Read," 266.

80. Van Duijn, "Printing, Public, and Power," 288.

81. Van Duijn, "Printing, Public, and Power," 291.

82. Rijcklof Hofman, "Inwardness and Individualization in the Late Medieval Low Countries: An Introduction," in Rijcklof Hofman, Charles Caspers, and Peter Nissen, eds., *Inwardness, Individualization, and Religious Agency in the Late Medieval Low Countries: Studies in the "Devotio Moderna" and Its Contexts* (Turnhout: Brepols, 2020), 1–26.

83. Sabrina Corbellini, Mart van Duijn, Suzan Folkerts, and Margriet Hoogvliet, "Challenging the Paradigms: Holy Writ and Lay Readers in Late Medieval Europe," *Church History and Religious Culture* 93, no. 2 (2013): 171–188.

84. Van Duijn, "Printing, Public, and Power," 297.

85. Van Liere, *Introduction to the Medieval Bible*, 102.

86. See Janet Ing, *Johann Gutenberg and His Bible: A Historical Study* (New York: Typophiles, 1988); Michael Matheus, Heidrun Ochs, and Kai-Michael Sprenger, eds., *Reviewing Gutenberg: Historische Konzepte und Rezeptionen* (Stuttgart: Franz Steiner Verlag, 2021); Eric Marshall White, *Editio Princeps: A History of the Gutenberg Bible* (London: Harvey Miller, 2017); and Guy Bechtel, *Gutenberg et l'invention de l'imprimerie: Une enquête* (Paris: Fayard, 1992).

87. De Hamel, *Book*, 196.

88. Quoted in Paul Needham, "The Paper Supply of the Gutenberg Bible," *Papers of the Bibliographical Society of America* 79, no. 3 (1985): 309.

Chapter 5: Renaissance and Reformation

1. Werner Greiling, Uwe Schirmer, and Elke Anna Werner, eds., *Luther auf der Wartburg 1521/22: Bibelübersetzung—Bibeldruck—Wirkungsgeschichte* (Cologne: Böhlau Verlag, 2023).

2. Andrew Pettegree, *Brand Luther: 1517, Printing, and the Making of the Reformation* (New York: Penguin, 2015); Lyndal Roper, *Living I Was Your Plague: Martin Luther's World and Legacy* (Princeton, NJ: Princeton University Press, 2021). On Luther's life, see Heiko A. Oberman, *Luther: Man Between God and the Devil* (New Haven, CT: Yale University Press, 1989); Lyndal Roper, *Martin Luther: Renegade and Prophet* (New York: Random House, 2017); and Heinz Schilling, *Martin Luther: Rebel in an Age of Upheaval*, trans. Rona Johnston (Oxford, UK: Oxford University Press, 2017).

3. Essential reading is Andrew Pettegree, *The Book in the Renaissance* (New Haven, CT: Yale University Press, 2011).

4. Andrew Pettegree, *Reformation and the Culture of Persuasion* (New York: Cambridge University Press, 2005).

5. Timothy J. Wengert, *Reading the Bible with Martin Luther: An Introductory Guide* (Grand Rapids, MI: Baker Academic, 2013), 8–21.

6. Jacob Burckhardt, *The Civilization of the Renaissance in Italy*, trans. S. G. C. Middlemore (London: Penguin, 1990).

7. See the essays in J. Marius J. Lange van Ravenswaay and Herman J. Selderhuis, eds., *Renaissance und Bibelhumanismus* (Göttingen, Germany: Vandenhoeck & Ruprecht, 2020); John Spencer Hill, *Infinity, Faith and Time: Christian Humanism and Renaissance Literature* (Montreal: McGill-Queen's University Press, 1997); and Henning Graf Reventlow, *History of Biblical Interpretation*, vol. 3, *Renaissance, Reformation, Humanism*, trans. James O. Duke (Atlanta: Society of Biblical Literature, 2010).

8. Debora Kuller Shuger, *The Renaissance Bible: Scholarship, Sacrifice, and Subjectivity* (Berkeley: University of California Press, 1994).

9. Christopher S. Celenza, *The Intellectual World of the Italian Renaissance: Language, Philosophy, and the Search for Meaning* (New York: Cambridge University Press, 2018); Christopher S. Celenza, *The Italian Renaissance and the Origins of the Modern Humanities: An Intellectual History, 1400–1800* (Cambridge, UK: Cambridge University Press, 2021).

10. Eugene F. Rice Jr., *Saint Jerome in the Renaissance* (Baltimore: Johns Hopkins University Press, 1985), 116–136.

11. On humanism and the Bible, see the following: Christine Christ-von Wedel, *Erasmus of Rotterdam: Advocate of a New Christianity* (Toronto: University of Toronto Press, 2013); Alan R. Perreiah, *Renaissance Truths: Humanism, Scholasticism and the Search for the Perfect Language* (Burlington, VT: Ashgate, 2014); Martin Dreischmeier, *Sprache als humanisierende Macht: Die Singularität des Lateinischen in Lorenzo Vallas Quintilian-Rezeption* (New York: Georg Olms Verlag, 2017); Douglas S. Pfeiffer, *Authorial Personality and the Making of Renaissance Texts: The Force of Character* (Oxford, UK: Oxford University Press, 2022).

12. Aaron D. Rubin, "Samuel Archivolti and the Antiquity of the Hebrew Pointing," *Jewish Quarterly Review* 101, no. 2 (2011): 233–234.

13. "Requerimiento, 1510," American Beginnings: The European Presence in North America, 1492–1690, National Humanities Center Resource Toolbox, accessed December 8, 2023, https://nationalhumanitiescenter.org/pds/amerbegin/contact /text7/requirement.pdf.

14. Quoted in Yvonne Sherwood, "Comparing the 'Telegraph Bible' of the Late British Empire to the Chaotic Bible of the Sixteenth Century Spanish Empire: Beyond the Canaan Mandate into Anxious Parables of the Land," in *In the Name of God: The Bible in the Colonial Discourses of Empire*, ed. C. L. Crouch and Jonathan Stökl (Leiden, the Netherlands: Brill, 2014), 6–7.

15. David M. Lantigua, *Infidels and Empires in a New World Order: Early Modern Spanish Contributions to International Legal Thought* (Cambridge, UK: Cambridge University Press, 2020), 194, 210.

16. See Diego von Vacano, "Las Casas and the Birth of Race," *History of Political Thought* 33, no. 3 (2012): 401–426.

17. Stephen G. Burnett, *Christian Hebraism in the Reformation Era (1500–1660): Authors, Books, and the Transmission of Jewish Learning* (Leiden, the Netherlands: Brill, 2012); Allison P. Coudert and Jeffrey S. Shoulson, eds., *Hebraica Veritas? Christian Hebraists and the Study of Judaism in Early Modern Europe* (Philadelphia: University of Pennsylvania Press, 2004).

18. Martin Wallraff, Silvana Seidel Menchi, and Kaspar von Greyerz, eds., *Basel 1516: Erasmus' Edition of the New Testament* (Tübingen, Germany: Mohr Siebeck, 2016); Robert D. Sider, ed., *Erasmus on the New Testament* (Toronto: University of Toronto Press, 2020).

19. Henk Jan de Jonge, "Novum testamentum a nobis versum: The Essence of Erasmus' Edition of the New Testament," *Journal of Theological Studies* 35, no. 2 (1984): 394–413.

20. Pierre-Yves Brandt, "Manuscrits grecs utilisés par Erasme pour son édition du *Novum Instrumentum* de 1516," *Theologische Zeitschrift* 54, no. 2 (1998): 120–124.

21. Henk Jan de Jonge, "The Character of Erasmus' Editions of the New Testament as Reflected in Translation of Hebrews 9," *Journal of Medieval and Renaissance Studies* 14 (1984): 81–87.

22. Quoted in Henk Nellen and Jan Bloemendal, "Erasmus's Biblical Project: Some Thoughts and Observations on Its Scope, Its Impact in the Sixteenth Century and Reception in the Seventeenth and Eighteenth Centuries," *Church History and Religious Culture* 96, no. 4 (2016): 603.

23. Erika Rummel, *Erasmus and His Catholic Critics*, 2 vols. (Nieuwkoop, the Netherlands: De Graaf, 1989).

24. See Robert Coogan, *Erasmus, Lee and the Correction of the Vulgate: The Shaking of the Foundations* (Geneva: Librairie Droz, 1992).

25. See Guy Bedouelle, *Lefèvre d'Étaples et l'intelligence des écritures* (Geneva: Droz, 1976); Christoph Schönau, *Jacques Lefèvre d'Etaples und die Reformation* (Gütersloh, Germany: Gütersloher Verlagshaus, 2017); and Richard Cameron, "The Attack on the Biblical Work of Lefèvre d'Étaples, 1514–1521," *Church History* 38, no. 1 (1969): 9–24. See also the essays in Erika Rummel, ed., *Biblical Humanism and Scholasticism in the Age of Erasmus* (Leiden, the Netherlands: Brill, 2008).

26. Richard Rex, "Humanist Bible Controversies," in *The New Cambridge History of the Bible*, vol. 3, *From 1450 to 1750*, ed. Euan Cameron (Cambridge, UK: Cambridge University Press, 2016), 63–67.

27. Paul Needham, "The Changing Shape of the Vulgate Bible in Fifteenth-Century Printing Shops," in *The Bible as Book: The First Printed Editions*, ed. Paul Saenger and Kimberly Van Kampen (London: British Library, 1999), 53–70.

28. J. Waterworth, trans., *The Canons and Decrees of the Sacred and Oecumenical Council of Trent* (London: Dolman, 1848), 17–21, https://history.hanover.edu/texts/trent/ct04.html.

29. On Stephanus, see Elizabeth Armstrong, *Robert Estienne, Royal Printer: An Historical Study of the Elder Stephanus* (Abingdon: Sutton Courtenay, 1986); and Basil Hall, "Biblical Scholarship: Editions and Commentaries," in *The Cambridge History of*

the Bible, vol. 3, *The West from the Reformation to the Present Day*, ed. S. L. Greenslade (Cambridge, UK: Cambridge University Press, 1963), 38–92.

30. Antonio Gerace, *Biblical Scholarship in Louvain in the "Golden" Sixteenth Century* (Göttingen, Germany: Vandenhoeck & Ruprecht, 2019).

31. Luke Murray, *Jesuit Biblical Studies After Trent: Franciscus Toletus and Cornelius a Lapide* (Göttingen, Germany: Vandenhoeck & Ruprecht, 2019), 102–104.

32. John Mervyn Gash, "Counter-Reformation Countenances: Catholic Art and Attitude from Caravaggio to Rubens," *Studies: An Irish Quarterly Review* 104, no. 416 (2015/2016): 373–387. See also Maurizio Marini, *Io Michelangelo da Caravaggio* (Rome: Bestetti e Bozzi, 1974).

33. Walter Friedlaender, *Caravaggio Studies* (Princeton, NJ: Princeton University Press, 1955), 122–130.

34. Alastair Hamilton, "In Search of the Most Perfect Text: The Early Modern Printed Polyglot Bibles from Alcalá (1510–1520) to Brian Walton (1654–1658)," in Cameron, *New Cambridge History*, 3:138–156; Erroll F. Rhodes, "Polyglot Bibles," in *The Oxford Companion to the Bible*, ed. Bruce M. Metzger and Michael D. Coogan (New York: Oxford University Press, 1993), 601–603.

35. Peter N. Miller, "The 'Antiquarianization' of Biblical Scholarship and the London Polyglot Bible (1653–57)," *Journal of the History of Ideas* 62, no. 3 (2001): 463–482.

36. Miller, "'Antiquarianization' of Biblical Scholarship," 465.

37. Adrian Schenker, "From the First Printed Hebrew, Greek, and Latin Bibles to the First Polyglot Bible, the Complutensian Polyglot: 1477–1517," in *Hebrew Bible / Old Testament: The History of Its Interpretation*, ed. Magne Saebo, vol. 2, *From the Renaissance to the Enlightenment* (Göttingen, Germany: Vandenhoeck & Ruprecht, 2008), 276–291; Antonio Alvar Ezquerra, ed., *La Biblia Políglota Complutense en su contexto* (Alcalá de Henares, Spain: Universidad de Alcalá, Servicio de Publicaciones, 2016); Miguel Anxo Pena González and Inmaculada Delgado Jara, eds., *A quinientos años de la Políglota: El proyecto humanístico de Cisneros; Fuentes documentales y líneas de investigación* (Salamanca, Spain: Servicio de Publicaciones, Universidad Pontificia de Salamanca, 2015); José Luis Gonzalo Sánchez Melero, *V centenario de la Biblia Políglota Complutense: La universidad del Renacimiento, el renacimiento de la Universidad* (Madrid: Universidad Complutense de Madrid, Servicio de Publicaciones, 2014).

38. Natalio Fernández Marcos, "The First Polyglot Bible," in *The Text of the Hebrew Bible and Its Editions: Studies in Celebration of the Fifth Centennial of the Complutensian Polyglot*, ed. Andrés Piquer Otero and Pablo Torijano Morales (Leiden, the Netherlands: Brill, 2017), 5.

39. Colin Clair, *Christopher Plantin* (London: Cassell, 1960); Léon Voet, *The Golden Compasses: A History of Evaluation of the Printing and Publishing Activities of the Officina Plantiniana at Antwerp*, 2 vols. (Amsterdam: Van Gendt, 1969–1972).

40. Hamilton, "In Search," 145.

41. Adrian Schenker, "The Polyglot Bibles of Antwerp, Paris, and London 1568–1658," in Saebo, *Hebrew Bible / Old Testament*, 2:774–784; Heather Madar,

Prints as Agents of Global Exchange, 1500–1800 (Amsterdam: Amsterdam University Press, 2021); Robert J. Wilkinson, *The Kabbalistic Scholars of the Antwerp Polyglot Bible* (Leiden, the Netherlands: Brill, 2007).

42. Hamilton, "In Search," 146.

43. Miller, "'Antiquarianization' of Biblical Scholarship," 468.

44. Maria Grossmann, *Humanism in Wittenberg, 1485–1517* (Nieuwkoop, the Netherlands: De Graaf, 1975).

45. Hans Volz, *Martin Luthers deutsche Bibel: Entstehung und Geschichte der Lutherbibel* (Hamburg: Friedrich Wittig Verlag, 1978); Jane O. Newman, "The Word Made Print: Luther's 1522 *New Testament* in an Age of Mechanical Reproduction," *Representations* 11 (1985): 95–133; John L. Flood, "Martin Luther's Bible Translation in Its German and European Context," in *The Bible in the Renaissance: Essays on Biblical Commentary and Translation in the Fifteenth and Sixteenth Centuries*, ed. Richard Griffiths (Burlington, VT: Ashgate, 2001), 45–71; Willem Jan Kooiman, *Luther and the Bible*, trans. John Schmidt (Philadelphia: Muhlenberg, 1961).

46. Martin Luther, "An Open Letter on Translating," ed. Michael D. Marlowe, Bible Research (website), June 2003, https://www.bible-researcher.com/luther01.html.

47. Pettegree, *The Book in the Renaissance*, 98–100.

48. Steven E. Ozment, *The Serpent and the Lamb: Cranach, Luther, and the Making of the Reformation* (New Haven, CT: Yale University Press, 2011); David Price, *In the Beginning Was the Image: Art and the Reformation Bible* (New York: Oxford University Press, 2021). See also the essays in Stefan Oehmig and Stefan Rhein, eds., *Wittenberger Bibeldruck der Reformationszeit* (Leipzig: Evangelische Verlagsanstalt, 2022); and Günter Frank and Maria Lucia Weigel, eds., *Reformation und Bildnis: Bildpropaganda im Zeitalter der Glaubensstreitigkeiten* (Regensburg, Germany: Schnell and Steiner, 2018).

49. Bruce M. Metzger, *The Canon of the New Testament: Its Origin, Development, and Significance* (New York: Oxford University Press, 1987), 242–245.

50. Stephan Füssel, *The Book of Books: The Luther Bible of 1534, a Cultural-Historical Introduction* (Cologne, Germany: Taschen, 2003).

51. Euan Cameron, "The Luther Bible," in *New Cambridge History*, 3:223.

52. Cameron, "Luther Bible," 235.

53. Bruce Gordon, *Zwingli: God's Armed Prophet* (New Haven, CT: Yale University Press, 2021), 164–181.

54. See Amy Nelson Burnett, *Teaching the Reformation: Ministers and Their Message in Basel, 1529–1629* (New York: Oxford University Press, 2006); and Wim Janse and Barbara Pitkin, eds., *The Formation of Clerical and Confessional Identities in Early Modern Europe* (Leiden, the Netherlands: Brill, 2006).

55. The literature is vast. Recommended are Stuart Murray, *Biblical Interpretation in the Anabaptist Tradition* (Kitchener, ON: Pandora, 2000); James M. Stayer, *The German Peasants' War and Anabaptist Community of Goods* (Montreal: McGill-Queens University Press, 1991); Hans Jürgen-Goertz, *The Anabaptists*, trans. Trevor Johnson (London: Routledge, 1996); Kat Hill, *Baptism, Brotherhood, and Belief in Reformation Germany: Anabaptism and Lutheranism, 1525–1585* (Oxford, UK: Oxford University

Press, 2015); and John D. Roth and James M. Stayer, eds., *A Companion to Anabaptism and Spiritualism, 1521–1700* (Leiden, the Netherlands: Brill, 2007).

56. Thieleman J. van Braght, *Martyrs Mirror: The Story of Seventeen Centuries of Christian Martyrdom, from the Time of Christ to A.D. 1660* (Scottdale, PA: Herald, 1950), 470.

57. Quoted in Michael G. Baylor, ed., *The Radical Reformation* (Cambridge, UK: Cambridge University Press, 1991), 147–148.

58. Cornelius J. Dyck, William E. Keeney, and Alvin J. Beachy, eds., *The Writings of Dirk Philips* (Scottdale, PA: Herald, 1992), 206–209.

59. Gerald Hammond, *The Making of the English Bible* (Manchester, UK: Carcanet, 1982); David Norton, "English Bibles from c. 1520 to c. 1750," in *New Cambridge History*, 3:305–344.

60. David Daniell, *William Tyndale: A Biography* (New Haven, CT: Yale University Press, 1994).

61. William Tyndale, "To the Reader," in *The First Printed English New Testament*, trans. William Tyndale (1526; reprint, London, 1871); "Tyndale's Prefaces," Bible Research, ed. Michael D. Marlow, accessed February 13, 2024, https://www.bible-researcher.com /tyndale2.html.

62. Debora Shuger, *Paratexts of the English Bible, 1525–1611* (Oxford, UK: Oxford University Press, 2022), 87–96.

63. Naomi Tadmor, *The Social Universe of the English Bible: Scripture, Society, and Culture in Early Modern England* (New York: Cambridge University Press, 2010).

64. William Tyndale, *Obedience of a Christian*, ed. David Daniell (London: Penguin, 2000), 19.

65. Quoted in Hannibal Hamlin and Norman W. Jones, eds., *The King James Bible After Four Hundred Years: Literary, Linguistic, and Cultural Influences* (Cambridge, UK: Cambridge University Press, 2010), 336.

66. Norton, "English Bibles," 312.

67. See David Daniell, "The Geneva Bible, 1560," in *The Bible in English: Its History and Influence* (New Haven, CT: Yale University Press, 2003), 291–319; Michael Jensen, "'Simply' Reading the Geneva Bible: The Geneva Bible and Its Readers," *Literature and Theology* 9, no. 1 (1995): 30–45; Femke Molekamp, "'Of the Incomparable Treasure of the Holy Scriptures': The Geneva Bible in the Early Modern Household," in *Literature and Popular Culture in Early Modern England*, ed. Matthew Dimmock and Andrew Hadfield (Burlington, VT: Ashgate, 2009), 121–137; Ian Green, "'Puritan Prayer Books' and 'Geneva Bibles': An Episode in Elizabethan Publishing," *Transactions of the Cambridge Bibliographical Society* 11, no. 3 (1998): 313–349; Crawford Gribben, "Deconstructing the Geneva Bible: The Search for a Puritan Poetic," *Literature and Theology* 14, no. 1 (2000), 1–16; Femke Molekamp, "The Geneva Bible in the Household," in *Women and the Bible in Early Modern England: Religious Reading and Writing* (Oxford, UK: Oxford University Press, 2013), 19–50; and Thomas Fulton, "Toward a New Cultural History of the Geneva Bible," *Journal of Medieval and Early Modern Studies* 47, no. 3 (2017): 487–516.

68. Maurice S. Betteridge, "The Bitter Notes: The Geneva Bible and Its Annotations," *Sixteenth Century Journal* 14, no. 1 (1983): 41–62.

69. Graham Tulloch, *A History of the Scots Bible* (Aberdeen: Aberdeen University Press, 1989).

70. See Hannibal Hamlin, *The Bible in Shakespeare* (Oxford, UK: Oxford University Press, 2013), esp. 43–76; and Hannibal Hamlin, "The Renaissance Bible," in *The Cambridge Companion to Shakespeare and Religion*, ed. Hannibal Hamlin (Cambridge, UK: Cambridge University Press, 2019), 34–51. See also the essays in Thomas Fulton and Kristen Poole, eds., *The Bible on the Shakespearean Stage: Cultures of Interpretation in Reformation England* (Cambridge, UK: Cambridge University Press, 2018).

71. James O. Wood, "Shakespeare, *Pericles*, and the Genevan Bible," *Pacific Coast Philology* 12 (1977): 82–89; Naseeb Shaheen, "Shakespeare and the Geneva Bible: *Hamlet* I.iii.54," *Studies in Bibliography* 38 (1985): 201–203; Hugh Craig, "Shakespeare's Vocabulary: Myth and Reality," *Shakespeare Quarterly* 62, no. 1 (2011): 53–74; John Harris, "William Shakespeare and His Geneva Bible," *St Mark's Review* 238 (2016): 106–129.

72. Norton, "English Bibles," 322.

73. Alexandra Walsham, "Unclasping the Book? Post-Reformation English Catholicism and the Vernacular Bible," *Journal of British Studies* 42, no. 2 (2003): 141–166.

74. A. A. den Hollander and Ole Peter Grell, "Bibles in the Dutch and Scandinavian Vernaculars to c. 1750," in Cameron, *New Cambridge History*, 3:249.

75. See Shelley Perlove and Larry Silver, *Rembrandt's Faith: Church and Temple in the Dutch Golden Age* (University Park: Pennsylvania State University Press, 2009).

76. Perlove and Silver, *Rembrandt's Faith*, 10–12.

77. On French Bible history, see Frédéric Delforge, *La Bible en France et dans la francophonie, histoire, traduction, diffusion* (Paris: Societé Biblique Française, 1991); and Bernard Chédozeau, "Bibles in French from 1520 to 1750," in Cameron, *New Cambridge History*, 3:285–304.

78. See Donald K. McKim, ed., *Calvin and the Bible* (Cambridge, UK: Cambridge University Press, 2006); Peter Opitz, *Calvins theologische Hermeneutik* (Neukirchen-Vluyn, Germany: Neukirchener, 1994); and G. Sujin Pak, *The Judaizing Calvin: Sixteenth-Century Debates over the Messianic Psalms* (New York: Oxford University Press, 2010).

79. Barbara Pitkin, *Calvin, the Bible, and History: Exegesis and Historical Reflection in the Era of Reform* (New York: Oxford University Press, 2020).

80. John Calvin, *The Form of Prayers and Ministration of the Sacraments*, online at A Puritan's Mind, accessed February 13, 2024, https://www.apuritansmind.com/puritan-worship/the-form-of-prayers-and-ministration-of-the-sacraments-by-john-calvin-1556/.

81. See Gijsbert Siertsema, "Psalm Translations in the Low Countries, 1539–1600, and Their European Context," in *From Revolt to Riches: Culture and History of the Low*

Countries, 1500–1700, ed. Theo Hermans and Reinier Salverda (London: UCL Press, 2017), 35–45; John Ottenhoff, "Recent Studies in Metrical Psalms," *English Literary Renaissance* 33, no. 2 (2003): 252–275; and Édith Weber, "La langue des Psaumes: Quelques exemples du problème de la paraphrase des Psaumes en langue vernaculaire," *Bulletin de la Société de l'Histoire du Protestantisme Français* 158 (2012): 259–282.

82. Timothy Duguid, *Metrical Psalmody in Print and Practice: English "Singing Psalms" and Scottish "Psalm Buiks," c. 1547–1640* (Burlington, VT: Ashgate, 2014).

83. Quoted in Emidio Campi and Mariano Delgado, "Bibles in Italian and Spanish," in Cameron, *New Cambridge History*, 3:381.

84. Graeme Murdock, "Bibles in Central and Eastern European Vernaculars to c. 1750," in Cameron, *New Cambridge History*, 3:345–357.

Chapter 6: Science and Reason

1. See Travis DeCook, "The Ark and Immediate Revelation in Francis Bacon's *New Atlantis*," *Studies in Philology* 105, no. 1 (2008): 103–122; and Suzanne Smith, "The *New Atlantis*: Francis Bacon's Theological-Political Utopia?," *Harvard Theological Review* 101, no. 1 (2008): 97–125.

2. Francis Bacon, *The New Atlantis* (Benediction Classics, 2008; Project Gutenberg, 2008), https://www.gutenberg.org/files/2434/2434-h/2434-h.htm.

3. Travis DeCook, "The Extrinsic Bible: Francis Bacon's *New Atlantis*, Concepts of Scripture, and the Question of Secularity," *Religion and Literature* 47, no. 1 (2015): 99–121.

4. The literature is enormous, but recommended are Maurice A. Finocchiaro, *On Trial for Reason: Science, Religion, and Culture in the Galileo Affair* (Oxford, UK: Oxford University Press, 2019); Jerome J. Langford, *Galileo, Science and the Church* (Ann Arbor: University of Michigan Press, 1971); and Richard J. Blackwell, *Behind the Scenes at Galileo's Trial: Including the First English Translation of Melchior Inchofer's "Tractatus syllepticus"* (Notre Dame, IN: University of Notre Dame Press, 2006).

5. Essential reading on the history of the Galileo affair is Maurice A. Finocchiaro, *Retrying Galileo, 1633–1992* (Berkeley: University of California Press, 2005).

6. Quoted in Douglas O. Linder, University of Missouri–Kansas City School of Law website, accessed February 13, 2024, http://law2.umkc.edu/faculty/projects/ftrials/galileo/recantation.html.

7. Mario Biagioli, *Galileo, Courtier: The Practice of Science in the Culture of Absolutism* (Chicago: University of Chicago Press, 1994).

8. On the intellectual culture of Galileo and the Jesuits, see Eva Del Soldato, *Early Modern Aristotle: On the Making and Unmaking of Authority* (Philadelphia: University of Pennsylvania Press, 2020). See also Eva Del Soldato, "If Aristotle Were Alive: Galileo and the Jesuits," University of Pennsylvania Press blog, June 3, 2020, https://www.pennpress.org/blog/if-aristotle-were-alive-galileo-and-the-jesuits/.

9. Jamie Doward, "When Milton Met Galileo: The Collision of Cultures That Helped Shape *Paradise Lost*," *Guardian*, August 19, 2017, https://www.theguardian

.com/books/2017/aug/20/john-milton-paradise-lost-galileo-collision-of-cultures
-bbc-documentary.

10. Richard J. Blackwell, *Galileo, Bellarmine, and the Bible* (Notre Dame, IN: University of Notre Dame Press, 1991); Ernan Mcmullin, "Galileo on Science and Scripture," in *The Cambridge Companion to Galileo*, ed. Peter Machamer (Cambridge, UK: Cambridge University Press, 1998), 271–347.

11. William E. Carroll, "Galileo and the Interpretation of the Bible," *Science and Education* 8 (1999): 151–187.

12. Galileo Galilei, "Letter to the Grand Duchess Christina of Tuscany," 1615, https://web.stanford.edu/~jsabol/certainty/readings/Galileo-LetterDuchessChristina.pdf.

13. Quoted in Kevin Killeen and Peter J. Forshaw, eds., *The Word and the World: Biblical Exegesis and Early Modern Science* (London: Palgrave, 2007), 4.

14. Galilei, "Letter to the Grand Duchess Christina."

15. Galilei, "Letter to the Grand Duchess Christina."

16. John Channing Briggs, "Bacon's Science and Religion," in *The Cambridge Companion to Bacon*, ed. Markku Peltonen (Cambridge, UK: Cambridge University Press, 1996), 172–199. See also Stéphane Guégan, "Jean Clair: 'Francis Bacon et quelques autres considérations," *Revue des deux mondes* (November 2019): 144–151.

17. Stephen A. McKnight, "Reconsideration: Francis Bacon's God," *New Atlantis* 10 (2005): 73–100.

18. Katherine Bootle Attié, "Prose, Science, and Scripture: Francis Bacon's Sacred Texts," in *Gathering Force: Early Modern British Literature in Transition, 1557–1623*, ed. Kristen Poole and Lauren Shohet (Cambridge, UK: Cambridge University Press, 2019), 178–196.

19. Quoted in Steven Matthews, "Reading the Two Books with Francis Bacon: Interpreting God's Will and Power," in Killeen and Forshaw, *Word and World*, 67.

20. See Stephen D. Snobelen, "The Theology of Isaac Newton's *Principia Mathematica*: A Preliminary Survey," *Neue Zeitschrift für Systematische Theologie und Religionsphilosophie* 52, no. 4 (2010): 377–412, https://isaacnewtonstheology.files.wordpress.com/2013/06/theology-of-the-principia.pdf; Bernard Cohen, "Isaac Newton's Principia, the Scriptures, and the Divine Providence," in *Philosophy, Science, and Method: Essays in Honor of Ernest Nagel*, ed. Sidney Morgenbesser, Patrick Suppes, and Morton White (New York: St. Martin's, 1969), 525–530; James E. Force, "Newton's 'Sleeping Argument' and the Newtonian Synthesis of Science and Religion," in *Standing on the Shoulders of Giants: A Longer View of Newton and Halley*, ed. Norman J. W. Thrower (Berkeley: University of California Press, 1990), 109–127; and Stephen D. Snobelen, "'God of Gods, and Lord of Lords': The Theology of Isaac Newton's General Scholium to the *Principia*," *Osiris* 16 (2001): 169–208.

21. Pablo Toribio, "Isaac Newton's Antitrinitarianism in Relation to His Natural Philosophy: Origins, Chronology and Continuities," in *Gegeneinander glauben—miteinander forschen? Paradigmenwechsel frühneuzeitlicher Wissenschaftskulturen*, ed. Kestutis Daugirdas and Christian Volkmar Witt (Göttingen, Germany: Vandenhoeck & Ruprecht, 2022), 177–202.

22. Newton to Bentley, December 10, 1692, in *Isaac Newton: Philosophical Writings*, ed. Andrew Janiak (Cambridge, UK: Cambridge University Press, 2012), 94.

23. Maurice F. Wiles, "Newton and the Bible," in *Language, Theology, and the Bible: Essays in Honour of James Barr*, ed. Samuel E. Balentine and John Barton (Oxford, UK: Clarendon, 1994), 338.

24. Richard H. Popkin, "Newton as a Bible Scholar," in *Essays on the Context, Nature, and Influence of Isaac Newton's Theology*, ed. James E. Force and Richard H. Popkin (Boston: Kluwer Academic, 1990), 103–118.

25. See Paul D. Cooke, *Hobbes and Christianity: Reassessing the Bible in Leviathan* (Lanham, MD: Rowman & Littlefield, 1996); Daniel J. Elazar, "Hobbes Confronts Scripture," *Jewish Political Studies Review* 4, no. 2 (1992): 3–24; Lodi Nauta, "Hobbes on Religion and the Church Between *The Elements of Law* and *Leviathan*: A Dramatic Change of Direction?," *Journal of the History of Ideas* 63, no. 4 (2002): 577–598; Noel Malcolm, "*Leviathan*, the Pentateuch, and the Origins of Modern Biblical Critics," in *Leviathan After 350 Years*, ed. Tom Sorell and Luc Foisneau (New York: Oxford University Press, 2004), 241–264; Frank M. Coleman, "Thomas Hobbes and the Hebraic Bible," *History of Political Thought* 25, no. 4 (2004): 642–669; Jeffrey L. Morrow, "*Leviathan* and the Swallowing of Scripture: The Politics Behind Thomas Hobbes' Early Modern Biblical Criticism," *Christianity and Literature* 61, no. 1 (2011): 33–54; and Johan Olsthoorn, "The Theocratic *Leviathan*: Hobbes's Argument for the Identity of Church and State," in *Hobbes on Politics and Religion*, ed. Laurens van Apeldoorn and Robin Douglass (Oxford, UK: Oxford University Press, 2018), 10–28.

26. Noel Malcolm, *Aspects of Hobbes* (Oxford, UK: Oxford Academic Books, 2002), 396–397.

27. Quoted in Travis DeCook, *The Origins of the Bible and Early Modern Political Thought: Revelation and the Boundaries of Scripture* (Cambridge, UK: Cambridge University Press, 2021), 109.

28. Quoted in DeCook, *Origins of the Bible*, 114.

29. The essential work is Anthony Grafton, *Joseph Scaliger: A Study in the History of Classical Scholarship*, 2 vols. (Oxford, UK: Clarendon, 1983).

30. Dirk van Miert, "Grotius's *Annotationes* on the Bible (1619–1645)," in *The Emancipation of Biblical Philology in the Dutch Republic, 1590–1670* (Oxford, UK: Oxford University Press, 2018), 133–169.

31. Quoted in van Miert, *Emancipation of Biblical Philology*, 142.

32. Dirk van Miert, "On the Eve of Spinoza: The Rise of Biblical Philology (1650–1670)," in *Emancipation of Biblical Philology*, 213–230.

33. Quoted in van Miert, *Emancipation of Biblical Philology*, 215.

34. Richard H. Popkin, "Spinoza and Bible Scholarship," in *The Cambridge Companion to Spinoza*, ed. Don Garrett (Cambridge, UK: Cambridge University Press, 1996); Harvey Shulman, "The Use and Abuse of the Bible in Spinoza's *Tractatus Theologico-Politicus*," *Jewish Political Studies Review* 7, no. 1/2 (1995): 39–55; Michah Gottlieb, "Spinoza's Method(s) of Biblical Interpretation Reconsidered," *Jewish Studies Quarterly* 14, no. 3 (2007): 286–317; Piet Steenbakkers, "Spinoza in the History of

Biblical Scholarship," in *The Making of the Humanities*, ed. Rens Bod, Jaap Maat, and Thijs Weststeijn, vol. 1, *Early Modern Europe* (Amsterdam: Amsterdam University Press, 2010), 313–326; Nancy Levene, "Does Spinoza Think the Bible Is Sacred?," *Jewish Quarterly Review* 101, no. 4 (2011): 545–573; Carlos Fraenkel, "Spinoza on Miracles and the Truth of the Bible," *Journal of the History of Ideas* 74, no. 4 (2013): 643–658; Warren Zev Harvey, "Spinoza on Biblical Miracles," *Journal of the History of Ideas* 74, no. 4 (2013): 659–675.

35. Clare Carlisle, *Spinoza's Religion: A New Reading of the Ethics* (Princeton, NJ: Princeton University Press), 13–15.

36. Quoted in Carlisle, *Spinoza's Religion*, 134.

37. See Andrew Hunwick, "Richard Simon (1638–1712): Sketch of Life and Career," in *Critical History of the Text of the New Testament: Wherein Is Established the Truth of the Acts on Which the Christian Religion Is Based*, by Richard Simon, trans. and ed. Andrew Hunwick (Leiden, the Netherlands: Brill, 2013), xxv–xxxiii. See also Jan Starczewski, "Richard Simon, Biblical Criticism, and Voltaire," *Religions* 13, no. 10 (2022), https://www.mdpi.com/2077-1444/13/10/995; and Guy G. Stroumsa, "Jewish Myth and Ritual and the Beginnings of Comparative Religion: The Case of Richard Simon," *Journal of Jewish Thought and Philosophy* 6 (1997): 19–35.

38. Quoted in Richard H. Popkin, *The History of Scepticism from Erasmus to Spinoza* (Berkeley: University of California Press, 1979), 221.

39. Quoted in Starzewski, "Richard Simon, Biblical Criticism," 7.

40. Ivano Dal Prete, *On the Edge of Eternity: The Antiquity of the Earth in Medieval and Early Modern Europe* (New York: Oxford University Press, 2022); Caroline Winterer, *American Enlightenments: Pursuing Happiness in the Age of Reason* (New Haven, CT: Yale University Press, 2016).

41. Lydia Barnett, "Giant Bones and the Taunton Stone: American Antiquities, World History, and the Protestant International," in *Empires of Knowledge: Scientific Networks in the Early Modern World*, ed. Paula Findlen (New York: Routledge, 2019), 225–246.

42. Barnett, "Giant Bones and the Taunton Stone," 215–216.

43. Quoted in Winterer, *American Enlightenments*, 226.

44. Barnett, "Giant Bones and the Taunton Stone," 215–216.

45. C. P. E. Nothaft, "Noah's Calendar: The Chronology of the Flood Narrative and the History of Astronomy in Sixteenth- and Seventeenth-Century Scholarship," *Journal of the Warburg and Courtauld Institutes* 74, no. 1 (2011): 191–211.

46. See Richard H. Popkin, *Isaac La Peyrère (1596–1676): His Life, Work, and Influence* (Leiden, the Netherlands: Brill, 1987); Richard H. Popkin, "Spinoza and La Peyrère," *Southwestern Journal of Philosophy* 8, no. 3 (1977): 177–195; Richard H. Popkin, "Jewish-Christian Relations in the Sixteenth and Seventeenth Centuries: The Conception of the Messiah," *Jewish History* 6, no. 1/2 (1992): 163–177; Ira Robinson, "Isaac de la Peyrère and the Recall of the Jews," *Jewish Social Studies* 40, no. 2 (1978): 117–130; and Yvan Loskoutoff, "L'arrestation et la conversion d'Isaac de La Peyrère d'après les sources romaines (1656–1657)," *Revue de l'histoire des religions* 236, no. 3 (2019): 545–576.

47. Colin Kidd, *The Forging of Races: Race and Scripture in the Protestant Atlantic World, 1600–2000* (New York: Cambridge University Press, 2006), 58.

48. Quoted in Kidd, *Forging of Races*, 100.

49. Gabrielle-Émilie Le Tonnelier de Breteuil, Marquise Du Châtelet-Lomond, introduction to *Examens de la Bible*, ed. Bertram Eugene Schwarzbach (Paris: Editions Honoré Champion, 2011), 440.

50. On Descartes and the Bible, see Brayton Polka, *Paradox and Contradiction in the Biblical Traditions: The Two Ways of the World* (Lanham, MD: Lexington, 2021), 115–180; Lloyd Strickland, "Taking Scripture Seriously: Leibniz and the Jehoshaphat Problem," *Heythrop Journal* 52, no. 1 (2011): 40–51; and Daniel J. Cook, "Leibniz on 'Prophets,' Prophecy, and Revelation," *Religious Studies* 45, no. 3 (2009): 269–287.

51. The following depends on Graham Gargett, "Voltaire and the Bible," in *The Cambridge Companion to Voltaire*, ed. Nicholas Cronk (Cambridge, UK: Cambridge University Press, 2009), 193–204.

52. See Jonathan Sheehan, *The Enlightenment Bible: Translation, Scholarship, Culture* (Princeton, NJ: Princeton University Press, 2005).

53. Sheehan, preface to *Enlightenment Bible*, xiii–xiv.

54. Douglas H. Shantz, *An Introduction to German Pietism: Protestant Renewal at the Dawn of Modern Europe* (Baltimore: Johns Hopkins University Press, 2013), 214.

55. Shantz, *Introduction to German Pietism*, 219.

56. Quoted in Shantz, *Introduction to German Pietism*, 226.

57. See David Johnston, "Bach and the Bible," *Proceedings of the Royal Musical Association* 90 (1963): 27–42; Howard Cox, "The Scholarly Detective: Investigating Bach's Personal Bible," *Bach* 25, no. 1 (1994): 28–45; Markus Rathey, *Bach's Major Vocal Works: Music, Drama, Liturgy* (New Haven, CT: Yale University Press, 2016); and Markus Rathey, *Bach in the World: Music, Society, and Representation in Bach's Cantatas* (New York: Oxford University Press, 2023).

58. Robin A. Leaver, "The Calov Bible from Bach's Library," *Bach* 7, no. 4 (1976): 16–22.

59. Quoted in Robin Leaver, "Sebastian Bach: Theological Musician and Musical Theologian," *Bach* 31, no. 1 (2000): 20.

60. Stephen J. Stein, "Jonathan Edwards and the Rainbow: Biblical Exegesis and Poetic Imagination," *New England Quarterly* 47, no. 3 (1974): 440–456. A selection of other writings includes Robert E. Brown, "Edwards, Locke, and the Bible," *Journal of Religion* 79, no. 3 (1999): 361–384; and David P. Barshinger and Douglas A. Sweeney, eds., *Jonathan Edwards and Scripture: Biblical Exegesis in British North America* (New York: Oxford University Press, 2018).

61. Quoted in David P. Barshinger, *Jonathan Edwards and the Psalms: A Redemptive-Historical Vision of Scripture* (New York: Oxford University Press, 2014), 111.

62. Quoted in Barshinger, *Jonathan Edwards and the Psalms*, 120.

63. Barshinger, *Jonathan Edwards and the Psalms*, 122–123.

Chapter 7: The King James Bible

1. The literature on the King James Bible (also known as the Authorized Version) is vast. Recommended recent reading: Adam Nicolson, *God's Secretaries: The Making of the King James Bible* (New York: HarperPerennial, 2005); David Norton, ed., *The Bible* (New York: Penguin, 2006); David G. Burke, ed., *Translation That Openeth the Window: Reflections on the History and Legacy of the King James Bible* (Atlanta: Society of Biblical Literature, 2009); David Crystal, *Begat: The King James Bible and the English Language* (New York: Oxford University Press, 2010); Helen Moore and Julian Reid, eds., *Manifold Greatness: The Making of the King James Bible* (Oxford, UK: Bodleian Library, 2011); Gordon Campbell, *Bible: The Story of the King James Version, 1611–2011* (New York: Oxford University Press, 2011); David Norton, *The King James Bible: A Short History from Tyndale to Today* (Cambridge, UK: Cambridge University Press, 2011); Harold Bloom, *The Shadow of a Great Rock: A Literary Appreciation of the King James Bible* (New Haven, CT: Yale University Press, 2011); David Lyle Jeffrey, ed., *The King James Bible and the World It Made* (Waco, TX: Baylor University Press, 2011); Donald L. Brake with Shelly Beach, *A Visual History of the King James Bible: The Dramatic Story of the World's Best-Known Translation* (Grand Rapids, MI: Baker, 2011); David G. Burke, John F. Kutsko, and Philip H. Towner, eds., *The King James Version at 400: Assessing Its Genius as Bible Translation and Its Literary Influence* (Atlanta: Society of Biblical Literature, 2013); Matthieu Arnold and Christophe Tournu, eds., *La Bible de 1611: Sources, écritures et influences, XVIe–XVIIIe siècles* (Strasbourg: Presses Universitaires de Strasbourg, 2013); Angelica Duran, ed., *The King James Bible Across Borders and Centuries* (Pittsburgh, PA: Duquesne University Press, 2014).

2. Quoted in David Norton, "English Bibles from c. 1520 to 1750," in *The New Cambridge History of the Bible*, vol. 3, *From 1450 to 1750*, ed. Euan Cameron (Cambridge, UK: Cambridge University Press, 2016), 329.

3. Jeffrey Alan Miller, "'Better, as in the Geneva': The Role of the Geneva Bible in Drafting the King James Version," *Journal of Medieval and Early Modern Studies* 47, no. 3 (2017): 517–543.

4. Norton, *King James Bible*, 61.

5. See the essays in Mordechai Feingold, ed., *Labourers in the Vineyard of the Lord: Erudition and the Making of the King James Version of the Bible* (Leiden, the Netherlands: Brill, 2018).

6. "The Translators to the Reader," preface to the 1611 King James Version, Christian Classics Ethereal Library (website), accessed February 13, 2024, https://www.ccel.org/bible/kjv/preface/pref10.htm.

7. "Translators to the Reader."

8. Miller, "'Better, as in the Geneva,'" 517.

9. See Jeffrey Alan Miller, "The Earliest Known Draft of the King James Bible: Samuel Ward's Draft of 1 Esdras and Wisdom 3–4," in Feingold, *Labourers in the Vineyard*, 187–265.

10. Thomas Cranmer, "Preface to the Bible," in *The Protestant Reformation*, ed. Lewis W. Spitz (Englewood Cliffs, NJ: Prentice-Hall, 1966), 167.

11. "The Translators to the Reader," 1611 King James Version, Bible Research (website), accessed February 13, 2024, https://www.bible-researcher.com/kjvpref.html.

12. Norton, *King James Bible*, 117.

13. Gordon Campbell, "The Commissioning of the King James Version," chap. 2 in *Bible*, https://academic.oup.com/book/5443/chapter/148310391.

14. Hannibal Hamlin, "The Noblest Composition in the Universe or Fit for the Flames? The Literary Style of the King James Bible," in *The Oxford Handbook of the Bible in Early Modern England, c. 1530–1700*, ed. Kevin Killeen, Helen Smith, and Rachel Willie (Oxford, UK: Oxford University Press, 2015), 469–482.

15. Quoted in Jason P. Rosenblatt, "Milton, Anxiety and the King James Bible," in *The King James Bible After 400 Years: Literary, Linguistic, and Cultural Influences*, ed. Hannibal Hamlin and Norman W. Jones (New York: Cambridge University Press, 2010), 184.

16. Campbell, *Bible*, 253.

17. Daniel Blank, *Shakespeare and University Drama in Early Modern England* (Oxford, UK: Oxford University Press, 2023).

18. Norton, *King James Bible*, 125.

19. See Kirsten Macfarlane, "Hugh Broughton and the King James Bible, Revisited," *Reformation* 25, no. 1 (2020): 92–108. See also Kirsten Macfarlane, *Biblical Scholarship in an Age of Controversy: The Polemical World of Hugh Broughton (1549–1612)* (Oxford, UK: Oxford University Press, 2021), 81–110, 209–214.

20. Macfarlane, "Hugh Broughton," 97–101. I am extremely grateful to Professor Macfarlane for email correspondence on these questions.

21. Eva Corlett, "Rare 'Wicked' Bible That Encourages Adultery Discovered in New Zealand," *Guardian*, May 2, 2022, https://www.theguardian.com/world/2022/may/02/rare-wicked-bible-that-encourages-adultery-discovered-in-new-zealand.

22. Quoted in Norton, *King James Bible*, 154.

23. Quoted in Norton, *King James Bible*, 188.

24. Quoted in Norton, *A History of the Bible as Literature*, vol. 2, *From 1700 to the Present Day* (Cambridge, UK: Cambridge University Press, 1991), 189.

25. Quoted in David Norton, *A History of the Bible as Literature*, vol. 2, *From 1700 to the Present Day* (Cambridge, UK: Cambridge University Press, 1991), 3.

26. Quoted in Norton, *King James Bible*, 190.

27. Norton, *King James Bible*, 189.

28. Simon Heighes, "How the King James Bible Inspired and Influenced Composers and Their Music," Classical Music (website), *BBC Music Magazine*, February 11, 2022, https://www.classical-music.com/features/articles/how-the-king-james-bible-inspired-and-influenced-composers-and-their-music/.

29. Campbell, *Bible*, 136.

30. Campbell, *Bible*, 142.

31. Quoted in Norton, *King James Bible*, 195.

32. Campbell, *Bible*, 167.

33. Michaela Giebelhausen, *Painting the Bible: Representation and Belief in Mid-Victorian Britain* (Burlington, VT: Ashgate, 2006), 4.

34. Sue Zemka, *Victorian Testaments: The Bible, Christology, and Literary Authority in Early-Nineteenth-Century British Culture* (Stanford, CA: Stanford University Press, 1997), 1–12.

35. Quoted in Jennifer Stevens, *The Historical Jesus and the Literary Imagination, 1860–1920* (Liverpool: Liverpool University Press, 2010), 9.

36. Stevens, *Historical Jesus*, 10.

37. Timothy Larsen, *A People of One Book: The Bible and the Victorians* (New York: Oxford University Press, 2011), 67–88.

38. Charles Bradlaugh, *A Few Words About the Devil, and Other Biographical Sketches and Essays* (New York: A. K. Butts, 1874; Project Gutenberg, 2013), https://www.gutenberg.org/files/36269/36269-h/36269-h.htm.

39. Quoted in Larsen, *People of One Book*, 71.

40. Quoted in Larsen, *People of One Book*, 79.

41. "A Conflict of Biblical Proportions: How the Bible Was Used to Turn the First World War into a Holy War," University of Cambridge website, November 8, 2015, https://www.cam.ac.uk/research/news/a-conflict-of-biblical-proportions-how-the-bible-was-used-to-turn-the-first-world-war-into-a-holy.

42. Quoted in Campbell, *Bible*, 255.

Chapter 8: The Transatlantic Bible

1. See Alec Ryrie, *Being Protestant in Reformation Britain* (Oxford, UK: Oxford University Press, 2013); Bruce Tucker, "Joseph Sewall's Diary and the Rhythm of Puritan Spirituality," *Early American Literature* 22, no. 1 (1987): 3–18; and J. A. Medders, "Grazing and Gazing: Meditation and Contemplation in Puritan Spirituality," *Journal of Spiritual Formation and Soul Care* 15, no. 1 (2022): 30–43.

2. See John Stachniewski, *The Persecutory Imagination: English Puritanism and the Literature of Religious Despair* (Oxford, UK: Oxford University Press, 1991); Margo Todd, "Puritan Self-Fashioning: The Diary of Samuel Ward," *Journal of British Studies* 31, no. 3 (1992): 236–264; Tom Webster, "Writing to Redundancy: Approaches to Spiritual Journals and Early Modern Spirituality," *Historical Journal* 39, no. 1 (1996): 33–56; Michael Mascuch, *Origins of the Individualist Self: Autobiography and Self-Identity in England, 1591–1791* (Cambridge, UK: Polity, 1997); Elaine McKay, "English Diarists: Gender, Geography and Occupation, 1500–1700," *History* 90, no. 2 (2005): 191–212; Andrew Cambers, "Reading, the Godly, and Self-Writing in England, Circa 1580–1720," *Journal of British Studies* 46, no. 4 (2007): 796–825; and James Daybell, "Women's Letters, Literature and Conscience in Sixteenth-Century England," *Renaissance Studies* 23, no. 4 (2009): 516–533.

3. Quoted in Effie Botonaki, "Seventeenth-Century Englishwomen's Spiritual Diaries: Self-Examination, Covenanting, and Account Keeping," *Sixteenth Century Journal* 30, no. 1 (1999): 9.

4. Julie Crawford, "Reconsidering Early Modern Women's Reading, or, How Margaret Hoby Read Her de Mornay," *Huntington Library Quarterly* 73, no. 2 (2010): 193–223.

5. Botonaki, "Seventeenth-Century Englishwomen's Spiritual Diaries," 3–21.

6. Quoted in John R. Knott Jr., *The Sword of the Spirit: Puritan Responses to the Bible* (Eugene, OR: Wipf and Stock, 2012), 47.

7. Quoted in John M. Major, "Milton's View of Rhetoric," *Studies in Philology* 64, no. 5 (1967): 696.

8. Mark Dever, "Richard Sibbes and the Centrality of the Heart," Ligonier (website), May 4, 2018, https://www.ligonier.org/learn/articles/richard-sibbes-and -centrality-heart.

9. Richard Rogers, "A Sweet Meditation," 1603, ReformedBooksOnline.com, https://reformedtheologybooks.files.wordpress.com/2014/07/rogers-richard-a-sweet -meditation-poem.pdf.

10. Meredith Marie Neuman, *Jeremiah's Scribes: Creating Sermon Literature in Puritan New England* (Philadelphia: University of Pennsylvania Press, 2013), 1–34.

11. Richard Baxter, *The Saints' Everlasting Rest* (New York: American Tract Society, 1851), Christian Classics Ethereal Library (website), accessed February 13, 2024, https://ccel.org/ccel/baxter/saints_rest/saints_rest.i.html.

12. Quoted in Knott, *Sword of the Spirit*, 89.

13. Natalie Spar, "The Politics of the Pure Language in Seventeenth-Century Quakerism: Speech, Silence, and the Founding of Pennsylvania," *Early American Studies* 13, no. 3 (2015): 702.

14. Quoted in Knott, *Sword of the Spirit*, 119.

15. Quoted in Knott, *Sword of the Spirit*, 134.

16. John Owen, *The Works of John Owen* (Edinburgh: Banner of Truth Press, 1968), 6:249.

17. Quoted in Crawford Gribben, "Reading the Bible: John Owen and Early Evangelical 'Biblicism,'" in *The Bible in Early Transatlantic Pietism and Evangelicalism*, ed. Ryan P. Hoselton, Jan Stievermann, Douglas A. Sweeney, and Michael A. G. Haykin (Philadelphia: Pennsylvania State University Press, 2022), 79.

18. Kate Narveson, *Bible Readers and Lay Writers in Early Modern England: Gender and Self-Definition in an Emergent Writing Culture* (New York: Routledge, 2016), 1.

19. Quoted in Narveson, *Bible Readers*, 184.

20. Quoted from Edmund S. Morgan, "John Winthrop's 'Modell of Christian Charity' in a Wider Context," *Huntingdon Library Quarterly* 50, no. 2 (1987): 145.

21. Quoted in Harry Stout, "Word and Order in Colonial New England," in *The Bible in America: Essays in Cultural History*, ed. Nathan O. Hatch and Mark A. Noll (New York: Oxford University Press, 1982), 27.

22. "John Winthrop's *City on a Hill*, 1630," website of Hans P. Vought, SUNY Ulster, accessed February 14, 2024, https://people.sunyulster.edu/voughth/John %20Winthrop's%20City%20upon%20a%20Hill.htm.

23. Quoted in Stout, "Word and Order," 30–31.

24. Lisa M. Gordis, *Opening Scripture: Bible Reading and Interpretive Authority in Puritan New England* (Chicago: University of Chicago Press, 2003), 3–4.

25. "The Massachusetts Bay Colony Case Against Anne Hutchinson (1637)," W. W. Norton website, accessed February 14, 2024, https://wwnorton.com/college/history /archive/resources/documents/ch02_03.htm.

26. Quoted in Gordis, *Opening Scripture*, 55.

27. Sean P. Harvey and Sarah Rivett, "Colonial-Indigenous Language Encounters in North America and the Intellectual History of the Atlantic World," *Early American Studies* 15, no. 3 (2017): 442–473.

28. Steffi Dipold, "The Wampanoag Word: John Eliot's *Indian Grammar*, the Vernacular Rebellion, and the Elegancies of Native Speech," *Early America Literature* 48, no. 3 (2013): 543–575; Sarah Rivett, "Learning to Write Algonquian Letters: The Indigenous Place of Language Philosophy in the Seventeenth-Century Atlantic World," *William and Mary Quarterly* 71, no. 4 (2014): 549–588.

29. Linford D. Fisher, *The Indian Great Awakening: Religion and the Shaping of Native Cultures in Early America* (New York: Oxford University Press, 2012), 25–26.

30. Quoted in Lori Anne Ferrell, *The Bible and the People* (New Haven, CT: Yale University Press, 2008), 110.

31. Quoted in Fisher, *Indian Great Awakening*, 28.

32. Linford D. Fisher, "Native Americans, Conversion, and Christian Practice in Colonial New England, 1640–1730," *Harvard Theological Review* 102, no. 1 (2009): 101–124.

33. Quoted in Fisher, "Native Americans, Conversion," 110.

34. Quoted in Fisher, "Native Americans, Conversion," 111.

35. Quoted in Fisher, "Native Americans, Conversion," 111.

36. Quoted in Fisher, "Native Americans, Conversion," 112.

37. Ryan P. Hoselton, "The Bible in Early Pietist and Evangelical Missions," in Hoselton, Stievermann, Sweeney, and Haykin, *Bible in Early Transatlantic Pietism*, 116.

38. Scott Richard Lynns, "The Bible in Native American Literature," *Religions* 13, no. 11 (2022), https://doi.org/10.3390/rel13111120.

39. Quoted in Lynns, "Bible in Native American Literature."

40. Quoted in Lynns, "Bible in Native American Literature."

41. Quoted in Lynns, "Bible in Native American Literature."

42. Hoselton, "Bible in Early Pietist," 111.

43. Quoted in Hoselton, "Bible in Early Pietist," 113.

44. Jonathan Edwards, "The Latter-Day Glory Is Probably to Begin in America," in *God's New Israel: Religious Interpretations of American Destiny*, ed. Conrad Cherry (Chapel Hill: University of North Carolina Press, 1998), 58.

45. Quoted in Hoselton, "Bible in Early Pietist," 115.

46. Philipp Jakob Spener, "The Necessary and Useful Reading of the Holy Scriptures," in *Pietists: Selected Writings*, ed. Peter C. Erb (New York: Paulist Press, 1983), 74.

47. Quoted in Ruth Albrecht, "Lay Appropriations and Female Interpretations of the Bible in German Pietism," in Hoselton, Stievermann, Sweeney, and Haykin, *Bible in Early Transatlantic Pietism*, 155.

48. Quoted in Hoselton, "Bible in Early Pietist," 124.

49. Quoted in Bruce Hindmarsh, "'At Any Price Give Me the Book of God!': Devotional Intent and Bible Reading for the Early Evangelicals," in Hoselton, Stievermann, Sweeney, and Haykin, *Bible in Early Transatlantic Pietism*, 226.

50. Quoted in Hindmarsh, "'At Any Price,'" 227.

51. Quoted in Hindmarsh, "'At Any Price,'" 232.

52. Quoted in Hindmarsh, "'At Any Price,'" 236.

53. Quoted in Ned Landsman, "Evangelists and Their Hearers: Popular Interpretation of Revivalist Preaching in Eighteenth-Century Scotland," *Journal of British Studies* 28, no. 2 (1989): 143.

54. John Wesley, preface to *Sermons on Several Occasions*, vol. 1, *First Series*, Christian Classics Ethereal Library (website), accessed February 14, 2024, https://ccel .org/ccel/wesley/sermons/sermons.iv.html.

55. Peter Vogt, "Moravians and the Bible in the Atlantic World: The Case of the Daily Watchwords in Bethlehem, PA, 1742–1745," in Hoselton, Stievermann, Sweeney, and Haykin, *Bible in Early Transatlantic Pietism*, 263.

56. Quoted in Vogt, "Moravians and the Bible," 271.

57. Quoted in Vogt, "Moravians and the Bible," 271.

58. Quoted in Benjamin M. Pietrenka and Marilyn J. Westerkamp, "Spirit of the Word: Scripture in the Lives of Evangelical and Moravian Women in the New World, 1730–1830," in Hoselton, Stievermann, Sweeney, and Haykin, *Bible in Early Transatlantic Pietism*, 245.

59. Quoted in Pietrenka and Westerkamp, "Spirit of the Word," 253.

60. Quoted in Pietrenka and Westerkamp, "Spirit of the Word," 254.

61. Quoted in Pietrenka and Westerkamp, "Spirit of the Word," 257.

62. Quoted in Hindmarsh, "'At Any Price,'" 225.

63. Quoted in Hindmarsh, "'At Any Price,'" 228–229.

64. Isaac Watts, "Preface to Hymns and Spiritual Songs" (London: J. Humphreys, for John Lawrence, 1707), iii.

65. "Isaac Watts," Center for Church Music website, accessed February 14, 2024, https://www.songsandhymns.org/people/detail/Isaac-Watts.

Chapter 9: The American Bible

1. Timothy Dwight, *The Conquest of Canaan: A Poem in Eleven Books* (Hartford, CT: Elisha Babcock, 1785), 22.

2. Bill Templer, "The Political Sacralization of Imperial Genocide: Contextualizing Timothy Dwight's *The Conquest of Canaan*," *Postcolonial Studies* 9, no. 4 (2006): 358–391; William C. Dowling, *Poetry and Ideology in Revolutionary Connecticut* (Athens: University of Georgia Press, 1990).

3. See Daniel L. Dreisbach, *Reading the Bible with the Founding Fathers* (New York: Oxford University Press, 2016).

4. Nathan O. Hatch, *The Democratization of American Christianity* (New Haven, CT: Yale University Press, 1989), 16, 81, 179–183; Mark A. Noll, *In the Beginning Was*

the Word: The Bible in American Public Life, 1492–1783 (New York: Oxford University Press, 2015), 235–237.

5. For an overview of the revivals, see Thomas S. Kidd, *The Great Awakening: The Roots of Evangelical Christianity in Colonial America* (New Haven, CT: Yale University Press, 2007).

6. Jonathan Edwards, *A Divine and Supernatural Light, Immediately Imparted to the Soul by the Spirit of God, Shown to Be Both a Scriptural and Rational Doctrine*, 1734, Electronic Texts in American Studies, DigitalCommons@University of Nebraska–Lincoln, https://digitalcommons.unl.edu/cgi/viewcontent.cgi?article=1056 &context=etas.

7. Harry S. Stout, *The Divine Dramatist: George Whitefield and the Rise of Modern Evangelicalism* (Grand Rapids, MI: William B. Eerdmans, 1991), 49–65.

8. Quoted in David T. Morgan Jr., "George Whitefield and the Great Awakening in the Carolinas and Georgia, 1739–1740," *Georgia Historical Quarterly* 54, no. 4 (1970): 531.

9. Quoted in Jonathan M. Threlfall, "George Whitefield's Delight in Scripture and Prayer," *Thoughts on Christian Theology and Pastoring* (blog), accessed February 14, 2024, https://jonathanthrelfall.com/2019/02/12/george-whitefields -delight-in-scripture-and-prayer/.

10. Quoted in Steven Lawson, "The Preeminence of Scripture in George Whitefield's Life," Ligonier (website), February 19, 2014, https://www.ligonier.org /learn/articles/preeminence-scripture-george-whitefields-life.

11. Quoted in Jan Stievermann, "Biblical Interpretation in Eighteenth-Century America," in *The Oxford Handbook of the Bible in America*, ed. Paul Gutjahr (New York: Oxford University Press, 2017), 102–104 (hereinafter referred to as *OHBA*).

12. Mark A. Noll, "Nineteenth-Century American Biblical Interpretation," in *OHBA*, 118–119.

13. Quoted in Todd M. Brenneman, "'Where the Scriptures Speak, We Speak': The Pennsylvania Frontier and the Origins of the Disciples of Christ," *Pennsylvania History: A Journal of Mid-Atlantic Studies* 85, no. 2 (2018): 153.

14. Alexander Campbell, *The Christian System, in Reference to the Union of Christians, and a Restoration of Primitive Christianity [. . .]* (Pittsburgh: Forrester and Campbell, 1839), https://icotb.org/resources/Campbell,Alexander-TheChristian System.pdf.

15. Paul C. Gutjahr, *An American Bible: A History of the Good Book in the United States, 1777–1880* (Stanford, CA: Stanford University Press, 1999), esp. chaps. 1 and 2.

16. David Paul Nord, *Faith in Reading: Religious Publishing and the Birth of Mass Media in America* (New York: Oxford University Press, 2004), 27–40. See also David Paul Nord, "Free Books, Free Grace, Free Riders: The Economics of Religious Publishing in Early Nineteenth-Century America," *Proceedings of the American Antiquarian Society* 106, no. 2 (1996): 241–272.

17. Michael S. Carter, "'Under the Benign Sun of Toleration': Mathew Carey, the Douai Bible, and Catholic Print Culture, 1789–1791," *Journal of the Early Republic* 27, no. 3 (2007): 437–469.

18. Quoted in Gutjahr, *American Bible*, 24.

19. Jeffrey Makala, "The Early History of Stereotyping in the United States: Mathew Carey and the Quarto Bible Marketplace," *Papers of the Bibliographical Society of America* 109, no. 4 (2015): 463–464.

20. Mark A. Noll, *America's Book: The Rise and Decline of a Bible Civilization, 1794–1911* (New York: Oxford University Press, 2022), 629.

21. See John Fea, *The Bible Cause: A History of the American Bible Society* (New York: Oxford University Press, 2016).

22. Paul C. Gutjahr, "Protestant English-Language Bible Publishing and Translation," in *OHBA*, 7–8.

23. David Daniell, *The Bible in English: Its History and Influence* (New Haven, CT: Yale University Press, 2003), 635–637.

24. See Gordon Campbell, "The Bible in America," in *Bible: The Story of the King James Bible, 1611–2011* (Oxford: Oxford University Press, 2010), 193–211.

25. Paul C. Gutjahr, "From Monarchy to Democracy: The Dethroning of the King James Bible in the United States," in *The King James Bible After 400 Years: Literary, Linguistic, and Cultural Influences*, ed. Hannibal Hamlin and Norman W. Jones (New York: Cambridge University Press, 2010), 164–187.

26. Gutjahr, *American Bible*, 70f; Frank Weitenkempf, "American Bible Illustration," *Boston Public Library Quarterly* 3 (1958): 154–157.

27. Quoted in Joseph P. Slaughter, "A 'True Commentary': The Gendered Imagery of *Harper's Illuminated and New Pictorial Bible* (1843–1846)," *Journal of the Early Republic* 41, no. 4 (2021): 595.

28. Slaughter, "A 'True Commentary,'" 593–595.

29. Monica L. Mercado, "'Have You Ever Read?': Imagining Women, Bibles, and Religious Print in Nineteenth-Century America," *U.S. Catholic Historian* 31, no. 3 (2013): 12–14.

30. See Russell W. Dalton, *Children's Bibles in America: A Reception History of the Story of Noah's Ark in US Children's Bibles* (London: Bloomsbury T&T Clark, 2015); and Ruth B. Bottigheimer, *The Bible for Children: From the Age of Gutenberg to the Present* (New Haven, CT: Yale University Press, 1996).

31. See Stephen R. Haynes, *Noah's Curse: The Biblical Justification of American Slavery* (New York: Oxford University Press, 2002).

32. Jeremy Schipper, *Denmark Vesey's Bible: The Thwarted Revolt That Put Slavery and Scripture on Trial* (Princeton, NJ: Princeton University Press, 2022), 31–34, 38–39.

33. See Paul Finkelman, *Defending Slavery: Proslavery Thought in the Old South; A Brief History with Documents* (Boston: Bedford, 2003); James Moorhead, *American Apocalypse: Yankee Protestants and the Civil War, 1860–1869* (New Haven, CT: Yale University Press, 1978).

34. Noll, *America's Book*, 226–228.

35. See David M. Goldenberg, *Black and Slave: The Origins and History of the Curse of Ham* (Berlin: Walter de Gruyter, 2017).

36. Quoted in Mark A. Noll, *God and Race in American Politics: A Short History* (Princeton, NJ: Princeton University Press, 2008), 41.

37. Noll, *America's Book*, 403–404.

38. Quoted in Abraham Smith, "The Bible in African American Culture," in *OHBA*, 197–201.

39. Quoted in J. Albert Harrill, "The Use of the New Testament in the American Slave Controversy: A Case History in the Hermeneutical Tension Between Biblical Criticism and Christian Moral Debate," *Religion and American Culture: A Journal of Interpretation* 10, no. 2 (2000): 159.

40. Quoted in Harrill, "Use of the New Testament," 159.

41. Quoted in Harrill, "Use of the New Testament," 159.

42. James W. C. Pennington, *The Fugitive Blacksmith* (London: Charles Gilpin, 1849), https://docsouth.unc.edu/neh/penning49/penning49.html.

43. Quoted in Noll, *America's Book*, 180–181.

44. Will Kynes, "Wrestle On, Jacob: Antebellum Spirituals and the Defiant Faith of the Hebrew Bible," *Journal of Biblical Literature* 140, no. 2 (2021): 291–307.

45. See "There Is a Balm in Gilead," Hymnary.org, accessed February 14, 2024, https://hymnary.org/text/sometimes_i_feel_discouraged_spiritual.

46. W. E. B. Du Bois, "Of the Sorrow Songs," chap. 14 in *The Souls of Black Folks* (Chicago: A. C. McClurg, 1903), https://etc.usf.edu/lit2go/203/the-souls-of-black -folk/4458/chapter-14-of-the-sorrow-songs/.

47. Rebecca Cox Jackson, *Gifts of Power: The Writings of Rebecca Jackson, Black Visionary, Shaker Eldress*, ed. Jean McMahon Humez (Amherst: University of Massachusetts Press, 1987).

48. Jackson, *Gifts of Power*, 108.

49. Jackson, *Gifts of Power*, 222.

50. Quoted in Andre E. Johnson, "God Is a Negro: The (Rhetorical) Black Theology of Bishop Henry McNeal Turner," *Black Theology* 13, no. 1 (2015): 36.

51. Quoted in Noll, *America's Book*, 183.

52. Frederick V. Armstrong, *The Archaeology of Harriet Tubman's Life in Freedom* (Syracuse, NY: Syracuse University Press, 2022), 85–114; Janell Hobson, *When God Lost Her Tongue: Historical Consciousness and the Black Feminist Imagination* (New York: Routledge, 2022), 93–121; Riché Richardson, *Emancipation's Daughters: Reimagining Black Femininity and the National Body* (Durham, NC: Duke University Press, 2021), 2–3, 6–7.

53. Noll, *America's Book*, 183–184.

54. Steven Greene, *The Bible, the School, and the Constitution: The Clash That Shaped Modern Church-State Doctrine* (New York: Oxford University Press, 2012), 11–44; Tracy Fessenden, "The Nineteenth-Century Bible Wars and the Separation of Church and State," *Church History* 74, no. 4 (2005), 784–811; James T. Sears and James C. Carper, *Curriculum, Religion, and Public Education: Conversations for an Enlarging Public Square* (New York: Teachers College Press, 1998), 25–35.

55. Quoted in Fessenden, "Nineteenth-Century Bible Wars," 788.

56. Fessenden, "Nineteenth-Century Bible Wars," 785–786.

57. Noll, *America's Book*, 316–317.

58. "Philadelphia Bible Riots of 1844," Building Knowledge and Breaking Barriers (website), Presbyterian Historical Society and Community College of Philadelphia, accessed December 13, 2023, https://bkbbphilly.org/source-set/philadelphia-bible -riots-1844.

59. "Philadelphia Bible Riots of 1844."

60. Gerald P. Fogarty, "The Quest for a Catholic Vernacular Bible in America," in *The Bible in America: Essays in Cultural History*, ed. Nathan O. Hatch and Mark A. Noll (New York: Oxford University Press, 1982), 163–180.

61. Noll, *America's Book*, 346–347.

62. Jon Gjerde, *Catholicism and the Shaping of Nineteenth-Century America* (New York: Cambridge University Press, 2012), 61–95.

63. James Gibbons, *The Faith of Our Fathers: Being a Plain Exposition and Vindication of the Church Founded by Our Lord Jesus Christ*, 63rd ed. (London: R. Washbourne, 1905), 21–22.

64. Gibbons, *Faith of Our Fathers*, 18–19.

65. Edward J. Blum, "Uncle Tom's Bibles: Bibles as Visual and Material Objects from Antebellum Abolitionism to Jim Crow Cinema," *Journal of Southern Religion* 21 (2019), jsreligion.org/vol21/blum.

66. See Claudia Setzer and David A. Shefferman, eds., *The Bible and American Culture: A Sourcebook* (London: Routledge, 2011), 264–265.

67. Herman Melville, *Moby-Dick* (London: Richard Bently, 1851), chap. 9, https: //etc.usf.edu/lit2go/42/moby-dick/634/chapter-9-the-sermon/.

68. Melville, *Moby-Dick*, chap. 9.

69. Melville, *Moby-Dick*, chap. 9.

70. Melville to Hawthorne, November 17, 1852, The Life and Works of Herman Melville (website), http://www.melville.org/letter7.htm.

71. Zachary Hutchins, "*Moby-Dick* as Third Testament: A Novel 'Not Come to Destroy but to Fulfill' the Bible," *Leviathan* 13, no. 2 (2011): 18–37.

72. Noll, *America's Book*, 606–607.

73. Noll, *America's Book*, 606–607.

74. Noll, *America's Book*, 260–262.

75. Mark A. Noll, *The Civil War as a Theological Crisis* (Chapel Hill: University of North Carolina Press, 2005), 34–50.

76. Harry S. Stout, *Upon the Altar of the Nation: A Moral History of the American Civil War* (New York: Viking, 2006), 277–278.

77. Abraham Lincoln, second inaugural address, March 4, 1865, https://www .nps.gov/linc/learn/historyculture/lincoln-second-inaugural.htm.

78. Drew Gilpin Faust, *The Republic of Suffering: Death and the American Civil War* (New York: Alfred A. Knopf, 2008), 164.

79. Quoted in Faust, *Republic of Suffering*, 173.

80. Gary Dorrien, *The Making of American Liberal Theology: Imagining Progressive Religion, 1805–1900* (Louisville, KY: Westminster John Knox, 2001).

81. For what follows I rely on Michael L. Kamen, "The Science of the Bible in Nineteenth-Century America: From 'Common Sense' to Controversy, 1820–1890," PhD diss. (University of Notre Dame, 2004).

82. Quoted in Kamen, "Science of the Bible," 3.

83. David P. Smith, *B. B. Warfield's Scientifically Constructive Theological Scholarship*, ed. June Corduan (Eugene, OR: Pickwick, 2011), 99–109; B. B. Warfield, *Evolution, Scripture, and Science: Selected Writings*, ed. Mark A. Noll and David N. Livingstone (Grand Rapids, MI: Baker, 2000), 51–58.

84. Benjamin B. Warfield, "Charles Darwin's Religious Life: A Sketch in Spiritual Biography," *Presbyterian Review* 9, no. 36 (1888): 575.

85. Warfield, "Charles Darwin's Religious Life," 576.

86. Quoted in Kamen, "Science of the Bible," 339.

87. Quoted in Kamen, "Science of the Bible," 339.

88. See Daniel J. Treier and Craig Hefner, "Twentieth- and Twenty-First-Century American Biblical Interpretations," in *OHBA*, 131–132.

89. Quoted in George M. Marsden, *Fundamentalism and American Culture*, 3rd ed. (New York: Oxford University Press, 2022), 199.

90. Quoted in Marsden, *Fundamentalism and American Culture*, 199.

91. Quoted in Marsden, *Fundamentalism and American Culture*, 204.

92. See Edward J. Larson, *Summer for the Gods: The Scopes Trial and America's Continuing Debate over Science and Religion* (New York: Basic, 1997).

93. Quoted in Marsden, *Fundamentalism and American Culture*, 212–213.

94. Noll, *America's Book*, 603–604.

Chapter 10: Missions Worldwide

1. Ayse Tekdal Fildis, "The American Board's Vision of Protestant Anatolia and Fostering Armenian Nationalism 1810–90," *Middle Eastern Studies* 48, no. 5 (2012): 735.

2. Quoted in Fildis, "American Board's Vision," 736.

3. See Michael Gladwin, "Mission and Colonialism," in *The Oxford Handbook of Nineteenth-Century Christian Thought*, ed. Joel D. S. Rasmussen, Judith Wolfe, and Johannes Zachhuber (Oxford, UK: Oxford University Press, 2017), 282–307; and Julius Bautista, "Christianity in Southeast Asia: Colonialism, Nationalism, and the Caveats to Conversion," in *The Oxford Handbook of Christianity in Asia*, ed. Felix Wilfred (New York: Oxford University Press, 2014), 215–230.

4. See Dana L. Robert, introduction to *Converting Colonialism: Visions and Realities in Mission History, 1706–1914*, ed. Dana L. Robert (Grand Rapids, MI: William B. Eerdmans, 2008), 3–5.

5. See Lamin Sanneh, "World Christianity and the New Historiography: History and Global Interconnections," in *Enlarging the Story: Perspectives on Writing World Christian History*, ed. Wilbert R. Shenk (Maryknoll, NY: Orbis, 2002), 94–114.

6. See Eleanor Jackson, "From Krishna Pal to Lal Behari Dey: Indian Builders of the Church in Bengal, 1800–1894," in Robert, *Converting Colonialism*, 166–206; and Dana L. Robert, introduction to *African Christian Outreach*, vol. 2, *The Mission*

Churches, ed. Dana L. Robert (Pretoria: South African Missiological Society, 2003), 1–18. See also the essays in David Lindenfeld and Miles Richardson, eds., *Beyond Conversion and Syncretism: Indigenous Encounters with Missionary Christianity, 1800–2000* (New York: Berghahn, 2012).

7. Quoted in R. S. Sugirtharajah, *The Bible and the Third World: Precolonial, Colonial, and Postcolonial Encounters* (Cambridge, UK: Cambridge University Press, 2001), 50.

8. Sugirtharajah, *Bible and the Third World*, 52–53.

9. Quoted in George Kam Wah Mak, "Laissez-Faire or Active Intervention? The Nature of the British and Foreign Bible Society's Patronage of the Translation of the Chinese Union Versions," *Journal of the Royal Asiatic Society* 20, no. 2 (2010): 169.

10. Quoted in Sugirtharajah, *Bible in the Third World*, 55.

11. Quoted in Sugirtharajah, *Bible and the Third World*, 62.

12. Lourens de Vries, "The Book of True Civilization: The Origins of the Bible Society Movement in the Age of Enlightenment," *Bible Translator* 67, no. 3 (2016): 332–333.

13. Quoted in de Vries, "Book of True Civilization," 334.

14. Quoted in de Vries, "Book of True Civilization," 337.

15. Quoted in de Vries, "Book of True Civilization," 348.

16. Kehinde Olabimtan, "The Basel Mission," in *The Encyclopedia of Christian Civilization*, ed. George Thomas Kurian, vol. 1, *A–D* (Malden, MA: Wiley-Blackwell, 2011), 214.

17. Quoted in de Vries, "Book of True Civilization," 337. See also Joris van Eijnatten, *Liberty and Concord in the United Provinces: Religious Toleration and the Public in the Eighteenth-Century Netherlands* (Leiden, the Netherlands: Brill, 2003), 479.

18. Quoted in Karl Rennstich, "The Understanding of Mission, Civilization, and Colonialism in the Basel Mission," *South East Asia Journal of Theology* 23 (1982): 11. See also Tiasa Basu Roy, "Intertwining Christian Mission, Theology, and History: A Case Study of the Basel Mission Among the *Thiyyas* and *Badagas* of Kerala, 1870–1913," *Religions* 12, no. 2 (2021), https://doi.org/10.3390/rel12020121; and Catherine Koonar, "'Christianity, Commerce and Civilization': Child Labor and the Basel Mission in Colonial Ghana, 1855–1914," *International Labor and Working Class History* 86 (2014): 72–88.

19. Quoted in Rennstich, "Understanding of Mission," 12.

20. Quoted in Rennstich, "Understanding of Mission," 11–12.

21. See Birgit Meyer, "'If You Are a Devil, You Are a Witch and, If You Are a Witch, You Are a Devil': The Integration of 'Pagan' Ideas into the Conceptual Universe of Ewe Christians in Southeastern Ghana," *Journal of Religion in Africa* 22, no. 2 (1992): 98–132.

22. Quoted in Rennstich, "Understanding of Mission," 13.

23. Quoted in Rennstich, "Understanding of Mission," 15.

24. Quoted in Nathan Nunn, "Religious Conversion in Colonial Africa," *American Economic Review* 100, no. 2 (2010): 150–151.

25. Johannes Fabian, *Language and Colonial Power: The Appropriation of Swahili in the Former Belgian Congo, 1880–1938* (Cambridge, UK: Cambridge University, 1986).

26. Birgit Meyer, "Christianity and the Ewe Nation: German Pietist Missionaries, Ewe Converts and the Politics of Culture," *Journal of Religion in Africa* 32, no. 2 (2002): 176. See also Birgit Meyer, *Translating the Devil: Religion and Modernity Among the Ewe in Ghana* (Edinburgh: Edinburgh University Press, 1999); and Benjamin Nicholas Lawrance, "Most Obedient Servants: The Politics of Language in German Colonial Togo," *Cahiers d'Etudes Africaines* 40, no. 159 (2000): 489–524. For wider background, see Werner Ustorf, *Die Missionsmethode Franz Michael Zahns und der Aufbau kirchlicher Strukturen in Westafrika: Eine missionsgeschichtliche Untersuchung* (Erlangen, Germany: Verlag der Ev.-Luth. Mission, 1989); and Klaus J. Bade, *Imperialismus und Kolonialmission: Kaiserliches Deutschland und koloniales Imperium* (Wiesbaden, Germany: Steiner, 1971).

27. Quoted in Meyer, "Christianity and the Ewe Nation," 176.

28. Meyer, "Christianity and the Ewe Nation," 179.

29. Quoted in Helen Bethea Gardner, "New Heaven and New Earth: Translation and Conversion on Aneityum," *Journal of Pacific History* 41, no. 3 (2006): 300.

30. Quoted in Gardner, "New Heaven and New Earth," 297.

31. Julius Gathogo, "The Birth of Protestant Education in East Africa: Sampling Johannes Ludwig Krapf (1810–1881)," *Studia Historiae Ecclesiasticae* 35 (2009), https://core.ac.uk/download/pdf/43167533.pdf.

32. Quoted in Gathogo, "Birth of Protestant Education," 174.

33. Quoted in Johnson Kiriaku Kinyua, "A Postcolonial Analysis of Bible Translation and Its Effectiveness in Shaping and Enhancing the Discourse of Colonialism and the Discourse of Resistance: The Gĩkũyũ New Testament—A Case Study," *Black Theology* 11, no. 1 (2013): 70.

34. Kiriaku Kinyua, "Postcolonial Analysis," 75–76.

35. Quoted in Kiriaku Kinyua, "Postcolonial Analysis," 79–80.

36. Kiriaku Kinyua, "Postcolonial Analysis," 82.

37. See Ben Fulford, "An Igbo Esperanto: A History of the Union Ibo Bible, 1900–1950," *Journal of Religion in Africa* 32, no. 4 (2002): 457–501.

38. Quoted in Fulford, "Igbo Esperanto," 486.

39. Quoted in Fulford, "Igbo Esperanto," 485.

40. Lamin Sanneh, "The CMS and the African Transformation: Samuel Ajayi Crowther and the Opening of Nigeria," in *The Church Mission Society and World Christianity, 1799–1999*, ed. Kevin Ward and Brian Stanley (Richmond, UK: Curzon, 2000), 184f.

41. See Hephzibah Israel, *Religious Transactions in Colonial Southern India: Language, Translation, and the Making of Protestant Identity* (London: Palgrave Macmillan, 2011).

42. Israel, *Religious Transactions*, 36.

43. Israel, *Religious Transactions*, 41.

44. Quoted in Israel, *Religious Transactions*, 54.

45. Quoted in Israel, *Religious Transactions*, 63.

46. John Bray, "Heinrich August Jaeschke: Pioneer Tibetan Scholar," *Tibet Journal* 8, no. 1 (1983): 50–55.

47. John Bray, "Language, Tradition and the Tibetan Bible," *Tibet Journal* 16, no. 4 (1991): 31.

48. Quoted in Bray, "Language, Tradition," 32.

49. Quoted in Bray, "Language, Tradition," 35.

50. Quoted in C. R. Bawden, "The English Missionaries in Siberia and Their Translation of the Bible into Mongolian," *Mongolian Studies* 6 (1980): 11.

51. Judith Bovensiepen, "*Lulik*: Taboo, Animism, or Transgressive Sacred? An Exploration of Identity, Morality, and Power in Timor-Leste," *Oceania* 84, no. 2 (2014): 121–137.

52. Manuel F. Ferreira, *Resumo da Historia Sagrada em Português e em Tètum para Uso das Crianças de Timor* (Lisbon: Imprensa Nacional, 1908), 18. Quoted in Kisho Tsuchiya, "Converting Tetun: Colonial Missionaries' Conceptual Mapping in the Timorese Cosmology and Some Local Responses, 1874–1937," *Indonesia* 107 (2019): 87. The following discussion is guided by this article.

53. Quoted in Alle Hoekema, *Dutch Mennonite Mission in Indonesia: Historical Essays*, Occasional Papers 22 (Elkhart, IN: Institute of Mennonite Studies, 2001), 237.

54. Quoted in A. Hoekema, "H. C. Klinkert: Missionary, Journalist, Bible Translator, Linguist," *Mennonite Quarterly Review* 67, no. 2 (1993): 237.

55. Eric Lindland, *Crossroads of Culture: Christianity, Ancestral Spiritualism, and the Search for Wellness in Northern Malawi* (Malawi: Mzuni, 2020), 241–242.

56. Quoted in Markku Hokkanen, "Scottish Missionaries and African Healers: Perceptions and Relations in the Livingstonia Mission, 1875–1930," *Journal of Religion in Africa* 34, no. 3 (2004): 229.

57. Min Suc Kee, "Translation of the Bible in Hangul," in *The Oxford Handbook of the Bible in Korea*, ed. Won W. Lee (Oxford, UK: Oxford University Press, 2022), 23–73.

58. Rose Greenfield, "Women's Work in the Indian Mission Field," in *Report of the Second Decennial Missionary Conference Held in Calcutta, 1882–83* (Calcutta: J. W. Thomas, Baptist Mission Press, 1883), 210.

59. Eliza F. Kent, *Converting Women: Gender and Protestant Christianity in Colonial South India* (New York: Oxford University Press, 2004), 149.

60. Quoted in Laura R. Prieto, "Bibles, Baseball and Butterfly Sleeves: Filipina Women and American Protestant Missions, 1900–1930," in *Divine Domesticities: Christian Paradoxes in Asia and the Pacific*, ed. Hyaeweol Choi and Margaret Jolly (Canberra: Australian National University Press, 2014), 376.

61. Quoted in Prieto, "Bibles, Baseball and Butterfly Sleeves," 376.

62. See Deanna Ferree Womack, *Protestants, Gender and the Arab Renaissance in Late Ottoman Syria* (Edinburgh: Edinburgh University Press, 2019), 274–327.

63. Quoted in Womack, *Protestants, Gender*, 274.

64. Quoted in Womack, *Protestants, Gender*, 292.

Chapter 11: Shangdi and Shen in China

1. The most recent scholarship on the Bible in China is found in K. K. Yeo, ed., *The Oxford Handbook of the Bible in China* (New York: Oxford University Press, 2021) (hereinafter referred to as *OHBC*).

2. Joseph Tse-Hei Lee, *The Bible and the Gun: Christianity in South China, 1860–1900* (New York: Routledge, 2003), 158–168.

3. Wang Shanshan, "Stones Indicate Earlier Christian Link?," *China Daily*, December 22, 2005, https://www.chinadaily.com.cn/english/doc/2005-12/22/content_505448.htm.

4. Roman Malek and Peter Hofrichter, eds., *Jingjiao: The Church of the East in China and Central Asia* (Sankt Augustin, Germany: Institut Monumenta Serica, 2006).

5. Daniel Kam-to Choi, "A History of the Chinese Bible," in *OHBC*, 23.

6. Song Gang, "The Basset-Su Chinese New Testament," in *OHBC*, 79.

7. Chan Kei Thong with Charlene L. Fu, *Finding God in Ancient China: How the Ancient Chinese Worshiped the God of the Bible* (Grand Rapids, MI: Zondervan, 2009), 189–191.

8. Quoted in Thong and Fu, *Finding God*, 205.

9. Nicolas Standaert, "The Bible in Early Seventeenth-Century China," in *Bible in Modern China: The Literary and Intellectual Impact*, ed. Irene Eber, Sze-kar Wan, and Knut Walf (Sankt Augustin, Germany: Institut Monumenta Serica, 1999), 31–54.

10. Choi, "History of the Chinese Bible," 24.

11. Quoted in Gang, "Basset-Su Chinese New Testament, " 80.

12. Zheng Haijuan, "De Poirot's Chinese Bible and Its Influence," in *OHBC*, 99.

13. Quoted in Michael G. Brown, "Who Was Robert Morrison?," Ligonier (website), May 29, 2023, https://www.ligonier.org/learn/articles/missionary-robert-morrison.

14. Quoted in Peter Burdge, "Translations of Christian Texts in Nineteenth-Century China," Linda Lear Center Digital Collections and Exhibitions (website), accessed February 14, 2024, https://lc-digital.conncoll.edu/exhibits/show/gold-journal/essays/translation.

15. Choi, "History of the Chinese Bible," 30–31.

16. Patrick Hanan, "The Bible as Chinese Literature: Medhurst, Wang Tao, and the Delegates' Version," *Harvard Journal of Asiatic Studies* 63, no. 1 (2003): 213–214.

17. George Kam Wah Mak, *The Colportage of the Protestant Bible in Late Qing China: The Example of the British and Foreign Bible Society* (Berlin: De Gruyter, 2015).

18. See the essays in Suzanne Wilson Barnett and John King Fairbank, eds., *Christianity in China: Early Protestant Missionary Writings* (Cambridge, MA: Harvard University Press, 1985).

19. Li Zhengrong, "The Eastern Orthodox Bible in China," in *OHBC*, 63–78.

20. An excellent history of the revolt is Carl S. Kilcourse, *Taiping Theology: The Localization of Christianity in China, 1843–64* (New York: Palgrave Macmillan, 2016).

21. Lian Xi, *Redeemed by Fire: The Rise of Popular Christianity in Modern China* (New Haven, CT: Yale University Press, 2010), 23.

22. Quoted in Lian, *Redeemed by Fire*, 25.

23. Wang Zi, "Localizing of Bible Printing in China," in *OHBC*, 367.

24. John T. P. Lai, "The Bible and Missionary Novels in Chinese," in *OHBC*, 283.

25. Quoted in Lai, "Bible and Missionary Novels," 296.

26. Quoted in Lai, "Bible and Missionary Novels," 296.

27. Quoted in Lai, "Bible and Missionary Novels," 286.

28. Lai, "Bible and Missionary Novels," 289.

29. Zi, "Localizing of Bible Printing," 365.

30. Paulos Huang and K. K. Yeo, "Confucian Classics and the Bible," in *OHBC*, 255.

31. Archie C. C. Lee, "The Bible and Daoist Writings," in *OHBC*, 223.

32. N. J. Girardot, *Myth and Meaning in Early Taoism: The Theme of Chaos (Hun-Tun)* (Berkeley: University of California Press, 1983), 11.

33. Quoted in Lee, "Bible and Daoist Writings," 219–220.

34. See Ann Cui'an Peng, *The Translation of the Bible into Chinese: The Origin and Unique Authority of the Union Version* (Eugene, OR: Pickwick, 2021); Jost Oliver Zetzsche, *The Bible in China: The History of the Union Version; or, The Culmination of Protestant Missionary Bible Translation in China* (Sankt Augustin, Germany: Steyler, 1999); and Chao-Chun Liu, "Discipled by the West? The Influence of the Theology of Protestant Missionaries in China on Chinese Christianity Through the Translation of the Chinese Union Version of the Bible," *Religions* 12, no. 4 (2021): 1–18.

35. Janice Wickeri, "The Union Version of the Bible and the New Literature in China," *The Translator: Studies in Intercultural Communication* 1, no. 2 (1995): 129–152.

36. See Kevin Xiyi Yao, "The Hunan Bible Institute (Biola-in-China): A Stronghold of Fundamentalist Bible Training in China, 1916–1952," *Studies in World Christianity* 27, no. 2 (2021): 124–144.

37. Melissa Wei-tsing Inouye, *China and the True Jesus: Charisma and Organization in a Chinese Christian Church* (New York: Oxford University Press, 2018); Pan Zhao, "The True Jesus Church and the Bible in Republican China," *Religions* 11, no. 2 (2020): 1–13, https://www.mdpi.com/2077-1444/11/2/89.

38. Quoted in Lian, *Redeemed by Fire*, 47.

39. Quoted in Lian, *Redeemed by Fire*, 63.

40. Zhao, "True Jesus Church."

41. Quoted in Zhao, "True Jesus Church."

42. George Kam Wah Mak, "The Belated Formation of the China Bible House (1937): Nationalism and the Indigenization of Protestantism in Republican China," *Bulletin of the School of Oriental and African Studies* 78, no. 3 (2015): 515–535.

43. Chu Sin-Jan, *Wu Leichuan: A Confucian-Christian in Republican China* (New York: Peter Lang, 1995), 46–59.

44. Sin-Jan, *A Confucian-Christian*, 53–62.

45. See Zhixi Wang, "Repressed Religious Modernity: Zhu Weizhi and the Rise of the Bible as Literature in Modern China," *Literature and Theology* 34, no. 4 (2020): 430–449.

46. Quoted in Wang, "Repressed Religious Modernity," 444.

47. Stephen Williams, "The Contribution of Ni Tuosheng (Watchman Nee)," in *Shaping Christianity in Greater China: Indigenous Christians in Focus*, ed. Paul Woods (Oxford: Regnum Books International, 2017), 204–215.

48. "Keh Nga Pit," in *Chinese SDA History*, ed. Samuel Young (Hong Kong: Chinese Union Mission of Seventh-day Adventists, 2002), 493–494.

49. Lian, *Redeemed by Fire*, 90.

50. Quoted in Paul P. Mariani, "China's 'Christian General' Feng Yuxiang, the Evangelist Jonathan Goforth and the Changde Revival of 1919," *Studies in World Christianity* 20, no. 3 (2014): 251.

51. Quoted in Benoît Vermander, "The Socio-political Impact of the Bible in China," in *OHBC*, 611.

52. Quoted in Lian, *Redeemed by Fire*, 92.

53. Quoted in Lian, *Redeemed by Fire*, 94.

54. See Daniel K. T. Choi and George K. W. Mak, "Catholic Bible Translation in Twentieth-Century China: An Overview," in *Catholicism in China, 1900–Present: The Development of the Chinese Church*, ed. Cindy Yik-yi Chu (New York: Palgrave Macmillan, 2014).

55. Tiangang Li and Ruth Hayhoe, "Christianity and Cultural Conflict in the Life of Ma Xiangbo," in *Ma Xiangbo and the Mind of Modern China*, ed. Ruth Hayhoe and Yongling Lu (New York: Routledge, 1996), 89–142.

56. Stacey Bieler, "Wu Jingxiong," Biographical Dictionary of Chinese Christianity (website), accessed December 14, 2023, http://bdcconline.net/en/stories/wu-jingxiong.

57. Choi and Mak, "Catholic Bible Translation," 105–123.

58. See the essays in Eber, Wan, and Walf, *Bible in Modern China*.

59. Eber, Wan, and Walf, *Bible in Modern China*, 905.

60. Quoted in Tim Ellsworth, "China House Church Leader Weighed Scripture and Culture," *Baptist Press*, August 28, 2008, https://www.baptistpress.com/resource-library/news/china-house-church-leader-weighed-scripture-culture/.

61. Quoted in Eber, Wan, and Walf, *Bible in Modern China*, 906.

62. Quoted in Kwok Pui-lan, "Christianity and Women in Contemporary China," *Journal of World Christianity* 3, no. 1 (2010): 11.

63. See Alle G. Hoekema, "Fan Pu (China): The Bible Interpreted Through the Art of Paper Cutting," *Exchange* 43, no. 4 (2014): 379–389.

64. Quoted in Hoekema, "Fan Pu," 387.

65. Alexander Chow, "You May Have Heard China Has 'Banned' the Bible App. But the Truth Is More Complicated," *Premier Christianity*, November 19, 2021, https://www.premierchristianity.com/opinion/you-may-have-heard-china-has-banned-the-bible-app-but-the-truth-is-more-complicated/5722.article.

Chapter 12: African Voices

1. Quoted in Jeremiah von Kuhn, "Can We Trust the 'Colonialist Bible'?," The Gospel Coalition Africa Edition (website), January 21, 2020, https://africa.thegospelcoalition.org/article/colonialist-bible/.

2. David Killingray, "Passing on the Gospel: Indigenous Mission in Africa," *Transformation* 28, no. 2 (2011): 93–102.

3. Killingray, "Passing on the Gospel," 95.

4. Quoted in Philip Jenkins, *The New Faces of Christianity: Believing the Bible in the Global South* (New York: Oxford University Press, 2006), 23.

5. See Aurélien Mokoko Gampiot, *Kimbanguism: An African Understanding of the Bible*, trans. Cécile Coquet-Mokoko (University Park: Pennsylvania State University Press, 2017): 1–2.

6. Quoted in Gerald West, "Reception of the Bible: The Bible in Africa," in *The New Cambridge History of the Bible*, vol. 4, *From 1750 to the Present*, ed. John Riches (Cambridge, UK: Cambridge University Press, 2015), 377.

7. Quoted in Jenkins, *New Faces of Christianity*, 64.

8. Gerald O. West, *The Stolen Bible: From Tool of Imperialism to African Icon* (Leiden, the Netherlands: Brill, 2016), 1.

9. Jenkins, *New Faces of Christianity*, 19–20.

10. Quoted in West, *Stolen Bible*, 108.

11. See David M. Goldenberg, *The Curse of Ham: Race and Slavery in Early Judaism, Christianity, and Islam* (Princeton, NJ: Princeton University Press, 2003).

12. Quoted in Mokoko Gampiot, *Kimbanguism*, 38.

13. Quoted in Mokoko Gampiot, *Kimbanguism*, 40.

14. Aloo Osotsi Mojola, *God Speaks My Language: A History of Bible Translation in East Africa* (Carlisle, Cumbria, UK: HippoBooks, 2020), 149.

15. Quoted in "Samuel Ajayi Crowther: A Translation Trailblazer," Wycliffe Bible Translators (website), accessed February 15, 2024, https://wycliffe.org.uk/story/samuel-crowther.

16. Brian Stanley, *Christianity in the Twentieth Century: A World History* (Princeton, NJ: Princeton University Press, 2018), 60.

17. Aloo Osotsi Mojola, "100 Years of the Luganda Bible (1896–1996): A General Survey," in *The Bible in Africa: Transactions, Trajectories, and Trends*, ed. Gerald O. West and Musa W. Dube (Leiden, the Netherlands: Brill, 2001), 525.

18. P. J. L. Frankl, "The Word for 'God' in Swahili," *Journal of Religion in Africa* 20, no. 3 (1990): 269–275.

19. Mojola, *God Speaks My Language*, 159–160.

20. Aloo Osotsi Mojola, "A 'Female' God in East Africa—or the Problem of Translating God's Name Among the Iraqw of Mbulu, Tanzania," *Bible Translator* 46, no. 2 (1995): 229.

21. Quoted in G. A. Mikre-Sellassie, "Missionary Translations of the Bible into Zulu," in *Bible Translation and African Languages*, ed. Gosnell L. O. R. Yorke and Peter M. Renju (Nairobi, Kenya: Acton, 2004), 45.

22. Quoted in Mikre-Sellassie, "Missionary Translations," 47.

23. Quoted in Mikre-Sellassie, "Missionary Translations," 47.

24. Quoted in Mikre-Sellassie, "Missionary Translations," 49.

25. An excellent overview is provided by David W. Shenk, *The Holy Book of God: An Introduction* (Achimota, Ghana: Africa Christian Press, 1981).

26. Quoted in West, *Stolen Bible*, 243.

27. Quoted in Mokoko Gampiot, *Kimbanguism*, 55.

28. Mokoko Gampiot, *Kimbanguism*, 56–57.

29. Quoted in Mokoko Gampiot, *Kimbanguism*, 66.

30. Quoted in Mokoko Gampiot, *Kimbanguism*, 84.

31. Quoted in Mokoko Gampiot, *Kimbanguism*, 100.

32. Quoted in Mokoko Gampiot, *Kimbanguism*, 67.

33. Quoted in Mokoko Gampiot, *Kimbanguism*, 67.

34. Humphrey M. Waweru, *The Bible and African Culture: Mapping Transactional Inroads* (Eldoret, Kenya: Zapf Chancery, 2011), 54–55.

35. Waweru, *Bible and African Culture*, 55.

36. Jenkins, *New Faces of Christianity*, 133. See also George Shepperson and Thomas Price, *Independent African: John Chilembwe and the Origins, Setting and Significance of the Nyasaland Native Rising of 1915* (Edinburgh: Edinburgh University Press, 1987).

37. Quoted in Jenkins, *New Faces of Christianity*, 135.

38. Quoted in Jenkins, *New Faces of Christianity*, 147.

39. Thabo Mbeki, Nelson Mandela Annual Lecture, University of Witwatersrand, Johannesburg, July 29, 2006, https://www.sahistory.org.za/archive/nelson-mandela -memorial-lecture-president-thabo-mbeki-university-witwatersrand-29-july-2006.

40. Mbeki, Nelson Mandela Annual Lecture.

41. West, *Stolen Bible*, 466.

42. Canaan S. Banana, "The Case for a New Bible," in *Rewriting the Bible: The Real Issues*, ed. Isabel Mukonyora, James L. Cox, and Frans J. Verstraele (Gweru: Mambo Press, 1993), 29.

43. Banana, "Case for a New Bible," 18.

44. Quoted in Masiiwa Ragies Gunda, *On the Public Role of the Bible in Zimbabwe: Unpacking Banana's "Re-Writing" Call for Socially and Contextually Relevant Biblical Studies* (Bamburg, Germany: University of Bamburg Press, 2015), 41.

45. S. A. Reed, "Critique of Canaan Banana's Call to Rewrite the Bible," *Religion and Theology* 3 (1996): 285–288.

46. Ragies Gunda, *On the Public Role*, 66.

47. Quoted in Ragies Gunda, *On the Public Role*, 73.

48. David T. Ngong, "Reading the Bible in Africa: A Critique of Enchanted Bible Reading," *Exchange* 43, no. 2 (2014): 175–176.

49. Justin S. Upkong, "Developments in Biblical Interpretation in Africa: Historical and Hermeneutical Directions," in West and Dube, *Bible in Africa*, 25.

50. West, "Reception of the Bible," 367.

51. Quoted in Jenkins, *New Faces of Christianity*, 36.

52. Quoted in West, "Reception of the Bible," 366.

53. West, *Stolen Bible*, 543.

54. Quoted in Don Silas, "How TB Joshua Healed Me of Skin Disease—Nigerian Singer, Victor AD," *Daily Post* (Nigeria), July 11, 2021, https://dailypost.ng/2021/07/11/how-tb-joshua-healed-me-of-skin-disease-nigerian-singer-victor-ad/.

55. "The Men Who Claim to Be Africa's 'Miracle Workers,'" BBC News, November 27, 2016, https://www.bbc.com/news/world-africa-38063882.

56. Nobantu Shabangu, "YouTube Shuts Down Homophobic Nigerian Megachurch Channel," OkayAfrica.com, April 21, 2021, https://www.okayafrica.com/nigera-tb-joshua-homophobic-church-shut-down-by-youtube/.

57. Quoted in Jenkins, *New Faces of Christianity*, 103.

58. Jenkins, *New Faces of Christianity*, 106.

59. Quoted in Jenkins, *New Faces of Christianity*, 106.

60. Quoted in Jenkins, *New Faces of Christianity*, 106.

61. Upkong, "Developments in Biblical Interpretation," 18.

62. Quoted in Jenkins, *New Faces of Christianity*, 55.

63. Catherine Gaynor, "The Bible in Africa," *Furrow* 20, no. 3 (1969): 8.

64. Waweru, *Bible and African Culture*, 28–29.

65. West, *Stolen Bible*, 369.

66. Joel Forster, "The Presence of African Missionaries and Churches Recognises the Fact That Europe Is a Mission Field," Evangelical Focus (website), June 9, 2022, https//evangelicalfocus.com/europe/17207/the-presence-of-african-missionaries-and-churches-recognises-the-fact-that-europe-is-a-mission-field.

67. Forster, "Presence of African Missionaries."

Chapter 13: Global Pentecostalism

1. See John Maiden, *Age of the Spirit: Charismatic Renewal, the Anglo-World, and Global Christianity, 1945–1980* (New York: Oxford University Press, 2023); Allan Heaton Anderson, *To the Ends of the Earth: Pentecostalism and the Transformation of World Christianity* (New York: Oxford University Press, 2013); Christopher A. Stephenson, *Types of Pentecostal Theology: Method, System, Spirit* (New York: Oxford University Press, 2013); Keith Warrington, *Pentecostal Theology: A Theology of Encounter* (New York: T&T Clark, 2008); and Guy P. Duffield and Nathaniel M. Van Cleave, *Foundations of Pentecostal Theology* (Los Angeles, CA: L.I.F.E. Bible College, 1983).

2. Excellent introductions to Pentecostal Bible reading and interpretation are found in the following: Craig S. Keener and L. William Oliverio Jr., eds., *The Spirit Throughout the Canon: Pentecostal Pneumatology* (Leiden, the Netherlands: Brill, 2022); William W. Menzies and Stanley M. Horton, *Bible Doctrines: A Pentecostal Perspective* (Springfield, MO: Logion, 1993); Kenneth J. Archer, *A Pentecostal Hermeneutic for the Twenty-First Century: Spirit, Scripture and Community* (New York: T&T Clark International, 2004)

3. See Charles H. Barfoot and Gerald T. Sheppard, "Prophetic vs. Priestly Religion: The Changing Role of Women Clergy in Classical Pentecostal Churches,"

Review of Religious Research 22, no. 1 (1980): 2–17; Susan C. Hyatt, *In the Spirit We're Equal: The Spirit, the Bible, and Women; A Revival Perspective* (Dallas, TX: Revival & Renewal Resources by Hyatt Press, 1998); and Julia Kuhlin, "'I Do Not Think I Could Be a Christian on My Own': Lived Religion Among Swedish Pentecostal Women," *Pneuma: The Journal of the Society for Pentecostal Studies* 39, no. 4 (2017): 482–503.

4. Marius Nel, "Pentecostalism and the Early Church: On Living Distinctively from the World," *Journal of Theology for Southern Africa* 153 (2015): 141–159; Douglas B. McGaw, "Meaning and Belonging in a Charismatic Congregation: An Investigation into Sources of Neo-Pentecostal Success," *Review of Religious Research* 21, no. 3 (1980): 284–301.

5. Marcelo Vargas A., *Faith That Indigenizes: Neo-Pentecostal Aimara Identity* (Carlisle, Cumbria, UK: Langham Global Library, 2022), 24–39; Jan-Åke Alvarsson, "The Bible, Pentecostalism, and 'Magic'," *Journal of the European Pentecostal Theological Association* 27, no. 2 (2007): 183–196.

6. Allan Anderson, "The Origins of Pentecostalism and Its Global Spread in the Early Twentieth Century," *Transformation* 22, no. 3 (2005): 175–185.

7. Fenggang Yang, Joy K. C. Tong, and Allan H. Anderson, eds., *Global Chinese Pentecostal and Charismatic Christianity* (Leiden, the Netherlands: Brill, 2017).

8. Paul J. Palma, *Grassroots Pentecostalism in Brazil and the United States: Migrations, Missions, and Mobility* (London: Palgrave Macmillan, 2022), 127–143.

9. Allan Anderson, *An Introduction to Pentecostalism: Global Charismatic Christianity* (Cambridge, UK: Cambridge University Press, 2004), 39–40. See also David Bundy, Geordan Hammond, and David Sang-Ehil Han, eds., *Holiness and Pentecostal Movements: Intertwined Pasts, Presents, and Futures* (University Park: Pennsylvania State University Press, 2022).

10. Richard Marin, "La Bible au Congrès: Pentecôtisme et politique au Brésil (1986–2016)," *Caravelle* 108 (2017): 65–82; Scott M. Thomas, "A Globalized God: Religion's Growing Influence in International Politics," *Foreign Affairs* 89, no. 6 (2010): 93–101; Abimbola A. Adelakun, *Performing Power in Nigeria: Identity, Politics, and Pentecostalism* (Cambridge, UK: Cambridge University Press, 2022), 1–28.

11. Ogbu Kalu, *African Pentecostalism: An Introduction* (New York: Oxford University Press, 2008), 250.

12. Grant Wacker, *Heaven Below: Early Pentecostals and American Culture* (Cambridge, MA: Harvard University Press, 2003), 1–2.

13. Jay R. Case, "And Ever the Twain Shall Meet: The Holiness Missionary Movement and the Birth of World Pentecostalism, 1870–1920," *Religion and American Culture: A Journal of Interpretation* 16, no. 2 (2006): 125–160.

14. Wacker, *Heaven Below*, 3.

15. Wacker, *Heaven Below*, 10.

16. See the essays in Amos Young and Estrelda Y. Alexander, eds., *Afro-American Pentecostalism: Black Pentecostal and Charismatic Christianity in History and Culture* (New York: NYU Press, 2011).

17. Quoted in Edmund J. Rybarczyk, "New Churches: Pentecostals and the Bible," in *The New Cambridge History of the Bible*, vol. 4, *From 1750 to the Present*, ed. John Riches (New York: Cambridge University Press, 2015), 593.

18. Quoted in Rybarczyk, "New Churches," 598.

19. Rybarczyk, "New Churches," 591.

20. Andrew Davies, "What Does It Mean to Read the Bible as a Pentecostal?," *Journal of Pentecostal Theology* 18, no. 2 (2009): 220.

21. Scott A. Ellington, "History, Story, and Testimony: Locating Truth in a Pentecostal Hermeneutic," *Pneuma* 23, no. 2 (2001): 262.

22. Rybarczyk, "New Churches," 592–593.

23. Rybarczyk, "New Churches," 601.

24. Davies, "What Does It Mean," 218.

25. Emiola Nihinlola, "'What Does This Mean?' A Theological Approach to the Bewilderment, Amazement and Perplexity of Pentecostalism," *Ogbomoso Journal of Theology* 13, no. 1 (2008): 134–143.

26. John Mansford Prior, "The Challenge of the Pentecostals in Asia, Part One: Pentecostal Movements in Asia," *Exchange* 36, no. 1 (2007): 12–13.

27. Obvious Vengeyi, "'The Bible Equals *Gona*': An Analysis of the Indigenous Pentecostal Churches of Zimbabwe's Magical Conception of the Bible," in *From Text to Practice: The Role of the Bible in Daily Living of African People Today*, ed. Joachim Kügler and Masiiwa Ragies Gunda (Bamberg, Germany: University of Bamberg Press, 2013), 78–105.

28. Rybarczyk, "New Churches," 600.

29. Raphael D. Warnock, speech, Cathedral of Mary Our Queen, Baltimore, April 12, 2018, transcript at https://www.archbalt.org/transcript-of-remarks-of-rev-dr -raphael-d-warnock-at-the-cathedral-of-mary-our-queen/.

30. Quoted in Wacker, *Heaven Below*, 73.

31. Quoted in Wacker, *Heaven Below*, 75.

32. Davies, "What Does It Mean," 219.

33. Quoted in Calvin L. Smith, "Pneumapraxis and Eschatological Urgency: A Survey of Latin American Pentecostal Theology and Its Outworking," in *Pentecostal Power: Expressions, Impact and Faith of Latin American Pentecostalism*, ed. Calvin Smith, Global Pentecostal and Charismatic Studies 6 (Boston: Brill, 2011), 192.

34. Rybarczyk, "New Churches," 600.

35. Daniel Topf, *Pentecostal Higher Education: History, Current Practices, and Future Prospects* (London: Palgrave Macmillan, 2021); Annang Asumang, "Reforming Theological Education in the Light of the Pentecostalisation of Christianity in the Global South," *Conspectus*, special edition (December 2018): 115–148.

36. Rybarczyk, "New Churches," 601.

37. Michael J. McClymond, "The Bible and Pentecostalism," in *The Oxford Handbook of the Bible in America*, ed. Paul Gutjahr (New York: Oxford University Press, 2017), 600.

38. Paul Gifford, "The Bible in Africa: A Novel Usage in Africa's New Churches,"

Bulletin of SOAS 71, no. 2 (2008): 205; Kudzai Biri, *African Pentecostalism, the Bible, and Cultural Resilience: The Case of the Zimbabwe Assemblies of God Africa* (Bamberg, Germany: University of Bamberg Press, 2020), 225–244.

39. Clinton N. Westman, "Pentecostalism and Indigenous Culture in Northern North America," *Anthropologica* 55, no. 1 (2013): 141–156.

40. Cephas N. Omenyo and Wonderful Adjei Arthur, "The Bible Says! Neo-Prophetic Hermeneutics in Africa," *Studies in World Christianity* 19, no. 1 (2013), https://www.euppublishing.com/doi/full/10.3366/swc.2013.0038.

41. Omenyo and Adjei Arthur, "Bible Says!"

42. Pew Research Center, *The Global Religious Landscape*, December 18, 2012, https://www.pewresearch.org/religion/2012/12/18/global-religious-landscape -exec/.

43. Quoted in Smith, "Pneumapraxis and Eschatological Urgency," 191.

44. Allan Heaton Anderson, "'Stretching Out Hands to God': Origins and Development of Pentecostalism in Africa," *Pentecostalism in Africa: Presence and Impact of Pneumatic Christianity in Postcolonial Societies*, ed. Martin Lindhardt (Leiden, the Netherlands: Brill, 2015), 63.

45. Lamin Sanneh, *Whose Religion Is Christianity? The Gospel Beyond the West* (Grand Rapids, MI: W. B. Eerdmans, 2003), 10–11.

46. Allan Heaton Anderson, "Contextualization in Pentecostalism: A Multicultural Perspective," *International Bulletin of Mission Research* 41, no. 1 (2016): 35–36.

47. Mark McLeister, "Popular Christianity, Sensation, and *Ling'en* Authority in Contemporary China," *Asian Ethnology* 78, no. 1 (2019): 136.

48. See Mitchell J. Neubert, Kevin D. Dougherty, Jerry Z. Park, and Jenna Griebel, "Beliefs About Faith and Work: Development and Validation of Honoring God and Prosperity Gospel Scales," *Review of Religious Research* 56, no. 1 (2014): 129–146; Sung-Gun Kim, "The Heavenly Touch Ministry in the Age of Millennial Capitalism: A Phenomenological Perspective," *Nova Religio* 15, no. 3 (2012): 51–64; Andrzej Kobyliński, "Ethical Aspects of the Prosperity Gospel in the Light of the Arguments Presented by Antonio Spadaro and Marcelo Figueroa," *Religions* 12, no. 11 (2021): 1–16; and Naomi Haynes, "'Zambia Shall Be Saved!': Prosperity Gospel Politics in a Self-Proclaimed Christian Nation," *Nova Religio* 19, no. 1 (2015): 5–24.

49. See Marius Nel, *The Prosperity Gospel in Africa: An African Pentecostal Hermeneutical Consideration* (Eugene, OR: Wipf and Stock, 2020), 43–113.

50. Lovemore Togarasei, "The Pentecostal Gospel of Prosperity in African Contexts of Poverty: An Appraisal," *Exchange* 40, no. 4 (2011): 339.

51. Natanael Disla, "Neo-Pentecostal Masculinities and Religion in the Public Sphere in Latin America," *Journal of Latin American Theology* 10, no. 2 (2015): 37.

52. Quoted in Bob Smietana, "Korean Pastor David Yonggi Cho, Founder of One of the World's Largest Churches, Has Died," Religion News Service, September 14, 2021, https://religionnews.com/2021/09/14/korean-pastor-david-yonggi-cho-founder -of-one-of-the-worlds-largest-churches-has-died/.

53. Quoted in Gifford, "Bible in Africa," 208.

54. Quoted in Gifford, "Bible in Africa," 210.

55. Quoted in Gifford, "Bible in Africa," 214.

56. See Lovemore Togarasei, "Mediating the Gospel: Pentecostal Christianity and Media Technology in Botswana and Zimbabwe," *Journal of Contemporary Religion* 27, no. 2 (2012): 262; J. Kwabena Asamoah-Gyadu, ""Christ Is the Answer": What Is the Question?' A Ghana Airways Prayer Vigil and Its Implications for Religion, Evil and Public Space," *Journal of Religion in Africa* 35, no. 1 (2005): 93–117; Marleen De Witte, "Altar Media's *Living Word*: Televised Charismatic Christianity in Ghana," *Journal of Religion in Africa* 33, no. 2 (2003): 172–202; and Fred Jenga, "Pentecostal Broadcasting in Uganda," *Journal of Communication and Religion* 40, no. 4 (2017): 53–71.

57. Togarasei, "Mediating the Gospel," 267.

58. Togarasei, "Mediating the Gospel," 267.

59. Katrien Pype, "The Liveliness of Pentecostal/Charismatic Popular Culture in Africa," in *Pentecostalism in Africa: Presence and Impact of Pneumatic Christianity in Postcolonial Studies*, ed. Martin Lindhardt, Global and Charismatic Studies 15 (Boston: Brill, 2015), 351.

60. Togarasei, "Mediating the Gospel," 268.

61. Margaret Everett and Michelle Ramirez, "Healing the Curse of the *Grosero* Husband: Women's Health Seeking and Pentecostal Conversion in Oaxaca, Mexico," *Journal of Contemporary Religion* 30, no. 3 (2015): 420–421.

62. Wacker, *Heaven Below*, 74.

Chapter 14: "World Without End"

1. Jorge Luis Borges, "The Book of Sand," *The New Yorker*, October 25, 1976, 38–39, https://www.newyorker.com/magazine/1976/10/25/the-book-of-sand.

2. Borges, "Book of Sand," 39.

3. Borges, "Book of Sand," 39.

4. Pew Research Center: "Frequency of Reading Scripture," Religious Landscape Study, 2014, https://www.pewresearch.org/religion/religious-landscape-study/frequency-of-reading-scripture/.

INDEX

Index

Index

Index

Index

Index

Index

Index

Index

Index

Index

Index

511

Index

Index

Index

Valla, Lorenzo, 137
Valladolid debate, 141
Vallotton, Annie *(pl. 35–36)*, 1–2
Vani Gospels, 105
Vatican library, 35, 37
vellum, 27
Vesey, Denmark, 278, 282
Victor AD, 398
Victorian world and society, 228–232
Vikings, 89
Vinegar Bible, 223
Visigoth Bible, 92
Voltaire, 197, 199–200
vowel pointing or points, 138
Vulgata Sixtina, 148
Vulgate and Vulgate Bibles, 96, 115, 133, 229
    as the Bible of the West, 119, 146,
        148–149, 153, 168
    revisions, 143, 146–147, 148

Wadé Harris, William, 389–390, 396
Walker, David, 280
Wallace, Lewis, 293–294
Walter, Theos, 355
Walton, Brian, 153–154
war, 280–281, 295–296, 301
Warfield, Benjamin Breckinridge (B. B.),
    297–298
Warnock, Raphael D., 414–415
"watchwords" of Moravians, 260–262
Watts, Isaac, 265–266
Weems, Mason Locke, 272, 273
Wei Enbo (Wei Baulo or Paul Wei), 357–358
Wei Yisa, 358
Welsted, Leonard, 224
Wesley, Charles, 259, 263–264
Wesley, John, 263–264, 409
Wessex Gospels, 63
White Monastery (Egypt), 68
Whitefield, George, 259, 269, 270
Whittingham, William, 164
Whore of Babylon *(pl. 20)*
Wicked Bible, 222–223

Willibrord, 86
Winstanley, Gerrard, 240
Winthrop, John, 247
witches, 112–113
women
    and home, 276–277
    in missionary work *(pl. 28)*, 330–333
    as owners of biblical texts, 21
    as Pietists, 201, 263
    portrayal in illustrated Bibles, 276
    as preachers, 262–263
    as scribes, 25
    in songs and hymns, 76
    words, with images, 75, 78–80, 82–84,
        92–93
World War I, 301
worship, 69–70, 71–72, 104–105
    See also liturgy
Wright, Henry C., 281
writing "in divinity," 243–244
Wu Jingxiong, 365–366
Wu Leichuan, 360
Wunnanauhkomun (minister), 251
Wycliffe, John, 119–120, 161
Wycliffite Bible, 119–121
Wylie, Ann, 259

Xi Jinping, 371
Xu, John (Johan Su), 340

Yiddish, 202
Yoido Full Gospel Church, 406, 420
Yoruba Bible, 319–320, 383, 384
Yoruba language and people, 319–320,
    396–397
YouVersion (app), 432
Yu Jie, 368

Zhu Weizhi, 360–361
Zimbabwe, 426
Zinzendorf, Nikolaus Ludwig von, 253, 260
Zulu language and people, 388, 397, 402
Zwingli, Huldrych, 138, 157–158

Melannie Ross

Bruce Gordon is Titus Street Professor of Ecclesiastical History at Yale Divinity School and has an appointment in Yale's Department of History. He is the author of the biographies *Calvin* and *Zwingli: God's Armed Prophet*, and of a number of other books on the history of Christianity. He lives in Vermont.